W9-AYL-921

BOARD and TABLE GAMES
From Many Civilizations

by
R.C. BELL

Revised Edition
Two volumes bound as one

Dover Publications, Inc.
New York

Published in Canada by General Publishing Company, Ltd., 30 Lesmill Road, Don Mills, Toronto, Ontario.

Published in the United Kingdom by Constable and Company, Ltd.

This Dover edition, first published in 1979, is a revised and corrected republication in a single volume of the work originally published by Oxford University Press, London, in two volumes. *Board and Table Games 1* was first published in 1960 (second edition, 1969) and *Board and Table Games 2* in 1969.

International Standard Book Number: 0-486-23855-5
Library of Congress Catalog Card Number: 79-51819

Manufactured in the United States of America
Dover Publications, Inc.
180 Varick Street
New York, N.Y. 10014

BOARD and TABLE GAMES
From Many Civilizations

by
R. C. BELL

Volume One

Tile from Sumerian gaming board *c*. 3000 B.C.

INTRODUCTION

This book has been written to introduce some of the best board and table games from the world's treasury to the reader. They have been arranged in six chapters:

RACE GAMES
WAR GAMES
POSITIONAL GAMES
MANCALA GAMES
DICE GAMES
DOMINO GAMES

Chapter 7 describes methods of making boards and pieces, and the Appendix contains ten biographies.

The games starred (*) in the table of contents have not been described in English before. Most of the remaining material is only to be found in reports of museums and learned societies, foreign articles and books long out of print. A short glossary of technical terms is given on p. xxiv; and to save space the bibliography also serves as a table of contents. Whenever possible the games have been described under English titles. The reader is advised to omit the lists of rules on a first reading; later any game that interests him can be studied in more detail.

Boards used for one game were sometimes taken for another; the chequered chess board was used for draughts (both war games), shaturanga (a war game) was played on the ashtapada board (a race game), and the board for fox and geese (a war game) was used for solitaire (a game of position). Such adaptations make game-reconstructions from antique fragments of doubtful value: because the x people of Upper Ruritania used a board for a particular game, it does not follow that the y people of lower Ruritania used the same board for the same game; nevertheless it is reasonable to assume that they may have done so until contrary evidence appears.

Books on card games are readily available and, therefore, they have not been included; international chess has been omitted for the same reason. Ninety-one games are described and the oldest was played some 5,000 years ago. May every reader find pleasure in these pages!

ACKNOWLEDGEMENTS

The author is indebted to the writers of all the publications in the bibliography, but there is an especial debt to the works of H. J. R. Murray, Stewart Culin and Willard Fiske. It is a pleasure to thank Dr. W. S. Mitchell, the Librarian of King's College Library, Newcastle-upon-Tyne, and his staff, for their unstinting help in procuring books and articles; Mr. Raymond S. Dawson for obtaining material during a recent visit to Peking and for help with Chinese writings; Mr. M. Caturani for help with Italian and Spanish; Miss Agnes Kramer for help with German; Miss K. Kasbekar for her account of Tablan; Mr. S. Afoakwa for help with Wari; Mr. A. P. Mohideen for Chinese Games; and Professor Eric Thompson for assistance with Mayan and Aztec games.

Prof. F. E. Hopper and Prof. H. D. Dickinson read the manuscript at an early stage and made valuable suggestions; Mrs. Norma Trelease prepared the typescript; the staff of the Oxford University Press have been most painstaking and helpful throughout the stages of publication; and last but not least, I wish to thank my wife who has shared her house for several years with numerous boards and pieces.

ACKNOWLEDGEMENTS TO THE
SECOND EDITION

THE author wishes to thank the many readers who have written to him over the last seven years; and whose comments and criticisms have brought about the changes and improvements in the present text, or have been incorporated into a second volume which is being published concurrently with this edition of *Board and Tables Games from many Civilizations, I.*

Especial thanks are due to the following: J. Barrs, Wembley; O. B. Brears, Rangoon; J. H. Campbell, Jackson, Michigan; D. W. Crowe, Ibadan; D. I. Duff, St. Andrews; R. H. Fox, Princeton, New Jersey; D. A. Fraser, Wembley; J. Gray, London; C. Haag, Birmingham; R. B. Hackett, London; H. Hoolim, Migdal, Ascalon; J. F. P. Hudson, Cambridge; V. Kramiduiu, Bangkok; Maria L. M. Lumbroso, Rome; V. Medley, Mount Merrion; A. H. Morehead, New York; L. Pijanowski, Warsaw; T. J. Ransley, Glasgow; W. H. Rawlings, Westmount, Canada; Margaret Rideout, Dedham; A. J. Roycroft, London; W. H. Shepherd, Manchester; P. Smith, Aberdeen; W. Stead, Great Ayton; D. Stewart, Kelantan, Malaya; G. D. Towner, Cambridge; W. W. Wallis, Randfontein, South Africa.

1968

CONTENTS AND BIBLIOGRAPHY

PAGE

INTRODUCTION   v

ACKNOWLEDGEMENTS TO FIRST EDITION   vi

ACKNOWLEDGEMENTS TO SECOND EDITION   vi

ILLUSTRATIONS   xix

GLOSSARY   xxiv

GAME   REFERENCES

Chapter One: RACE GAMES

1. CROSS AND CIRCLE RACE GAMES

NYOUT   Culin, S., *Korean Games*, Philadelphia,   1
1895, pp. 66–73.
Ruiz, Alberto, *Anales del Instituto
Nacional de Antropologia e Historia*,
Mexico, 1952, Vol. 5, p. 27.
Ruppert, K., *The Mercado Chichen
Itza*, Yucatan, Carnegie Inst. Washington Pub. 546, Contribution No.
43, 1943, fig. 4c.
Thompson, Eric, personal communication 1956. I am indebted to him for
drawing my attention to the last two
articles and also for the estimation of
the age of the board at Palenque.

ZOHN AHL   Culin, S., *Chess and Playing Cards*,   4
Washington, 1898, p. 686.

PATOLLI   Taylor, E. B., 'On the Game of Patolli   6
in Ancient Mexico, and its probable
Asiatic Origin', *Anthropology*, London, 1881, p. 116.

PACHISI   Falkener, E., *Games Ancient and Orien-*   9
tal, London, 1892, p. 257.
Culin, S., *Chess and Playing Cards*,
Washington, 1898, p. 851.

LUDO   12

2. SPIRAL RACE GAMES

THE HYENA GAME   Davies, R., 'Some Arab Games and   12
Riddles', *Sudan Notes and Records*,
viii, 1925, p. 145.

THE ROYAL GAME OF GOOSE   Strutt, J., *The Sports and Pastimes of*   14
the People of England, 3rd ed., 1845,
p. 336.

GAME	REFERENCES	PAGE
THE ROYAL GAME OF GOOSE (*cont.*)	Whitehouse, F. R. B., *Table Games of Georgian and Victorian Days*, 1951, p. 57.	14

3. SQUARE BOARD RACE GAMES

*THAAYAM	Dr. Thillai-nayagam, personal communication 1956.	17

4. PEG SCORING BOARDS

THE PALM TREE GAME	Lord Carnarvon and Carter, H., *Five Years' Excavation at Thebes*, quoted by Peet, T. E., *Universal History of the World*, ed. Hammerton, p. 562. Gadd, C. J., 'An Egyptian game in Assyria', *Iraq*, 1, 1934, p. viiib and p. 46. *Illustrated London News*, 23 October 1937, p. 709.	20

5. THE BACKGAMMON GROUP

THE SUMERIAN GAME	Woolley, Sir Leonard, *Ur, The First Phase*, London, 1946.	23
THE GAME OF THIRTY SQUARES	Ridgeway, W., *Journal of Hellenic Studies*, 1896, Vol. XVI, p. 288. Towry-White, E., 'Types of Ancient Egyptian Draughtsmen', *Proceedings of the Society of Biblical Archaeology*, Vol. XXIV, 1902, p. 261. Nash, W. I., 'Ancient Egyptian Draughtsboards and Draughtsmen', *Proceedings of the Society of Biblical Archaeology*, Vol. XXIV, 1902, p. 341. Murray, H. J. R., *History of Board Games other than Chess*, Oxford, 1952, p. 12.	26
LUDUS DUODECIM SCRIPTORUM	Austin, R. G., 'Roman Board Games. I', *Greece and Rome*, Vol. IV (1934), p. 30.	30
TABULA	Emery, Walter B., *Nubian Treasure*, London, 1948, p. 46 and Pl. 32. Austin, R. G., 'Roman Board Games. II', *Greece and Rome,*. IV (1934-5), p. 76. Austin, R. G., 'Zeno's Game of Table', *Journal of Hellenic Studies*, 1934, Vol. LIV, p. 202.	34

GAME	REFERENCES	PAGE
TABULA (*cont.*)	Austin, R. G., *Archaeologia Cambrensis*, 1938, p. 250. Lanciani, R., 'Gambling and Cheating in Ancient Rome', *North American Review*, 1892, pp. 97–105. Gusman, P., *Pompei. The City, Its Life and Art*, London, 1900, p. 220. Murray, H. J. R., *History of Board Games other than Chess*, Oxford, 1952, p. 29.	34
CHASING THE GIRLS	Fiske, W., *Chess in Iceland*, Florence, 1905, pp. 89, 353.	37
TOURNE-CASE	Fiske, W., *Chess in Iceland*, Florence, 1905, p. 183.	38
SIXE-ACE	Fiske, W., *Chess in Iceland*, Florence, 1905, pp. 88, 356. Cotton, C., 'The Compleat Gamester', *Games and Gamesters of the Reformation*, London, 1930, p. 78.	39
FAYLES	Fiske, W., *Chess in Iceland*, Florence, 1905, pp. 167, 295.	41
BACKGAMMON	Fiske, W., *Chess in Iceland*, Florence, 1905, pp. 173–294. Richard, W. L., *Complete Backgammon*, 1st Eng. ed., London, 1938. Murray, H. J. R., *History of Chess*, Oxford, 1913, footnote p. 120.	42

Chapter Two: WAR GAMES

1. THE ALQUERQUE GROUP

ALQUERQUE	Parker, H., *Ancient Ceylon*, London, 1909, pp. 579, 644. Fiske, W., *Chess in Iceland*, Florence, 1905, footnote p. 255.	48
THE STONE WARRIORS	Culin, S., *Games of the North American Indians*, Washington, 1907, p. 799.	48
FIGHTING SERPENTS	Culin, S., *Games of the North American Indians*, Washington, 1907, p. 801.	50
THE SIXTEEN SOLDIERS	Parker, H., *Ancient Ceylon*, London, 1909, p. 583.	51

2. THE CHESS GROUP

SHATURANGA	Forbes, D., *History of Chess*, 1860. Murray, H. J. R., *History of Chess*, Oxford, 1913, pp. 55–77.	51

GAME	REFERENCES	PAGE
SHATRANJ	Murray, H. J. R., *History of Chess*, Oxford, 1913, pp. 220–338.	57
CIRCULAR OR BYZANTINE CHESS	Strutt, J., *Sports and Pastimes of the People of England*, 1845 ed., p. 311. Murray, H. J. R., *History of Chess*, Oxford, 1913, pp. 177, 342.	62
THE COURIER GAME	Murray, H. J. R., *History of Chess*, Oxford, 1913, p. 482. McBride, H. A., 'Masterpieces on Tour', *National Geographical Magazine*, December 1948.	62
MODERN INTERNATIONAL CHESS	. . . . .	65
THE MAHARAJAH AND THE SEPOYS	Falkener, E., *Games Ancient and Oriental*, 1892, pp. 217–24.	65
CHINESE CHESS	Hyde, T., *Historia Shahiludii*, Oxford, 1694, p. 158. Culin, S., *Korean Games*, Philadelphia, 1895, p. 82. Murray, H. J. R., Oxford, *History of Chess*, 1913, p. 119.	66
*THE JUNGLE GAME	I am indebted to Mr. A. P. Mohideen who sent this game to me from Hong Kong, and to Mr. R. Dawson, Department of Oriental Studies, Durham University, for the translation of the Chinese instruction sheet.	68
3. DRAUGHTS		
ENGLISH DRAUGHTS	Murray, H. J. R., *History of Board Games other than Chess*, Oxford, 1952, p. 72. La Roux, M., *The Complete Draughts Player*, London, 1955, pp. 7–16.	71
THE LOSING GAME	. . . . .	72
DIAGONAL DRAUGHTS	. . . . .	73
ITALIAN DRAUGHTS	Murray, H. J. R., *History of Board Games other than Chess*, Oxford, 1952, p. 78, quoting Mallet, P., *Le Jeu des Dames*, Paris, 1668.	73
TURKISH DRAUGHTS	Falkener, E., *Games Ancient and Oriental*, 1892, p. 237.	73
REVERSI	*Hoyle's Games Modernised*, London, 1923, p. 447.	74

GAME	REFERENCES	PAGE
CONTINENTAL OR POLISH DRAUGHTS	*Hoyle's Games*, London, 1853, pp. 404–21.	75

4. THE TAFL GROUP

FOX AND GEESE	Fiske, W., *Chess in Iceland*, Florence, 1905, p. 146. Redstone, V. B., 'England among the Wars of the Roses', *Trans. R. Hist. Soc.*, n.s. XXI, 1902, p. 195.	76
TABLUT	Linneus, C., *Lachesis Lapponica*, London, 1811, ii. 55.	77
SAXON HNEFATAFL	Robinson, J. A., *Time of St. Dunstan*, Oxford, 1923, p. 69. Murray, H. J. R., *History of Board Games other than Chess*, Oxford, 1952, pp. 55–64.	79
COWS AND LEOPARDS	Parker, H., *Ancient Ceylon*, London, 1909, p. 581.	81

5. THE LATRUNCULORUM GROUP

SEEGA	Lane, E. W., *Modern Egyptians*, 1890, p. 320. Petrie, F., *Objects of Daily Use*, British School of Archaeology in Egypt, 1927, p. 56.	82
HIGH JUMP	Marin, G., 'Somali Games', *Journal of the Royal Anthropological Institute*, LXI, 1931, p. 506.	84
LUDUS LATRUNCULORUM	Varro, M. T., *De Lingula Latina*, vii. 52. Ovid, P. O. N., *Ars Amatoria*, ii. 208; iii. 358. Bassus, S., *Laus Pisonis*, in the first part of the fourth volume of Wernsdorf's *Poetae Latinae Minores*, p. 236, v. 192. (These three authors are quoted by Austin, R. G., 'Roman Board Games', *Greece and Rome*, IV (1934–5), p. 24.)	84

6. RUNNING–FIGHT GAMES

*TABLAN	Dr. K. V. Kasbekar, personal communication. The board in fig. 143 has belonged to her family for at least fifty years and is probably much older than this.	87

GAME	REFERENCES	PAGE
*PULUC	Sapper, von K., *Boas Anniversary Vol.*, article 190, p. 238. (I am indebted to Professor E. Thompson for drawing my attention to this article and to Miss Kramer for her translation.)	89

Chapter Three: GAMES OF POSITION

1. MORRIS GAMES

NOUGHTS AND CROSSES	White, A. B., *British Chess Mag.*, 1919, p. 217.	91
THREE MEN'S MORRIS	Ovid, P. O. N., *Ars Amatoria*, iii. 365–6. Hyde, T., *De Historia Nerdiludii*, Oxford, 1694, p. 211. Fiske, W., *Chess in Iceland*, Florence, 1905, pp. 122–38. Murray, H. J. R., *History of Board Games other than Chess*, Oxford, 1952, p. 37.	91
SIX MEN'S MORRIS	Murray, H. J. R., *History of Board Games other than Chess*, Oxford, 1952, p. 43.	92
NINE MEN'S MORRIS	Parker, H., *Ancient Ceylon*, 1909, p. 507. Macalister, R. A. S., *Archaeology of Ireland*, London, 1928, p. 123. Sjovold, T., *The Viking Ships*, Oslo, 1954, p. 7. Fiske, W., *Chess in Iceland*, Florence, 1905, p. 105.	93

2. THREE-IN-A-ROW GAMES

| DARA | Fitzgerald, R. T. D., 'The Dakarkari People of Sokito Province, Nigeria. Notes on their material Culture', *Man*, XLII, 1942, p. 26. | 95 |

3. FIVE-IN-A-ROW GAMES

| GO-MOKU | Volpicelli, Z., 'Wei-Chi', *Journal of China Branch, Royal Asiatic Society*, n.s. 26, 1894, p. 80. | 96 |
| HASAMI SHOGI | Harbin, E. O., *Games of Many Nations*, New York, Nashville, 1955, p. 107. | 97 |

4. REPLACEMENT GAMES

| FIVE FIELD KONO | Culin, S., *Korean Games*, Philadelphia, 1895, p. 102. | 98 |

GAME	REFERENCES	PAGE

HALMA   Hedges, S. G., *The Home Enter-*   98
                         tainer (undated), p. 76.

5. TERRITORIAL POSSESSION

WEI-CH'I   Volpicelli, Z., 'Wei-chi', *Journal of*   99
                         China Branch, Royal Asiatic Society,
                         n.s. 26, 1894, p. 80.
                         Culin, S., *Korean Games*, Philadelphia,
                         1895, p. 91.
                         Falkener, E., *Games Ancient and*
                         Oriental, 1892, p. 239.
                         Pecorini, D. and Tong Shu, *The*
                         Game of Wei-chi, 1929.
                         Cheshire, F., *Goh or Wei-chi*, Hastings,
                         1911.
                         Lasker, E., *Go and Go-Moku*, New
                         York, 1960.
                         Smith, A., *The Game of Go*, Vermont,
                         1958.
                         Takagawa, K., *How to play Go*, printed
                         in Japan, 1956.
                         Takagawa, K., *The Vital Points of Go*,
                         printed in Japan, 1958.
                         Segoe, K., *Go Proverbs Illustrated*,
                         Tokyo, 1965.

6. PATIENCE GAMES

SOLITAIRE   Hedges, S. G., *The Home Entertainer*   111
                         (undated), p. 79.

Chapter Four: MANCALA GAMES

1. TWO-RANK MANCULA

MANKALA'H   Lane, E. W., *An Account of the Manners*   113
                         and Customs of the Modern Egyp-
                         tians, reprint from the 3rd edition
                         of 1842, Minerva Library, 1890,
                         p. 315.
                         Petrie, F., *Objects of Daily Use*, British
                         School of Archaeology in Egypt,
                         1927, p. 55.
                         Parker, H., *Ancient Ceylon*, London,
                         1909, pp. 224, 594.

PALLANGULI   Mohandas, S., personal communica-   115
                         tion 1957.
                         Durai, H. G., 'Pallanguli', *Man*, No-
                         vember 1928, p. 185.

GAME	REFERENCES	PAGE
WARI	Afoakwa, S., personal communication 1957. Bennett, G. T., in *Religion and Art in Ashanti* by R. S. Rattray, Oxford, 1927, pp. 382–98. Jobson, R., *The Golden Trade*, 1623, reprinted 1904, p. 48. Herskovits, M. J., 'Wari in the New World', *Journal of the Royal Anthropological Institute*, Vol. XLII, 1923, pp. 23–37.	116

2. FOUR-RANK MANCULA

CHISOLO	Smith, E. W. and Dale, A. M., *The Ila-speaking Peoples of Northern Rhodesia*, London, 1920, Vol. 2, pp. 232–7. Chaplin, J. H., 'A note on Mancala Games in Northern Rhodesia', *Man*, Vol. LVI, 1956, p. 168.	123

Chapter Five: DICE GAMES

DICE	Culin, S., *Chinese Games with Dice and Dominoes*, Washington, 1895, p. 535. Tacitus, C., *Germania A.D. 99*, Cap. XXIV. Fiske, W., *Chess in Iceland*, Florence, 1905, footnote p. 249. Sturluson, S., *Heimskringla*, translated by S. Laing, 2nd ed. London, 1889, iii. pp. 1–2. (Quoted by W. Fiske.) Wright, T., *History of Domestic Manners and Sentiments in England during the Middle Ages*, London, 1862. Lanciani, R., 'Gambling and Cheating in Ancient Rome', *North American Review*, 1892, p. 97.	125

1. GAMES WITH TWO-SIDED DICE

HEADS AND TAILS	Strutt, J., *Sports and Pastimes of the People of England*, London, 1845 ed., p. 337.	127
THE BOWL GAME	Brown, Mrs. N. W., 'Some Indoor and Outdoor Games of the Wabanak Indians', *Trans. Roy. Soc. Canada*, Sec. II, 1883, p. 41. (Quoted by S. Culin, *Chess and Playing Cards*, Report Nat. Museum, 1896, p. 707.)	127

GAME	REFERENCES	PAGE

2. GAMES WITH SIX-SIDED DICE

THIRTY-SIX — Scarne, J., *Scarne on Dice*, 1946, p. 381. — 129

PIG — Scarne, J., *Scarne on Dice*, 1946, p. 178. — 130

ACES IN THE POT — Wood and Goddard, *The Complete Book of Games*, 1940, p. 351. — 130

BARBUDI — Scarne, J., *Scarne on Dice*, 1946, p. 367. — 130

HAZARD — Hoyle, E., *Hoyle's Games Improved*, edited by C. Jones, 1786, pp. 252–5. Cotton, C., *Compleat Gamester*, 1674. Reprinted in the English Library, 1930, as *Games and Gamesters of the Restoration*, p. 82. Ashton, J., *The History of Gambling in England*, London, 1898. Quinn, J. P., *Fools of Fortune*, 1890. — 132

BUCK DICE — Scarne, J., *Scarne on Dice*, 1946, p. 371. — 136

MARTINETTI — Scarne, J., *Scarne on Dice*, 1946, p. 388. — 136

DROP DEAD — Scarne, J., *Scarne on Dice*, 1946, p. 374. — 137

INDIAN DICE — Scarne, J., *Scarne on Dice*, 1946, p. 369. — 137

SHIP, CAPTAIN, MATE AND CREW — Scarne, J., *Scarne on Dice*, 1946, p. 390. — 138

SEQUENCES — Wood and Goddard, *The Complete Book of Games*, 1940, p. 363. — 138

TWENTY-SIX — Scarne, J., *Scarne on Dice*, 1946, p. 356. — 139

ACES — Scarne, J., *Scarne on Dice*, 1946, p. 384. — 139

3. GAMES WITH SPECIAL DICE

BELL AND HAMMER — Card of Instructions in a Bell and Hammer Set in the author's possession, c. 1850, maker unknown. Rogers, A., personal communication 1958. — 140

CROWN AND ANCHOR — King, T., *Twenty-one Games of Chance*, London (undated), p. 54. — 142

LIAR DICE — Ogbourn, Miss L. A., personal communication. (A form played at Oxford University) — 143

4. CHINESE DICE GAMES

STRUNG FLOWERS — Culin, S., *Chinese Games with Dice and Dominoes*, Washington, 1895, p. 493. — 145

GAME	REFERENCES	PAGE
THROWING HEAVEN AND NINE	Culin, S. *Chinese Games with Dice and Dominoes*, Washington, 1895, p. 494.	146
PUT AND TAKE	Traditional form (Durham miners).	148

Chapter Six: DOMINO GAMES

FISHING	Culin, S., *Chinese Games with Dice and Dominoes*, Washington, 1895, pp. 508–18.	150
DISPUTING TENS	Culin, S., *Korean Games*, Philadelphia, 1895, p. 117.	151
COLLECTING TENS	Culin, S., *Korean Games*, Philadelphia, 1895, p. 118.	152
MA-JONG	Culin, S., *Chinese Games with Dice and Dominoes*, Washington, 1895, pp. 518–21. 'East Wind', *Mah Jongg*, London, 1923. Harr, L. L., *How to Play Pung Chow*, New York, 1923. Bray, J., *How to Play Mah Jong*, New York, 1923. Racster, O., *Mah-jongg*, London, 1924. Anonymous, *The Standard Rules of Mah-jongg*, Chad Valley Co., 1924. Reeve, E. G., *Advanced Mah Jongg*, London, 1924. Ranger, L., *Directions for playing Ma jong*, Shanghai (undated). Higginson, C. M. W., *Mah Jongg, How to play and score* (undated).	153
EUROPEAN DOMINOES	Strutt, J., *Sports and Pastimes of the People of England*, 3rd ed., 1845, p. 322.	162
THE BLOCK GAME	Hedges, S. G., *The Home Entertainer*, Odhams (undated), p. 87.	163
THE BERGEN GAME	Dawson, L. H., *Hoyle's Games Modernised*, 1923, p. 469.	164
FORTY-TWO	Morehead, A. H., *The Modern Hoyle*, Winston, 1944, p. 255. Harbin, E. O., *The Fun Encyclopaedia*, 1940, p. 36.	165
BINGO	Dawson, L. H., *Hoyle's Games Modernised*, 1923, p. 470.	165
DOMINO CRIB	As played in the Officers' Mess, R.C.A.F. Station, Topcliffe, Yorks., 1945.	167

GAME	REFERENCES	PAGE
THE MATADOR GAME	Dawson, L. H., *Hoyle's Games Modernised*, 1923, p. 467.	170
CYPRUS	Anonymous Pamphlet, published by the Embossing Co., Albany, New York, U.S.A. (undated).	171
TIDDLE-A-WINK	Anonymous Pamphlet, published by the Embossing Co., Albany, New York, U.S.A. (undated).	172

Chapter Seven: MAKING BOARDS AND PIECES   173

Appendix: BIOGRAPHIES

AUTHOR	REFERENCES	
AS-SULI	Murray, H. J. R., *History of Chess*, Oxford, 1913, p. 199.	179
CHARLES COTTON	*Dictionary of National Biography*, London, 1908, Vol. IV, p. 1223. Beresford, J., *Poems of Charles Cotton 1630–1687*, London, 1923, Preface. Walton, I. and Cotton, C., *The Complete Angler*, London, 1823 ed.	181
THOMAS HYDE	*Dictionary of National Biography*, London, 1908, Vol. X, p. 403.	184
EDMOND HOYLE	*Dictionary of National Biography*, London, 1908, Vol. X, p. 133. Pole, W., *The Evolution of Whist*, 1895, pp. 35–69.	187
JOSEPH STRUTT	*Dictionary of National Biography*, London, 1909, Vol. XIX, p. 65.	189
DUNCAN FORBES	*Dictionary of National Biography*, London, 1908, Vol. VII, p. 386.	191
EDWARD FALKENER	*Dictionary of National Biography*, Supplement Vol. XXII, p. 624.	193
STEWART CULIN	*Who Was Who in America 1847–1942*, Marquis, Chicago. Dorsey, G. A., *The American Magazine*, June 1913. Wechsler, M., (Dept. Primitive Art, Brooklyn Museum, New York), personal communication.	194
WILLARD FISKE	*Dictionary of American Biography*, Vol. VI, p. 417.	196

xviii   *CONTENTS AND BIBLIOGRAPHY*

AUTHOR	REFERENCES	PAGE
WILLARD FISKE (*cont.*)	White, H. S., *Willard Fiske, Life and Correspondence*, 3 vols., Oxford, 1925. Fiske, W., *Chess in Iceland*, Florence, 1905.	196
H. J. R. MURRAY	Obituary in *British Chess Magazine*, August 1955. Miss K. M. E. Murray, personal communication.	198
INDEX		201

LIST OF ILLUSTRATIONS

Tile from Sumerian gaming board	*Frontispiece*
Diagram of row and column	**xxiv**

Chapter One: RACE GAMES

Figure 1. Nyout   1
2. Nyout ring and pam-nyout   1
3. Mayan game from Palenque   3
4. Mayan game from Chichen Itza   3
5. Zohn Ahl   4
6. Dicing sticks for Zohn Ahl   5
7. Patolli cross, counters and beans   6
8. Pachisi cloth   10
9. Pachisi pieces, dice and shells   10
10. Ludo   12
11. Hyena   13
Plate I. Royal and pleasant game of Goose   *facing p.* 14
IIa. Shaturanga   *facing p.* 15
IIb. Indian chess   *facing p.* 15
Figure 12. Thaayam   17
13. Board from Thebes   20
14. Board from Megiddo   20
15. Board from Ur   22
16. Cribbage   22
17. Board from Royal Tombs of Ur   23
18. Diagram of Movement in Sumerian game   24
19. Tau   25
20. Game of Thirty Squares (Senat)   26
21. Board from Ak-hor   27
22. Wall drawing from Benihassan   27
23. Board from Qustul   29
24. Fritillus   29
25. Silver mirror-back   30
26. Ludus Duodecim Scriptorum board from Holt   31
27. Ludus Duodecim Scriptorum boards from Italy   32
28. Wall-painting of gamblers with dice (Pompeii)   33
29. Wall-painting of a fight (Pompeii)   33
30. Zeno's game of Tabula   34

31. Chasing the Girls   37
32. Tourne-case   39
33. Sixe-Ace (two players)   40
34. Sixe-Ace (four players)   40
35. Fayles   41
36. Medieval Tables   42
37. Backgammon   44
Tailpiece: Antique Chinese Tableman in filigree ivory   46

Chapter Two: WAR GAMES

38. Alquerque board (Ancient Egypt)   47
39. Alquerque   47
40. Stone Warriors   49
41. Fighting Serpents   50
42. Sixteen Soldiers   50
43. Ashtapada board   51
44. Moves in Shaturanga   52
45. Shaturanga   53
46. Concourse of shipping   55
47. Muslim chessmen   58
48. Shatranj   59
49. Circular or Byzantine chess   61
50. Courier chessmen   62
51. Courier chess positions   62
Plate III.   'The Chess Players' (Van Leyden)   facing p. 64
Pl.IV,Fig.52.Blind player's chess set   facing p. 65
Figure 53. Maharajah and the Sepoys   65
        54. Chinese chess board   66
        55. Chinese chess pieces   67
        56. Jungle game   69
        57. English draughts   72
        58. Draughtsmen   72
        59. Diagonal draughts   73
        60. Turkish draughts   74
        61. Polish draughts   74
        62. Fox and thirteen Geese   76
        63. Fox and seventeen Geese   76
        64. Tablut   77
        65. Tablut pieces and custodian capture   78
        66. Board from Wimose   79
        67. Hnefatafl pieces   80
        68. Hnefatafl   80
Plate V.   Hnefatafl in a tenth-century manuscript   facing p. 80
Plate VI.   Two consecutive pages from *De Ludis
              Orientalibus*   facing p. 81

Figure 69. Cows and Leopards   81
       70. Seega   82
       71. Multiple custodian capture   83
       72. High Jump   83
       73. Stone Ludus Latrunculorum board   85
       74. Tablan   88
       75. Puluc   89
Tailpiece: English dicing cup   90

Chapter Three: GAMES OF POSITION

76. Noughts and Crosses   91
77. Three Men's Morris   92
78. Three Men's Morris (another form)   92
79. Six Men's Morris   93
80. Nine Men's Morris   93
81. Board from the Gokstad ship   94
82. Dara   95
83. Go-Moku   96
84. Hasami Shogi   97
85. Custodian capture in Hasami Shogi   97
86. Five Field Kono   98
87. Halma   99
88. Wei-ch'i: Korschett notation   101
89. Wei-ch'i: Single and multiple captures   102
90. Wei-ch'i: Illegal play   103
91. Wei-ch'i: Multiple capture   103
92. Wei-ch'i: Multiple capture   104
93. Wei-ch'i: True and false eyes   104
94. Wei-ch'i: Repeating position or ko   104
95. Wei-ch'i: An impasse or seki   105
96. Wei-ch'i: End of game, before neutralization   106
97. Wei-ch'i: End of game, final count   106
98. Wei-ch'i: Building fences   107
99. Wei-ch'i: Construction of territories   108
100. Wei-ch'i: Opening plays   109
101. Wei-ch'i: Cross over or matari   110
102. Wei-ch'i: Handicap positions   110
103. Solitaire   111
Tailpiece: Wooden Wei-ch'i bowl filled with tze   112

Chapter Four: MANCALA GAMES

104. Mankala'h   113

105. Mancala, Ancient Egypt   113
106. Wari   117
107. Awari   122
108. Chisolo   123
Tailpiece: Antique Pallanguli board (redrawn from Durai)   124

Chapter Five: DICE GAMES

109. Etruscan dice   125
110. Grotesque dice   126
111. All-tes teg-enuk bowl   128
112. All-tes teg-enuk tallies and dice   128
113. Martinetti   136
114. Bell and Hammer cards   140
115. Crown and Anchor dice   142
116. Exploded Crown and Anchor die   142
117. Crown and Anchor board   142
118. Poker dice   143
119. Exploded Poker die   143
120. Strung Flowers: Six Triple Throws   145
121. Strung Flowers: Sequence   145
122. Strung Flowers: Two Alike   146
123. Strung Flowers: Dancing Dragon   146
124. Throwing Heaven and Nine   147
125. Put and Take   148
Tailpiece: Antique Chinese dicing cup of ivory   148

Chapter Six: DOMINO GAMES

126. Chinese Dominoes   149
127. Domino wood-pile   150
128. Wood-pile for Collecting Tens   152
Plate VII.   Ma-jong tiles and counters   *facing p.* 154
Plate VIII. Lorry drivers playing Chinese chess *facing p.* 155
Figure 129. Ma-jong: Wind discs and Tong   155
130. Ma-jong: Dead Wall   156
131. Ma-jong: Change of direction   159
132. Development of Dominoes   162
133. The Block game   163
134. Domino Crib   169
135. Matador   170
136. Cyprus   171
Tailpiece: Ma-jong Flower tile   172

Chapter Seven: MAKING BOARDS AND PIECES

Tailpiece: Bell and Hammer mallet, dice and cup   178

137. *Poker work*. Fighting Serpents
138. *Wood carving*. Wari
139. Diagram of hollowing out a cup
140. *Chip-carving*. Ludus Latrunculorum
141. *Inlaying*. Medieval Tables
142. *Marquetry*. Continental Draughts
143. *Paint work on white wood*. Tablan
144. *Paint on matting*. Patolli
145. *Formica on plywood*. Cows and Leopards
146. *Pottery*. Ancient board (Palenque)
147. *Gilt on rexine*. Nine Men's Morris
148. *Beadwork on leather*. Zohn-ahl
149. *Embroidery*. Pachisi   *Plates*
150. *Paper*. Chinese chess   *IX–XXIV*
151. *Paper on linen*. Game of Goose   *between*
152. *Metalwork*. Pallanguli   *pp.* 178–9
153. *Perspex inlay*. Tau
154. *Ivory*: Shatranj pieces
155. *Bone*. Hnefatafl pieces
156. *Bone*. Domino casket
157. Dominoes
158. *Pottery*. Pieces for Game of Thirty Squares
159. Gambling sticks
160. *Ivory billiard balls*. Sundry dice
161. *Wood-turning*. All-tes teg-enuk
162. Cypher of Charles Cotton
163. Signature of Charles Cotton
164. Signature of Edmond Hoyle (?)

Tailpiece: Rajah from Indian chess set (From Hyde's *De Ludis
               Orientalibus*)   200

GLOSSARY

COLUMN	See diagram below.
CROWNHEAD	Spaces on which a piece becomes promoted to a king.
CUSTODIAN CAPTURE	Capture by trapping an enemy piece between two of one's own.
DIAGONAL MOVE	The piece moves diagonally across the board.
DIE	The singular of dice.
EN PRISE	A piece is en prise when it is liable to capture at the opponent's next move.
FILE	See diagram below.
HUFF	Confiscation of a piece which has infringed a rule.
INTERVENTION	Capture by a piece occupying the point immediately between two enemy pieces, when the latter are removed from the board.
LONG DIE	A four-sided die.
LONG LEAP	A jump by a piece over another piece to land beyond, but vacant squares may intervene on either side of the captured piece.
ORTHOGONAL MOVE	The piece moves along a rank or file.
RANK	See diagram below.
REPLACEMENT	A capture made by a piece moving on to a space occupied by an enemy piece and removing it from the board.
ROW	See diagram below.
SHORT LEAP	A capture made by a piece jumping over an enemy piece on an adjacent space to land on the space immediately beyond.

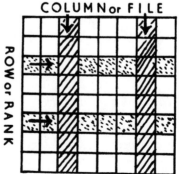

CHAPTER ONE

Race Games

1. CROSS AND CIRCLE RACE GAMES

In 1949 North Korea invaded South Korea across the Thirty-ninth parallel and the war that followed made this obscure country a household word throughout the western world. The Kingdom of Korea was founded in 1122 B.C. and before the Christian era the Koreans were highly civilized. One of their games, Nyout, is an example of a Cross and Circle game that has survived unchanged down countless centuries.

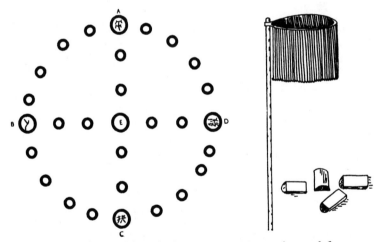

FIG. 1. Nyout board (after Culin, *Korean Games*)

FIG. 2. Nyout ring and four pam-nyout (after Culin, *Korean Games*)

NYOUT

The Nyout board consists of twenty-nine marks which are often drawn on a piece of paper. Those in the centre and at the four quarters are larger than the others. The mark at the top is 㐄 CH'UT—Exit.

The pieces are called MAL or horses, and are made of wood, stone or paper and are moved according to the throws of four dice known as PAM-NYOUT. These are about 1 in. in length, white, and flat on one side, convex and blackened by charring on the other. They are usually made of the wood of a thick bushy tree like the prunus. Ebony makes an excellent substitute. To prevent cheating the dice are thrown through a ring of straw about 2 in. in diameter, which is fastened to the end of a stick a foot long which is stuck in the ground.

Scores

4 black sides up	..	5	and the player
4 white sides up	..	4	has another turn
3 white sides up	..	3	
2 white sides up	..	2	
1 white side up	..	1	

If a block falls in an upright position it counts as though it fell with the black side up.

Rules of Play

1. All the players throw the blocks in turn, the highest becoming the leader and the others follow in the order of their throws.

2. Throwing a five or a four allows the player another throw which is made before moving his piece.

3. The players enter their men on the mark to the left of that marked EXIT, and move anti-clockwise according to their throws. The object of the game is to get an agreed number of horses around the circle and out at A. If a horse lands on one of the cardinal marks it short-circuits along a limb of the cross.

4. If two play, each player has four horses; if three play each has three horses; and if four play the players sitting opposite are partners and have two horses each.

5. If a player's horse catches up with another of his own, he may double them up as a team and then move them around as one piece.

6. If a player's horse moves on to a mark occupied by an opponent's piece the latter is caught and must go back to the beginning and start again. When a player makes a capture he has an extra turn.

7. When a player throws a 5 or a 4 and has a second throw he may divide the throws between two horses.

8. A player may move his partner's horses instead of his own.

9. When a horse is about to enter the board a throw of 5 takes it

to the spot marked B (fig. 1), and it may move towards the exit by the radius BE. If the throw is less than 5 but the next throw brings it to B it may travel along the radius BE and EA, otherwise it must continue on to C. If it lands on C it can travel along CE and EA, otherwise it must continue on towards A, the exit.

Nyout is popular among the Korean lower classes and is played as a gambling game for money in the public houses. There are records of a game similar to Nyout being played in Korea in the third century A.D.

There is considerable evidence that North America was populated from North-east Asia and this theory is supported by Amerindian games. Fig. 3 shows a drawing of a flagstone found by the Mexican archaeologist Alberto Ruiz in the temple of the Inscriptions at Palenque, a Mayan city in Central America which was inhabited about A.D. 800.

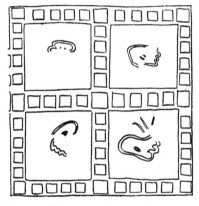

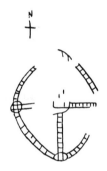

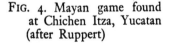

FIG. 3. Mayan game cut into a flagstone at Palenque, *c*. A.D. 800 (after Alberto Ruiz)

FIG. 4. Mayan game found at Chichen Itza, Yucatan (after Ruppert)

Fig. 4 shows a tracing one-tenth actual size of a board cut into the stucco top of a bench in a gallery at the south-eastern corner of the market place in the ruins of Chichen Itza, Yucatan. The building is thought to have been used as a barracks or as a club house for the young warriors belonging to the military orders of the Jaguars and Eagles. The board is placed conveniently for the players to sit facing each other. The stucco is damaged in places but enough remains to indicate the likeness of this board to a contemporary one for Nyout.

The Cross and Circle pattern may be modified by omitting the cross. Many North American Indian games consist of a circle (often with vestigial remains of a cross) scratched on the ground, and the progress of the pieces is controlled by the throws of marked sticks. Zohn Ahl, played by the women and girls of the Kiowa Indians, Oklahoma, may be taken as representative.

ZOHN AHL

The board is marked out on the ground with forty small stones, the points being the intervals between the stones. In the centre is a flat stone, known as the AHL stone, on to which the dicing sticks are thrown. The wide gaps at the North and South represent a river in flood, while those at the East and West are dry streams (figs. 5 and 148 on Plate XIV).

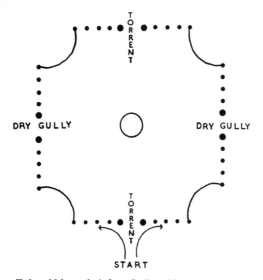

FIG. 5. Zohn Ahl track (after Culin, *Chess and Playing Cards*)

Runners. Each team has one runner and the moves of the runners are controlled by the throw of four dice sticks, the runners moving in opposite directions round the track.

Dice Sticks. These are flat on one side and round on the other. They are about 7 in. long, $\frac{3}{8}$ in. wide, and $\frac{3}{10}$ in. thick. Three of the sticks have a red stripe running down the middle of the flat side, while the fourth, known as the SAHE, has a green stripe, and its convex side is marked with a star (figs. 6 and 159 on Plate XXI).

Scoring

One flat side up	..	1 and if this is the blue, another turn
Two flat sides up	..	2
Three flat sides up	..	3 and if the blue is included, another
Four flat sides up	..	6 and another turn [turn
Four convex sides up	..	10 and another turn

Counters. Each team starts with four pebbles, shells, or white sticks which are used as counters.

RED STICKS   GREEN STICK

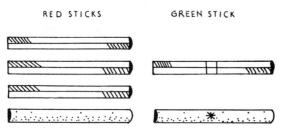

FIG. 6. Dicing sticks for Zohn Ahl (after Culin, *Chess and Playing Cards*)

Method of Play

1. The players are divided into two teams and a player from each team throws the sticks alternately, each player in a team throwing in turn and advancing her side's runner with her throw.

2. If a runner lands in the torrent at the North she must return to the start and her team must pay their opponents one counter. If a runner falls into the dry river bed at East or West the team loses one throw.

3. If the two runners meet on the same point the last to arrive sends her opponent back to the beginning and her side wins a counter.

4. When the first runner arrives back at the start the opponents have to pay a counter and the first lap is over. If the throw is big enough to take the runner beyond the start she moves the surplus number of points along the second lap. The runner winning each lap gains a counter.

5. The game ends when one side holds all the counters or, if a time limit has been set, the side holding most at that moment is the winner.

PATOLLI

The Cross and Circle can also be modified by omitting the circle. This happened in Patolli, the favourite gambling game of the Aztecs. Unfortunately, the Christian priests with misplaced zeal destroyed the native records and manuscripts and no Aztec description of the game has survived. The earliest Spanish account is Gomara's (1552), written thirty-one years after the conquest in 1521 but unfortunately it is very short. He mentions that the Emperor Montezuma sometimes watched his nobles playing at Court.

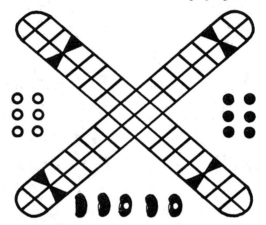

FIG. 7. Patolli cross, counters and beans (after Duran)

Duran describes these Mexican gamesters walking about with a patolliztli mat rolled up under an arm and carrying a little basket containing coloured stones used as markers. Before a game they called for a bowl of fire and threw incense into it, or sacrificed offerings of food to their dice and then they would gamble with all the confidence in the world. The nobility played for high stakes in precious stones, gold beads and very fine turquoises.

The Mexican God of Sport and Gambling was Macuilxochitl, the God of Five Flowers, and as they played the gamblers invoked his aid by rubbing the five beans between their hands, and then, as they threw them on the mat, they shouted 'Macuilxochitl!' and clapped their hands together, craning forward to see their score.

The following description is based on four early works: Sahagun (c. 1545), Gomara (1553), Duran (c. 1560) and Torquemada (1615). Father Sahagun prepared his *Historia universal de Nueva-Espana* about 1545, but it was suppressed by the ecclesiastical authorities for nearly 300 years, finally being published in 1829 by Bustamente in Mexico. Father Diego Duran (1538–1588) wrote his history *Antiguallas e Historia de los mejicanos* about 1560. It was first published under the title *Historia de las Indias de Nueva-Espana & Islas de Tierra Firme* in Mexico (1867–1880).

The board was a thin mat and painted on it in liquid rubber was a great diagonal cross reaching to the corners. Each limb was divided into sixteen compartments. Some mats were decorated with the figure of fortune as a lucky device or with its symbol, two clubs.

Twelve small stones were used as pieces, six red and six blue, and if two played each took six. (This remark suggests that more than two could play, but it is not recorded if the players formed partnerships or were independent, and if they shared the twelve pieces or increased the total number.)

Five large black beans, called patolli, each with a hole drilled in one side to act as a white pip, were rubbed between the player's hands and then thrown on to the mat to make the cast.

Scoring (Duran)

1 pip up ..	1
2 pips up ..	2
3 pips up ..	3
4 pips up ..	4
5 pips up ..	10

The stones were moved along the divisions according to the throws. Little more is known about patolli and this is not enough to play the game. By comparison with other North American games it is probable that the marked squares were penalty areas and the player was penalized for trespassing on them—possibly a turn was lost, or a forfeit paid (figs. 7 and 144 on Plate XII).

Suggested Additional Rules (for two players)

1. The players put an agreed sum into a pool and decide on the size of the forfeits.

2. One player takes six red pieces, the other six blue.

3. Each player casts the patolli in turn and the higher scorer starts the game by casting again.

4. The opening player introduces a piece on to his nearest

central square and then moves it the indicated number of compart-ments in either direction round the board, but whichever way his first piece moves the others must do likewise. His opponent at his opening throw also has a free choice of direction but having once chosen, the remaining pieces must travel the same way. The op-posing forces may, therefore, be moving in the same or opposite directions.

5. After the entry of the first piece the others must enter the board on the player's nearest central square with a throw of 1.

6. No piece may move on to a compartment occupied by any other piece.

7. If two or more of a player's pieces can be moved to satisfy a particular throw, the player has free choice which it shall be, but if only one piece can move, the move must be made even if it is to the player's disadvantage.

8. If a player cannot move any piece he pays a forfeit into the pool.

9. A player landing on a compartment which has been reduced in size by the markings pays two forfeits to his opponent.

10. A player moving a piece on to one of the rounded compart-ments at the end of the limbs of the cross is awarded another turn.

11. Pieces travel round the cross and are borne off on the side of the fourth limb nearest the player with exact throws, as in back-gammon. The four central squares, which have been traversed in the circuit of the piece, are excluded in the bearing off.

12. As each of the player's pieces leaves the cross his opponent pays him one forfeit.

13. The player removing all his pieces from the cross first wins the stake in the pool.

14. For three players it is suggested that each player should have five counters of his own colour making 15 counters in all. The rules remain unchanged.

15. For four players each player should have four counters, of his own colour, and the players may decide to play ALL AGAINST ALL, or that the players sitting opposite each other shall be partners and share the profits or losses of each hand. Cowrie shells, beads, dried peas, etc., can be used as forfeits.

In Asia the Cross and Circle game became variously modified as it spread westwards. The circle was invaginated against the side of the cross to form a bigger cross of three rows of squares. This increased the length of the track and removed the short cuts along the cardinals.

PACHISI

Pachisi, or Twenty-five, is the national game of India, and is found in palaces, zenanas, and cafés alike. The Emperor Akbar played in a truly regal fashion on courts made of inlaid marble. In the centre of the court was a dais four feet high on which he and his courtiers sat, while sixteen young slaves from the harem, wearing appropriate colours, moved about the red and white squares as directed by the throws of cowrie shells. Traces of these royal boards are still visible at Agra and Allahabad.

Modern boards are usually made of cloth, cut into the shape of a cross, and then divided into squares by embroidery (figs. 8 and 149 on Plate XV). The marked squares represent castles in which the pieces are free from capture. A castle occupied by a player's piece is open to his partner's pieces, but closed to the enemy.

Each player has four bee-hive shaped wooden pieces marked with his own colours (fig. 9). Six cowrie shells are used as dice.

Scoring

2 cowries with mouths up	..	2
3 cowries with mouths up	..	3
4 cowries with mouths up	..	4
5 cowries with mouths up	..	5
6 cowries with mouths up	..	6 and another throw
1 cowrie with mouth up	..	10 and another throw
0 cowries with mouth up	..	25 and another throw

The game is played by four players each having four pieces. The players sitting opposite each other are partners, and yellow and black play against red and green. Each piece enters the game from the central space known in Hindustani as the Char-koni, and travels down the middle of his own limb and then round the board, returning up the middle of his own limb back to the Char-koni. On arriving back at the middle row of their own limb the pieces are turned on their sides to show that they have completed the circuit. They can only reach home by an exact throw. The moves are controlled by six cowries.

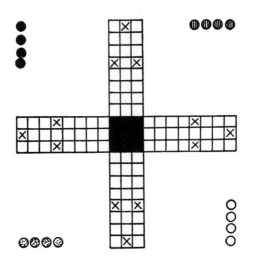

FIG. 8. Pachisi cloth and pieces (from author's collection)

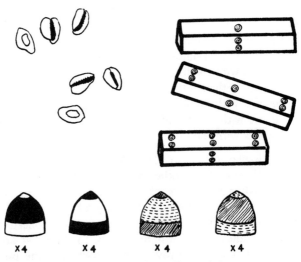

X 4   X 4   X 4   X 4

FIG. 9. Pachisi pieces, three long dice and six cowrie shells
(from author's collection)

frameatthe top:

Rules

1. The cowries are thrown from the hands. When 6, 10, or 25 is thrown the player has an extra turn and he continues until he throws a 2, 3, 4, or 5; when his turn of play ends. On finishing a turn the player moves his pieces before the next player begins his turn. Each throw allows the player to move a piece the indicated number of squares and if he throws more than once in a turn, the different throws may be used to move different pieces; but a single throw cannot be split, i.e. on a throw of 4, a piece moves four squares, the player is not allowed to move two pieces two squares each.

2. A capture is made by a player moving a piece on to a square other than a castle square, occupied by an enemy piece. The latter is removed from the board and must re-enter the game at the Charkoni, with a throw of 6, 10, or 25. A player making a capture has another throw.

3. At the beginning of a game a player's first piece may enter the board whatever the throw, but the other pieces can only be entered on throwing a 6, 10, or 25.

4. The pieces move anti-clockwise.

5. A player may refuse to play when it comes to his turn, or he may throw and then refuse to make use of it. He may do this to avoid the risk of capture or to help his partner. On reaching the castle at the end of the third limb, he may wait there in safety until he throws a 'twenty-five' and then move out in one throw.

6. Pieces may double up on any square, but doubled men can be sent back to start again if they are hit by an equal or larger number of men belonging to the enemy, unless they are resting on a castle square.

Tactics

If a player's partner is behind in the game it may be wise to keep pieces back to help him by blocking the way to opposing pieces, or by capturing them if they threaten him. Both partners win or lose together and if one of them rushes ahead and out of the game the opponents have two throws to the remaining partner's one, and they can keep just behind him and then send him back to the beginning again with a capturing throw. Sometimes when a leading player reaches his own limb he will continue on a second circuit to help his partner instead of turning his piece over and moving up the centre.

The cowries may be replaced by three long dice (fig. 9) marked 1 and 6, and 2 and 5, on the opposing faces. If dice are used the game is called Chausar.

LUDO

About 1896 Pachisi was modified and introduced into England as Ludo, patent 14636, a cubic die being used (fig. 10). The boards and rules are available in any games shop.

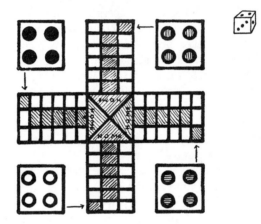

FIG. 10. Modern Ludo board and cubic die

2. SPIRAL RACE GAMES

THE HYENA GAME

Li'b el Merafib or the Hyena game is played by the Baggara Arabs of the Sudan. The board is made by tracing a spiral groove in the sand and making a random number of holes along its course. Each hole represents a day's journey. A larger hole at the centre is a well and the beginning of the track is a village. Each player has a marker which represents his mother.

The dice consist of three pieces of split stick, each about six inches long, on which the bark has been left, so that each stick has one rounded green surface and one flat white one. They are tossed up into the air.

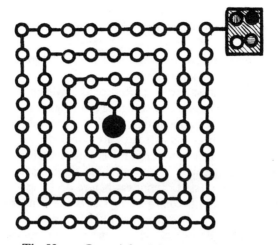

FIG. 11. The Hyena Game (after Hillelson, *Week-end Caravan*)

Scores

One white side up	..	a taba
Two white sides up	..	2 and the turn ends
Three white sides up	..	3
Three green sides up	..	6

Rules

1. The players throw the sticks in turn, each player continuing his turn until he throws a 2; when he passes the sticks to the next player.

2. A player must throw a taba before his mother can leave the village.

3. After throwing a taba the player's mother moves along the spiral two, three, or six days as indicated by the next throw. She does not move for a taba but tabas are marked down on the sand to her credit to be used later.

4. Two mothers can share the same day (hole).

5. A mother must reach the well exactly. If she is short, however, she may make up the missing days by paying the equivalent number of tabas from her son's store.

6. At the well she requires two tabas to wash her clothes, and two to start the return journey. If the player hasn't the required tabas to his credit his mother has to wait until he has collected them

for her. If this happens, however, the player is allowed to mark down for later use any other scores of 2, 3, or 6, which he may throw in the meantime.

7. The women return from the well to the village in the same way as on the outward journey.

8. The mother first arriving back at the village lets a hyena loose and her son controls this savage creature which is allowed to leave the village on a payment of two tabas. It travels at twice the speed of the other pieces as its scores are doubled.

9. At the well it is held up until it has paid ten tabas for a drink.

10. On leaving the well it still moves at double speed and eats any women it overtakes. It cannot eat before drinking.

11. The player who becomes the hyena is the winner but there are degrees of defeat. A player whose mother is eaten by the hyena is ribbed unmercifully by one who manages to guide his maternal parent home safely.

This amusing game can be made up quite simply in wood using coloured marbles for the mothers.

Flinders Petrie, the archaeologist, described in his book *Objects of Daily Life in Ancient Egypt* a spiral board which figured in the tomb of Hesy, with 545 divisions between the tail and the centre which represented a serpent's head. A similar serpent in limestone with seventy-two divisions between the head and tail was found in a tomb of the early dynasties. These may have been used for similar games.

THE ROYAL GAME OF GOOSE

In the eighteenth century A.D. Spiral Games again became popular. One of the first was the ROYAL GAME OF GOOSE and this served as a prototype for numerous similar games. It was imported into England from the continent. Plate 1 (opposite) shows an uncoloured copy which was engraved on hand-made paper with a water-mark of vertical lines and a coat of arms. It was found in 1958 in a Northumberland farmhouse between the pages of a large atlas, published by F. Senex in 1720.

The game is undated but the portrait in the upper right-hand corner, 'JACK SHEPHERD drawn from life', shows him in handcuffs. He was born in Stepney in December 1702 and was brought up in the Bishopsgate workhouse. He was apprenticed to a carpenter, but ran away in 1723 and took to crime. He escaped from jail twice in

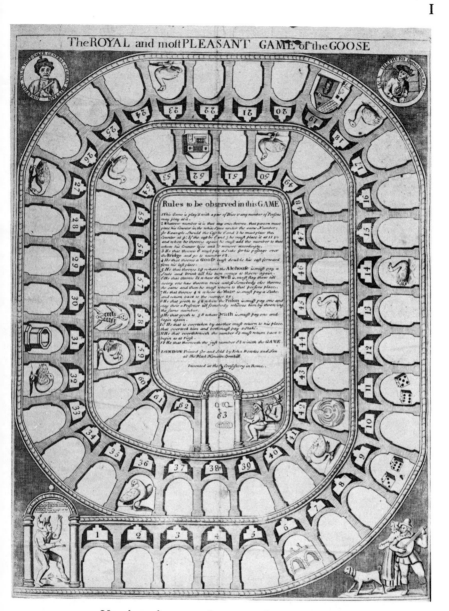

Uncoloured copper-plate engraving, *c.* A.D. 1725

(a) Shaturanga pieces found in London by Falkener, on a modern board
(From his *Games Ancient and Oriental*)

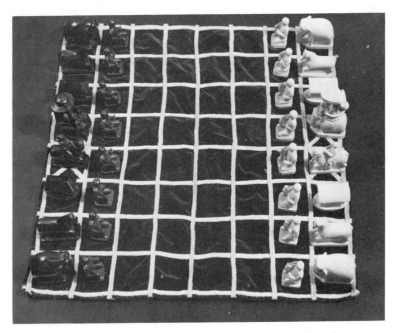

(b) Indian chess cloth and carved wooden pieces found
by the author in Edinburgh

the first half of 1724, and towards the end of that time was responsible for almost daily robberies in the London area. He was captured, tried, and condemned to death in July, but escaped and returned to his old haunts. In September he was re-arrested and imprisoned in the strongest part of Newgate, being chained to the floor of his cell, but escaped through the chimney to the roof of the prison and then climbed on to a neighbouring house. A few days later he was recaptured, hopelessly drunk, in a Clare Market tavern and on 16 November 1724 was hanged at Tyburn shortly before his twenty-second birthday.

The upper left-hand corner has an illustration of 'JONATHAN WILD, Thief-taker General of Great Britain'. Wild was born about 1682 in Wolverhampton and became a receiver of stolen goods. He also arranged robberies and then claimed a reward for recovery. Any property which could not be restored to the owners with profit was taken abroad in his own sloop. He betrayed Shepherd and numerous other thieves who would not work for him and in return his activities were overlooked for a time by the authorities, but he was eventually arrested for receiving a piece of stolen lace, tried at the Old Bailey, and hanged at Tyburn on 24 May 1725.

This version of the game was apparently engraved after the capture and death of Shepherd in 1724, but while Wild was still enjoying popularity as a thief-taker; and before he fell from grace and perished at Tyburn in 1725. If these deductions are correct this version is some twenty years earlier than the suggested date of the game's importation into England from Rome given in Whitehouse's book. This particular copy bears the imprint of John Bowles and Son and was probably printed between 1754 and 1764.

The rules are given in quaint English in the central panel beneath which is written:

LONDON. Printed for and sold by John Bowles and Son at the Black Horse in Cornhill. Invented at the Consistory in Rome.

RULES

1. *This game is played with a pair of dice and any number of players may play at it.*

2. *Whatever number it is that anyone throws, that person must place his counter in the white space under the same number: for example, should the cast be 6 and 3 he must place the counter at 9: If the cast be 6 and 5 he must place it at 11: and when he throws again he must add the number to that where his counter lies and so remove accordingly.*

3. *He that throws 6 must pay a stake for his passage over the bridge and go to number 12.*

4. *He that throws a goose must double his cast forward from his last place.*

5. *He that throws 19 where the* ALE HOUSE *is must pay a stake and drink till his turn comes to throw again.*

6. *He that throws 31 where the* WELL *is, must stay there until every one has thrown twice, unless somebody else throws the same and then he must return to 'That Persons' place.*

7. *He that throws 42 where the* MAZE *is must pay a stake and return back to the number 29.*

8. *He that goeth to 52 where the* PRISON *is must pay one and stay there a Prisoner till somebody relieves him by throwing the same number.*

9. *He that goeth to 58 where* DEATH *is, must pay one and begin again.*

10. *He that is overtaken by another must return to his place that overtook him and both must pay a stake.*

11. *He that overthroweth the number 63 must return back and begin as at the first.*

12. *He that throweth the just number 63 wineth the* GAME.

Each player started with twelve counters and paid his debts into a pool which became the winner's property.

In his poem *The Deserted Village* published in 1770 Oliver Goldsmith wrote:

> The pictures place'd for ornament and use,
> The Twelve good rules, the Royal Game of Goose.

The games of pure amusement were soon followed by a host of others based on the same principles and designed for educational purposes, teaching the children history, geography, architecture, botany, and astronomy. Occasional copies may still be found in old book or antique shops: delightful hand-coloured sections mounted on canvas and contained in slip cases or between boards, similar to modern road maps mounted on cloth.

3. SQUARE BOARD RACE GAMES

THAAYAM

When the rice is nearly ripe women and girls in Southern India spend days in the paddy frightening away the birds, and to pass the time they play several games, the most popular being Thaayam. The board (fig. 12) is marked out on the ground and little sticks are used for pieces. The dice are made from tamarind seeds which are chocolate brown in colour and cubical in shape, each of the surfaces being slightly convex. They are used in making curries. When one side of a seed is rubbed on a stone the outer husk can be rasped away leaving the white kernel exposed. Four prepared seeds, with three sides white and three left dark, are used.

Scoring   1 white side up   ..   1
                    2 white sides up   ..   2 and turn ceases
                    3 white sides up   ..   3 and turn ceases
                    4 white sides up   ..   4
                    0 white sides up   ..   8

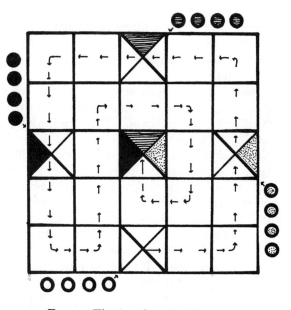

FIG. 12. Thaayam board and markers

If four cowries are used instead of seeds the mouth side up is the equivalent of white and the convex side up of black.

The middle squares of each side of the board are marked and represent a player's palace, while the central square is a keep or castle. Each player has four pieces which start the game off the board.

Rules

1. Each player in turn throws the dice and the highest scorer begins the game. Tying players rethrow. When a player's turn is finished the dice are passed to the player on his right who begins his turn.

2. A player continues to throw the dice until he scores a 2, or a 3, and then the turn ceases and the dice are passed to the next player.

3. A player must move a piece by the indicated amount of each throw unless it is impossible to do so. He may use the throws in any order.

4. A player can only enter a piece on to the board with a throw of 1, and the piece is placed in the player's palace. No score counts until he throws a 1, but after a 1 is thrown the piece is moved as indicated by the dice, e.g. if a player's four pieces were all off the board and he threw 8, 4, 1, 4, 2, he would introduce a piece into his palace with the throw of 1, and then with the 4, and the 2, he would move it on six squares.

5. Any throw may be shared between a player's pieces: e.g. if he threw 1, 4, 1, 4, 1, 3, the 1's could be used to introduce pieces into his palace, or to move pieces on their journey, while the 4, 4, 3, could be used to move on one piece 4 plus 4 plus 3=11 squares; or two or three pieces by any desired combination of the throws. A turn can be split between two or more pieces.

6. The pieces move anti-clockwise round the board until they reach the square contiguous with their palace when they turn into the inner path and travel clockwise until they again reach the square contiguous with their palace when they turn to enter the centre; and when all a player's pieces have assembled in the keep the final bearing off begins; and with each 1 thrown a piece is removed from the board. The first player to remove all his pieces from the board wins the game.

7. A player may have any number of his pieces on one square.

8. If a piece lands on a square occupied by a hostile piece the latter is hurt in battle and is removed from the board, and can only enter again via his own palace on a throw of 1, and begins his journey all over again.

9. If a player moves a piece on to a square occupied by two or more enemy pieces—except a TWIN—the latter are sent home in the same way that a single piece would have been.

10. If a player's piece hits an enemy piece the player has another turn.

11. Rule 8 does not apply to pieces resting on the marked squares which are havens of safety. This symbolizes the sanctity of a guest in a house—even if he is an enemy he is free from harm while under the host's roof. Any number of pieces of any colour may thus congregate on a palace square, and all are safe from attack. The central keep is also a common sanctuary.

12. If a player has two pieces on the palace square immediately opposite his own palace he has the option of declaring them a TWIN, or playing on in the ordinary way. A twin resting on an ordinary square can only be attacked and sent home by another twin; a single enemy piece may move on to the same square with it, or a twin may move on to a square occupied by a single enemy piece, but does not harm it. Twins are neither attacked by nor can attack, single pieces; twins can only attack or be attacked by each other.

13. A twin moves only half the number of squares thrown by the dice: e.g. a throw of 4, 1, 4, 2=11, and would only allow a twin to move five squares, one half of ten squares. The player could of course move the twin four squares representing eight of the throw and then move some single piece three squares, utilizing the whole of the other three points scored.

14. If a twin is hit by a twin and sent off the board there are two alternative methods of play and it should be decided at the start of the game which is to be used.

(*a*) On being hit and sent off the board the twin becomes two single pieces again and they are entered singly on throws of 1, in the ordinary way.

(*b*) When a twin is sent off the board it can only be reintroduced as a twin, and only on throwing two 1's in a single throw, e.g. 4, 1, 4, 1, 8, 2. The first 4 could be used to move a piece on the board, then the two 1's could reintroduce the twin to the palace, the 8 and 2 could be used to move the twin on five squares or some

other piece on ten squares and the 4 between the 1's could move
some other piece four squares.

15. When a twin reaches the central keep it becomes two single
pieces, and a double throw of 1 is not required in the final escape
from the board.

I am indebted to Dr. M. Thillai-nayagam for the account of this
game. He also mentioned a more elaborate form known as 'The
King's Thayyam'. The boards are double the size and eight tamarind seeds are used instead of four. The game is played in Tamil
schools but he was unable to give any details.

4. PEG SCORING BOARDS

THE PALM TREE GAME

In his five years excavating at Thebes Lord Carnarvon found a
gaming board in a tomb of the Late Middle Kingdom, which is
usually regarded as embracing the Twelfth Dynasty (2000 to 1788
B.C.) and is generally known as The Feudal Age.

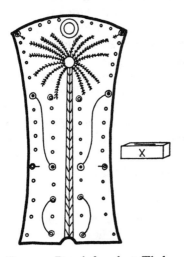
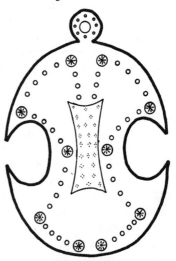

FIG. 13. Board found at Thebes;   FIG. 14. Ivory and gold board from
   c. 2000 B.C. (redrawn from   Megiddo in Palestine, *c.* 1300
   Lord Carnarvon and H. Car-   B.C. (drawn from a photograph
   ter's *Five Years' Excavations*   of a fragment in *Illustrated*
   at Thebes)   *London News*, 23 October
                                   1937, p. 709)

The board (fig. 13) is six inches long and three inches wide with an ivory top, and dog- and jackal-headed pieces which were contained in a drawer secured by copper staples and an ivory bolt.

Suggested Rules for the Palm Tree Game

1. The right side of the board belongs to Black, and the left to White. The pieces travel from the gold point beside the trunk of the palm nearest its fronds down the tree, round the perimeter of the board, and back up the other side of the tree; the five pieces taking up the upper five positions along the tree trunk on the opponent's side of the board. Exact throws are needed to enable them to take up these positions.

2. The two players throw the four-sided die alternately and only on the throw of four (X) can a piece be introduced on to the board at the gold point near the top of the tree. In virtue of Rule 3 the player then throws again and he may use this extra turn to move any of his pieces in play the indicated amount.

3. A piece landing on a gold point earns the player an extra turn.

4. If a piece lands on a point connected with a gold line it moves to the other end. This may be a promotion or a demotion, the line acting as either a snake or a ladder.

5. If a piece lands on a gold point marked with a short horizontal line the player loses a turn.

6. A player cannot move a piece on to a point already occupied.

7. A player must move if he can; if he is unable to use a score his opponent may do so in addition to his own turn which follows.

8. If the pieces become blocked and neither player can pass those of the opponent, the game is drawn.

9. The first player to marshal his five pieces on the upper five points of his opponent's side of the tree wins the game.

Archaeologists know the Palm Tree Game as the game of Dogs and Jackals as the pieces are often in the likeness of these animals. It appears to have originated in Egypt and the board from Thebes is one of the oldest known.

The board shown in fig. 14 was made in the thirteenth century B.C. of ivory and gold and was found at Megiddo in Palestine.

The board in fig. 15 was found at Ur by Sir Leonard Woolley in 1932. It is 13 cms. long and has the broken ends of gaming pieces protruding from the short side of the board. It was probably made during the Assyrian occupation of Ur, about 700 B.C. Similar boards have been found in Assyria itself and one has an inscription on its reverse which reads:

'Palace of Esarhaddon, the great king, the mighty king, king of all, king of Assyria, governor of Babylon, king of Sumer and Akkad, son of Sennacherib, the mighty king, king of all, king of Assyria, son of Sargon, the mighty king, etc. . . .'

Esarhaddon conquered Egypt *c.* 675 B.C.

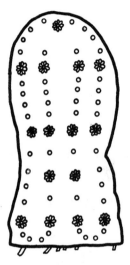

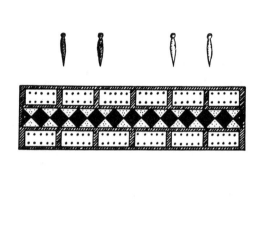

FIG. 15. Board of baked clay found at Ur by Sir L. Woolley; *c.* 700 B.C. (redrawn from Murray's *History of Board Games other than Chess*)

FIG. 16. Cribbage board of inlaid woods (author's collection)

An eighteenth- or early nineteenth-century cribbage board in the author's collection is shown in fig. 16. The resemblance to the earlier boards is striking. Cribbage was invented by Sir John Suckling (1609–1642) and was an improvement on an older card game, Noddy. There seems little doubt that an existing form of score board was utilized for the new games, and the humble cribbage board obtainable in any games shop may have a lineage reaching back to the board from Thebes.

5. THE BACKGAMMON GROUP

GAMING BOARDS FROM THE ROYAL
TOMBS AT UR

Sir Leonard Woolley found five gaming boards in the royal
tombs at Ur in Mesopotamia which were of the same type,
though each had individual variations in the decoration of the
squares. The boards date from about 3000 B.C. Sir Leonard's
book *The First Phases* contains a plate showing two of these
boards. One is very simple and consists of little discs of shell
with red or blue centres set in bitumen which covered the wood
and formed a background. The more elaborate board is completely
covered with an incrustation of shell plaques inlaid with lapis

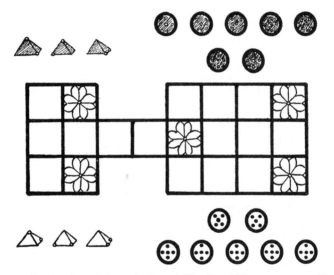

Fig. 17. Gaming board from the Royal Tombs of Ur, *c.* 3000 B.C. (drawn
from photographic plate in Sir L. Woolley's *The Royal Cemetery*)

lazuli and red limestone and divided by lapis lazuli strips; in other
examples the majority of the plaques and also the white 'pieces' are
engraved with animals (see frontispiece); but all agree in having the
coloured rosette in the middle row of the larger section next to the
'bridge'. The boards were hollow and inside were found seven
black and seven white counters and six curious dice, pyramidal in

shape with two of the four points dotted with inlay. Three white
and three lapis lazuli dice made a set; perhaps three for each player.
No account of how to play the game has survived but one may guess
that there were lucky and unlucky squares. The two sides of the
elaborate board are identical, suggesting that one side belonged to
each player. The middle rank may have been neutral territory.

Suggested Rules for the Sumerian Game

1. Each player places an agreed sum into a pool which becomes
the property of the winner at the end of the game. (In one of the
finds there were twenty-one small white balls which may have been
tallies.)

2. One player throws a single die, the other forecasting while
it is in the air whether a tipped or an untipped corner will be uppermost. If he is correct he has the choice of colour, side of the board ,
and the opening move.

ENTER

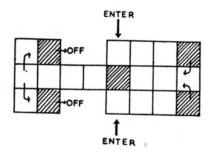

ENTER

FIG. 18. Diagram to show the direction of movement of the
pieces on the board

3. Both 'teams' start off the board. The direction of movement
is shown in fig. 18.

4. The opening player throws his three dice and the possible
scores are:

Three jewelled corners up .. 5 and another throw
Three plain corners up   .. 4 and another throw
Two plain corners up   .. 0 and the turn finishes
One plain corner up   .. 1 and another throw

5. A piece can only be entered on the board on the throw of
five and then it moves forward by the indicated numbers on the
additional throws.

6. If a piece moves on to a marked square the opponent pays a fine into the pool.

7. When a piece moves on to the central file it is at war with the enemy pieces and if it lands on a square occupied by an enemy piece the latter is sent off the board and must start again with a throw of 5. There are eight 'fighting' squares and six 'safe' squares on the board for each player.

8. An exact throw is needed to bear a piece off the board.

9. A player may have any number of pieces on the board at once but only one piece is allowed on one square at a time.

10. The first player to bear all his pieces off the board wins the pool.

Fifteen hundred years later the Egyptians used boards which appear to have been derived from those of Ur, and several have been found in tombs of the 'Empire' age, about 1580 B.C. A board found at Enkomi in Cyprus which was within the Egyptian Empire is shown in fig. 19. See also fig. 153 on Plate XVII.

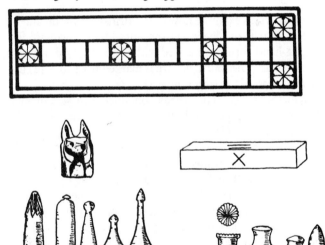

FIG. 19. Board for the Egyptian game of Tau found in Enkomi in Cyprus; *c*. 1580 B.C. (redrawn from *Journal of Hellenic Studies*, 1896, p.288). A long die and types of pieces used at that time are included

The group of squares at the smaller end of the Sumerian board have been unfolded into a straight tail but the rosettes have been retained and the game may have been played in a similar way. The Egyptian boards were usually made in a box form containing a drawer to hold the pieces and dice. The game was called Tau by the Egyptians. The under-surface of the box often had a second game of 3 × 10 or 3 × 12 squares.

THE GAME OF THIRTY SQUARES (SENAT)

F IG. 20. Egyptian Senat board now in the British Museum marked with the cartouche of Queen Hatshepsut, *c.* 1500 B.C., with one of twenty lion-headed pieces found with it. The gambling-sticks were found elsewhere

Fig. 20 shows an example now in the British Museum and marked with the cartouche of Queen Hatshepsut. The fifth square from the lower right-hand corner is marked with the hieroglyph which means a door or an exit. The fourth square is marked with an X (4) the third III (3), the second II (2), and the first I (1).

Many of these Egyptian boards contained two sets of men, one side being pawn shaped and the other like cotton reels (figs. 19 and 153 on Plate XVII).

The drawer of the board which is now in the British Museum contained twenty lion-headed pieces (fig. 20), ten of a light coloured wood, nine of a dark coloured wood, and one of ivory which may have been a replacement for a lost piece of the set. In addition to pieces there were four staves. A board from Tutankhamen's tomb contained two knuckle bones, and in the board from Ak-hor (fig. 21) was a long die. Four elaborate gaming pieces are also shown in fig. 21.

There is a picture in the Fifth Dynasty tomb of Rashepses at Sakkarah, *c.* 2500–2400 B.C., of two men squatting on the ground playing a game.

The pieces are placed alternately along the board, although the Egyptian artistic convention of only drawing in profile makes this observation of limited value. A similar painted relief from the Eleventh Dynasty tomb of Baqt at Benihasan, *c.* 2000–1780 B.C., shows two boards and four players. Over one board is written in hieroglyphs 'To play with five'. Over the other board is 'Consumed', possibly meaning that the game was finished. These two pictures are close together and may show two stages of the same game (fig. 22).

FIG. 21. Board from Ak-hor now in the Cairo Museum. The four elaborate gaming-pieces were found elsewhere

Several papyri exist containing similar drawings but the texts give no clue whatever to the method of play. It appears to have been a race game of the backgammon type and may have been an early forerunner of Nard, later so popular among the Arab peoples.

FIG. 22. Wall drawing from a tomb at Benihassan, *c.* 2000 B.C. (redrawn from Falkener's *Games Ancient and Oriental*)

Suggested Rules for Senat

1. Each player has ten men. At the beginning of the game the men are placed alternately on the top and second row (fig. 158 on Plate XXI).

2. The players throw the long die and the higher throw gives the advantage of first move, though this player's pieces occupy the second positions.

3. The opening player throws the die again and moves a piece the indicated number of squares, landing on an empty square, or one containing an enemy piece which is captured and removed. A piece may not move on to a square occupied by one of its own team.

4. If an opening player's first throw is a 2, he can only move his front piece, all the others being blocked, and if he throws a four (X) then only one of his two forward pieces can be moved. With a throw of 1, he can move any piece and make a capture, and with a throw of 3, he can make a capture with any piece except his front one.

5. The players throw the die alternately, making their moves before passing the die to their opponent. The pieces can only move towards the end of the board, They cannot move backwards.

6. A piece reaching one of the marked squares—X, III, II, I— cannot be captured but rests on it until an exact throw allows the piece to escape from the board and wins the player a point. A piece reaching the square marked ♂ is safe from attack, but must move on to a marked square as soon as possible.

7. A piece must vacate a marked square at the first possible throw.

8. The player guiding most pieces safely off the board wins the game.

In 1929 the Egyptian Government decided to raise the level of the Aswan Dam which involved the flooding of the southern area of Lower Nubia and the destruction of archaeological sites from Wadi es Sebua to Adindan on the Sudan frontier. An expedition under Walter B. Emery was sent to explore the area and to rescue as much material as possible before it was covered with water. In the six winter-months of 1931 they explored the tombs at Ballana and Qustul. Those at Qustul were constructed about the fourth century A.D. and belonged to the kings and nobility of a race known to archaeologists as the X-group people. They were probably the Blemyes, a powerful nation who lived south of the First Cataract. Between A.D. 250 and their final defeat in the middle of the sixth century, they were often at war with Roman forces in Egypt. About A.D. 550 Silko, the king of the Notabae who were allies of Rome, attacked and utterly routed the Blemyes and drove them out into the desert where they lingered for a few years and finally disappeared from history, and with them the last traditions of Pharaonic Egypt.

The Qustul tombs were buried beneath tumuli and in the base of tomb 3 near the surface the expedition found an elaborate gaming board lying face downwards, and beneath it a leather bag containing fifteen ivory and fifteen ebony gaming pieces; a dice box and five ivory dice. The board was 32 in. long and 15 in. wide and was made of a single piece of wood with a framed border, strengthened at the corners with silver brackets attached with small silver nails. There was a loop handle also of silver which was fastened to the frame with gudgeon pins. The playing surface of the board contained thirty-six squares marked by a delicate fretwork of ivory in conventional floral design. The squares were arranged in three rows of twelve, and each row was divided by centre markings, also of ivory fretwork. The outer rows were bisected by half circles, and the middle row by a full circle (fig. 23).

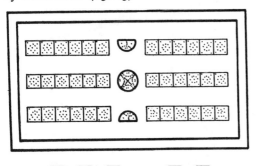 

FIG. 23. Gaming-board from Qustul, *c.* A.D. 350 (drawn from
plate XXXII in Emery's
Nubian Treasure)

FIG. 24. Copy of a fritillus or dice-
box based on plate XXXII in
Emery's *Nubian Treasure*

The five dice were cube-shaped and of ivory. They were marked from one to six with tubular drill holes which were filled with red paint. The dice box (fig. 24) was made of wood and was $6\frac{1}{2} \times 3 \times 3$ in. The fittings were of silver. The dice were dropped through the open top and fell onto an inclined grooved board which turned them over before they rolled out through the opening at the bottom between two carved dolphins. Similar dice boxes were used by gamesters throughout the Greco-Roman world as late as the end of the fifth century. They prevented cheating by sleight of hand.

The Qustul board, pieces, dice, and box were used for a game probably similar to those played by their ancestors, the Ancient Egyptians.

LUDUS DUODECIM SCRIPTORUM

There are frequent references in Roman literature to a popular game called 'Ludus Duodecim Scriptorum'—the game of the twelve lines. On the back of a silver mirror which was made in the second or third century B.C. and found in Palestrina is an engraving of a youth and a maiden both partially undressed sitting in front of a gaming table (fig. 25).

FIG. 25. Back of a silver mirror, *c.* 200 B.C. (redrawn from D. Comparetti, Rendiconti della reale accademia dei Lincei, 17 Feb. 1887)

The youth has his hand half closed and looks as if he is about to throw a die. There are no pieces shown on the table; possibly the game has only just begun and the pieces were entered on the board according to the throws of the dice. The word OFEINOD is archaic and unknown. DEVINCAMTED may be translated 'I believe I shall beat you'. Comparetti who examined the mirror when it was in a private collection believed the work was Roman even though it was in the style of Greek art, and he suggested that the game may be the original form of Ludus Duodecim Scriptorum. Apparently this indigenous game was later replaced by the more elaborate thirty-six space game, coming either directly from Egypt or via Greece. The newcomer soon supplanted the native Roman game and also took its name in the same way that 'Sphairistike' invented by Major Wingfield in England about 1874 became known as 'Lawn Tennis', and within fifty years as 'Tennis'. Real tennis is an entirely different game played in a penthouse and there are barely a score of courts left in the whole of Europe.

A crude board made of buff ware but closely resembling the Qustul board was found at Holt in Denbighshire and is now in the National Museum of Wales. It apparently belonged to a soldier of the Twentieth Legion stationed on the Marches of Wales in the first half of the second century A.D. A raised moulded border surrounds the playing area which consists of two outer rows of twelve roughly inscribed ivy leaves, separated into groups of six by a central geometrical pattern. The middle row consists of twelve pairs of scrolls bisected by a compass-drawn pattern of a circle with a six-armed rosette inside it (fig. 26).

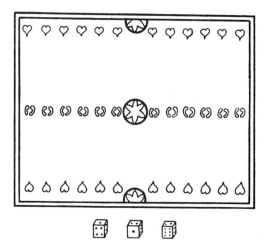

FIG. 26. Ludus Duodecim Scriptorum board from Holt in Denbighshire, c. A.D. 125; now in the National Museum of Wales (redrawn from Austin's *Roman Board Games*)

More than a hundred boards for this game were found in the city of Rome alone during the lifetime of Rodolfo Lanciani, professor of Archaeology in the University, clear evidence of its one-time popularity. The commonest form consisted of three horizontal lines, each line being split up into twelve spaces. These spaces varied in almost every board; there were circles, squares, vertical bars, leaves, letters, monograms, crosses, crescents, and even erotic symbols. Sixty-five of the boards contained six words of six letters. See fig. 27.

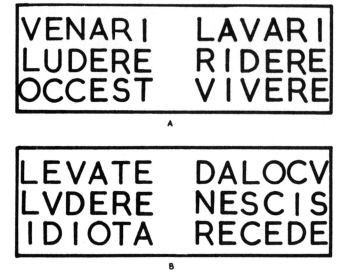

FIG. 27. Ludus Duodecim Scriptorum boards found at Timgad (A) and Rome (B) (redrawn from Austin's *Roman Board Games*)

   (A) was found at Timgad; a rough translation is:

> To hunt—to bathe
> To play—to laugh
> This is—to live.

   (B) was found in Rome.

> Jump up—push off
> You can—not win
> Get out—Baboon.

The players used three dice marked from 1 to 6, and the highest throw was three sixes, called by Cicero 'Venereus' (*de Divin.* 1. 13). The lowest throw was three aces known as 'Canis'. Cheating was prevented by throwing the dice into a Fritillus or Pyrgus, a wooden tower about a foot high which had a spiral staircase inside.

   In the later days of Rome gambling became a mania. Nero played for huge stakes, up to 400,000 sesterces a point (about £6,000), while Lampridius tells us that Commodus turned the Imperial Palace into a casino replete with every form of shameless dissipation. Once, when he was pressed for money, he pretended that he was about to visit the African Provinces of the Empire, but when the Treasury made him a grant for the purpose, his enthusiasm evaporated rapidly and he spent it all in gambling and in immoral excesses.

In 1876 two paintings were found in a tavern in Pompeii, a Roman city partially buried with lava in A.D. 63, and finally over-whelmed by Vesuvius in A.D. 79. In one painting two players are seated opposite each other on stools, holding a gaming-table on their knees, and on it arranged in various lines are several LATRUNCULI of yellow, black, and white. The player on the left is shaking a yellow dice box and shouts 'Exsi!' (I am out!) The other points to the dice and answers 'Non tria, dvas est!' (Not three points, but two!) See fig. 28.

FIG. 28. Tavern wall-painting in Pompeii, *c.* A.D. 70 (redrawn from Gusman's *Pompeii, the City, its Life and Art*)

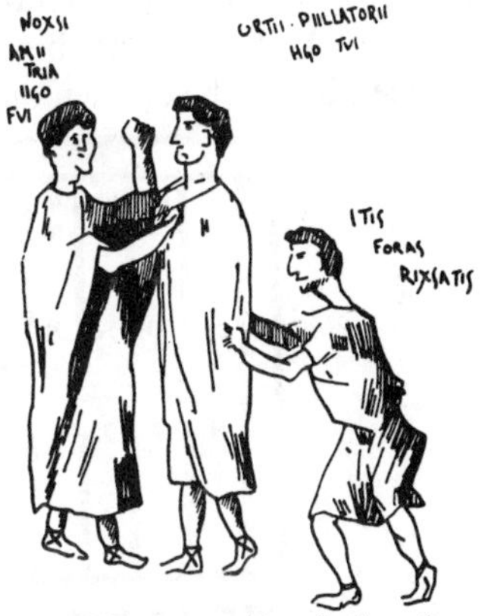

FIG. 29. Tavern wall-painting from Pompeii, *c.* A.D. 70 (redrawn from Gusman's *Pompeii, the City, its Life and Art*)

In the next picture the same players have sprung to their feet to fight, and the innkeeper, acting as his own chucker-out, is pushing them into the street, shouting 'Itis foras rixsatis!' (Get out if you want to fight!).

The game is mentioned by Ovid (*A.A.* iii. 363 f., *Trist.* ii. 475) and other writers but unfortunately no description of the rules has survived.

During the first century A.D. Ludus Duodecim Scriptorum became obsolete in fashionable circles and was replaced by Tabula, a variant with only two rows of points. Emperor Claudius (A.D. 41–54) was very fond of the game and Suetonius states that he wrote a book on the subject and had a board fixed to his chariot so that he could play while travelling.

Four centuries later Emperor Zeno (A.D. 475–81) suffered so re-markable a misfortune in a game that the position was described in an epigram half a century later by Agathias, a scholastic of Myrine in Asia (A.D. 527–67). The position has been recovered by M. Becq de Fourquière and this sixth-century record enables us to reconstruct the game of Tabula with a fair degree of certainty.

TABULA

Fig. 30 shows the board and the position of the pieces. The Emperor was playing White and the throw of his three dice was 2, 5, 6. As he was unable to move the men on (6) which were blocked by the black men on (8), (11), (12): or the singleton on (9),

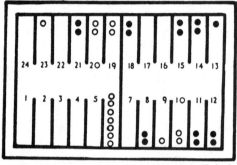

FIG. 30. Diagram of Zeno's disastrous throw at Tabula, *c.* A.D. 480 (redrawn from Austin's *Zeno's Game of Table*)

which was blocked by the black pieces on (11), (14), (15): he was forced to break up his three pairs, a piece from (20) going to (22), one from (19) going to (24), and one from (10) going to (16). No other moves were possible and he was left with eight singletons and a ruined position.

Rules for Tabula

1. The game was played on a board of twenty-four points by two players, each having fifteen pieces of a distinguishing colour.

2. The moves of the pieces were controlled by the alternate throws of three six-sided dice. If, for example, the numbers 1, 3, 5, were thrown:

(*a*) Three pieces could be moved, one 1 point, one 3 points, and one 5 points, as long as each resting point was not blocked by enemy pieces; or (*b*) two pieces could move, e.g. one piece by 1 point, and the other piece by 3 plus 5, or 5 plus 3, or any other combination desired; or

(*c*) one piece could move 9 points if each resting place were free, i.e. 1 plus 3 plus 5, or any reorientation of these numbers, e.g. 5 plus 1 plus 3.

3. The pieces were entered on the board in the first quarter and travelled anti-clockwise round the track. Apparently both colours travelled in the same direction, and it improves the game if no piece is allowed to enter the second half of the board until all the player's pieces are entered into the first half.

4. If a player had two or more men on a point, this point became closed to the enemy and the pieces on it could not be captured. They were called PILED MEN or ORDINARII.

5. If a player moved a piece on to a point occupied by an enemy singleton, the latter was sent off the board and had to re-enter the game at the next possible throw. Probably no other piece could be moved until it was re-entered. Singletons were known as VAGI.

6. Pieces unable to move because they were blocked by enemy ordinarii were known as INCITI. A player was forced to use the whole of his throw if this was possible even if, as happened to the unfortunate Emperor Zeno, it was to the player's disadvantage: any part of a throw, however, which was unplayable was lost and the turn passed to his opponent.

7. An additional rule not mentioned by classical writers which improves the game is that no piece may be borne off the board until all the player's pieces have entered the last quarter. If a player starts bearing off and a vagus is hit, no further pieces can be borne off until it has re-entered the final quarter again.

All gambling games were forbidden by law except during the festive licence of the Saturnalia at least as early as the time of Cicero (106–43 B.C.) but the laws were never rigidly enforced, and under many emperors were entirely disregarded.

Towards the end of the sixth century the name Tabula became replaced by Alea. Isidore of Seville who was born in the sixth century and died in the seventh, wrote in his *Origines*, 'Alea, id est ludus tabulae. . . .' (Alea, that is the game of tabula. . . .)

The Codex Exoniensis, a collection of Anglo-Saxon verse given to Exeter Cathedral by Leofric, the city's first bishop, about A.D. 1025, contains the first English references to Tables. Two lines run:

'Hy twegen sceolon
Taefle ymsittan.'

meaning in modern English:

'These two shall sit at Tables.'

A superb manuscript was compiled between A.D. 1251 and 1282 at the command of Alfonso X, King of Léon and Castile. It is now in the library of the monastery of St. Lorenzo del Escorial, a few miles from Madrid. It contains ninety-eight pages, 16·5 in. high and 11·7 in. wide, bound in sheepskin. The manuscript is written in two columns to the page in a beautiful hand with many illuminated initials, both small and large. It is also illustrated with 150 richly coloured drawings, ten being full plates. The book is divided into four sections. Part one deals only with chess; part two with games played with three dice; part three with some fifteen varieties of Tables; and part four contains a miscellaneous collection of games starting with an enlarged chess, the Grande Acedrez, then a game consisting of a combination of chess and tables, Tablas de Alcedrez, and it ends with the game of Alquerque.

Some of the medieval boards used for Tables were magnificent works of art. One of them on view at the Munich Art Exposition of 1876 had been found in 1852 in the *mensa* of the altar of the diocesan church of St. Valentine in Aschaffenburg and had served as a reliquary. The plain points were pieces of red-veined oriental jasper, which were polished only on their upper surfaces, the sides being inlaid; and the adorned points were overlaid with thick pieces of split rock-crystal, themselves inlaid, and beneath were small terra-cotta figures, variously painted with green, red, yellow, blue, and white tints lying on a gold ground. They represented partly twin-tailed sirens, partly dragon-like monsters, centaurs, and battles between beasts and men. The spaces between the points as well as the borders and edges of the sides were covered with very thin silver leaf laid on hard cement, in which foliage and other ornamental designs were impressed by means of metal stamps, which appeared as if they were in high relief when seen from the front. The flowers and leaves on the two sides were enamelled in red, green, and blue. At each end of the board were small drawers for holding the men which were missing. The covers of these containers were of rock crystal adorned with silver.

Backgammon boards were favourite objects for the expression of a craftsman's skill and it is not surprising that this superb board became a treasured piece of church furniture in spite of its secular origin.

In isolated parts of Iceland, Table boards are still used whose points are made of wooden strips tacked to an underlying plank similar to the Tabula boards of the late Roman period. One of the rustic games, AD ELTA STELPUR, or CHASING THE GIRLS, may date back to this period. Fig. 31 shows the opening positions of the two players' pieces.

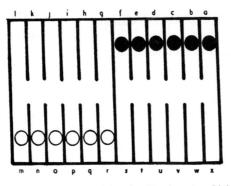

FIG. 31. Opening position in Chasing the Girls

CHASING THE GIRLS

Rules   One player has six white pieces, and the other six black.

1. The players throw a single die and the lower score gives the advantage of first move.

2. Two cubic dice are thrown but only throws of 6, 1, and any doublet are used. On throwing a doublet the player has another turn.

3. A throw of 6, 6, counts as a double double and the player may move four of his pieces six places each.

4. A throw of any other doublet allows two pieces to move the indicated number and the player has another turn.

5. A throw of 6, or of 1, allows one piece to move this number of points.

6. No other throw scores.

7. All the pieces move in an anti-clockwise direction and continue to circulate round the board until one player has lost all his men.

8. If a piece lands on a point occupied by an opponent's piece the latter is removed from the board and is out of the game.

9. Doubling up on a point is not allowed and if a throw brings a piece to a point on which the player already has a piece the former is placed on the first vacant point beyond.

10. When a player has only one man left, called a HORNASKELLA or CORNER-RATTLER, the method of play changes:

(*a*) The corner-rattler can only land on the corner points of the four quarters of the board, e.g. on a, f, g, l, m, r, s, and x.

(*b*) A throw of 1 moves it on to the next corner point.

(*c*) A throw of 6 moves it on two corner points.

(*d*) Throws of 1, 1, and 6, 6, count double a single throw of these numbers, but no other double enables the corner-rattler to move. The player, however, wins another throw: e.g. if a piece became a corner-rattler on p and the player threw 6, 1, then it would move to point r in virtue of the 1, and then to point x in virtue of the throw of 6. If he then threw 2, 2, he would have another throw. If this were 5, 1, he would move to a, etc.

11. The corner-rattler can only capture pieces standing on corner points and can itself only be attacked on these points. It is also safe from capture if it stands between enemy pieces; e.g. if Black has men on q, r, s, and White has a corner-rattler on m, and White throws 3, 1, the corner-rattler moves to r and captures the Black man on the point. If Black then throws 1, 2, the black piece on q cannot move to r and capture the corner-rattler because it is between two hostile pieces. Thus Black can only move his piece on s to t, or his piece on q to t, the next vacant point.

If Black threw 1, 6, however, the black piece on s could move to a, using the 6, and then the black piece on q could move to r and capture White's corner-rattler and win the game. Both players may be reduced to corner-rattlers, when the game may develop into a long chase before one of them is beaten.

TOURNE-CASE

This simple game from France is played with a Tabula or Backgammon board and two cubic dice.

Rules

1. Each player has three pieces which are entered on the player's side of the board and travel along it to the twelfth or HOME point.

2. A player's pieces remain in their order of entry. No piece can pass over one in front of it, nor can two pieces rest on the same point except on the home point.

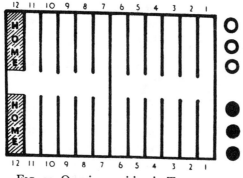

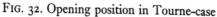

FIG. 32. Opening position in Tourne-case

3. If a player plays a piece on to a point, other than the home point, and an enemy piece is on the point immediately opposite, the latter is sent off the board and has to re-enter at the next throw.

4. Doublets count only as a single throw: e.g. a throw of 4, 4, allows the player to move only one piece four places.

5. The first player with three pieces home wins the game. If he does so before his opponent has any pieces home he gains a double win.

SIXE-ACE

The Alfonsine codex mentions this game as 'sies dos e as' and it is therefore at least seven hundred years old. Twelve pieces of the same colour are taken and each player arranges six on his side of the board (fig. 33).

Two dice are used and the score of a die is reckoned as:

1: A piece is handed over to the opponent and added to his pieces.
6: A piece is borne off the table and is laid aside.
5: A piece is put in the central pool between the tables.
2: A piece is taken from the pool and added to the player's pieces.
3 and 4: These throws are disregarded.

Each die's score must be taken separately and uncombined. On a throw of 3, 2, the 3 is disregarded and a piece is taken from the pool (if there is one in it) and is added to the player's pieces. The throw cannot be counted as 5.

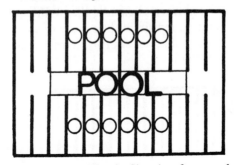

FIG. 33. Opening position in Six-Ace for two players

If doublets are thrown each die counts separately and the player has another throw, unless he casts 2, 2, when he has to pick up two pieces from the pool (if it contains so many) and he does not get another turn. Alternatively, it was sometimes played that on a throw of 2, 2, the player had to add all the pieces in the pool to his own, but he had another turn as well. When a player has cleared his side of the board he must throw a 6 to win.

In the *Compleat Gamester* by Charles Cotton (1674) there is a drinking variant of this game, which paraphrased might read:

'Up to five may play at Six-Ace, each having six pieces. [There are thirty pieces in a backgammon set.] On the throw of a 1, a player passes a piece to his neighbour; on the throw of 6, he bears a piece off; and a player throwing a 2, must drink and throw again. The last two players on the board, or sometimes the last one, pay for the drinks.'

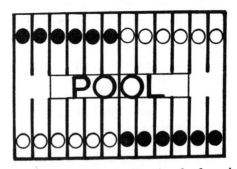

FIG. 34. Opening position in Six-Ace for four players

Fig. 34 shows the opening position in a four-handed game. The turn moves anti-clockwise round the table and on the throw of an Ace a piece is passed to the player on the right.

FAYLES

Fayles is also mentioned in the Alfonso manuscript under the name of Fallas and was still played in the time of Ben Jonson (1572–1637). See figs. 35 and 141 on Plate XI.

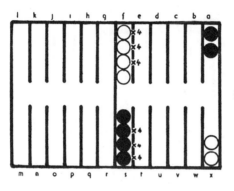

FIG. 35. Opening position in Fayles

Rules

1. Black started with 13 of his men on s and 2 on a and moved his pieces in the direction a to x. White had 13 men on f and 2 on x and moved in the direction x to a.

2. Three dice were used or, if only two, then at each throw the smaller score of the pair was counted twice, e.g. 6, 4, was scored as 6, 4, 4.

3. A piece was moved for the throw of each die or the same piece could be moved again if desired, and if a piece landed on a BLOT or singleton the latter was sent back to its starting point.

4. A piece could not move on to a point held by two or more enemy pieces.

5. If a player at any stage of the game threw a number which could not be played he FAILED and immediately lost; otherwise the player first bearing all his men off the board was the winner.

BACKGAMMON

Nard was a favourite game of the Arab world and was apparently invented before A.D. 800 in south-west Asia or, according to one tradition, in Persia. A Babylonian Talmud, the Gemara, compiled between A.D. 300 and 500, contains the word Nerdshir, and several early European Hebrew philologers, including Nathan ben Jechiel (Rome, 1103), suggested that it represented a game similar to or identical with Nard.

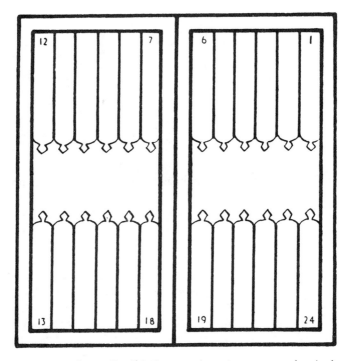

Fig. 36. Tables in an English fourteenth-century manuscript (redrawn from Fiske's *Chess in Iceland*)

Nard and its variants are found throughout Asia. Himly collected the Chinese references and the Hun Tsun Sii which was written during the Sung period (A.D. 960–1279) states that t'shu-p'u, its Chinese name, was invented in western India, spread to China in the time of the Wei Dynasty (A.D. 220–265) and became popular in China between A.D. 479–1000. Each player had sixteen pieces in the Chinese game. An antique ivory specimen forms the tailpiece of this chapter (p. 46). In Japan the game was called Sugoroko and it was declared illegal by the Empress Jito who reigned from A.D. 690–697.

Nard appears to have been introduced into Europe by the Arabs either into Spain or into Italy during the Arabic occupation of Sicily. Thirty pieces were used on a board of twenty-four points and the movements were controlled by the casts of two dice. King Alfonso's manuscript (A.D. 1251–1282) refers to 'Todas tablas' which was almost certainly the Tables of the Middle Ages. Fig. 36 shows an illustration of a board from an English thirteenth-century manuscript.

By 1475 chess had become the popular game and by the end of the sixteenth century the word Tables was used as a generic term for any game played on a flat surface or table, and was no longer applied to a specific game. Early in the seventeenth century a new variant appeared and, coupled with improvements in the boards, finer dice boxes and other attractive changes, the old game enjoyed a tremendous revival and swept through Europe, being played in England as backgammon, in Scotland as gammon, in France as tric-trac, in Germany as puff, in Spain as tablas reales, in Italy as tavole reale.

Just before the 1939–45 war there was a craze for backgammon among the intellectuals, especially the London literary set, but by the middle of the twentieth century the game was once more suffering an eclipse. The 1970's saw an unexpected boom in the game in the West, and boards, pieces and rule books can now be bought at any good game shop. In the Middle East tric-trac (backgammon) has maintained its popularity and is played by all classes in Lebanon and neighboring countries of the eastern Mediterranean.

Unfortunately, backgammon has inherited a number of technical terms but they are reduced to a minimum in the following account.

POINTS. Each player's side of the board contains two sets of six elongated triangles known as points, separated from each other by the BAR.

INNER TABLE. This consists of the player's first six points.

OUTER TABLE. This consists of the points from seven to twelve.

THE BAR. This separates the inner from the outer table.

Fig. 37 shows the initial positions of the pieces. By a convention the inner tables are always those nearer the source of light. The object of the game is to bring all one's pieces home to one's inner table and when they are all assembled there they are BORNE OFF the board. The first player to remove all his pieces wins the game.

BLACK

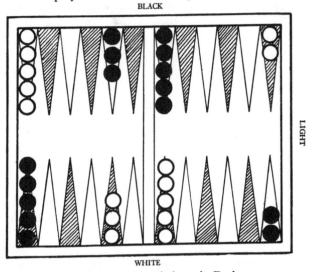

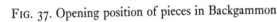

WHITE

Rules FIG. 37. Opening position of pieces in Backgammon

1. At the beginning of the game each player throws a single die and the player with the higher score has a choice of the sides of the board and the colour of his men. He then makes the first move using the numbers of both the dice to move his pieces. His opponent then throws both dice and moves his pieces accordingly and throughout the rest of the game the players throw both dice alternately. The players retain the same sides and pieces in succeeding games.

2. The pieces move in a direction from the opponent's inner table to the opponent's outer table and then from the home outer table to the home inner table and when all the pieces are congregated in the inner table the player begins to bear them off the board.

3. The opposing pieces travel in opposite directions.

4. The two units of a throw may be used separately to move two pieces the indicated amounts, or they may be combined to move one piece the sum of the units as long as it is possible to move the piece first by the throw of one die and then the other. Either number may be played first; if only one number can be played and there is a choice, the higher must be played.

5. When a pair is thrown this throw is known as a DOUBLET and the player plays double the score, i.e. if 2, 2, is thrown the player counts it as a throw of 2, 2, 2, 2, and can move four men two points, or one man eight points or any other possible combination.

6. When a player has two or more men on the same point his opponent is barred from moving on to the point. This is called MAKING A POINT. A player may have more than five men on any point.

7. A player must play the whole of a throw if he can, and any part of a throw which cannot be played is lost.

8. If a single man rests on a point this is known as a BLOT, and if the opponent plays a piece on to that point the blot is hit and is removed from the table and placed on the bar where it remains until it can be played into the opponent's inner table. If a player elects to move only one piece on a throw he may hit a blot on his first or second resting point, or on both.

9. If a player has a man on the bar he cannot move any other piece until it has been re-entered into the game and this is only possible if the pips of one of the dice thrown corresponds to a point on the opponent's inner table which is not held by him. If a player is unable to enter the man on the bar the throw is lost and the opponent follows with another throw. A player unable to enter a man may lose several throws in succession.

10. A player may hit two or more blots in the same throw and he also has the choice of hitting or not hitting a blot, unless no other move is possible.

11. When a player has moved all his men to his own inner table he begins to bear them off. The numbers on the dice may be used to move men forward or to bear them off, or both.

12. If a number higher than any point covered is thrown, a man from the highest point must be borne off.

13. If a number is thrown for an unoccupied point, no men below can be borne off if any man remains on a higher point.

14. A doublet may enable a player to bear off four men at the same time.

15. If a player has begun bearing his pieces off and has a blot hit, it must be placed on the bar and then re-entered into the opponent's inner table and must travel round the board to his own inner table again before any more of his men can be borne off.

16. The player first bearing all his men off the board is the winner

but there are degrees of victory. The simplest form of scoring is the points game.

A. THE POINTS GAME

The winner gets four points for each opposing piece in his inner table or on the bar; three points for each piece in his outer table; two points for each piece in the opponent's outer table, and one point for each piece in the opponent's inner table.

B. THE TRADITIONAL GAME

In the older method of scoring a player wins by:

A SINGLE GAME if his opponent has borne off one or more of his pieces;

A DOUBLE GAME (GAMMON) if no opposing piece has been borne off;

A TRIPLE GAME (BACKGAMMON) if no opposing piece has been borne off and there are one or more pieces on the bar or in the winner's inner table. The stakes for a single win are decided before the game and if a gammon or a backgammon is made the loser pays twice or three times the agreed stake.

DOUBLES. In the modern method of scoring if a doublet is thrown by the players on their initial throw of one die each to decide who moves first, the basic stake is automatically doubled and each tie of the opening throw may either double the previous basic stake or add one to the previous basic stake as decided upon by the players. This is known as AUTOMATIC DOUBLING.

At any time during the game either player may offer to double the stake. If the offer is refused his opponent loses the game and

pays the stake in force at the time of the refusal. If the double is accepted, the game goes on with a doubled stake but an additional double can only be made by the player who accepted the previous double. This is known as VOLUNTARY DOUBLING. A voluntary double may only be offered by the player whose turn it is to play and before he has thrown the dice.

Antique Chinese Tableman in filigree ivory (author's collection)

Modern backgammon sets contain a die with the faces marked 2:4:8:16:32:64, which is used to record the number of doubles pertaining at the moment of play.

CHAPTER TWO

War Games

1. THE ALQUERQUE GROUP

Seven different types of gaming boards were found cut into the great roofing slabs of the temple at Kurna in Egypt, which was built about 1400 B.C. One of these boards was unfinished, probably owing to a mistake in the cutting of a diagonal line (fig. 38).

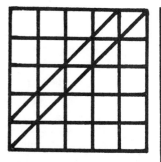

FIG. 38. Abandoned Alquerque board, Ancient Egypt, *c.* 1400 B.C. (from Parker's *Ancient Ceylon*)

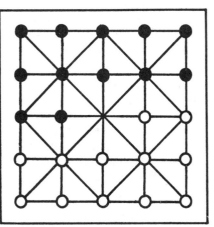

FIG. 39. Opening position of the pieces in Alquerque

Two thousand years later a game called Quirkat is mentioned in the Arabic work *Kitab-al Aghani*, whose author died in A.D. 976. When the Moors invaded Spain they took El-quirkat with them and it appears in the Alfonso X manuscript under its Spanish name of Alquerque (A.D. 1251–1282).

ALQUERQUE

Fig. 39 shows the Alquerque board with the pieces arranged ready for play. The pieces move from any point to any adjacent empty point along a marked line. If the adjacent point is occupied by an enemy piece and the next point beyond it on the line is empty, the player's piece can make a short jump over the hostile piece and remove it from the board. If another piece is then EN PRISE it is taken in the same move by a second short leap, a change of direction being allowed. Two or more pieces may be captured in one move. If a piece can make a capture it is forced to do so, otherwise it is HUFFED and is removed from the board. These rules from the Alfonso manuscript are not sufficient to play a game.

Suggested Additional Rules

1. No piece can move backwards; only forwards, diagonally forwards, or sideways.
2. No piece may return to a point that it has been on before.
3. A piece reaching the opponent's back line is unable to move except by making a capture by a short leap over an enemy piece.
4. The game is over when:

(*a*) *One player has lost all his pieces.* He then pays two points for losing the game and two points for each of the victor's pieces left on the board.

(*b*) *A player cannot move any of his pieces.* He then pays two points for losing the game and a single point for each enemy piece on the board in excess of his own. Should the loser have more pieces on the board than his opponent he pays two points for defeat, minus one point for each piece he has in excess of the winner.

When the Spaniards settled in New Mexico they introduced a quadruple alquerque which the Zuni Indians modified into a new game.

THE GAME OF THE STONE WARRIORS

The boards were often cut into one of the stone slabs used in the flat roofs of the native houses. There were 168 squares (fig. 40) and at the beginning of a game between two players each had six warriors in the six nearest squares on his side of the board. The warriors were discs of pottery about 1 in. in diameter, plain for one side and and with a hole drilled through the centre for the other. The object of the game was to cross over and take the opponent's place, capturing as many men as possible on the way. The pieces moved diagonally one square at a time.

A capture was made by a player blocking an enemy piece diagonally between two of his own, when it was removed from the board (custodian capture). The first piece a player lost was replaced by a special piece called the PRIEST OF THE BOW which could move diagonally or orthogonally. No piece could move backwards.

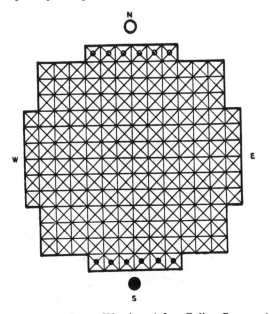

FIG. 40. Game of the Stone Warriors (after Culin, *Games of the North American Indians*)

When the game was played by four, North and West played against South and East. Each player had six pieces making a total of twelve perforated and twelve plain, and each side had one Priest of the Bow, a larger piece, which was exchanged for the first piece captured by the enemy.

The Zuni Indians played another game on the roof-tops called Kolowis Awithlaknannai. (Kolowis is a mythical serpent and Awithlaknannai means 'stones kill'.)

FIGHTING SERPENTS

The length of the board and the number of pieces was not constant. Fig. 41 shows a common size. Small black and white stones

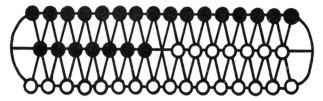

FIG. 41. Board for Fighting Serpents (after Culin, *Games of the North American Indians*)

except for the central one. The opening player moved a piece onto an empty point. This piece was captured by a short leap at the opponent's next move and was taken off the board, taking being compulsory. The players moved alternately and the pieces could move one intersection in any direction along the lines. Capture was by the short leap and more than one piece could be lifted in one turn of play. The game ended when one player had lost all his pieces. See fig. 137 on Plate IX.

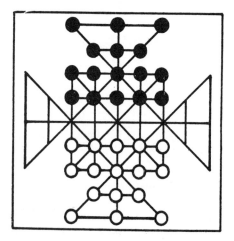

FIG. 42. Board for The Sixteen Soldiers (author's collection)

THE SIXTEEN SOLDIERS

This game is played in Ceylon and parts of India. The initial position is shown in fig. 42. The players move alternately and all pieces can move in any direction along the lines of the board, orthogonally or diagonally, to the next point of intersection.

A capture is made by jumping over an enemy piece on to a vacant point beyond and any number of pieces may be captured in one move by a series of jumps similar to the move of a king in English draughts. The player capturing all the opposing soldiers wins.

As a variant each player may have seven more men placed on the points of the triangle on his left. Three empty points remain along the central transverse line. The same board is used for the game of COWS AND LEOPARDS described on p. 81.

2. THE CHESS GROUP

SHATURANGA

In Ancient India a race-game called Ashtapada was played on a board of sixty-four squares (fig. 43). It was probably similar to Thayaam (p. 17). See also Plate II*a* facing p. 15.

About the fifth century A.D. the Ashtapada board was used for a new game, Shaturanga, which was a miniature battle between four armies each under the control of a Rajah and each containing four corps: Infantry, Cavalry, Elephants, and Boatmen. In this game two players were loosely allied against two opponents.

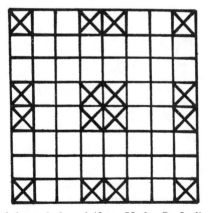

FIG. 43. An Ashtapada board (from Hyde, *De Ludis Orientalibus*)

One of the early Sanskrit writings, the Bhavishya Purana, con-tains the tale of a prince who lost all his possessions including his wife, playing at dice. He went to an old friend to learn the mysteries of Shaturanga hoping to win his fortune back. His instruction is contained in a poem and the following account is based on the translation by Professor Duncan Forbes, Department of Oriental Languages, at King's College, London (1860).

The pawns in Shaturanga represent the infantry, a ship the boat-men, a horse the cavalry, an elephant the elephants, and a human figure the rajah. Each piece had a different type of move.

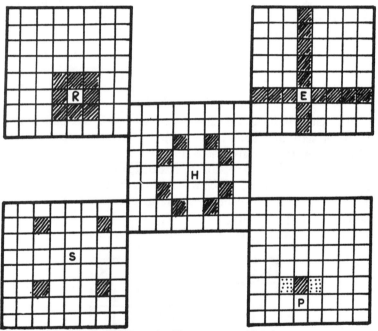

FIG. 44. Moves of the pieces in Shaturanga. The pieces indicated by a letter can move to any shaded square at the next move
R=rajah, E=elephant, H=horse, S=ship, P=pawn

Power of Movement

The RAJAH moved orthogonally or diagonally one square in any direction (fig. 44).

The ELEPHANT moved orthogonally forwards, sideways, or back-wards any number of unoccupied squares. The elephant could not jump over a piece (fig. 44).

The HORSE moved one square orthogonally and one square diagonally (the knight's move in modern chess). The horse could jump over any intervening piece (fig. 44).

The SHIP moved two squares diagonally and could jump over any intervening piece (fig. 44).

The PAWNS moved one square orthogonally forwards, unless they were making a capture when they moved one square diagonally forwards (fig. 44).

Ships and pawns were minor pieces and could capture each other but were not allowed to capture the major pieces. The moves of the pieces were controlled by a long die marked 2, 3, 4, 5. On a throw of:

2: The ship moved   4: The elephant moved
3: The horse moved   5: The rajah or a pawn moved.

If a piece moved onto a square occupied by an enemy piece, the latter was removed from the board. (Minor pieces could not move onto squares occupied by major pieces.)

Fig. 45 shows the arrangement of the board with the Black Army

YELLOW   BLACK

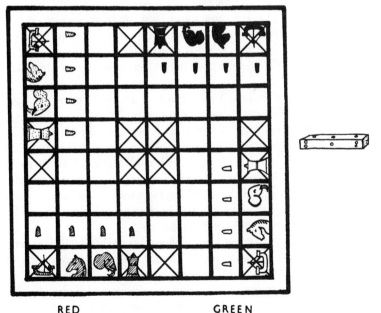

RED   GREEN

FIG. 45. Shaturanga pieces arranged for a game on an ashtapada board.

at the north, the Red at the south, the Green at the east and the Yellow at the west. Each army is drawn up in the same formation with a boat on the marked corner square, next is a horse, then an elephant, and the king stands on a marked central square known as the THRONE. The pawns stand in front of these pieces and move orthogonally forwards towards their ally's side of the board. This opening position of the pieces is taken from al-Beruni's work *India*. Al-Beruni was a Persian born in Khiva in Khwarizm in A.D. 973 and he lived in Hyrcania on the southern shores of the Caspian. He travelled to India and wrote extensively about the people of the Punjab. He died at Ghazna in A.D. 1048.

Rules

(Additions in italics fill obvious deficiencies in the ancient account.)
   1. *At the beginning of the game each player puts an agreed stake into a pool. This is shared by the victorious allies at the end of the game.*
   2. *Each player throws a die in turn and the player with the highest number throws again and makes his opening move in accordance with this throw, unless it is a 4: when the elephant is unable to move and the turn passes clockwise to the player on the left.*
   3. An indicated piece must move if this is possible, even if it is to the player's disadvantage. A throw can sometimes be satisfied by a choice of pieces, e.g. if a 5 is thrown the rajah or a pawn may move, or if the ally's troops have been taken over, one of his pawns or rajah.
   4. If the piece indicated by a throw is unable to move the turn is lost and the die passes to the next player.
   5. SEIZING A THRONE. When a rajah occupies the throne of an enemy rajah he seizes a throne and wins a single stake from the despoiled opponent. If he captures either adverse rajah at the same move he wins a double stake. If a rajah mounts the throne of his ally he assumes command of the allied forces as well as his own . . . *and at his own or his partner's throws he may move either his own or his ally's pieces: a considerable advantage.*
   6. REGAINING A THRONE. If a player whose ally's rajah has been captured captures a hostile rajah, he may propose an exchange of prisoner rajahs with the player owning the remaining rajah, but the latter has the option of accepting or refusing the exchange. . . . *Rescued rajahs re-enter the board on their own throne squares, or, if these are occupied, on the nearest vacant square.*

7. If a player whose own rajah is still on the board but whose ally's rajah is a prisoner captures both enemy rajahs he may claim the restoration of his ally's rajah without exchange or ransom. . . . *This would, however, also restore to his ally the control of his pieces.*

8. BUILDING AN EMPIRE. A player who succeeds in seizing his ally's throne and in capturing both enemy rajahs builds an empire.

(*a*) If the player's rajah made the capture on the hostile rajah's throne square he wins a quadruple stake . . . *from both opponents.*

(*b*) If the player's rajah made the capture on some other square he wins a double stake . . . *from both opponents.*

(*c*) If the capture of the second hostile rajah was made by any other piece the player wins a single stake . . . *from both opponents.*

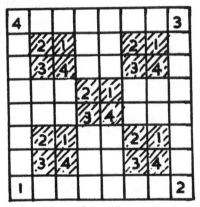

FIG. 46. The original positions of the ships are marked 1, 2, 3, 4. The five possible Concourses of shipping are shaded

9. CONCOURSE OF SHIPPING. Each ship sails on a different course and controls different squares and they can never attack each other directly, but if three ships are on adjacent squares and the fourth moves into position to occupy the fourth square this player completes a concourse of shipping and he captures the two enemy vessels and takes control of the moves of his ally's ship . . . *and when he throws a 2, he may move his own or his ally's ship on to a square favourable to himself even if it is not in his ally's interests!* There are only five positions on the board where a concourse of shipping can occur (fig. 46).

10. PROMOTION OF PAWNS. If a pawn reaches an unmarked square on the opposite side of the board it is promoted to the piece of that square, either a horse or an elephant. Promotion only occurs,

however, if the player has already lost one or more pawns. He is not allowed to have a promoted piece and three pawns on the board, and promotion is delayed until a pawn has been lost. . . . *A pawn reaching a marked square is not promoted and can take no further part in the game except to be captured by an enemy piece unless he should become a* PRIVILEGED PAWN.

11. PRIVILEGED PAWN. If a player has only a ship and a pawn left, this pawn becomes privileged and on reaching any square on the opposite side of the board can be promoted to any piece at the choice of his owner. This appears to be a chivalrous courtesy towards a weak adversary.

12. DRAWN GAME. If a player loses all his pieces except his rajah he is considered to have fought to an honourable peace and the game is drawn. . . . *His ally may still be in a position to fight on alone.*

13. *When a player has lost all his pieces he is out of the game. His turn does not pass to his partner who is forced to fight on with only one turn to his opponents' two.*

14. *Each player pays any special debts acquired in the course of the game to the player winning them; e.g. a stake to the first enemy player seizing his throne; a double stake if his rajah is captured in the same move; and a quadruple stake if one of his opponents builds an empire. The allies do not win from each other.*

Gambling became forbidden at an early date in Hindu culture and in the ninth book of the Laws of Manu is written:

'Let the king punish corporally, at discretion, both the gamester and the keeper of the gambling house, whether they play with inanimate objects such as dice, or shaturanga, or with living creatures as in the blood sports of cock and ram fighting.'

Shaturanga players evaded the gambling laws by discarding the die and removing the element of luck. Other changes followed. One of the first appears to have been the amalgamation of the allied forces into a single army and the game for four players became one for two. This explains the duplication of the pieces in modern chess. The allied kings were reduced in rank to prime ministers and their power of movement was halved, making them weak pieces.

About the same time the moves of the ship and the elephant were transposed, the elephant moving diagonally two squares, while the ship, called in Sanskrit *roka*, assumed the powerful orthogonal moves of the ancient elephant. With these changes the game ceased to be Shaturanga; it had developed into the early medieval variety of chess, Shatranj.

SHATRANJ

There is a tradition which places the introduction of Shatranj from India into Persia during the reign of Naushirawan (A.D. 531–79). He is better known in the west as Chosroes I. The earliest reference to Shatranj occurs in a Persian work called the *Karnamak-i-Artakh shatr-i-Papakan* which was written about A.D. 600. The poet Firdausi writing four centuries after Chosroes' death composed a great epic poem of a hundred and twenty thousand lines called the *Shahnama*, based on earlier historical works which have been lost. In the poem he relates a traditional story of how chess came to Persia. Forbes made a collation of six manuscripts in the British Museum and the following account is taken from his work.

'One day an ambassador from the king of Hind arrived at the Persian court of Chosroes, and after an oriental exchange of courtesies, the ambassador produced rich presents from his sovereign and amongst them was an elaborate board with curiously carved pieces of ebony and ivory. He then issued a challenge.

'"Oh great king, fetch your wise men and let them solve the mysteries of this game. If they succeed my master the king of Hind will pay you tribute as an overlord, but if they fail it will be proof that the Persians are of lower intellect and we shall demand tribute from Iran."

'The courtiers were shown the board, and after a day and a night in deep thought one of them, Buzurjmihr, solved the mystery and was richly rewarded by his delighted sovereign.'

(Perhaps the twenty-four hours were spent in bribing the Indian ambassador rather than in heavy thinking.)

In the following fifty years Shatranj became known to the Arabs and also to the Byzantine Court through the marriage of Khusru Parviz, the grandson of Chosroes I, to the daughter of the Byzantine emperor Maurice. In A.D. 591 Khusru became king of Persia and after the assassination of his father-in-law, the Emperor Maurice, he declared war on the Roman Empire. At first he was successful and conquered Asia Minor, Syria, Egypt, and North Africa, but after a crushing defeat by the Emperor Heraclius he lost them all again.

The Greeks probably knew the game soon after A.D. 600 and about the same time it reached the cities of Mecca and Medina. Shatranj was in high favour at the court of the Caliphs of Damascus from A.D. 661 to 774. The first Arabian writer on chess of whom we have any record was as-Sarakhsi, a physician of Bagdad who died in A.D. 899. As-Suli, the greatest of the Arab chess players, died in the city of Basra about A.D. 946 and several of his games have been preserved.

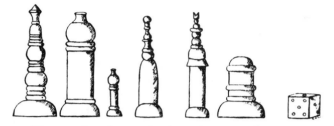

FIG. 47. Chess set based on early eleventh-century fragments found at Bambra-ka-Thul

The oldest-known Muslim chessmen (fig. 47) were found in 1855 in India by Mr. A. F. Bellasis while excavating the ruined Muslim city of Mansura at Bambra-ka-thul, 47 miles north-east of Haidarabad. The city was destroyed by an earthquake a little before the time of .al-Beruni (A.D. 1030). They are now in the British Museum. A long die (2, 5; 1, 6;), a cubic die (1, 6; 2, 5; 3, 4;), and fragments of a small box were found with them.

When and where Shatranj entered Europe is uncertain but claims have been made for at least three routes. In the seventh century A.D. the Saracens captured North Africa, and they crossed the Straits of Gibraltar and settled in Andalusia early in the eighth. They probably took chess with them and the game may have spread from Spain to the court of Charlemagne in France about A.D. 760.

The game may also have reached France from the Byzantine Court. There is a story that at one time a marriage was contemplated between Charlemagne and the Empress Irene. The two monarchs exchanged courtesies and presents and among those from the aged Empress was a chess set in which the two prime ministers were replaced by two queens whose power had been increased beyond that of any piece on the board. Charlemagne sensed future difficulties and the marriage did not materialize!

The most frequently suggested avenue of entry was the Crusades. In 1171 Saladin founded the Ayubite dynasty in Egypt and Syria, and Shatranj was held in considerable respect at his court. We know that the Christians learnt medical secrets from the Arab physicians and Shatranj also may have appealed to the knights of the Cross. On their return home the game would have reached every castle in Christendom.

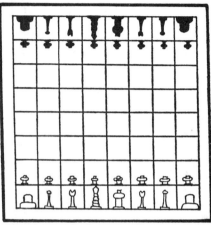

Fig. 48. Arrangement of pieces in Shatranj (using thirteenth-century symbols from Alfonso X and Cotton manuscripts)

A Shatranj board is shown in fig. 48 and the symbols used for the pieces are taken from the thirteenth-century Alfonso and Cotton manuscripts. There are no chequered squares and the advantage of the first move was decided with a die. See also fig. 154 on Plate XVIII.

Moves of the Pieces

The KING (Shah) moved one square orthogonally or diagonally in any direction.

The PRIME MINISTER (Firz) moved one square diagonally forwards or backwards. The two prime ministers could not attack each other.

The ELEPHANT (Fil) moved diagonally two squares. He could jump over a piece on the intervening square but could not attack it. The four elephants were unable to attack each other as each had a different circuit.

The WAR HORSE (Faras) moved one square orthogonally and one square diagonally. He was allowed to jump over intervening pieces.

The RUHK moved orthogonally any number of vacant squares in any direction. He could not jump over a piece.

The PAWNS (Baidaq) moved one square orthogonally forwards, but captured by moving one square diagonally forwards. When a pawn reached the far side of the board he was promoted to the rank of a prime minister and he could then move diagonally one square at a time backwards or forwards. There could be any number of promoted pawns on the board at the same time.

There were three ways of winning:

1. By CHECKMATE. If a checked king was unable to move out of check, or it was impossible to capture the checking man, or to interpose another man to protect him from the check, the game was lost.

2. By A BARE KING (Isolation of a king). If a player captured all the opponent's pieces except his king, he won the game.

3. By STRANGLED STALEMATE. If a player was stalemated in Shatranj, he was allowed to exchange his king with any other piece on the board as long as the king was not in check in the new position. This counted as the king's move, and the game then continued. The exchanged piece was known as the VICTIM because it was usually captured in the new position. If a stalemated king was unable to exchange position with any of his remaining forces the game was lost.

DRAWN GAME. Because of the peculiar powers and limited range of some of the pieces a powerful force was sometimes unable to defeat a much weaker one stationed on favourable squares, and in spite of there being three ways of winning, drawn games were frequent.

PERPETUAL CHECK was considered a drawn game.

The opening moves of Shatranj were rather tedious as several of the pieces were more restricted than their modern counterparts, and so the players often agreed to allow the opening player to make ten moves at once to arrange his forces; no piece, however, was allowed to cross the middle of the board. The second player then made his first ten moves in reply and from this opening position, called the Ta'biyat, or battle array, the play proceeded by alternate moves. Sometimes twelve moves constituted the Ta'biyat instead of ten.

During the next four centuries there was little change in the game and the European form of medieval chess described in Caxton's *The Game and Playe of the Chesse* printed in Bruges in 1474 was little different from the Persian Shatranj of the Crusades. Caxton's work was a translation of a translation of the famous chess morality of Jacobus de Cessolis, a native of Lombard who was a

friar belonging to the order of the Friars Preachers, now known as
Dominicans. The monk's work was in four books, written in Latin
and called *Liber de Moribus Hominum et Officiis Nobilium*. It was
written between A.D. 1275 and 1300, and was immensely popular.
Several manuscripts have survived.

Caxton's *The Game and Playe of the Chesse* was reprinted in
London in 1480 with the addition of twenty-four woodcuts. Several
reprints were made during the nineteenth century, the last being
in 1883 by W. E. A. Axon, London. At an auction of Lord Cunliffe's library a copy of the 1474 edition sold for £1,900. The book
had been bought for £54. 12s. od. in 1813.

During the long evolution of chess many exotic forms were invented, enjoyed an ephemeral popularity, and then passed away.
One such was Tamberlane's or the Great Chess which was the
form played by the Mogul conqueror. After it had been forgotten
for several hundred years it was recovered from a Persian manuscript in the possession of the Royal Asiatic Society and it is fully
described in Forbes's *History of Chess*. There were twenty-eight
pieces on each side and the game was played on a large board of
112 squares. Another medieval form which may be of more interest
to the modern player was the Circular, or Byzantine Chess.

FIG. 49. Byzantine
chess (after Strutt,
*Sports and Pas-
times of the People
of England*). Bland
(*Persian Chess*)
gives an alternative
arrangement with
the King and
Queen at the peri-
phery, then the
Bishops, then
Knights and the
Rooks placed
centrally

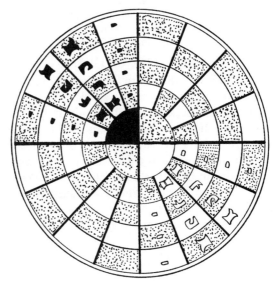

CIRCULAR CHESS

The circular board contained sixty-four spaces and four citadels. Ordinary chessmen were used. The board and opening position of the pieces is shown in fig. 49. The pieces had the same moves and powers as in Shatranj with one exception. There was no pawn promotion, and if two of a player's pawns were played around the board and met face to face blocking each other, the opponent removed them both and then made his own move.

If a player's king was hard pressed and he managed to enter his opponent's citadel he was considered to have reached a sanctuary and the game was drawn.

FIG. 50. Courier chessmen   FIG. 51. Opening positions
    from Van Leyden's *Chess*   in Courier chess
    Players; c. A.D. 1520   (after Murray's *History of Chess*)

THE COURIER GAME

Early in the thirteenth century this enlarged form of chess appeared in Germany and was played for several centuries. The village of Ströbeck near Halberstadt, in the Hartz mountains, still possesses a board which was presented to the village in 1651 by the Elector-Prince Frederick William of Brandenburg. The original silver pieces were lent in the eighteenth century and were never returned; but there is a complete set of wooden men for the game. A set based on Van Leyden's 'Chess Players' is shown in fig. 50. See also Plate III facing p. 64.

Fig. 51 shows the arrangement of the pieces.

Moves

The KING moved one square in any direction. He had no power of leaping and could not castle.

The QUEEN moved one square diagonally forwards or backwards but in the opening move she jumped to the third square.

The BISHOP moved two squares diagonally and had the power of jumping over a piece on the intervening square.

The KNIGHT moved one square orthogonally and one square diagonally or vice-versa. It had the power of leaping over an intervening piece.

The ROOK moved any number of vacant squares orthogonally.

The COURIER moved any number of empty squares diagonally. This is the move of the modern bishop.

The JESTER moved to an adjacent square horizontally or vertically.

The SAGE moved to any adjacent square, and unlike the king was not limited by being in check.

The PAWNS could only move a single square forwards with the exception of the Queen's and Rooks' pawns which could make a double step forwards on their first move.

Rules

1. The board was placed with a white corner square at the player's right hand.

2. To develop the game more quickly the opening player moved his two rooks' pawns and his queen's pawn to the fourth square, and the queen made a JOY-LEAP to her third square. His opponent replied with the same four moves and then the game continued one move alternately as in other forms of chess.

3. Nothing is known about the pawn promotion of Courier chess but it may have been the same as in another variety of chess played in Ströbeck. In this a pawn reaching the eighth row had to make three joy-leaps to the sixth, fourth, and second rows on the same file before it was promoted. It then became a queen only. It could not leap over, or take a piece during the joy-leaps. It was immune from capture when on the eighth row, but not in its leaps backwards to its original square. These leaps did not have to be in consecutive moves.

The game is mentioned in the *Wigalois* of Wirnt v. Gravenberg (A.D. 1202) and therefore it was played at least as early as this date. Gustavus Selenus in *Das Schach-oder König-Spiel* (Leipzig, 1616) gives woodcuts of the pieces. The courier was a man galloping on horseback with a horn to his lips; the sage had a long beard; and the jester, cap and bells. Plate III (opposite), a painting of 'The Chess Players', *c.* A.D. 1520, shows a Courier game in progress. It is attributed to Van Leyden, and before the Second World War formed part of the famous collection of the Kaiser Friedrich Museum in Berlin. In September 1939 these works of art were removed to the vaulted stone cellars, but in 1943, when the air-raids increased and the building was severely damaged, the collection was placed in an air-raid shelter in Dönhoffstrasse, and a little later in a huge concrete anti-aircraft flak tower near the Alexanderplatz.

Early in 1945 the air-raids became excessive and the art experts urged the military authorities to transfer the treasures to a safer home. All requests were refused until a direct order was received in March from Hitler himself for the immediate evacuation of the most valuable items. By this time only two small open trucks could be spared but the removal began on 12 March 1945. The two drivers left the city a little before 8 p.m. when the raids usually began. As they could not drive by night for fear of accidents in the blackout, they stopped and slept in the woods a few miles from Berlin. There was no covering of any sort for the priceless cargo but fortunately it did not rain. When they arrived at Merker's salt mine which is south-west of Erfurt the treasures were placed 2,000 ft. below ground. The two trucks made several journeys until conditions became impossible.

On 7 April 1945 General Patton's Third Army entered the area and two elderly French women who were in a German slave-gang stopped Lt.-Col. Russell of the American 90th Infantry Division and indicated with gesticulations and a torrent of French that he should follow them into the mine. There he found a fantastic reincarnation of Aladdin's cave. There were millions of pounds' worth of gold coins, bullion, jewels, art treasures, and crate after crate of great paintings, Van Leyden's being among them.

Nazi loot was returned to its rightful owners while the Kaiser Friedrich collection was taken to Wiesbaden. In November 1945 instructions arrived for their transfer to the U.S.A. The roads were appalling; ice and snow added to the dangers from bomb craters and weakened bridges, and it was decided to send them by rail. The only rolling stock left in the shattered railway yard were two German hospital cars complete with huge red crosses. The masterpieces were placed inside, and the journey to Le Havre began.

A game of Courier chess, *c.* A.D. 1520. Reproduced from Van Leyden's oil-painting 'The Chess Players'

FIG. 52. Blind player's chess set, twentieth century. The white pieces have pointed tops and the black smooth. The black squares are raised above the general level of the board. The pieces have pegs to prevent accidental displacement

In America the pictures were stored in the National Gallery of Art in Washington until a home was ready for them in Germany. Early in 1948 they returned to the Fatherland, to a modern exhibition hall in Munich, the Haus der Kunst.

MODERN INTERNATIONAL CHESS

Information is so readily available that it will not be described here. Fig. 52 (opposite) shows a twentieth-century chess set for blind players.

THE MAHARAJAH AND THE SEPOYS

A chess board and set is used. One player arranges his pieces in the normal way; the other has a single piece, the Maharajah, which can move as a Queen or a Knight and is placed on any free square on the board (fig. 53).

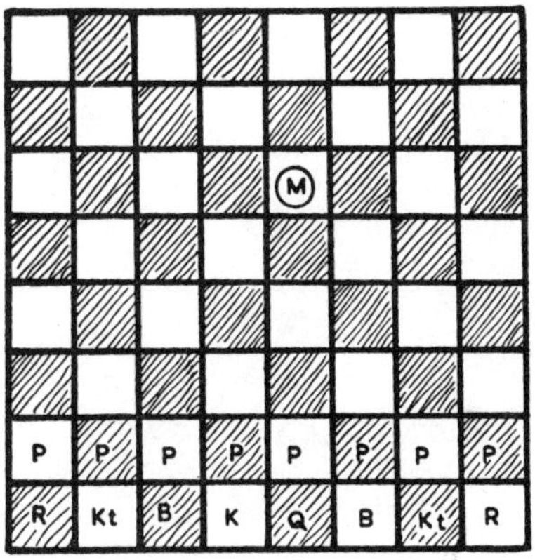

FIG. 53. Opening position in The Maharajah and the Sepoys

The game provides interesting problems, though a careful player who never leaves a piece unsupported will finally hem the Maharajah in. If he makes a mistake, however, the Maharajah's great mobility may allow him to win quickly by trapping the King behind his own men; or later when the board is clear, he may drive the King into a corner which is followed by an inevitable checkmate.

ORIENTAL CHESS

When Shatranj spread westwards into Europe it also re-entered Northern India and travelled eastwards into Burma, China, and

Japan. Each of these countries developed its own form. Only the Chinese will be described.

CHINESE CHESS (Siang k'i)

The original Shatranj was considerably modified and elephants, horsemen, infantry, cannon, and war-chariots fight for the capture of the enemy general. Each army has a fortress within which the general and his mandarins direct operations; the enemy fortress must be taken by storm to win the game. Between the two armies is a river which the heavily-laden elephants are unable to cross. The other field pieces pass over it at will.

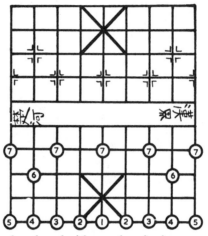

Fig. 54. Chinese chess board with one player's pieces arranged in opening positions

The Chinese chess board consists of two halves of 8 × 4 squares which are separated by a space one square wide known as the river. Each half of the board contains four squares marked with diagonals. The resulting square of nine points is known as the fortress. The pieces are placed on the intersections of the lines instead of on the spaces, and the board becomes one of 9 × 10 points (figs. 54 and 150 on Plate XV, also Plate VIII).

The chessmen are circular discs of wood, ivory, or other material, all alike in size and shape. The ranks are written on the upper face, one side in red and the other in green or black. Some of the green characters differ from those of the red on pieces of the same power, as if one side were given English titles and the other German. This increases

the atmosphere of rival armies but it makes recognition more difficult for players who do not read Chinese. The author has found it
helpful to add small triangular marks to the pieces confined to the
fortress, and small circular marks to the field pieces outside, the
soldiers being left unmarked (fig. 55).

FIG. 55. Chinese chess pieces. The characters for the Horse, Chariot and
Cannon are the same for both colours (from pieces in author's
collection)

Moves of the Pieces

The GENERAL moves one point vertically or horizontally, but he
is confined to the nine points of the fortress.

The MANDARINS move one point diagonally, but they are confined to the fortress, being limited to the five points marked by the
heavy lines.

The ELEPHANTS move diagonally to the next point but one, the
intervening point must be unoccupied and they are unable to
cross the river into enemy territory.

The other pieces are free to move over the whole board.

The HORSEMEN move one point vertically or horizontally followed
by a point diagonally; the intervening point must be unoccupied.

The CHARIOTS move any distance vertically or horizontally, if
the intervening points are unoccupied.

The CANNONS move any distance vertically or horizontally, but they can only capture if they have jumped over some piece on the way to the point which they are attacking. The intervening piece, known as the SCREEN, may be of any power and of either side. The cannons cannot, however, jump over more than one piece in a single move, and do not jump unless they make a capture.

The SOLDIERS move one point vertically forwards on their own side of the board. In enemy territory they can move one point forwards or sideways, but on reaching the opponent's back line they can only move sideways. There is no promotion.

The object of the game is to checkmate or stalemate the opposing General. A player cannot give perpetual check, he must vary the move. A General is in check:

1. When he is under attack by any piece, and could have been taken on the following move, if nothing were done to thwart the attack.

2. When the Generals face one another upon the same file with no intervening piece. The player moving the piece which exposes the two Generals on the same file makes the check.

When a check is given there are three possible replies:

1. The attacking piece may be taken and removed from the board.

2. The General may move out of check.

3. The check may be covered. If a horseman is the attacking piece, a man placed on the ANGLE of its move blocks its attack.

If a cannon is attacking, either the screen may be removed, as a cannon can only attack over an intervening piece, or a second piece may be interposed which protects the General as a cannon can only jump over one piece at a time. If the check cannot be relieved the General is defeated and the game is lost.

Chess is the game of the middle and lower classes and they usually play for small stakes; the aristocracy and the intelligentsia prefer Wei-ch'i. The earliest reference to Siang k'i is in the *Book of Marvels* (Hüan Kwai Lu) attributed to Nui Seng-ju who died in A.D. 847. Chinese chess is regarded as the national game in Hong Kong and one television channel spends considerable time in relaying games between champions.

THE JUNGLE GAME

No information is yet available about the history of this curious game. It may be a development of Chinese chess comparable to Draughts in Europe.

The board is shown in fig. 56. The pieces of one side are blue, and the other red. Each player has eight animals. In the list below the numbers represent their respective strengths.

Piece	Power
Elephant	8
Lion	7
Tiger	6
Panther	5
Dog	4
Wolf	3
Cat	2
Rat	1
Trapped	0

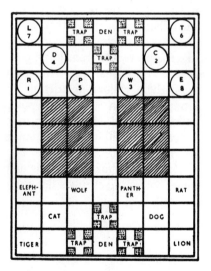

FIG. 56. Board for The Jungle Game. The shaded squares represent water. One player's pieces are arranged in the opening positions (author's collection)

At the beginning of the game the pieces are placed on the appropriately marked squares. Blue moves first.

Rules

1. Each turn consists of moving one piece one square orthogonally in any direction. Only one piece may occupy any square.

2. An animal may eat any animal smaller than itself by moving on to its square. (The method of capture in chess.) The only exception to this rule is that the rat can kill the elephant since it can run into the elephant's ears and so gnaw into its brain. If similar animals meet, the animal moving on to a square eats the animal already there.

3. Three pieces have special powers.

(*a*) When the rat reaches the river it can enter it and move on the water squares as if it were on dry land. If it is in the river no other animal can attack it since they cannot move on to a water square. The rat, however, is unable to attack the elephant from a water square. If both rats meet in the river the moving piece eats the stationary one.

(*b*) When a lion or a tiger reaches a square on the edge of the river, at the next move it can jump over the water in any orthogonal direction, landing on the nearest land square. It destroys any smaller animal that may occupy that square: if, however, there is a rat in the river in the line of the jump, it blocks the way and the lion or tiger is prevented from leaping over the water.

4. Each side has three trap-squares and the player's own pieces may move on and off them without restriction, but if an enemy animal occupies a trap-square, it loses all its power and becomes weaker than any defending piece. On entry or as soon as it moves out of the trap it regains its full strength. Animals of either side may enter and leave traps at will.

5. A player may not move any of his animals on to his own den.

6. When any animal enters the enemy's den the game is won.

3. DRAUGHTS

About A.D. 1100 someone unknown, probably living in the south of France, invented a new game using tablemen on a chequered chess board with the moves of Alquerque. Each player had twelve pieces called FERSES, the name of the queens in medieval chess, and the ferses in the new game moved in the same way as in the old, one square diagonally in any direction. A piece in FIERGES, however, made a capture by jumping diagonally over the enemy piece to land on an empty square immediately beyond.

In the *Chronique* of Philip Mouskat (A.D. 1243), lines 23617–20, is a reference to a KING of Fierges, indicating that a fers could be promoted to a king at this early period. When the name of the fers in chess was changed to dame, the same change occurred in the new game, a piece being known as a DAME, and the game as DAMES. In Dames there was no compulsion to take an enemy piece, a survival of chess practice. When a compulsion rule was introduced in France about 1535 the old non-huffing game became known as LE JEU PLAISANT DE DAMES or simply as PLAISANT in contrast to the huffing game called JEU FORCÉ. Modern English draughts is the jeu forcé of the sixteenth century.

ENGLISH DRAUGHTS

The board is shown in fig. 57. The pieces move only on the black squares and Black begins. The players change colours at the end of each game. The double-black corner must be on the player's right. The draughtsmen move diagonally forwards one square at a time. They cannot move backwards.

The object of the game is to capture or immobilize the twelve opposing pieces. A capture is made by a piece jumping over an enemy piece and landing on a vacant square immediately beyond. If the capturing piece can continue to leap over other enemy pieces they are also captured and removed from the board. When a piece finally comes to rest the move is finished.

If a draughtsman reaches the opponent's back line it becomes a king (fig. 58). Crowning ends a move. After crowning a king can move diagonally backwards or forwards one square at a time, and captures by a SHORT JUMP over an enemy piece. There may be several kings on the board at the same time.

If a player has a choice of captures he may take a smaller rather than a larger number if he wishes, but if he chooses the larger then he must capture all the pieces possible. If he does not make a complete capture he becomes liable to one of the three penalties below, which are also levied against a piece failing to make a single capture when this is possible.

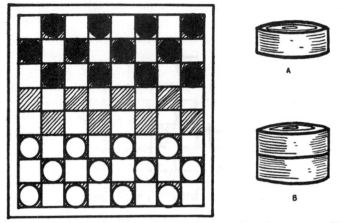

FIG. 57. English draughts board   FIG. 58. A, a draughtsman; B, a king

Penalties for failing to take an Enemy Piece

1. The opponent may insist that the piece which was moved is returned to its position, and the proper capturing move made.

2. The opponent may accept the move which was made and let it stand. If this is done the piece able to make the capture must do so at the player's next move or the penalties may be inflicted a second time.

3. The opponent may remove the piece which should have made the capture, and then continue with his own move. This is called HUFFING and does not constitute a move in itself.

The early settlers took the English game to North America where it is known as CHECKERS. There are two variants of the English draughts which make a pleasant change from the orthodox game.

THE LOSING GAME

Each player has twelve men arranged in the conventional manner and the moves and methods of capture are as in the English game except that only Rule 1 under penalties applies. Each player tries to force his opponent to capture his pieces, and the first player to lose them all wins the game.

DIAGONAL DRAUGHTS

The rules are the same as in the English game except that the pieces are arranged as in fig. 59.

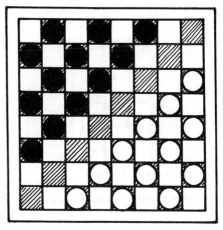

FIG. 59. Opening position in Diagonal draughts

ITALIAN DRAUGHTS

This game was played in Italy at the end of the sixteenth century. The two differences from English draughts were:

1. A man could not take a king.

2. A player had to take when possible or lose the game, and if he had a choice of capture he was forced to take the greater number; and if the number were equal, then the more valuable pieces: e.g. he was compelled to take a king in preference to a man. This rule was known in Italy as 'il più col più' ('the greater to the greater').

TURKISH DRAUGHTS

An uncheckered board is used but the familiar one is satisfactory. Each player has sixteen men and the opening arrangement is shown in fig. 60.

Rules

1. A man moves one square forwards or sideways but not diagonally, and on reaching the eighth row becomes a king.

2. A man captures by the short jump forwards or sideways and may take more than one piece in a turn of play.

3. Captured pieces are removed as taken and a turn continues until the piece can make no more captures.

4. A king can move forwards, sideways, or backwards any number of vacant squares, and the king can place himself on any vacant square beyond the captured piece to make further captures.

5. The first player to capture or immobilize all his opponent's pieces, or reduce the enemy to a single man against a king, wins the game.

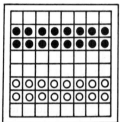

FIG. 60. Opening position in Turkish draughts

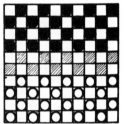

FIG. 61. Opening position in Polish draughts

REVERSI

Reversi was invented in 1888* and is played on a draughts-board. There are sixty-four pieces which are black on one side and white on the other.

Black begins by placing a piece black side up on one of the four central squares on the empty board. White replies by placing his first piece white side up on another of these squares. The central four squares must be filled first and then the players play alternately, each piece being placed on a square adjacent to one occupied by an enemy piece. Any enemy pieces directly intervening between this piece and another of the player's own colour, orthogonally or diagonally, are captured and turned over to show the player's colour uppermost. A piece may change owners several times in a game. When all the squares of the board are covered with pieces, the player with most of his colour showing wins the game.

* Information supplied by Victor Medley.

CONTINENTAL OR POLISH DRAUGHTS

The jeu forcé (English draughts) only lasted a few years in France and was replaced about 1650 by a variety known as 'Le Grand Forçat'. This also became obsolete within fifty years and was replaced by the game now known as Polish or Continental draughts, first played in the cafés of Paris in 1727. Modifications in the rules have been made and as now played, Polish draughts must rank as one of the great board games of the world. See fig. 142 on Plate XI. The first book on Continental draughts was published in 1727 by Quercetano, a pseudonymn, and was probably written about five years earlier.

Rules

1. The opening position of the pieces is shown in fig. 61.
2. A man moves one square diagonally forwards.
3. A man captures by the short leap either diagonally forwards or backwards. Capturing is compulsory.
4. A king can move diagonally any number of unoccupied squares.
5. A king may land any number of vacant squares beyond a captured piece. Rules 4 and 5 may occur together (a long leap).
6. If a player has a choice of captures he must choose the one in which the greatest number of captures are made, or if equal numbers are at risk, then the player has the choice of which piece he captures. (In Friesland, and only there, if equal numbers of pieces are at risk, then the more powerful pieces must be taken. In Frisian draughts men and kings can leap diagonally or orthogonally [G. Bakker. Utrecht. Aug. 1970].)
7. Captured pieces are only lifted at the end of the move and a dead piece forms an impassable barrier.
8. A man is only promoted to a king when he remains on the opponent's back line; if on reaching the crownhead more captures are possible, they must be made and the move completed, the man remaining unpromoted until he again reaches the crownhead and remains there at the end of the move.

4. THE TAFL GROUP

These games originated in northern Europe and are miniature battles fought between unequal forces. The smaller force has a piece, or pieces, with special powers and the larger force tries to hem them in; while the smaller force tries to break out, or destroy the larger.

FOX AND GEESE

Thirteen geese are arranged on the board as in fig. 62 and the fox is placed on any vacant point. The fox and the geese can move in any direction along a line to the next contiguous point. If the fox jumps over a goose and lands on an empty point beyond, the goose is killed and removed from the board. Two or more geese can be killed in one move by a series of short jumps by the fox. The geese cannot jump over the fox, but they try to crowd him into a corner

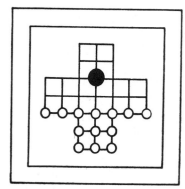 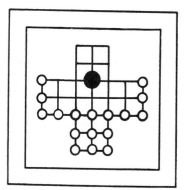

FIG. 62. An early form of Fox and Geese

FIG. 63. Fox and Geese. A later form with seventeen geese

and make it impossible for him to move. If the fox is immobilized he loses the game, but if he can deplete the gaggle of geese until they are unable to trap him he wins.

If the geese are correctly played the fox must lose. In later forms of the game the geese were increased to seventeen, but were deprived of the power of moving backwards (fig. 63).

Hala-tafl, the Fox Game, is mentioned in the Icelandic 'Grettis saga'. Dr. Finnur Jonsson, the literary historian, believed that this saga was written after A.D. 1300 by an anonymous priest who lived in the northern part of the island.

During the reign of Edward IV of England (1461–83) an entry was made in the accounts of the Royal Household for the purchase of two foxes and twenty-six hounds of silver over-gilt for two sets of Marelles.

Fiske suggested that Fox and Geese may be the same game as Freystafl which is mentioned in the late sagas. Tafl itself, frequently appearing in the early literature of northern Europe, was later replaced by Hnefatafl. No record of either game has survived.

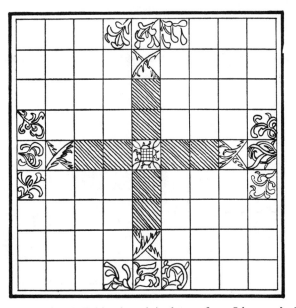

FIG. 64. Embroidered Tablut board (redrawn from Linnaeus's *Lachesis Lapponica*)

In 1732 Linnaeus, the Swedish botanist, visited Lapland when he was a young student and his diary contains the description of a game played there by the Alpine Lapps called Tablut which appears to be closely related to Hnefatafl. The following account is taken from the entry in his diary for 20 July.

TABLUT

The Tablut board (fig. 64) is marked out with 9 × 9 squares, the central one being distinctive and known as the Konakis or throne. Only the Swedish king can occupy this square. One player has

eight blonde Swedes (fig. 65A) and their monarch (fig. 65B); the other
has sixteen dark Muscovites (fig. 65C). The king is larger than the
other pieces. The Muscovites are placed on the embroidered
squares. (This remark suggests that the board was made of reindeer
skin ornamented with needlework as the Lapps had no cloth.)

Rules

1. All the pieces move orthogonally any number of vacant squares
(the move of the rook in chess).

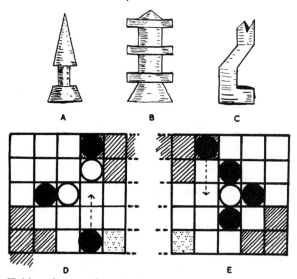

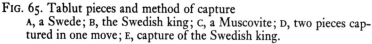

FIG. 65. Tablut pieces and method of capture
    A, a Swede; B, the Swedish king; C, a Muscovite; D, two pieces cap-
tured in one move; E, capture of the Swedish king.

2. A piece is captured and removed from the board when the
opponent occupies both adjacent squares in row or column (fig. 65D).
This is the CUSTODIAN method of capture. A piece may move safely
on to an empty square between two enemy pieces.

    3. The king is captured if all four squares around him are occu-
pied by enemy pieces (fig. 65E); or if he is surrounded on three sides
by enemy pieces and on the fourth by the Konakis. When the king
is captured the game is over and the Muscovites are victorious.

    4. The Swedes win if the king reaches any square at the peri-
phery of the board. When there is a clear route for the king to a
perimeter square the player must warn his opponent by saying

'Raichi!' When there are two clear routes he must say 'Tuichi!' This is the equivalent of 'Checkmate' since it is impossible to block two directions in the same move.

Linnaeus's journey through Lapland was an incredible feat. He travelled 3,798 miles on foot and by small boat in 153 days, an average of 24 miles a day, in spite of most of the route being over trackless wastes. He depended for food upon the hospitality of the peasant people. His diary, written in a mixture of Swedish and Latin, is crammed with observations and drawings: pages of records of flowers and plants, descriptions of animals, fish, insects, parasites, and geology; details of diseases and their treatment; folk-lore; cooking recipes, marriage ceremonies, scythes, skis, cross-bows, making garments, building houses. . . .

Before he died this traveller occupied a professorial chair and became a preceptor of the learned world, invented a system of plant classification still in use today, and was honoured throughout Europe.

SAXON HNEFATAFL

A fragment of a gaming board (fig. 66) was found at Wimose in Fyn, the second largest of the Danish islands, in a Roman Iron-Age grave. This period ended about A.D. 400.

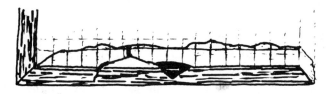

FIG. 66. A fragment of a board found at Wimose, Denmark, *c*. A.D. 400 (from Du Chaillu's *The Viking Age*, Vol. I, p. 216). ⅙ real size.

Eighteen squares are visible along one side and if the board was symmetrical it contained at least 18 × 18 squares, and each square was about 1 in. × 1 in. in area. The Scandinavians took tafl with them to Iceland and Britain. The later sagas mention the development of tafl into hnefatafl and an English manuscript written during the reign of King Athelstan (A.D. 925–40) contains a diagram of the Saxon form of hnefatafl which corresponds with the Wimose fragment. See Plate V, opposite.

The Latin text describes the game as a religious allegory, but it is valuable in preserving the form of hnefatafl played in England in the tenth century.

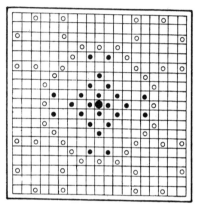

FIG. 67. Saxon Hnefatafl pieces. A, a hnefi; B, a hunns found at Woodperry (after Murray's *A History of Board Games other than Chess*)

FIG. 68. Saxon Hnefatafl board and opening position of the pieces (reconstruction)

A bone piece found at Woodperry in Oxfordshire gives the shape of the hunns or ordinary pieces (fig. 67B). The king or hnefi was larger and more ornate (fig. 67A). (This is a reconstruction.)

The following reconstruction of the game is based on the translation of the Athelstan manuscript in J. Armitage Robinson's *Time of St. Dunstan* (Oxford, 1923). The board (fig. 68) has been modified to allow the pieces to move on the squares instead of on the points. See also fig. 155 on Plate XVIII.

Reconstructed Board and Suggested Rules

1. The two forces begin in the positions shown in fig. 68. The king is on the central square.

2. The king's force has the first move and then the players move alternately.

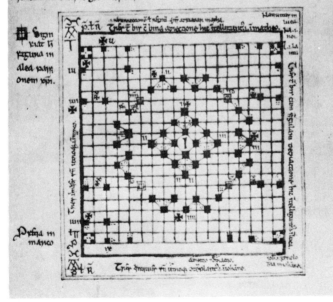

Photograph of a page from a tenth-century manuscript with a diagram of a Hnefatafl board

PROLEGOMENA CURIOSA.

اول نع طرقها وزرركه اور زركك
جاسر ازر دار انزرر صلح وحنك
دخی خزار قلخذی دی دنی بن زركك
صلح المزاول قلخذی دی دنی بن بزركك
جنك معمور العر ادی بی زركك

Illud quâ plagâ fiat Castellum, ubi duorum colorum
Examines viri sunt qui faciunt pacem & Bellum?
Pax facit illud Castellum momento desolatum:
Bellum verò illud statim habitatum reddit?

Nempe *Scaccarium* assimilatur Castello, quia armatis viris defenditur; quod in pace (quando nempe non luditur,) incolis vacuum & quasi desolatum est, quòd non adsint Scachi seu Milites. In bello autem, (viz. quando luditur,) tum incolis frequens est, & Scachis seu Militibus refertum. Adeò ut Bellum quod omnia vastare solet, hîc è contra istud Castellum non desolatum, sed habitatum, reddat.

Hieronymus Vida etiam suum Librum cui Tit. *Scachias,* sic inchoat,

Ludimus effigiem belli simulataque veris
Prælia, buxo acies fictas, & ludicra regna:
Ut gemini inter se Reges albusque nigerque
Pro laude oppositi certent bicoloribus armis.

Et *Sokeikt Damascenus* in Libello Arabico quidé folo
(a 2)

DE SHAHILUDIO

cè vocant *Shatrangi: non enim dicitur Fortuna aut Infortunium* (i. e. bona fortuna aut mala fortuna,) in Bello Shatrangico, quemadmodum dicitur de duobus Regibus contra (e invicem belligerantibus. *Causæ enim Belli Shatrangici comperte sunt, ut sapiens prudenti ducto suo semper vincat, & non metuat causam naturalem.*

Impressa exemplaria pro *Cubia,* meliùs legunt אשקוש *Escaqués.* At in illis pessimâ interpolatione interseritur אשטרוש *Astashir,* ut legatur אשטרוש אסתשיר *aut* infortunium in *Astashir & in Bello Scachorum.* Pessima inquam est hæc interpolatio: cum enim Author Philosophicè differendo, introduxisset exemplum Ludi *Shatrangi* seu *Scachorum* tanquam rei quæ fortunæ & casui non esset subjecta; Interpolator injicit mentionem τοῦ *Astashir* seu *Tesserarum Ludi,* qui fortunæ & casui omnino obnoxius est; quod itaque Authoris scopo non quadrat, sed potiùs totius Argumenti vim enervat, & loci sensum planè pervertit.

.In dictâ pericope etiam innuitur hunc Ludum esse repræsentationem Belli. Ideòque *Achmetes* in *Oneirocriticis* observat, quòd ὁ Βασιλεὺς, ἢ Μέγιστος, ἢ Ἄρχων πολέμιος, ἐὰν ἴδῃ ὅτι τὸ Ζατρίκιον αὐτῷ ἀπώλετο, ἢ ἐκλάσθη, ἢ ἐκλάπη, ἀπολέσει τὸν ἑαυτοῦ. Et *Ahmed Bashâ* Epigrammatista idem innuit, in suâ Epigrammatum Turcicorum collectione adducens لغز شطرنج *de Shatrangi* ænigma elegans, MS Seld. superius, p. 236.
لغز

Reproduction of two consecutive pages from Hyde's *De Ludis Orientalibus.*
Note the extraordinary mixture of languages (see page 184)

3. Any piece can move orthogonally any number of vacant squares (the rook's move in chess).

4. A capture is made by trapping an enemy piece between two of the player's pieces on rank or file but not diagonally.

5. A piece may move onto the square between two enemy pieces without being captured.

6. The king can only be captured by being surrounded on all four sides by enemy pieces.

7. Black wins if the king reaches any square on the periphery of the board and loses if the monarch is captured.

COWS AND LEOPARDS

This game is not one of the Tafl group, but the sides are unequal and the objectives of the two players are different. It is the best of a

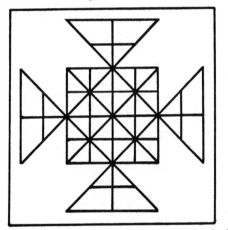

FIG. 69. Board for Cows and Leopards (after Parker's *Ancient Ceylon*)

group of related games which are widely played throughout southern Asia and appear to be quite independent of Scandinavia. One player has two leopards, and the other has twenty-four cows which try to imprison the leopards. The leopards can KILL a cow by jumping over her on to a vacant point beyond. Cows and leopards move from one point to the next orthogonally or diagonally.

The leopard player begins the game by placing a leopard on any point, usually the centre one. A cow is next put down, and then the second leopard on any other chosen point. Another cow follows, and then a cow is added to the board after each move of a leopard, until they are all in play. Only then can the cows on the board be moved. While the cows are being introduced some will be KILLED and if the leopards can kill eight cows they should win, but with careful play the cows always succeed in trapping the leopards. A cow 'at risk' must be taken. See fig. 145 on Plate XIII.

5. THE LATRUNCULORUM GROUP

War games with the custodian method of capture are played in north-east Africa, but the two sides are equal and the games have two phases: the first when the pieces are introduced on to the board, and the second when they fight for supremacy.

SEEGA

In *The Modern Egyptians* Lane described the game of Seega which was popular with the fellaheen in the early nineteenth century. Marin, a hundred years later, found the same game played by the Somali.

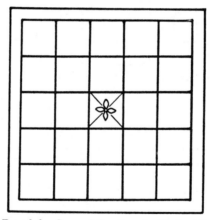

FIG. 70. Board for Seega (after Lane's *Modern Egyptians*)

A board of 5 × 5 squares is marked out on the ground (fig. 70). The two players each use a set of twelve coloured stones.

First Phase

1. The players place two stones at a time on any vacant squares except the centre square which is left uncovered in the first phase.

2. When the twenty-four stones have been placed, the player placing the last couple in position begins the second phase.

Second Phase

3. A stone can move orthogonally to any adjacent vacant square, including the central one.

4. If a player can trap an enemy stone between two of his own (the custodian capture), he removes it from the board and continues to move the same stone as long as he makes captures with it.

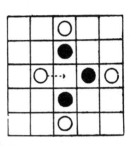

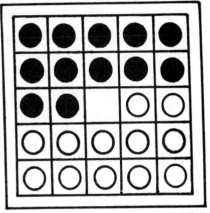

FIG. 71. Multiple custodian capture

FIG. 72. Opening positions in High Jump

5. A stone may make more than one capture in a single move. In fig. 71 the white stone captures three black ones by moving on to the centre square.

6. A player can move a stone between two enemy stones without harm.

7. A stone on the centre square cannot be captured even though it is trapped between two enemy pieces.

8. When a player cannot move, his opponent must make an opening for him by taking an extra turn.

9. The boards may be increased to 7×7 or 9×9 squares, each player then having 24 or 40 pieces.

A weak feature of the game is the frequency of a draw.

Each player may make a barrier behind which there are only his own pieces and he can move these without any chance of attack. The placing of the stones in the first phase is an important factor in planning such barriers. If a player captures all the enemy stones he has a clear win; if a barrier position arises the player with most pieces has a points win; if each player has the same number of pieces in a barrier position the game is drawn.

HIGH JUMP

The Somalis play another game called High Jump on the same board. The initial positions of the stones are shown in fig. 72. The stones move as in Seega but they capture an opponent's piece by jumping over it orthogonally, and several pieces can be taken in succession in one turn of play. It is not compulsory to make a capture.

LUDUS LATRUNCULORUM

In the museum at Chesters, Northumberland, is a stone board which was found on Hadrian's Wall (fig. 73). Several small pieces of tile were lying near and are now in the Black Gate Museum, Newcastle-upon-Tyne. Some are plain and others have a hole drilled through the centre. They appear to have served as pieces for the game.

In a Richborough find there was a board of 8 × 8 squares with eighteen flat discs; eleven were marked with concentric circles and seven were plain. Many other boards have been found in Roman sites in Britain. They are usually marked with 7 × 8, 8 × 8, or 9 × 10 squares. Their frequency suggests a popular game which may have been Ludus Latrunculorum. The first reference to this game was made by Varro (116–27 B.C.) but it was probably much older. He implies that it was played on a board marked with lines and spaces.

Ovid tells us that the pieces were of different-coloured glass or even precious stones. He also states that a piece was taken by being surrounded by two enemy pieces in rank or file and that backward moves were allowed. Our chief source of information about the game comes from an obscure account in a poem known as *Laus Pisonis* which was written by Saleius Bassus during the middle of the first century A.D. The following translation is taken from Professor Austin's article, 'Roman Board Games'.

'Cunningly the pieces are disposed on the open board, and battles are fought with soldiery of glass, so that now White blocks Black, now Black blocks White. But every foe yields to thee, Piso; marshalled by thee, what piece ever gave way? What piece on the brink of death dealt not death to his enemy? Thousand-fold are thy battle tactics: one man in fleeing from an attack himself overpowers him, another, who has been standing on the look-out, comes up from a distant coign; another stoutly rushes into the mêlée, and cheats his foe now creeping on his prey; another courts blockade on either flank, and under feint of being blocked, himself blocks two men; another's objective is more ambitious, that he may quickly break through the massed phalanx, swoop into the lines, and razing the enemy's rampart do havoc in the walled stronghold. Meantime, although the fight rages fiercely the hostile ranks are split, yet thou thyself are victorious with serried lines unbroken, or despoiled may be of one or two men, and both thy hands rattle with the prisoned throng.'

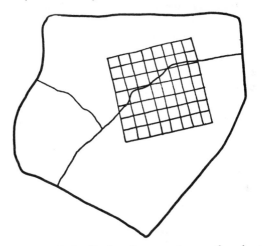

FIG. 73. Stone board for Ludus Latrunculorum found at Chesters, Northumberland; *c.* A.D. 150–400

Allowing for the demands of the metre and rhetoric this is a fair description of the game of Seega; the cunning disposition of the pieces on the open board refers to the first phase of the game when the pieces are placed in position. The attack by trapping an enemy piece between two of one's own is described, while a piece may be supported by moving another alongside; impregnable lines of pieces may be created, and the captured pieces are removed from the board and held in the hands. The game was won by the player who succeeded in making most captures.

Becq de Fouquière and others have suggested that some of the pieces may have had increased power: perhaps there was a leader who could move more than one square at a time by jumping over an enemy piece and trapping another of the player's pieces. This would allow a player to break up an otherwise impregnable position and thus prevent a game finishing with many pieces still on the board. There is nothing in the literature to support these suggestions, nor is there anything to contradict them. One of the Pompeii wall-paintings shows a board with yellow, black, and white pieces on it, while in 1924 twenty-one white, five black, and two blue counters were found in a room of one of the barrack buildings in a late first-century deposit at Chester. No trace was found of a board or dice. The game may have been played on the ground marked out into squares. The two blue counters may have been leaders.

Egypt was within the frontiers of the Roman Empire in the days of Trajan, and Somaliland was just outside. Ludus Latrunculorum may well have survived among the unsophisticated fellaheen and Somali tribesmen while it was forgotten elsewhere after the fall of the Roman Empire. Seega and High Jump may be survivals of the Roman game, each preserving one of its forms of movement. The last reference to Latrunculorum being played in the interior of the Empire was about A.D. 400 when Macrobius rebuked those who played at Tabula and Latrunculi. See fig. 140 on Plate X.

Suggested Rules for Ludus Latrunculorum

1. Using an 8×7 board each player has 16 pieces. They are placed two at a time by alternate turns of play anywhere on the board. During this first phase no captures are made.

2. When the thirty-two pieces are in position each player adds a blue piece to the board. This is the DUX. The second phase then begins. The pieces can move one square orthogonally in any direction.

3. A capture is made by trapping an enemy piece between two of one's own pieces on rank or file.

4. When a piece makes a capture it has another turn, and from this it follows that an isolated piece may endanger itself and several of its fellows by starting a sequence of captures.

5. The dux may move in the ordinary way, or it may make a short orthogonal jump over an enemy piece, landing on an empty square beyond. It does not capture by this manœuvre, unless it traps another enemy piece between itself and one of its own men. The power of jumping enables it to penetrate a defensive position which may start a whole series of captures from within a walled stronghold. It is captured in the same way as any other piece.

6. A piece may move between two enemy pieces without being captured.

7. The game continues until one player has lost all his pieces, or a blockade has developed which neither player can break. The player with most pieces left on the board then wins.

8. If no captures have been made in thirty moves a blockade has been established and the game is over.

6. RUNNING-FIGHT GAMES

Lane's *Modern Egyptians* contains the description of a game TAB which is played on a board of 9×4 squares. The board is very similar to the 10×3 board of Ancient Egypt and it may be another example of a race board being adapted for a war game. TABLAN is simpler than TAB although it belongs to the same group.

TABLAN

This traditional game is still played in some of the villages in Mysore in south-west India. See fig. 143 on Plate XII.

Rules

1. The board (fig. 74A) consists of four rows of twelve squares and each player has twelve pieces of his own colour. At the beginning of the game one piece stands on each square of the player's back row.

2. The four dicing sticks are painted on one side and plain on the other. They are thrown from the hand into the air, caught and thrown up again two or three times before they are allowed to fall to the ground.

Scores

1 plain surface up	..	2 and throw again
4 plain surfaces up	..	8 and throw again
4 painted surfaces up	..	12 and throw again

No other throw scores and the sticks are passed to the opponent.

3. The first move of a piece can only be made on a throw of 2, though this throw can be split into two 1's if required, and two pieces can be moved one square, instead of one piece two squares.

4. Throws of 8 and 12 can similarly be split in half into two 4's or two 6's.

5. The pieces move in the directions shown in the diagram (fig. 74B). White's pieces move A to L, L to X, X to m, m to x and then into Black's back row. Black's pieces move in the opposite direction and finish in White's back row.

6. The pieces can only capture enemy pieces when they are on the two central rows, or when displacing them on the opponent's back row. Captured pieces are removed from the board.

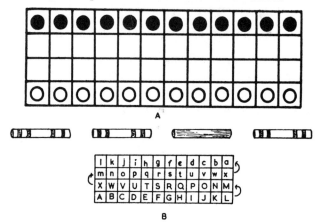

FIG. 74. Tablan board with the pieces in the opening position. Below are four dicing-sticks. (The diagram shows the direction of movement.) (author's collection)

7. Once a piece lands on a square on the opponent's back row it is immobilized and does not move again during the game. It cannot be captured.

8. The enemy home row is captured, square by square, starting from a to l. (This rule is optional.)

9. More than one piece can be moved in any turn of play and more than one capture can be made; but the pieces must move in the directions shown, and when they reach their last square on the middle rows they must turn off into the enemy home row and become immobilized. If they displace a home piece in doing so it is captured.

10. There is no DOUBLING UP of pieces.

11. At any stage of the game a player has to use a throw, convenient or not, unless he has only one piece left near the end of the middle row next to the enemy camp and the throw does not allow him to occupy a square in the enemy camp. These squares must be occupied one after another in the order of a to l (Rule 8).

12. The player occupying most enemy home squares wins the game.

PULUC

This is another running-fight game played by the Kekchi Indians of Central America who are descended from the Mayas. This description is taken from the German text of von Karl Sapper in the Boas Anniversary volume, article 190, p. 283. I am indebted to Miss Agnes Kramer, F.R.C.S. Ed., for her translation.

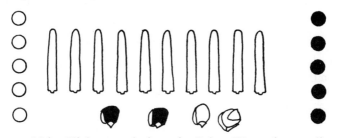

FIG. 75. Maize Highway and pieces for Puluc. The maize-ear dice are drawn to a larger scale

Ten corn cobs are laid on the ground like the rungs of a ladder. The players sit at either end of the MAIZE HIGHWAY and each has five counters of his own colour, made of little pieces of stick. Four flat maize ears are used as dice with one surface blackened and the other left natural (fig. 75).

Scores   2 yellow surfaces up .. 2
            3 yellow surfaces up .. 3
            4 yellow surfaces up .. 5
            4 black surfaces up   .. 4

Rules

1. At the beginning of the game each player throws the dice, and the higher scorer throws again to begin the game; the players then throw alternately.

2. At the player's first throw he enters one of his team on to the highway. At his next throw he may enter another piece or move his first piece on the indicated number of spaces. Any number of his team may be on the highway at the same time. He must not move a piece on to a space which is already occupied by one of his own pieces; there is no doubling up.

3. A player may move a piece forwards on to a space occupied by an enemy piece; the latter is taken prisoner by being placed beneath the winning piece and is moved backwards along the highway by its conqueror in his journey towards the far end of the board.

4. If the victor and the vanquished reach the end of the board (an exact throw is not required), the victor returns to his team ready to be re-entered on the highway for another journey along it, while the poor prisoner is SLAIN and is out of the game.

5. If a player moves a piece on to a space occupied by an enemy piece in charge of a prisoner, the player's piece is placed on the top of the stack, and the whole stack reverses its direction towards the goal of the new victor. Possession of the stack may change sides several times before it eventually arrives at the end of the highway when the top piece and all the others of the same colour are returned to their team ready for new journeys, while the prisoners are out of the game.

6. If a piece journeys along the highway to the far end without incident, it returns to its team to begin the journey again.

7. A stack may capture a single piece or another stack.

8. When a player has no pieces left he has lost the game.

The hat unscrews, and inside are two dice. The hat serves as a dicing cup. Probably Victorian English.

CHAPTER THREE

Games of Position

1. MORRIS GAMES

NOUGHTS AND CROSSES

This simple game is played on a diagram drawn on a slate or piece
of paper (fig. 76).

FIG. 76. Noughts and Crosses

The opening player places an X in any position on the board. His
opponent then adds an O and the players make their marks alternately until one of them has three of his symbols in a straight line.
This wins the game. If neither player can make a line the game is
drawn. The players alternate in having first move in successive
games.

A. S. White pointed out that the opening player has only three
possible moves: centre, middle of side, and corner of side. There
are only twelve positions after the second player has moved and in
seven of these the first player should win, and in five draw. The
second player can never win unless his opponent makes a mistake.

THREE MEN'S MORRIS

The board contains nine points and each player has four counters
of his own colour. The players place one counter alternately on a

point, and if one player can place three in a straight line he wins the game (fig. 77).

A more complicated board was cut into the roofing slabs of the temple at Kurna in Egypt, *c.* 1400–1333 B.C. (fig. 78).

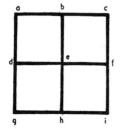

FIG. 77. Three Men's Morris (from Fiske's *Chess* ← *in Iceland*)

FIG. 78. A second form of Three Men's Morris (from Fiske's *Chess in Iceland*) →

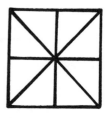

Each player had three men of his own colour and entered them in turn on any vacant point on the board, and then the game continued with alternate moves until one player succeeded in placing his three men in a straight line. As the first player could always force a win by correct play, dice may have been used to decide the advantage of first entry.

More than a thousand years later Ovid mentions the game in his *Ars Amatoria*. The Roman boards were usually of wood or stone, though exotic materials were sometimes used to satisfy the eccentricities of the rich. Trimalchio had one of turpentine-tree, and Martial speaks of an ivory board.

The game was widely played in England in A.D. 1300 and visitors to the cathedrals of Norwich, Canterbury, Gloucester, Salisbury, and Westminster Abbey can see boards cut into the cloister seats by monks who found their long devotions tedious.

Hyde tells us that on the other side of the world the Chinese were playing the same game, Luk tsut K'i, in the time of Confucius, *c.* 500 B.C.

SIX MEN'S MORRIS

Six Men's Morris was popular in Italy, France, and England during the Middle Ages but was obsolete by 1600. Each player had six pieces and they were entered alternately, one at a time; each player trying to form a row along one of the sides of either square. If a player succeeded in this he removed any one of his opponent's pieces. When all the pieces had been entered the game continued by alternate moves of a piece along a line to an adjacent empty point. When a player was reduced to two men the game was over (fig. 79).

NINE MEN'S MORRIS

Two players have nine men each and enter them alternately one at a time, on any vacant point. Each time a player forms a row or MILL of three pieces along a line he removes one of his opponent's pieces from the board, but not one which is in a mill. When all the men have been entered the turns continue by moving a piece to an adjacent vacant point along a line, with the object of making a mill and capturing an enemy piece. A player blocking all his opponent's men so that they cannot move, or reducing him to two pieces, wins the game. See fig. 147 on Plate XIV for an end of the first stage.

A mill can be made and broken any number of times; an enemy piece being captured each time the mill is made. If a player only has three pieces in a mill left on the board and it is his turn to move, he must do so even if this means losing a piece and the game at his opponent's next move.

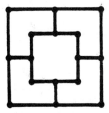

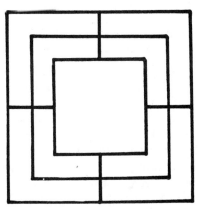

FIG. 79 (*above*). Six Men's Morris (from Fiske's *Chess in Iceland*)

FIG. 80 (*right*). Nine Men's Morris (from Fiske's *Chess in Iceland*)

Cut into the roofing slabs at Kurna is a design 15½ in. square for this game, *c.* 1400 B.C. Two similar diagrams are cut into the great flight of steps which ascend the lower part of the hill at Mihintale in Ceylon. They were carved by the masons who laid the thirty-foot-wide stairway during the reign of Mahadathika Maha-Naga, A.D. 9–21. The design has been used in Ceylon as a charm against evil influences. In Europe it has been found on articles from Lake Dwellings, the first city of Troy, and a burial site of the Bronze Age at Cr Bri Chualann (Bray), Co. Wicklow, Ireland.*

In 1880 a large grave-mound was opened on the Gokstad farms near Sandefjord in Norway. Inside was a Viking ship and on the

* The town has reverted to its original name.

deck was the burial chamber of a king. Many of his possessions were with him, including a portion of a gaming board, cut on one side for Nine Men's Morris (fig. 81) and on the other for a game which may have been Hnefatafl (fig. 66).

The Alfonso X manuscript of the thirteenth century A.D. describes a variant using three cubic dice. During the entry phase throws of 6, 5, 4, or 6, 3, 3, or 5, 2, 2, or 4, 1, 1, gave the caster the right to break into an enemy mill and capture a piece, in addition to introducing one of his own pieces on to the board, and if a mill was formed with this piece he removed two of the opponent's men. With any other throw only a single piece was entered. At the end of the first phase the dice were discarded and the game continued in the usual way.

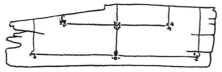

FIG. 81. Fragment of a Nine Men's Morris board from the Gokstad ship, *c.* A.D. 900 (after Du Chaillu)

Nine Men's Morris reached its zenith in the fourteenth century. Superb illustrations of the game are contained in the codices of the North Italian Academies; manuscripts designed for the use of the court. There is an illustrated account of the game in one of the redactions of the *Civis Bononiae*, a remarkable volume in the Victor Emmanuel library at Rome. The perimeters of the boards are drawn with double lines in two colours while the pieces are dissimilar and each player controls the movements of MOONS, STARS, SHIELDS, CROSSES, SQUARES, and ROUNDS. The Moon is shown as a crescent orb, the Star has long shimmering rays, the Shield is triangular, the Cross is in the Greek form, and the Squares and Rounds are in solid colour.

These codices contain collections of Morris positions, with the sides differentiated in red or gold, contrasting with the black and white of chess diagrams. Unfortunately, the manuscripts contain very little information on how to play the games. Only six names are given for the pieces and in some of the diagrams more than one Square or Round is shown. All the pieces seem to have had the same value and movement and von der Lasa has suggested that the names and shapes may merely represent a method of recording the order of play.

Triple-purpose boards built in the form of a shallow box with a hinged lid were popular in Europe from the fourteenth century onwards. When closed, one surface was used for chess, and the other for Nine Men's Morris; when open, the interior displayed a backgammon table. Some were most elaborately worked in mother-of-pearl, ivory, and metals.

2. THREE-IN-A-ROW GAMES
DARA

Several games of this group are played in North Africa, one of the best being Dara of the Dakarkari people, Nigeria. The board consists of thirty small depressions made in the ground in five rows of six each.

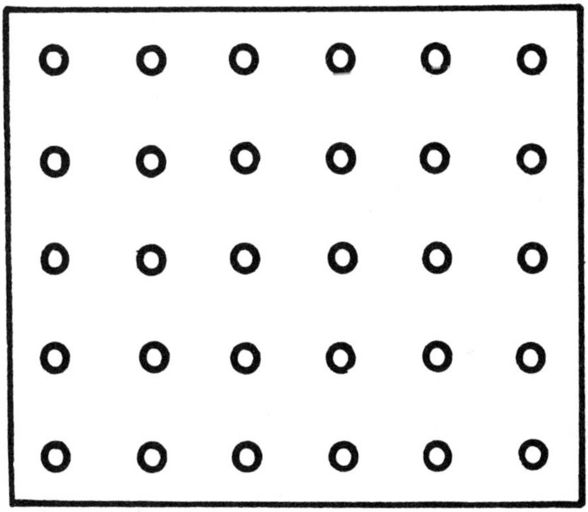

FIG. 82. Arrangement of holes in Dara (after Fitzgerald)

First phase. Each player has twelve distinctive stones or pieces of pottery. They are placed one at a time in the holes in alternate turns of play. When all the pieces have been positioned the second phase begins.

Second phase. Alternately, one piece is moved orthogonally to the next hole, the object being to form a line of three pieces in consecutive holes orthogonally, but not diagonally. When a THREE is formed the player removes one of his opponent's pieces from the board.

The game ends when one player is unable to make further lines of three pieces. Lines of four pieces do not count. Skilful placing of the pieces in the first phase of the game may be decisive in the second.

3. FIVE-IN-A-ROW GAMES

GO-MOKU (RENJU)

This Japanese game is played chiefly by children, women and Occidental visitors. It is a poor relation of the intellectual Go, described on pp. 99ff. under its Chinese name of Wei-ch'i.

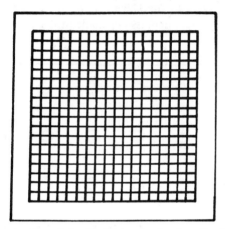

FIG. 83. Board for Go-Moku (author's collection)

Go-moku, also known as Renju, is played on the Go board of 19 × 19 points.

1. At the beginning of the game the board is empty. The players place their pieces by alternate turns of play on any unoccupied point.

2. Players are not permitted to construct open-ended forks with branches of three stones each. Forks of three and four, or four and four, are allowed.

3. The first player to form a continuous line of five pieces on a row, column, or diagonal wins the game.

Go-moku was introduced into Europe about 1885. Known in England as Spoil Five, it was played on the squares instead of the points.

HASAMI SHOGI (1)

This game, also from Japan, is played on a quarter of the I-go board (9 × 9 squares). Each player has 18 pieces of his own colour and they are placed on the two back rows. The object is to form five men in a row excluding the two home rows. No diagonal moves are allowed. A piece may move any number of unoccupied squares orthogonally in any direction.

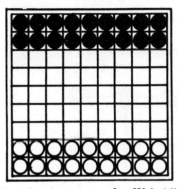

FIG. 85. Custodian capture in a corner in Hasami Shogi (2)

FIG. 84. A quarter of a Wei-ch'i board arranged for playing Hasami Shogi (1)

Method of Play

1. A piece cannot land on a square occupied by another piece.

2. A piece can jump over an adjacent piece to land on a vacant square beyond; but it cannot jump over a vacant square and an occupied square in the same move.

3. When a player traps an opposing piece between two of his own on a rank or file (custodian capture), it is removed from the board. Any number of pieces may be trapped between two opposing pieces as long as there are no gaps.

4. A piece may move between two enemy pieces safely.

5. A player wins the game when he has five pieces in a row on a file, rank, or diagonally.

HASAMI SHOGI (2)

The first variety of Hasami Shogi belongs to the games of position but the second is a war game.

1. Each player has one row of men on his back row.

2. The moves and the method of capture are as in the first form.

3. The object of the game is to capture all an opponent's pieces and remove them from the board. A man on a corner square may be captured by blocking his movement with pieces on the two adjacent orthogonal squares (fig. 85).

4. REPLACEMENT GAMES

FIVE FIELD KONO

The board and opening position are shown in fig. 86. The players move one piece one point at a time diagonally across the squares,

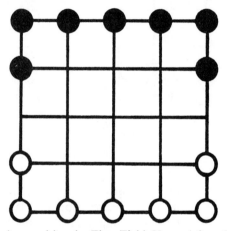

FIG. 86. Opening position in Five Field Kono (after Culin's *Korean Games*)

either backwards or forwards. The object of the game is to move the pieces across to the other side of the board to occupy the places vacated by the opponent, and the first player to do so wins the game.

HALMA

This game was invented about 1880 and in the two-handed form each player has nineteen men arranged in his own CAMP, the walls of which are marked by a thicker or double line. Only one man may be moved in any turn of play: either as a single step in any direction on to an empty adjacent square, or by leaping over a man in any direction on to an empty square immediately beyond. A number of leaps may be made over his own or hostile pieces, and each player tries to make ladders to enable his pieces to move several squares in

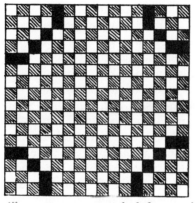

FIG. 87. Halma. Two corners are marked for 19 pieces (two-handed game). If four play each player has 13 pieces

a single turn of play. Each also tries to use an opponent's ladder, or alternatively tries to block it to prevent its use by his adversary. The first player to move all his pieces into the enemy camp wins the game. In a four-handed game each player has thirteen men arranged in his own corner.

Cheap boards are made of cardboard and the pieces are wooden or plastic; expensive boards are of veneered wood with light and dark squares and in the centre of each is a drill hole to receive the pegs of the halma men which are made of bone or ivory.

5. TERRITORIAL POSSESSION

WEI-CH'I

This Chinese game, pronounced Way Chee, was first mentioned in Chinese writings from Honan dating from about 625 B.C. The first books on the subject were written much later during the Tang Dynasty, A.D. 618–906. Wei-ch'i was introduced into court circles in Japan about A.D. 500, probably during the reign of Empress Suiko, at a time when the Roman Empire was falling into decay. In the museum at Nara is a Go board (Go is the Japanese name for the game) said to have been used by the Emperor Shomu, A.D. 724–48. About the time William the Conqueror invaded England in A.D. 1066, Go was beginning to be played by the common people in Japan, and in the thirteenth century it was popular with the Samurai class, and boards and stones were regarded as essential pieces of military equipment and were taken on active service. As soon as the fighting was over, Go contests began.

In the sixteenth century a State Academy was founded for the advancement and tuition of the game, and several master players were installed as professors with substantial salaries: the director, Honinbo Sansha, receiving 1,400 square yards of land and an annual income of 1,000 bushels of rice. Private schools were also established, and professional itinerant players toured the country playing exhibition games and instructing pupils. The Academy awarded professional players degrees, the first or lowest carrying the title 'Shodan', and the highest or ninth, which has been granted very rarely, 'Kudan'. A strict system of handicapping was also devised, the weaker player being allowed first move; or being granted two, three, or four stones, the last being the highest handicap permissible among players holding degrees.

In the first half of the nineteenth century considerable advances were made in the science of the game, but with the fall of the Shogunate in 1868, state regulation of the game ceased and the Go Academy came to an end. The influx of foreigners created interests in imported goods and customs; the native arts and pastimes declined, and many of the Go masters became destitute.

There was a revival of the old national game about 1880, and today there are some eight million Go players and nearly one hundred professionals in Japan; while most Japanese newspapers carry a Go column as a standard feature. In China Wei-ch'i is played widely, and the same game Pa-tok is popular in Korea, though the standard of play in both these countries is well below that in Japan.

Traditional Japanese boards are made of a solid block of wood about eighteen inches long and sixteen broad, and some five inches thick, fitted with four detachable feet about three inches high. The board and feet are stained yellow. A square depression is cut into the underside of the board to lighten it, and also to increase its resonance; the pieces making a pleasant click when placed upon it. The Koreans have gone a stage further and some of their boards have wires stretched beneath to produce a musical note when the stones are played.

The upper surface of a Go board is marked out with thin black lines of lacquer into a grid of 19 × 19 forming 361 intersections or 'points'. Nine of these are marked with little circles to assist in rapid orientation and in handicapping (see later).

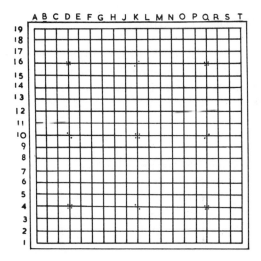

FIG. 88. Diagram of a Go board and the Korschett system of notation. 10E16 means that on the 10th play White placed his stone on E16. 73A4+2 means on the 73rd play Black put his stone on A4 and captured 2 white stones. (Black moves are odd, and White even, unless Black receives a handicap.)

Each player has a bowl containing his 'stones' which are discoidal in shape and some ⅞ inch in diameter, Black having 181 and White 180. In the best sets the white stones are made of shell from the provinces of Hitachi and Mikawa, while the black are a kind of slate from the Nachi cataract in Kishiu. Cheaper 'stones' may be made of glass (see tailpiece, p. 112).

The players sit on the floor facing each other across the board.

Rules.

1. The board is empty at the beginning of the game.

2. There is a slight advantage in playing first and this privilege is granted to the weaker player, Black, who starts by putting one of his stones on any point of the board. Play then alternates, only one stone being placed at each turn. Once played the stones cannot move, and remain in position until the end of the game, unless they are captured when they are removed from the board.

3. The object of the game is to control vacant points in such a way that they cannot be occupied by the opponent. The player controlling most points or 'territory' at the end of the game is the winner.

4. Stones completely surrounded by those of the opposite colour and without any empty points orthogonally adjacent to them are captured and removed from the board; but this is not the primary object of the game, just as in chess the object is not to capture pieces, but to checkmate the rival king. In both games it is possible to win without making a single capture.

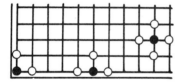
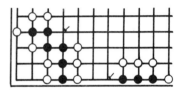

FIG. 89A. Positions of single capture

FIG. 89B. Multiple capture. A white stone placed as arrowed would capture the Black group attacked

5. If a stone is surrounded orthogonally by enemy stones, it is captured and removed from the board. (FIG. 89A.) Stones arranged orthogonally on adjacent points are considered a single unit, and however large, all the stones of the group survive or are captured together. (FIG. 89B.)

6. A stone cannot be placed on a point completely surrounded by enemy stones unless it makes a capture by so doing. (FIGS. 90 and 91.) Nor can a stone occupy the last free point of one of its own groups, unless enemy stones are captured by this action. (FIG. 92.)

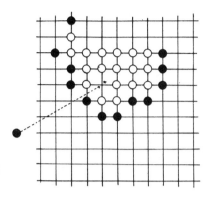

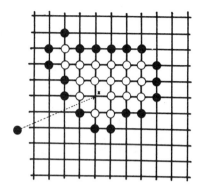

FIG. 90. Black cannot play onto *x* as it would be captured immediately (rule 6)

FIG. 91. A Black stone on *x* leaves the White stones without contact with an empty point and they are therefore captured and removed, Black's stone remaining on *x*

7. Vacant points completely controlled by stones of one colour are called EYES, and as an eye can only be occupied by an opponent when it results in the capture of the surrounding stones, it follows that a group with two eyes is impregnable. (FIG. 93A.)

8. A group of stones not in orthogonal contact may contain empty points, but the disconnected stones can be attacked and then the whole formation becomes dead. These empty points are false or temporary eyes, and are often constructed by the novice in error for real eyes. (FIG. 93B.)

9. A player may place a stone on any vacant point except to make an illegal play, rule 6, or when his opponent has just captured a stone in a repetitive position known as a *ko*, when he must make one play elsewhere on the board. Without this rule a perpetual position would arise and a drawn game. When fighting for a vital *ko* players hunt everywhere for forcing plays which their opponents must answer, and thereby allow them to attack the *ko* once more. (FIG. 94.)

10. If there are three *kos* on the board at once the game is declared drawn.

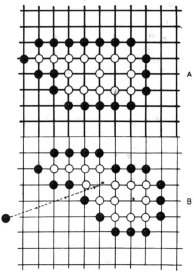

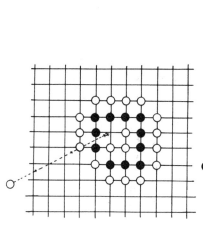

FIG. 92. A White stone on *x* captures the Black stones, but if
any of the encircling White
stones were missing, the play
would be illegal as the central
white formation would be captured

FIG. 93A, Safe White formation
with two eyes; 93B, false eyes.
If Black plays onto *x* five White
stones are captured; and at the
next turn a Black stone on *y*
captures the rest; though
Black would leave the 'dead'
formation and play elsewhere
unless his own encircling
stone were threatened

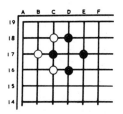

FIG. 94. Repeating position or *Ko*. If White plays onto D17 capturing the
Black stone on C17, Black may not attack the White stone until he
has made one play elsewhere on the board

11. Sometimes opposing formations of stones are interlocked so that neither player can attack the opponent's pieces without losing his own. This impasse is known as *seki*, and these positions are left alone until the end of the game when they are neutralized and all the free points within it are ignored and do not count to either score. (FIG. 95.)

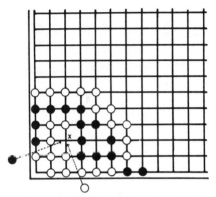

FIG. 95. An impasse or *seki*. Neither player can enter a stone at *x* without losing his own formation. Expert players rarely form *seki* positions

12. At the end of the game there will be isolated vacant points between the opposing formations which are neutral and profitless to both players. They are filled in to help in adding up the final score, but it is immaterial by whom.

13. Stones which, while not actually surrounded, can inevitably be so, are *dead*, and are removed at the end of the game without further play.

14. When the profitless points have been filled, and the dead stones removed from each player's territories, each player places his opponent's captured stones on vacant enemy points, thus reducing the opposing score by the number of pieces held. (FIGS. 96 and 97.)

Tactics

Only a few basic principles can be mentioned in this brief account:

1. Do not make purposeless moves and lose time and space.

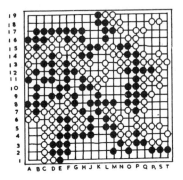
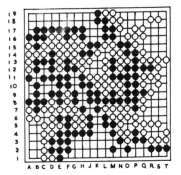

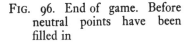

FIG. 96. End of game. Before
neutral points have been
filled in

FIG. 97. End of game. Captured
and dead stones have been
placed in enemy territories.
Ready for the final count

2. Abandon indefensible stones, but fight out all doubtful positions.

3. As the players wish to enclose territory quickly, the fences should be as light as possible, consistent with enough strength to resist attack. The size of an enclosure must be balanced against the number of stones required to defend it. The wider the space the further the fence is from support and the stronger it must be. (See FIG. 98.)

Fences built of alternate stone and space are usually secure, and the opponent cannot play between without loss, but if the pieces are further apart a struggle for the intervals may develop, and the success of the defence will depend upon the position of other groups.

4. If a lightly constructed fortification is attacked it is often better to extend it and gain other territory, or to counter-attack enemy positions rather than spend stones in strengthening: solid walls around small plots lead to inevitable defeat.

5. When trying to prevent the development of an enemy stone in a clear field it is generally unwise to play onto an adjacent point. This invites attack. It is better to leave a vacant point between the pieces, and then any attack will develop too slowly to be successful.

6. Every effort should be made to prevent the opponent from linking dead formations with living ones.

7. When a player places a stone which forces his opponent to defend, he has obtained the *sente*, and it is sometimes worth losing a few pieces to seize or retain this advantage.

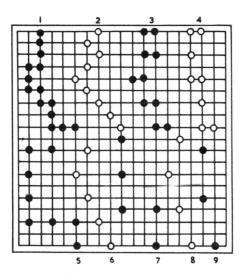

FIG. 98. Building fences:

1. Very strong but slow
2. Faster and still strong
3. Strong
4. Nearly as strong as 3, and faster
5. Strong and fast for penetrating new territory
6. A variant of 5
7. } Rather flimsy but sometimes useful
8. }
9. Weak, but fast and quickly converted into 5 or 6

8. An eye of three points cannot be defended against the turn, but with it two eyes of one point each can be formed. An eye of four vacant points in a straight line can be defended with or without the *sente*, but if they are in a square they are indefensible even with it. Four empty points like a stunted T can be defended with the turn, but not against it.

A fortification with more than seven empty points is usually safe and it is wasteful to strengthen it unless it is attacked. There are, however, positions in a corner when eyes of seven, eight, or even nine points can be attacked, resulting in loss, *seki*, or *ko*.

9. Neutralization of enemy territory is always profitable. If White holds a territory of four vacant points in a square it will cost Black $3+2+1 = 6$ stones before the formation is captured, but there must be at least five stones in the wall of White's formation, and three more will have been played into it making a loss of eight pieces which will be placed in White's final territories at the end of the game. White has also lost four vacant points and therefore is $8+4 = 12$ points poorer, while Black gains $8-6 = 2$ points; a total improvement of Black's position by $12+2 = 14$ points.

Strategy

The corners of the board are natural fortresses against attack, and territories formed there require fewer stones. (FIG. 99.)

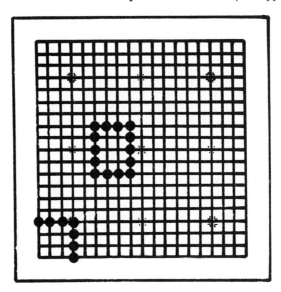

FIG. 99. Seven stones control nine points in the corner, whereas fourteen stones only control six points in the centre

The sides of the board are less protected; and the centre is the most difficult to fortify. Play usually begins at the corners, spreads to the sides, and finishes in the centre.

In fig. 100A Black has used his first eight stones mapping out a territory of about twenty-five points, while White has laid claim to most of the rest of the board, and is in a position to shift his play wherever it may be most profitable. A game of Go resembles

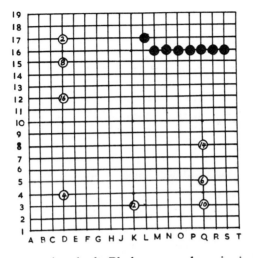

FIG. 100A, poor opening play by Black; B, a sound opening by both players

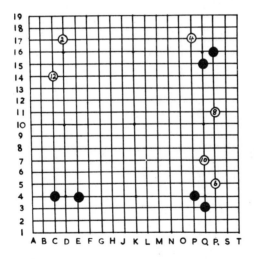

five simultaneous games of chess; one at each corner and the fifth in the middle of the board, with the additional interest that the position of stones in one area influences the other four.

An opponent may be prevented from forming an eye in a disputed territory by playing a stone on one of the four points he needs to complete it. Sometimes this is done before he has filled the other three necessary positions.

Two groups of stones can often be joined by a 'cross over' or *watari* (FIG. 101.)

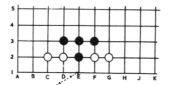

FIG. 101. White plays onto EI and links his two groups. Black cannot play onto CI or FI without losing his stone at the next turn

Handicapping

Equal players play Black alternately; but if one wins three times consecutively he usually gives his opponent a handicap of two stones, and if he continues to win, the number is gradually increased.

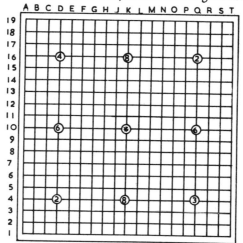

✳ 5. 7. 9.

FIG. 102.

Handicap	Positions
2 stones	D4, Q16
3	D4, Q4, Q16
4	D4, D16, Q4, Q16
5	D4, D16, K10, Q4, Q16
6	D4, D10, D16, Q4, Q10, Q16
7	D4, D10, D16, K10, Q4, Q10, Q16
8	D4, D10, D16, X4, K16, Q4, Q10, Q16
9	D4, D10, D16, K4, K10, K16, Q4, Q10, Q16

The player receiving a handicap plays Black and plays second. Handicap stones are placed in standard positions. (FIG. 102.)

If a nine handicap game were played by two professionals Black would win by about 100 points; but novices may be given 11, 13, 17, or even 25 stones and still lose!

Casual games last one to three hours, and professional matches up to three days. Beginners are advised to play on a quarter of the board and to concentrate on fundamental corner problems; corner play analyses, called *joseki*, are described at length by most Japanese Go writers.

6. PATIENCE GAMES

SOLITAIRE

In the eighteenth century a new game reached England from the Continent called Solitaire. It was a form of patience for one player using a traditional Fox and Geese board and said to have been invented by a French count when in prison.

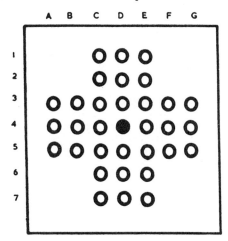

FIG. 103. Fox and Geese board used for Solitaire

Fig. 103 shows a Fox and Geese board with a notation to record solutions of solitaire problems. The basic problem is to remove the marble in D4, and then at each turn of play one marble must jump orthogonally over an adjacent marble into a vacant hole beyond. The marble passed over is removed. The object of the game is to remove all the marbles from the board except one, and this should be left in the central hole.

Method

1.	D2 into D4 remove D3			17.	C2	C4	C3
2.	F3	D3	E3	18.	A3	C3	B3
3.	E1	E3	E2	19.	D3	B3	C3
4.	E4	E2	E3	20.	A5	A3	A4
5.	C1	E1	D1	21.	A3	C3	B3
6.	E1	E3	E2	22.	D5	D3	D4
7.	E6	E4	E5	23.	D3	B3	C3
8.	G5	E5	F5	24.	B3	B5	B4
9.	D5	F5	E5	25.	B5	D5	C5
10.	G3	G5	G4	26.	D5	F5	E5
11.	G5	E5	F5	27.	F4	D4	E4
12.	B5	D5	C5	28.	C4	E4	D4
13.	C7	C5	C6	29.	E3	E5	E4
14.	C4	C6	C5	30.	F5	D5	E5
15.	E7	C7	D7	31.	D6	D4	D5
16.	C7	C5	C6				

This sequence of moves leaves the last marble in the centre, D4. Other problems can be set and solved.

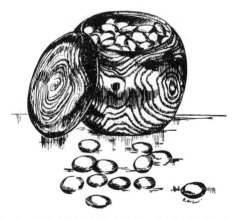

Wooden Wei-ch'i bowl filled with tze (author's collection)

CHAPTER FOUR

Mancala Games

1. TWO-RANK MANCALA

MANKALA'H

In Lane's *Modern Egyptians*, written when he was living in Egypt in the 1830's, is a description of MANKALA'H, a popular game in the coffee shops. The loser paid for the coffee! The board (fig. 104) consisted of two rows of six small pits.

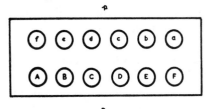

FIG. 104. Board for Mankala'h (after Lane's *Modern Egyptians*)   FIG. 105. Limestone mancala board from Ancient Egypt (from Petrie's *Objects of Daily Use*)

Those marked A, B, C, D, E, F, belonged to P, and a, b, c, d, e, f, to p. Each began the game with thirty-six pebbles. One player took all the pebbles and without counting, distributed them in one or more pits on each side; usually choosing the central pits and leaving the end pits empty. Another common arrangement was to place about half into pit A and the remainder in pit a. If the other player did not like his opponent's arrangement he could turn the board round but he then surrendered his right to first move.

The player opening the game started from any one of his pits by lifting all the pebbles out of it and sowing one in each pit in an anticlockwise direction. When he reached the end of his row he passed over into the opponent's row, sowing a pebble into each pit in turn. At the end of the opponent's row, if he still had pebbles left in his hand, he returned to the beginning of his own row and continued sowing until he had used them up. If the last pebble was sown into an empty pit his turn ceased and his opponent began to play.

If the last pebble was sown into a pit containing one or three pebbles, making two or four, the player took these pebbles together with those of the pit opposite and put them into his store as captured pieces. If one or more of the preceding pits also contained either two or four pebbles, with no pit with any other amount intervening, he also took the contents of these preceding pits together with the contents of those opposite.

If the last pebble fell into a pit containing two, four, or some other even number, thus making an odd number after the sowing, he lifted all the pebbles out and sowed them in the same way as before: e.g. if the last pebble was placed in pit D, he lifted out all the pebbles in it and sowed one into E, another into F, and a third into a, etc. and he continued in this way until either his last pebble fell into an empty pit or into a pit with one or three pebbles, thus making two or four, when he captured them.

After the first win of a lap, the player could play from any pit on his side of the board. After any other win in a lap he had to lift the pebbles in the next loaded pit on his side of the board.

When one player had more than one pebble on his side of the board, and his opponent had none, he was obliged to put one of his pebbles into his opponent's first hole. When only two pebbles remained on the board they became the property of the player first having them both on his side of the board. When the board was empty each player counted his pebbles, and the winner scored the difference for that round. A new round then began, and the score of each round was added to the last until one player reached sixty.

Professor Flinders Petrie found a rough block of limestone at Memphis containing three rows of fourteen pits which appears to be an early form of Mankala'h (fig. 105). The store suggests that pieces were captured and the pits are so small that the pieces were probably beans or seeds.

There are several sets of deeply cut holes in the roofing slabs of the Kurna temple at Thebes, *c.* 1400 B.C. Other sets of boards are cut into the summit of the damaged portion of the great pylon built in Ptolemaic times at the entrance of the temple of Karnak, and also at the Luxor temple. The boards consist of two rows of six, seven, and eight saucer-shaped holes, the largest being 3½ in. wide and 1 in. deep.

Boards have been found in Arabia dating from before the time of Muhammad, and the followers of the prophet carried variations of the game to the countries influenced by their culture. MANCALA is used as a generic noun for all the games of the Mankala'h type.

PALLANGULI

Pallanguli is played by the Tamil women of southern India and Ceylon, though it is sometimes used as a gambling game by men. Antique boards were made of wood or ivory and were usually plain, though they might be beautifully carved and ornamented. The modern board in fig. 152 on Plate XVII came from Ernakulam in Travancore-Cochin and is made of a white metal chromium-plated. The little wheels are an unexpected embellishment!

The players start with seven holes and place six seeds in each. The opening player then lifts the seeds from any hole on his side of the board, leaving it empty, and moving anti-clockwise sows one seed into each pit. If he reaches the end of his side of the board he continues sowing in his opponent's holes, still in an anti-clockwise direction. When the last seed of a lift falls into a hole, either on his own side of the board or his opponent's, he picks up all the pieces in the next hole and continues sowing as before in the same direction. If the last seed of a lift falls into a hole with an empty hole beyond, any seeds in the hole immediately beyond the empty hole are captured and put into the player's store hole; he then continues play from the next loaded hole beyond; but if the last seed of a lift falls into a hole with two empty holes beyond he wins nothing and his turn ceases.

His opponent then plays by lifting the seeds or seed from any hole on his side of the board and sowing in an anti-clockwise direction. His turn also ceases when he sows the last seed of a lift into a hole next to two empty ones. The game continues by alternate moves.

Four seeds in a hole are called a COW and, irrespective of the sower, becomes the property of the owner of the hole and is lifted at once and put in his store while play continues.

At the end of the first round each player lifts the seeds from his store hole and puts six into as many of the holes on his side of the board as he can, any remainder being returned to his store. The loser of the first round will be unable to fill all his holes and these are marked with a little stick and are known as RUBBISH HOLES. The winner of a round fills all his seven holes and the surplus remains in his store.

The player having the first move in the first round, has second move in the second round, and first move in the third round, etc., each round being played in the same way as the first except that the rubbish holes are not used. The game ends when one player is reduced to less than six seeds and is unable to fill even one hole at the beginning of a round.

During any round the losing player may win enough seeds to re-open one or more rubbish holes, and eventually he may turn the tables and finally defeat his opponent. A game between well-balanced players can last a very long time. A player is not allowed to count his pieces before making a move, but a good player can tell at a glance the best moves on the board. An antique Pallanguli board is shown as the tailpiece on p. 124.

WARI

The beautiful board carved from one piece of Osese wood in fig. 138 (Plate IX, facing p. 178) came from Ghana. The stem is hollow and contains the seeds when they are not in use. The design is traditional.

Each player begins with four seeds in each hole on his side of the board (fig. 106).

Rules

1. The opening player lifts all the seeds out of one of the holes on his side of the board and sows one into each of the holes in an anti-clockwise direction, cup F being followed by cup a and cup f by cup A.

Example. If the opening player P emptied cup C at the beginning of the game the position would become $\frac{444445}{440555}$.

The second player, p, then lifts the seeds from any hole on his side of the board. If he chose cup e he would sow one seed in cups f, A, B, C, and the position would be $\frac{504445}{551555}$.

2. If the last seed of a lift drops into an enemy hole to make a

final score of 2 or 3, these seeds are captured and are placed in the player's store. The seeds of any unbroken sequence of 2's and 3's on the opponent's side of the board contiguous with and behind the plundered hole are also lifted. A player is not, however, allowed to capture all the pieces on the opponent's side of the board as this would leave him nothing to lift at the next turn of play.

Example. If the position were $\frac{121122}{442710}$ and it was P's turn to play, and he emptied D, he would capture 3 from e, 2 from d, 2 from c, 3 from b, and 3 from a, leaving 1 in f for p to lift at the next turn.

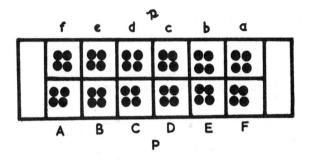

FIG. 106. Wari board at the beginning of a game (redrawn from Rattray's *Religion and Art in Ashanti*)

If the position were $\frac{121710}{111108}$ and P emptied cup F, he would capture 2 from f, 3 from e, and 2 from d. The new position would become $\frac{000821}{111100}$.

3. A heavily loaded cup may contain more than 12 seeds and the sowing from such a cup will be more than one complete cycle of the board. The emptied cup is omitted from the sowing on the second or subsequent cycles and remains empty.

Example. If the position were $\frac{361100}{428008}$ and P lifted the fifteen seeds in cup F, he would drop the last seed in cup d making 3 in that cup and would capture 3, 3, 2, 2, from cups d, c, b, a.

4. When an opponent's cups are empty a player must, if possible, feed seeds into them. If he cannot do so the game is over and all the seeds left on the board become the player's.

Example. If the position were $\frac{000000}{103218}$ and it was P's turn to play he would be obliged to empty cup F. No other cup would feed seeds into p's side of the board.

If the position were $\frac{000000}{103210}$ P could not pass seeds over into p's cups by any lift and therefore the game would be finished, and all the seeds on the board would belong to P.

An extreme example occurs when it is P's turn to play and the position is $\frac{0\,0\,0\,0\,0\,0}{5\,4\,3\,2\,1\,0}$. The game is finished and the fifteen seeds left on the board all belong to P.

5. If all a player's cups are empty and it is his turn to play, the game is over.

6. When only a few seeds remain in play they may circulate with no captures possible for either player. Each then takes the seeds on his own side of the board.

Example. If the position were $\frac{1\,0\,0\,0\,0\,0}{0\,0\,0\,0\,0\,1}$ each player would take the seed on his own side.

Tactics of Wari

A threat occurs to a cup containing one or two seeds when any enemy cup contains a number of seeds equal to the number of cups intervening between them.

Example. If cup B contains 1 or 2 seeds, it is threatened by 2 in f, 3 in e, 4 in d, 5 in c, 6 in b, or 7 in a. In looking for a threat it is quicker to count backwards from the threatened cup, noting when the number of intervening cups agrees with the number of seeds in the cup reached. If a cup contains more than eleven seeds the same rule applies after the subtraction of eleven.

A player's position is strongest when his cups are bearing on several different enemy cups. It is usually a weakness to have several cups all bearing on one opposing cup.

Example. If p has 3 in e, 4 in d, and 6 in b, they all threaten cup B.

If a single seed is threatened it may be defended by:

1. Moving it on to the next cup.

2. Adding a seed to the threatening hole and then the sowing will overshoot the singleton.

3. The player may leave the threat undefended and prepare an immediate reprisal which equals or exceeds it.

Two seeds in a cup may be defended in the same ways and in addition they may be converted into a three by playing a seed into it.

A cup loaded with more than eleven seeds may threaten an empty cup, or one containing one seed. An empty cup is difficult to defend. Only overloading the threatening cup, or preparing reprisals are possible. A singleton may be defended by increasing it to two, which would make four seeds in the cup after the opponent's sowing.

If the singleton were moved on, an empty cup is left which would entail the loss of two seeds when the opponent has finished his sowing.

Example. If the position were $^{14}\frac{00000}{111000}$ and it was P's turn to play, his only move to save immediate loss of seeds is to lift the seed in B, making 2 in cup C which is then safe from the threat of the 14 seeds in f.

If the position were $^{14}\frac{00000}{110001}$, loss is inevitable, but if P played from cup A, only two would be lost while if he played from B or F he would lose eight.

The position after p's move in the first alternative would be $\frac{011111}{242112}$.

The position after p's move in the second alternative would be $\frac{011111}{323112}$; and if the seeds in F were moved it would be $\frac{011112}{332111}$.

In the position $\frac{540500}{202005}$ with P to play he is presented with a difficult problem. He is threatened with losing 3 at C if p at his next move plays e. He may:

1. Empty the threatened cup C, then p can play f and win four, 2 from D and 2 from E.

2. Overload e by playing F, but p can win 3 at C by playing c.

3. If P plays A, converting C into a safe 3, p can win 2 at B by playing c. This move gives the smallest loss and appears to be the most attractive, but it should be noted that the move giving the smallest *immediate* loss is not always the best in the end.

The End Game

Each player tries to retain as many seeds in his own cups and as few in his opponent's as possible. By keeping the seeds spread in many cups instead of a few, and by playing from lightly loaded cups in preference to the heavier, a player can slow the progress of seeds on his side of the board, and may manage to make the outflow smaller than the inflow.

> Lifting one seed from a cup advances 1 unit.
> Lifting two seeds from a cup advances 3 units.
> Lifting three seeds from a cup advances 6 units.
> Lifting four seeds from a cup advances 10 units.

Example. The effect of slow-motion play is seen in the position $\frac{000000}{300001}$. If it is P's turn to play he can win all four seeds. The play is FaAbDcCdBeCf. Any other play will not win all four pieces. This introduces the problem of recording Wari games.

Notation

As player P must always start from a cup on his side of the board (A, B, C, D, E, F) and p must start from one on his side (a, b, c, d, e, f), it is possible to record a game by noting the letters representing the holes, and then the game may be replayed later and the positions recovered. If the opening four moves of a game were CeFd the resulting position would be $\frac{620558}{862550}$. The reader is advised to check

this for himself to make sure he understands this method of notation. Player p would win 2 from cup C.

Group Movement

When the board is nearly empty, a diminishing sequence of seeds in consecutive cups with empty cups ahead may be advanced unaltered. If P has 432100 in his cups and he plays from A, the new position is 043210. If p leaves this unaltered, on the next move P may play from B and the position becomes 004321. This process may continue round the corner Fa. An important application of this principle occurs when a player has two cups with a 1 in front of a 2 and empty cups ahead.

Example. Assume that P has advanced 2 seeds in one cup and 1 in the cup in front with empty holes ahead to the end of his row, 2 seeds being in E and 1 in F. On playing from E, he has two seeds in E and 1 in a. If b is empty p cannot play from cup a without allowing P to make a capture at b from F. This 2 and 1 method may be used repeatedly to capture seeds that must be passed to the other side of the board. Of the 3 passed, 2 are captured.

In the position $\frac{000000}{011121}$ with P to play, he may win 5 of the 6 seeds by playing EaFaDbCcBdCeDfEaF. The two seeds remaining in B and a would circle perpetually and are, therefore, shared by the players.

Heavily Loaded Cups

A heavily loaded cup may have a devastating effect on an opposing row of nearly empty cups, and this effect may sometimes be increased by delaying its use for a few moves.

Example. In the position $\frac{000001}{003211}$ with P to play, if he played F at once the position would become $\frac{111113}{114320}$ and he would win the three seeds in a.

If P played the moves EaDbEcCdEeDfF he would then gain 10 seeds at the last move.

If p had had 2 or 3 seeds in his cups he might have manœuvred so that the cup threatened by P always contained 2 seeds, or at least that a 2 occurred close behind the cup threatened and thus prevented a wholesale sweep by P from cup F.

Match Play

At the end of a game the players count their seeds, the one with most being the winner. If they are playing a match the winner of a game fills the holes on his side of the board and then begins to fill the holes on his opponent's side; and each hole filled with 4 seeds, or a hole with one or more of the leading player's seeds, becomes an extension of his side of the board for the next game. When a player has only two or three holes left he usually concedes the match to his opponent.

Early in the seventeenth century Richard Jobson saw Wari played in the Gambia territory and wrote:

'In the heat of the day, the men will come forth, and sit themselves in companies, under the shady trees, to receive the fresh aire, and there passe the time in communication, having only one kind of game to recreate themselves withall, and that is in a peece of wood, certaine great holes cut, which they set upon the ground betwixt two of them, and with a number of some thirty pibble stones, after a manner of counting, they take one from the other, until one is possessed of all, whereat some of them are wondrous nimble.'

AWARI

In the New World African slaves played their native games and taught them to their children. It is still possible to trace the ancestral origins of some West Indian negroes by their form of mancala. Four variants of Wari are found among the negroes of Guiana and the Caribbean which match with the games of Dahomey, Togoland, and Nigeria. The games have several names, one being Awari. As an intellectual exercise it is on a level with chess. The negroes play for amusement and the prestige accruing to a good player. They will not play for money.

Awari is a masculine pastime though women occasionally play. Herskovits saw an elder of the Saramacca people teaching a young girl, but if a woman became a strong player the men refused to play with her, for no man's reputation would bear the ridicule following defeat by a woman.

Awari also has a religious significance and is often played in a House of Mourning to amuse the spirit of the dead awaiting burial. It is only played during daylight; for when the shadows fall the Yorkas, or ghosts, would join the living players in their game and at the end carry off the spirits.

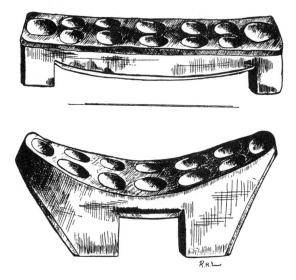

FIG. 107. Awari boards (redrawn from Herskovits' *Wari in the New World*)

Making Awari boards involves spiritual danger, and only old men who have lost a wife are allowed to make them. Although the Bush Negroes are fine carvers, their Awari boards are crude affairs roughly hacked out of a log; they feel that a board should not be brought to immediate perfection, but that the fingers of many players should caress the cups in many games to make them smooth.

The boards are made in two shapes, one with a straight top and the other curved. A village will have both types so that when a man dies who preferred to play on one shape, the villagers will use the other for a time to lessen the chance of his ghost joining in.

A negro on the island of St. Kitts explained that Awari was not played at night because of devils.

'But we're not as afraid of djombies as we used to be.'

'Why not?'

'There aren't so many now, sir. The motor cyars run 'em over, sir.'

2. FOUR-RANK MANCALA

Mancala games with four rows of holes are found mainly in eastern and southern Africa, but extend as far north as the Central African Republic, and westward beyond the bend in the Zaire River to Lisala and Mbandaka. The Swahili, Baganda, and a few other advanced tribes used beautifully made and finished boards, but most

CHISOLO

This is played by the Ba-ila speaking peoples of Northern Rhodesia. The board consists of four rows of seven holes scooped out of the earth. There is a larger store hole at one end. The counters are small stones and each player starts with thirty-three arranged as in fig. 108.

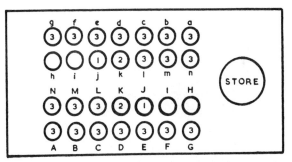

FIG. 108. The beginning of a game of Chisolo

Method of Play

1. The players move alternately and only along the two rows on their own side of the board.

2. On the first move each player must move clockwise; in the second move he may move either clockwise or anti-clockwise, but for the rest of the game he must move in the same direction as he did on his second move. The two players may, therefore, be moving in the same or different directions.

3. The player may begin his move from any hole on his side of the board. He lifts all the stones out of a hole and sows one into each

of the holes beyond. If the last stone of a lap falls into a loaded hole, he lifts all the stones in it and begins a second lap, sowing one stone into each hole beyond. A move may consist of several laps.

4. When the last stone of a lap falls into an empty hole the move is finished. If the empty hole was in the front row the player captures all the stones in the two holes on the same file on the opponent's side of the board; and when he makes a capture he also has the privilege of robbing all the stones out of one extra hole belonging to his opponent. If the two enemy holes on the same file are empty, and no capture is made, the player is also barred from robbing a third hole.

If the last stone of a lap falls into an empty hole in the back row the move finishes, but no captures are made.

5. When a player has no stones left on his side of the board the game is over and he has lost.

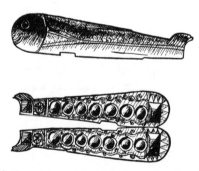

Antique Pallanguli board (redrawn from Durai)

CHAPTER FIVE

Dice Games

The history of lots is as old as the history of man. The pyramidal dice of Sumer have been described in the first chapter, also four-sided dice from Egyptian tombs. Etruscan dice found near Rome (fig. 109) and made about 900 B.C. are similar to the dice of today, with the opposite faces adding up to seven: 1:6, 2:5, 3:4. Similar dice have been found in Britain in the prehistoric earthworks of Maiden Castle.

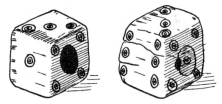

FIG. 109. Etruscan dice, *c*. 900 B.C. (after Culin's *Chinese Games with Dice and Dominoes*)

Gambling sticks have been found with Senat boards of the Empire Age of Egypt, *c*. 1500 B.C., and are still used today by the fellaheen for the game of Tab. The Arabs use them for Hyena, the Koreans for Nyout, and the Amerindians for many related games.

Gambling fever has not been confined to any nation or period in time. Tacitus wrote of the Germani in A.D. 99:

'They practise dice play, at which one will naturally wonder, soberly, and quite as if it were a serious business, with such hardihood in winning and losing, that, when they have nothing more left, they stake their freedom, and their person on the last cast of the die. The loser resigns himself voluntarily to servitude, and even if he is younger and stronger than his adversary, he allows himself to be bound and sold. Thus great is their staunchness in an affair so bad: they themselves call it "Keeping their word".'

During the twelfth and thirteenth centuries A.D. dicing spread throughout England. Hazard was the favourite game in low taverns, and although men could no longer stake their personal liberties on a throw, they played for everything else, even their clothing, on which the tavern-keeper, who acted as a pawnbroker, readily lent small sums of money. There are many accounts of travellers falling into the taverner's hands and playing and drinking themselves destitute; and in an early fourteenth-century manuscript there is an illumination depicting two such players; the older is stark naked, while the younger is reduced to his shirt!

Dice have even taken part in the destiny of nations. King Olaf of Norway, and his contemporary, King Olaf of Sweden, met at Konungahella in Norway in A.D. 1020 to decide the ownership of the isolated district of Hising. They agreed to throw two dice for its possession. The Swedish king threw two sixes, and smiled and said it was hardly worth the Norwegian's while to make a throw. King Olaf replied, while shaking the dice in his hands, 'Although these be two sixes on the dice, it would be easy, sire, for God to let them turn up again in my favour!' Then he threw and had sixes also. The Swede re-threw, and again had two sixes. On Olaf's second throw one die showed a six but the other split in two and there were seven pips showing. Norway gained the district and the kings parted at the end of the meeting staunch friends.

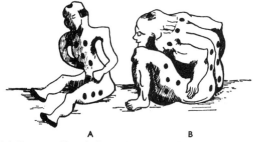

A   B

FIG. 110. (A) Roman die of silver. Some versions have the pips arranged with Rabelaisian humour. (B) Sixteenth-century German die of box-wood (redrawn from Wright's *History of Domestic Manners and Sentiments in England during the Middle Ages*, 1862)

Grotesque dice in human form have been made from time to time and the two shown in fig. 110 are separated by more than a thousand years. The first is Roman, and made of silver. Several Roman dice of the same type are known. The second is larger and is carved in box-wood. In was apparently made in Germany at the beginning of the sixteenth century. Both were in the collection of Lord Londesborough.

1. GAMES WITH TWO-SIDED DICE

HEADS AND TAILS

Although this game is now only of interest to children or used for gambling by the unintelligent, during the reign of Edward II it even appeared at court. In one of his wardrobe rolls is the entry: 'Item, paid to Henry, the King's barber, for money which he lent to the King to play at Cross and Pile [Heads and Tails]—Five Shillings. Item, paid to Pires Barnard, usher of the King's Chamber, money which he lent to the King, and which he lost at Cross and Pile to Monsieur Robert Wattewille, Eight Pence.'

These sums were not trifles. A penny in those days had the purchasing power of at least two modern pounds; a whole sheep cost 3*d*., and a hind earned 6*d*. a week!

The Romans played the same game with a copper coin, the AS, with the head of Janus on one side and the prow of a galley on the other. They called the game CAPITA AUT NAVIM. Professor Lanciani found a coin of Nero which had been sawn in two, and an iron weight placed between the two halves to make one side come up more often. Similar crooked coins are still used by a few pitmen today when playing pitch and toss. Occasionally one may also find a coin which has been split and joined to the halves of another so that one coin has two 'heads' and the other two 'tails'.

Heads and tails is played by one player tossing a coin into the air and the other calling when it is still in flight. If his guess is correct he wins, if not he loses.

THE BOWL GAME

Long before Columbus discovered America the Amerindians played bowl games. All-tes teg-enuk of the Passamaquoddy of Maine is typical of the group. Three pieces of equipment are required.

1. A bowl or shallow wooden dish about 12 in. across and 2 in. deep (fig. 111).

2. The dice are six thin bone discs about ¾ in. in diameter, plain on one side and carved and coloured on the other (fig. 112).

3. Four dozen small sticks about 6 in. long, four larger ones, and a fifth stick which is notched (fig. 112; see also fig. 161 on Plate XXIII).

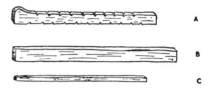

FIG. 111. Wooden bowl for All-tes teg-enuk. The dice are made of plum-stones (bone described in the text) (after Culin's *Chess and Playing Cards*)

FIG. 112. Equipment for All-tes teg-enuk: (A) Notched tally. (B) Four large tallies. (C) Forty-eight small tallies. (D) Six bone discs, plain on one surface and marked on the other

Method of Play

Two players sit facing each other with the bowl between them containing the dice which are arranged haphazardly. The sticks are heaped up in a store pile. One of the players takes the bowl and bangs it down on the ground, causing the dice to jump into the air. If a player scores he has another turn, otherwise the bowl passes to the opponent who also bangs it down and the turn of play passes alternately back and forth. If a die jumps out of the bowl the turn ceases. There are two phases in the game.

First Phase. If five of the discs are the same way up, either marked or plain, the player wins three small tallies from the store pile and places them in a cache.

If he succeeds twice in succession he wins nine small tallies from the pool.

If three times in succession he wins twelve small tallies or one big one; his turn then ceases.

If six discs are alike the player wins a big tally from the pile, or twelve small ones.

If this happens twice in succession the player wins three big tallies or thirty-six small ones.

If it happens three times in succession the player takes sixteen small tallies from the opponent's cache, or if this is impossible he turns a stick up on end; and then claims his win when it is possible and adds them, together with the marker stick, to his own cache.

If all the small tallies have been taken and only large ones are left in the pile, when a player throws five alike he places one of his sticks in front of his cache to show that he has a credit of three tallies. When a player has four sticks out, he takes a large tally from the pool and adds it together with the four marker sticks to his cache.

The notched tally is worth three small tallies and must be the last tally taken from the pile. When it has been won the second phase begins.

Second Phase. The values of the throws alter:

Five alike wins four small tallies from the opponent.

Five alike twice in succession wins twelve small tallies.

Five alike three times in succession wins a large tally or sixteen small tallies from the opponent's cache.

Six alike wins one large tally or sixteen small ones.

Six alike twice in succession wins three large tallies or forty-eight small ones.

When a player has no sticks left he has lost the game.

All-tes teg-enuk may become wearisome in a drawn-out second phase. A quicker ending is achieved by placing any tallies won from the opponent in the second phase back into the pool and out of play. The first player to lose all his tallies loses the game.

2. GAMES WITH SIX-SIDED DICE

GAMES USING ONE DIE

THIRTY-SIX

In this game for any number of players each puts a stake into a pool, and then throws the die to determine the order of play, the lowest cast opening and the highest having the advantage of playing last. Each player in turn throws the die, adding each number thrown to his previous score; the object being to reach thirty-six, or approach it as closely as possible without passing it. Players throwing more than thirty-six go OVER THE TOP and are out of the game. The player nearest to thirty-six wins, and if there is a tie the pool is divided between the winners.

PIG

Any number of players may play and each throws the die in turn. The player with the lowest throw begins the game and the one with the highest plays last. The opening player throws the die as many times as he wishes, each time adding the number on the upper face of the die to his score. If he throws an ace, however, he loses all the points for that turn, and has to pass the die on to the next player. He may stop throwing at any time and hand the die on, when he keeps the points scored in that turn and adds it to his total score. The first player to reach 100 points wins. In succeeding games the advantage of an early throw is decided afresh by each player casting the die, lowest starting and the highest being last.

GAMES USING TWO DICE

ACES IN THE POT

Any number can play and each player starts with two counters. The players make a single throw with two dice in rotation. On a throw of 1 one counter is placed in the pot; if two 1's are thrown both counters are put in. On a throw of 6 a counter and the dice are passed to the player on the left. On a throw of 6:6 the dice and both counters are passed to the left. The dice pass clockwise around the players until there is only one counter left outside the pot. A player without a counter cannot throw the dice but passes them on. The player with the last counter makes three consecutive throws and if he does not throw a 6 he wins the game; but if a 6 is thrown the counter and the dice pass to the player on the left who in turn throws three times. The first player to throw three times without a 6 wins the game.

BARBUDI

This popular Mexican gambling game is played by any number with two dice thrown from a cup.

Rules

1. Each player rolls one die and the highest scorer starts the game. He is known as the SHOOTER and the player on his right becomes the FADER who makes a bet on any amount up to an agreed

limit that the shooter will not win; and he places his bet in the centre of the table.

2. The Shooter may place an equal sum into the centre, or he may allow other players to make up part of, or even the whole of the second stake; or he may refuse the wager entirely and pass up the dice.

3. The Fader also has the right to refuse to fad, and if he does so the opportunity to fad is passed on to the next player on the right.

4. The other players make side bets on whether the Shooter, or the Fader, will make a winning, or losing, throw.

5. When the Fader makes his bet he calls for a ONE-SHOT or a TWO-SHOT decision (Rules 7 and 8).

6. When the Fader's bet has been covered the Shooter rolls the dice once. If the number thrown is not decisive the dice are passed to the Fader who rolls once. If this roll is also ineffectual the Shooter throws again, and they continue throwing alternately until a decisive throw is made.

7. In a One-shot decision the winning numbers are throws of 6:6, 5:5, 3:3, and 6:5, while the losing numbers are 4:4, 2:2, 1:1, and 1:2.

8. In the Two-shot decision if either the Shooter or the Fader throws a 6:5, he wins only half the bet, while a throw of 1:2 loses only half the bet. Either player can then call off the rest of the bet, or they may continue shooting for it.

When the Shooter loses with a throw of 1:2, or the Fader wins with a throw of 6:5, and the second half of the wager is refused by either player, the Shooter passes the dice to the Fader who becomes the new Shooter, and the player on his right the new Fader. If, however, they decide to shoot for the second half of the wager they change roles, the Fader of the first half of the bet becomes the Shooter, and the late Shooter becomes the new Fader. When a decisive throw is cast the dice are passed to the player on the new Shooter's right who becomes the next Shooter.

9. Except when the second half of a Two-shot decision has been contested, when a Shooter throws a losing number or the Fader throws a winning one, the dice pass to the Fader who becomes the new Shooter.

10. A Shooter retains the dice and continues to shoot as long as he continues to win.

HAZARD

In Flaundres whylom was a companye
Of yonge folk that haunteden folye
As ryot, *hazard*, stewes and tavernes.
Chaucer. *Pardoner's Tale*, 1-3.

This game for any number of players became a mania among gamblers in the seventeenth and eighteenth centuries, and it survives in a modified form in the modern American game of Craps, so widely played by the United States and Canadian troops in the Second World War. Two dice were thrown from a cup by one of the players known as the CASTER.

Rules

1. The Caster threw the two dice to determine the MAIN point. This had to be a 5, 6, 7, 8, or a 9; any other throw was disallowed and he threw again until one of the valid points came up.

2. He then threw the two dice to determine the CHANCE point. This had to be a 4, 5, 6, 7, 8, 9, or 10.

3. Then he continued to throw the two dice until either he duplicated the CHANCE point when he won the stakes on the table, or he threw the MAIN point when he lost them.

4. When the Caster was throwing to determine the CHANCE point he lost the stakes outright if he threw an OUT.

A throw of 12 was OUT if the MAIN point was 9, 7, or 5.

A throw of 11 was OUT if the MAIN point was 9, 8, 6, or 5.

A throw of 2 or 3 known as CRABS was OUT regardless of the MAIN point.

5. There were also advantageous throws for the Caster when he was throwing for the CHANCE known as NICKS. If he duplicated the MAIN point, i.e. if the MAIN was 5, and he threw a 5, he scored a NICK and won the stakes.

He also won a NICK:

On throwing a 12 when the MAIN point was a 6 or an 8.

On throwing 11 when the MAIN point was a 7.

Methods of Betting

Any player wishing to lay money with the Caster placed it in a marked circle in the centre of the table. The Caster had the option of accepting or refusing the stake. A player betting with the Caster could bar any throw if he did so before the throw was made, and with the agreement of the Caster. The players also wagered side bets among themselves and the table below taken from the 1786 edition of Hoyle give the odds accepted at that time against the Caster.

Table of Odds Against the Caster for Side Betting

Main	Chance	Odds
7	4	2 to 1
6	4	5 ,, 3
5	4	4 ,, 3
7	9	3 ,, 2
7	6	3 ,, 2
7	3:3	6 ,, 5
7	5	3 ,, 2
6	5	Evens
3:3	5	5 to 4
8	5	Evens
4:4	5	5 to 4
9	4	4 ,, 3
9	5	Evens

Great fortunes were won and lost at Hazard. William Crockford was born in 1775, the son of a fishmonger with a small business adjoining Temple Bar. After his father's death he sold fish for a time, but also made money at gambling and joined a gaming house in King Street, St. James's. He became a bookmaker at Tattersall's and later a race-horse owner. One of his horses, Sultan, won the Derby in 1836.

In 1821–22 luck went against Crockford's gaming establishment, and night after night his capital shrank. At last the evening came when there was only £5,000 left; and in the first hour's play £3,000 of it had been lost. Crockford left the room, meditating whether to hang or to drown himself, but scarcely was his back turned when the run of luck changed and within two hours the house had easily recouped their losses. By the end of the season he had won over £200,000. He opened a new club-house in 1827 and Captain Gronow has given us a contemporary description.

'In the reign of George IV a new star rose upon the horizon in the person of Mr. William Crockford; and the old-fashioned games of faro, macao and lansquenet gave place to the all-devouring thirst for the game of hazard. Crockey, when still a young man, had relinquished the peaceful trade of a fishmonger for a share in a "hell" where, with his partner Gye, he managed to win, after a sitting of twenty-four hours, the enormous sum of one hundred thousand pounds from Lords Thanet and Granville, Mr. Ball Hughes, and two other gentlemen whose names I do not now remember. With this capital added to his former gains, he built the well-known palace in St. James's Street, where a club was established, and play organized on a scale of magnificence and liberality hitherto unknown in Europe.

'No one can describe the splendour and excitement of the early days of Crockey. A supper of the most exquisite kind, prepared by the famous Ude, and accompanied by the best wines in the world, together with every luxury of the season, was furnished gratis. The members of the club included all the celebrities of England, from the Duke of Wellington, to the youngest ensign of the Guards; and, at the gay and festive board, which was constantly replenished from midnight to early dawn, the most brilliant sallies of wit, the most agreeable conversation, the most interesting anecdotes, interspersed with grave political discussions and acute logical reasoning on every conceivable subject, proceeded from the soldiers, scholars, statesmen, poets and men of pleasure, who, when the "House was up" and balls and parties at an end, delighted to finish their evening with a little supper, and a good deal of hazard at old Crockey's. The tone of the club was most excellent. A most gentleman-like feeling prevailed, and none of the rudeness, familiarity and ill-breeding which disgraced some of the minor clubs would have been tolerated for a moment.

'The great foreign diplomatists, Prince Talleyrand, Count Pozzo di Borgo, General Alava, the Duke of Palmella, Prince Esterhazy, the French, Russian, Spanish, Portuguese, and Austrian ambassadors, and all persons of distinction and eminence who arrived in England, belonged to Crockford's as a matter of course; but many rued the day when they became members of that fascinating but dangerous coterie. The great Duke himself, always rather a friend of the dandies did not disdain to appear now and then at this charming club; whilst the late Lord Raglan, Lord Anglesey, Sir Hussey Vivian, and many more of our Peninsula and Waterloo heroes, were constant visitors. . . .

'In the play-room might be heard the clear ringing voice of that agreeable reprobate, Tom Duncombe, as he cheerfully called "Seven" and the powerful hand of the vigorous Sefton in throwing for a ten.

'Who that ever entered that dangerous little room can forget the large green table, with the croupiers, Page, Darking and Bacon, with their suave manners, sleek appearance, stiff white neck-cloths, and the almost miraculous quickness and dexterity with which they swept away the money of the unfortunate punters when the fatal cry of "Deuce ace", "Aces", or "Sixes out" was heard in answer to the caster's bold cry of "Seven", or "Nine", or "Fives the main" . . . .

'A number of men who did not care to play at hazard used purposely to lose a hundred or two a year at the tables, to have the pleasure of dining and supping with their friends, who all flocked to the magnificent rooms. . . . '

Crockford won all the ready money of his generation. Twelve hundred thousand pounds were netted by the fortunate fishmonger, but when he died he was worth less than a sixth of this sum; unlucky speculations disposing of the rest.

Hazard was never very popular in America except among the negroes around New Orleans who began to play it about 1800. They soon simplified the intricate rules and betting odds and played a form known as THE NEGRO'S GAME, later developing into CRAPS. The sharper John Philip Quinn who reformed, and later when on an evangelical tour was imprisoned quite unjustly, wrote while in jail an exposition on gambling called 'Fools of Fortune'. He mentions travelling on the Mississippi steamboat *City of Chester* and hearing a negro calling, 'Come seven or eleven!' and 'Chill'en crying fo' bread!' Quinn tried his luck and lost fifteen dollars to the 'Crap Roller'.

While the new game of Craps was spreading up the Mississippi, its many variations settled into a standard form played by the workers on the steamboats, the wharves and docks, in the cotton fields and the saloons. About 1890 it began to appear in the clubs and gambling houses, competing with Faro as a banking game, and developing step by step into the Open Craps of the casino.

Private, or Military Craps, however, needs no layout, bank, or book: only two or more players with cash in their pockets, a pair of dice, and time on their hands. G.I. Joe has played Craps all over the world, for millions of pounds, but it is a dull game and its attraction depends entirely on money.

GAMES USING THREE DICE

BUCK DICE

Any number can play and each player throws the dice to determine the order, the highest leading and the lowest having his turn last. The low man throws a single die to give the POINT NUMBER. The opening player throws three dice and scores one point for each point number thrown and he continues to throw as long as he throws point numbers and they are added up as he goes along. When he fails to throw a point number on any throw the dice are passed to the next player. Each player drops out of the game as he reaches exactly fifteen points. The last player left in the game is the loser.

If a player reaches a total above fifteen the whole throw does not count and he passes the dice on. Any three of a kind except that of the point number is a LITTLE BUCK and counts five points. When a triple point number is thrown it is a BIG BUCK and the player is immediately credited with fifteen, whatever his previous score may have been. The player shooting first has a slight advantage.

MARTINETTI

Each player has a coloured counter and the board is marked from 1 to 12 (fig. 113). Each player throws the dice from a cup, the highest scorer starting the game, while the lowest has his turn last. Ties are thrown again.

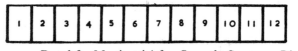

| 1 | 2 | 3 | 4 | 5 | 6 | 7 | 8 | 9 | 10 | 11 | 12 |

FIG. 113. Board for Martinetti (after Scarne's *Scarne on Dice*)

If the opening player throws an ace he places his marker on space 1 on the board. If he throws a 1 and a 2 on the same throw, he would put his marker on the second space, while a throw of 1:2:3 would advance it to the third compartment. Numbers may also be added together to make required numbers. A throw of 1:4:6 could be used to make 5 or 7 or 10 or 11. Each player's turn lasts as long as he is using the numbers thrown. If he fails to score on any throw the dice are passed to the player on his left.

If a player misses a number that he could have used any player may make use of it by calling it out as soon as the player passes the

DROP DEAD

dice on and before they are rolled again. If two players call the number together the one who is nearest the player's left takes precedence.

The first player to travel from 1 to 12 and back to 1 again wins the game.

GAMES USING FIVE DICE

DROP DEAD

Any number can play and each player throws a single die to decide the order of play, low man going first and high last. Tying players throw again. Each player in turn throws the five dice, using a cup, and scores the sum of the numbers thrown, unless a 2 or a 5 appears, when he scores nothing on that roll and any die with 2 or 5 is put aside. The player puts the remaining dice back in the cup and rolls again and continues to score whenever 2 or 5 does not appear, eliminating any die that shows 2 or 5 until all the dice are dead. The next player then has his turn and the highest scorer wins.

INDIAN DICE

The players each throw a die to decide the order of play, high man playing first, the next highest second, etc. Sixes are high, deuces low, while aces are wild and can count as any number.

The opening player has a choice of making one, two, or three throws; the other players are only allowed the same number as he has chosen. After his first throw the opening player may put aside any of the five dice and place the others in the cup for a second throw, or he may re-throw all five. After his second throw, he may throw any or all of the five dice in a third throw, including any which were previously put aside.

Scoring Values

Five of a kind (five 6's being above five 5's, etc.)
Four of a kind
Three of a kind and a pair (known as a FULL HOUSE)
Three of a kind
Two pairs
One pair

A hand without a pair scores nothing and a sequence is useless. Whatever the dice show after the last throw is the final value of the hand.

Example. The first player throws 5:5:2:3:4. He may throw all five again hoping to get better than a pair; or he may put the 5:5 aside and throw the remaining three dice. If he throws 1:3:4 he would add the 1 to the 5:5 making three of a kind, as the ace is wild, and then he might stand or attempt a third roll, hoping to get another 5 or a pair which would give him a full house.

Each round is called a leg. If there are only two players the winner of two out of three legs wins the game. When there are more players they all enter in the first two legs, and the high man in the first leg plays a two-handed deciding game with the winner of the second leg. Alternately the two low men may play off and the loser pays a forfeit.

SHIP, CAPTAIN, MATE AND CREW

Each player throws a single die to decide on the order of play, the highest going first and the lowest last. Players tying throw again. Each player, in turn, is allowed three throws and first tries to get a 6:5 and 4 in that order, the 6 being the ship, the 5 the captain, and the 4 the mate. If 6 and 5 appear on the first throw they are put aside and the three remaining dice are rolled again trying for a 4. When a player has 6:5:4 in that order the points on the remaining two dice are his score, or the crew. If he has not used all his three throws he may, if he wishes, use any remaining throws of the two dice to try to make a higher total. If a 6 and a 4 appear on the first roll, only the 6 can be put aside, and the player then throws the remaining four dice trying for a 5 and then a 4.

The player with the highest score at the end of the round is the winner. If the two high players tie, the round is drawn for everyone and another round is thrown. The player on the left of the shooter in one round becomes the new shooter in the next.

GAMES USING SIX DICE

SEQUENCES

Any number can play and each throws the six dice once, and then passes them on clockwise around the table. A throw of 1:1:1 cancels

a player's whole score and he has to start again. The first to reach a
hundred wins.

Scoring

Throw	Points
1:2	5
1:2:3	10
1:2:3:4	15
1:2:3:4:5	20
1:2:3:4:5:6	25

1:1:1 cancels whole score. Start again.

GAMES USING TEN DICE

TWENTY-SIX

One of the players acts as banker and has a large pile of counters,
the rest have smaller piles. A cup and ten dice are used. The player
on the left of the banker chooses any number from one to six as his
POINT, and puts a number of counters into the centre of the table
and then throws the ten dice thirteen times, counting the number
of times the point number appears. The banker pays:

4 to 1 if the player scores	26 or 27 point numbers	
5 to 1 for	28 or 29 ,,	,,
6 to 1 for	30 or 31 ,,	,,
7 to 1 for	32 or 33 ,,	,,
8 to 1 for	any higher number.	

If the player fails to score 26 point numbers he forfeits his stake to
the banker, except when he scores fewer than 11 points, when the
banker pays him 4 to 1.

GAMES USING FIFTEEN OR MORE DICE

ACES

This is one of the best of the dice games. Any number may play
but each player must have a dice cup and five dice. Each player puts
an agreed stake into a pool and then throws his five dice and the
player with the highest hand takes any seat and is the first shooter,
the player throwing the second highest sits on his left and shoots
second, etc. Tying players throw again. Aces count as 7.

The first shooter begins by throwing five dice. Each 1 is placed in the centre of the table; all 2's are passed to the player on his left, all 5's to the player on his right. The player continues to throw until he fails to throw a 1, a 2, or a 5, or until he has no dice left. The player on the left then begins his throw. Players with no dice are still in the game as they may receive dice from the players on either side of them.

When all the dice but one have been placed in the centre of the table the player throwing the last 1 with the last die is the winner and takes the pool.

3. GAMES WITH SPECIAL DICE

BELL AND HAMMER

Schimmel, or Bell and Hammer, came from Germany and was played in England at least as early as 1816 and as late as 1870.

FIG. 114. The five cards used in Bell and Hammer (author's collection)

Equipment

Eight cubic dice are used, each with five plain surfaces and the
sixth is marked with a 1 or a 2, a 3, a 4, a 5, a 6, a Bell, or a Hammer.

There are five picture cards:

> An Inn
> A White Horse
> A Hammer
> A Bell
> A Bell and Hammer

A dicing cup, and a small ivory or wooden mallet for the auctioneer completes the set (see tailpiece, p. 176). Any number of players
may take part in this fascinating game which is in three phases.

First Phase. Each player starts with 36 counters and throws the
eight dice in turn, the player throwing the highest number becoming the auctioneer. The latter calls for four counters from each player
to form a pool. He then offers up the five picture cards one at a time
for sale, each being exchanged for counters from the successful
bidder; and the proceeds are added to the pool. A player not having
a card does not take part in the round; and any player being out of
two successive rounds is out of the game and his remaining counters
are confiscated and are added to the pool.

Second Phase. The players throw the eight dice in rotation round
the table, the auctioneer throwing first.

Method of Scoring

1. If all the dice are blanks, each player pays one counter to the
owner of the White Horse.

2. If the Bell, or Hammer, or Bell and Hammer turn up, the other
dice being blank, the owners of the corresponding cards pay one
counter to the owner of the White Horse.

3. If the Bell, or the Hammer, or the Bell and Hammer turn up
with one or more numbers showing as well, the auctioneer pays this
number of counters from the pool to the owner of the card.

4. If only numbers and blanks are thrown the auctioneer pays the
player making the throw the number of counters from the pool
equivalent to the number shown on the dice.

5. When the same number is thrown as there are counters in
the pool the game ends; but if a larger number is thrown than

there are counters in the pool, the player making the throw pays the difference to Mine Host, the holder of the Inn Card. As soon as the inn is open the third phase of the game begins.

Third Phase.

6. When any player throws all blank dice Rule 1 no longer applies but the owner of the White Horse pays 1 counter to the innkeeper.

7. If the Bell, or the Hammer, or the Bell and Hammer are thrown, the other dice being blank, the owners of these cards pay one counter to the innkeeper.

8. If a number is thrown with either the Bell, or Hammer, or Bell and Hammer, the owners of these cards must pay the innkeeper the difference between the number thrown and the counters remaining in the pool.

9. A player wins the counters from the pool when he throws a smaller number than there are counters in it; he wins the game by throwing the same number as the number of counters left in the pool, which he adds to his store. The winner of one game becomes the auctioneer in the next and the whole game ends when one player has won all the counters from his rivals.

FIG. 115. Three Crown and Anchor dice

CROWN AND ANCHOR

Crown and Anchor is popular in the British Navy and Fishing

FIG. 116. Exploded Crown and Anchor die to show positions of the symbols

FIG. 117. Crown and Anchor board (author's collection)

Fleet. Three special dice are used marked with a crown, an anchor, a heart, a spade, a diamond, and a club. The players sit round a board or cloth marked with the same symbols (fig. 117).

The players place their bets on the devices of their choice and the banker throws the three dice from a cup. He pays even money on singles, two to one on pairs, and three to one on three of a kind. The banker's advantage is such that eventually he will always be well in pocket and everyone else well out! The bank should, therefore, pass to each player in turn.

LIAR DICE

This game can be played with five standard dice, but is more enjoyable when using five poker dice which are marked with an Ace, King, Queen, Jack, Ten, and Nine. Fig. 119 is an exploded drawing.

FIG. 118. Five poker dice

The opening player casts the dice on to the table from a cup and hides them behind his left hand from the other players. He declares a score which may be accepted or challenged by the player on his left. If it is challenged and the throw is found to be at least as high as the declaration the challenger loses a life. If it is below the declaration the caster loses a life.

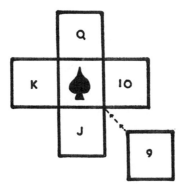

FIG. 119. Exploded drawing of poker die to show positions of symbols

If the declaration is accepted the dice, still concealed, are passed on to the next player who may retain or throw any number of dice. The number re-thrown must be stated, e.g. 'Throwing three'. He then makes his declaration which must be higher than the one he accepted and the player on his left in turn may accept the new call or challenge it.

Order of Scoring

Five of a kind (Aces count high, e.g. above five Kings)
A Royal Flush (the five dice in sequence, Ace high)
A low Flush (the five dice in sequence, King high)
Four of a kind
Full house (three of a kind and a pair)
Three of a kind
Two pairs
One pair
Pryle

Except for the royal and low flushes, sequences do not count. A hand without a scoring combination is called a PRYLE.

If a declaration of five aces is made the next player may challenge or accept it. If he accepts he is allowed five throws of the dice to equalize. If he succeeds the caller loses a life; if not, the acceptor. Each player has three lives and when these are lost he is out of the game. The first player to lose three lives, however, is granted an extra or fourth life. This grace is known as being ON THE PARISH. The last player left in the game is the winner.

4. CHINESE DICE GAMES

Standard Chinese dice are small cubes $\frac{1}{5}$ in. to $\frac{2}{3}$ in. in size, usually made of bone or ivory and marked with incised pips from one to six which are arranged so that the sum of the opposite faces is seven. The ONE pip is uncoloured and is much larger and more deeply incised than the others which are black except the FOUR, whose pips are painted red, a relic of the dice which were imported into China from India many centuries ago. The dice are usually thrown from the hands into a porcelain bowl, the players throwing in turn in a clockwise direction.

STRUNG FLOWERS (Sz'ng luk)

Three dice are used and only four combinations score.

1. TRIPLES. Three sixes are high and three aces low (fig. 120).

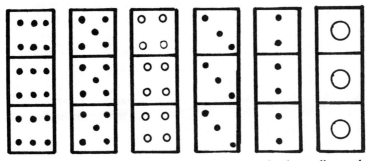

FIG. 120. Strung Flowers: The six triple throws in descending order
(after Culin's *Chinese Games with Dice and Dominoes*)

2. STRUNG FLOWERS. This is a sequence of 4:5:6 and gives the game its name (fig. 121).

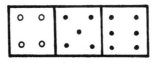

FIG. 121. The sequence of Strung Flowers (after Culin's *Chinese Games with Dice and Dominoes*)

3. TWO ALIKE. The highest score is the Two Alike Six High and the lowest is the Two Alike One High which is known as the Ace Negative (fig. 122).

The composition of the pair is immaterial.

4. THE DANCING DRAGON. This is the sequence 1:2:3 and is the lowest scoring combination (fig. 123).

Method of Play

The players throw the dice in turn and the one with the highest number of red spots becomes the banker. The other players place their stakes, usually divisible by three, on the table. The banker throws until a scoring combination appears. If he throws a Triple, Strung Flowers, or Two Alike Six High, each of the players pays him the full amount of their stakes and then the banker calls for new bets and throws the dice again.

If he throws a Dancing Dragon 1:2:3 or an Ace Negative the banker pays each player the full amount of their stakes.

If he throws Two Alike and Five, Four, Three, or Two High, he hands the dice to the player on his left. If this player makes a higher cast, the banker must pay him, but if a lower cast, the player pays the banker. If the player also throws Two Alike and an odd die, the amounts paid by the player or the banker are usually proportionate to the difference between the scores of the odd die; if it is 4 or 3, the full stake is paid; if 2 then $\frac{2}{3}$ of the stake; and if 1, $\frac{1}{3}$ of the stake. If the banker was the winner, the next player on the left throws against him and the game continues until someone out-throws the banker. The next player on the banker's left becomes the new banker and a new lap begins.

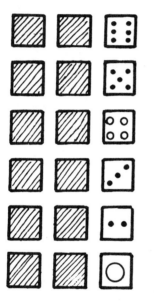

FIG. 122. Strung Flowers: Two-Alike throws in descending order (after Culin's *Chinese Games with Dice and Dominoes*)

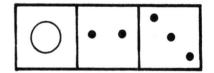

FIG. 123. Strung Flowers: The Dancing Dragon (after Culin's *Chinese Games with Dice and Dominoes*)

THROWING HEAVEN AND NINE (Chak t'in kau)

Two dice are used in this game for any number of players, and the twenty-one possible throws are divided into two series, CIVIL and MILITARY. The throws, their names, and their order of scoring are shown in fig. 124 in descending scales.

Each player throws the two dice in turn and the one with the highest number of pips becomes the banker. The banker calls for the stakes and all the other players put their bets on the table in front of them. The banker then throws and his cast determines the suit, whether civil or military, for that round. Any throw of the other suit does not count and the player must cast again until he makes a cast in the reigning suit.

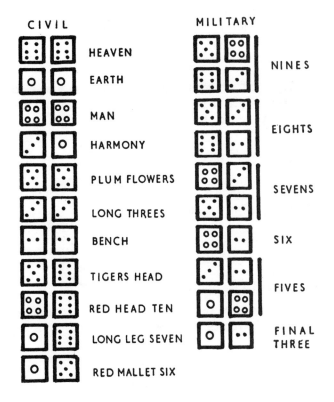

FIG. 124. Throwing Heaven and Nine: The twenty-one possible throws arranged in the Civil and Military series (after Culin's *Chinese Games with Dice and Dominoes*)

If the banker throws the highest pair of the reigning suit, that is HEAVEN of the civil or the NINES of the military, each player gives him his stake; but if he throws the lowest of the reigning suit, that is the RED MALLET SIX of the civil or the FINAL THREE of the military, the banker pays each player the amount of his stake.

If the banker throws any other pair than the highest or the lowest of either suit, the second player throws and is paid his stake if he throws higher than the banker, or pays the banker if he throws lower. There is no exchange if the throws are the same. The game continues until the banker is out-thrown, when he is succeeded by the second player as the new banker. When all the players have been banker in turn the game may finish or another round be started. A player may withdraw at the end of any round.

PUT AND TAKE

Each player puts an equal number of counters into a pool and then the opening player spins a six-sided teetotum and obeys the instructions on the face falling uppermost (fig. 125).

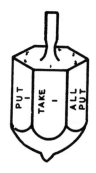

1. Take one 3. Take all 5. Take 2
2. All put   4. Put 2   6. Put 1
   (one into pool)

FIG. 125. Put and Take Spinner

The players spin the teetotum in turn, and when a player loses all his counters he retires from the game.

Antique Chinese dicing cup of ivory (author's collection)

CHAPTER SIX

Domino Games

CHINESE DOMINOES

Cubic dice were imported into China from India in the distant past; but dominoes, little tablets representing the throw of two dice, appear to have been a Chinese invention. The tiles have the same names as in the corresponding dice throws, and they are divided into the same Civil and Military series. All the tiles in the civil series are in duplicate. A domino set consists of thirty-two tiles and there

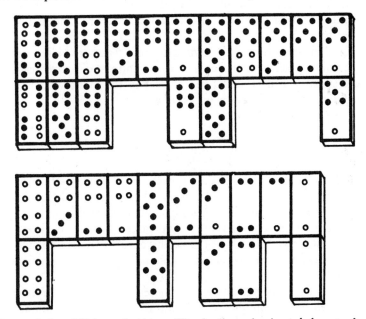

FIG. 126. Set of Chinese dominoes. The duplicate dominoes belong to the Civil series. (author's collection)

are no blanks (fig. 126). It makes playing easier if the military tiles are marked with a little horizontal line in the middle though this is not Chinese custom.

Chinese dominoes are made of ivory, bone, or wood, and are known as kwat p'ai (bone tablets). They are usually longer than the European type, being about 3 in. long, $\frac{7}{8}$ in. wide and $\frac{3}{8}$ in. thick, with incised spots which are painted red or white.

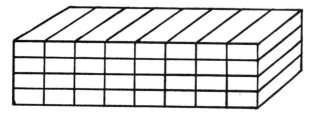

FIG. 127. A wood pile of dominoes

Most games start with the tiles stacked in a WOOD PILE (fig. 127).

The ONE and FOUR spots are marked in red, all the others are white except for the double six tile which is half red and half white (fig. 126).

The identical tiles of the civil series pair together, while those of the military pair in total counts. The 2–4 and 1–2 tiles together form the SUPREME pair which is the highest in the military series, but separately they rank as the lowest tiles.

FISHING (Tiu ü)

This simple game is played by two or three players with two sets of dominoes. The pieces are well mixed and then piled face downwards in a wood pile four tiles high. Four stacks of four each are drawn from one end of the pile and placed face up on the table. When two play both players draw three stacks (twelve dominoes), or if three play, two stacks (eight dominoes), from the same end of the pile.

The players then examine their pieces, and the first player tries to match one of his pieces with one having the same number of spots among those turned up on the table. If he succeeds he places the matched pair face up in front of himself. Whether successful or not he draws the top domino of the stack at the end of the wood-pile from which the last stacks were drawn and tries to match it with one of those on the table. If successful, he takes the pair, but if not, he places the piece drawn with those on the table.

The second player then tries to match one of his pieces, and also draws one from the pile, and the game is continued until the pile is exhausted. A pair of double SIXES in a player's hand is laid out at once.

The two pieces composing the SUPREME, mate with each other and form an exception to the rule in this game that all pieces having the same number of spots mate with each other without reference to their belonging to the civil or military series.

If a player holds a piece in his hand identical with two pieces on the table, and the fourth piece of the same kind has not been played, he may, at his turn, pile the three pieces that are alike one on the other with the faces up, at the opposite end of the stack from which tiles are being drawn. The player who lays out the fourth piece then takes the other three.

When the last domino is drawn, the players examine those they have taken. The tiles with eight or more spots are called LARGE FISH and count two points for each spot of either colour. The tiles with less than eight spots are called MINNOWS and count one point for each red spot only. If the score of the minnows is between decades, the higher decade is counted, e.g. if a player's score in minnows is 12 he is credited with 20.

The player with the highest count becomes the winner, and is paid by each of the players for each point he has in excess of their total.

DISPUTING TENS (Tsung shap)

One set of dominoes is used in this game for two players. The tiles are piled face down, side by side, in a woodpile four high and eight long. The players divide it between them, each taking four of the stacks. The first player draws the top piece from the stack at the right of his pile and lays it face up on the table. The second player then draws a piece from his pile and lays it face up alongside the piece played by the first player. They continue to draw and place the pieces on the table at either end of the row of upturned tiles.

Rules

1. If a player puts down a tile which is a duplicate of one of the pieces at either end of the row, he takes both pieces to make a PAIR. They count ten for each spot on them at the end of the game.

2. If a player puts down a domino and its spots make a multiple of ten when added to those on the pieces at both ends of the row, or with the two tiles at either end of the row, he lifts the three pieces and at the end of the game each spot on them counts one point.

3. If there are only two pieces on the table and a player takes them, he piles them on top of each other to mark a SWEEP which counts forty. He then draws from his pile and lays out another piece.

4. If a player fails to take up a winning combination of two or three tiles his opponent may take it, then lay out a piece, and continue the game.

5. The game ends when one of the players has laid out all his pieces and the player with the highest count wins.

COLLECTING TENS (K'ap t'ai shap)

This is the favourite domino game in the Chinese gambling houses in the U.S.A. and can be played by any number from two upwards. Many sets of dominoes are used and they are carefully mixed by the players and piled face down, five pieces high, in a long woodpile down the centre of the table.

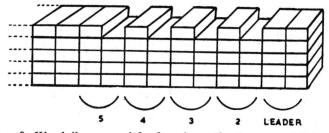

FIG. 128. Woodpile prepared for five players for the game of Collecting Tens

At the start of the game all the players place equal stakes in a box on the table. Five per cent. of the total is taken by the House and the rest goes to the winning player. The croupier, or one of the players, shakes four dice under a cup and counts anti-clockwise around the players starting with the player on his right, to the number thrown. This player becomes the leader.

The top piece on the third stack from one end of the pile is then removed and placed at the far end of the pile; and the top piece from each alternate stack up to one less than the number of players is also removed and placed with it; fig. 128 shows a pile prepared for a game of five players.

The leader takes the two stacks at the end containing ten pieces; the second player on his right takes the next two stacks containing nine pieces; and the remaining players each take nine pieces.

The players examine their pieces and if the leader has not drawn a winning hand he discards a piece which is placed face up on the table.

The next player on his right may take up this piece to complete a winning hand, or exchange it for a piece from his hand, which he places face up on the table. He also draws a piece from the top of the exposed stack of the woodpile. If it does not complete a winning hand he may either place it face up on the table or keep it and discard a piece from his hand.

The third player may then take one of the pieces from the table and draw one from the top of the exposed stack. The game continues until one of the players wins by collecting ten pieces consisting of a MATCHING PAIR of two identical tiles, and four DECIMAL PAIRS, the sum of the spots of each pair being ten or a multiple of ten. The piece 2-4 only counts as three in making up tens.

The winner of a game takes the contents of the stake box and a new game begins.

Collecting Tens and a game called Playing Heavens and Nines (Ta t'in kau) were the forerunners of a game which swept the western world in the 1920's and is best known as Ma-jong. Modified dominoes were used with three suits and twenty-eight special tiles.

MA-JONG

Estimates of the age of this game vary from the time of Confucius, twenty-five centuries ago, to about one hundred and fifty years. The latter is more likely as it only became popular in China about 1900. Stewart Culin, writing in 1895, was unaware how Ma-jong was played, and he described in some detail curious dominoes from Fuchau, and other sets from Shanghai and Ningpo. These sets varied in the number of the tiles and the inscriptions on them, but they belonged to games related to the now well-known Ma-jong.

There are considerable differences in the methods of playing the game in the north and the south of China, and the quality of the translations also varies considerably. No two books on the subject are in complete agreement, and if any points of dispute arise in a game, the rules in the hosts' book should be accepted as final. The account given here is taken from several sources and should be acceptable to most players.

Ma-jong was introduced into the clubs of Canton, Shanghai, and other foreign settlements in China, and sets made for foreigners had numerals added to the upper left hand corner. From the Far East the game spread to America, and then to Europe.

Equipment

The game is played with pieces of bone or ivory, backed with bamboo. Some of the most valuable sets are made of mother-of-pearl and jade, and are housed in richly carved or lacquered caskets. Cheaper modern sets of plastic materials have lowered the price though even these cost from £5 upwards. Players are advised to buy the best they can afford; a good set is a delight to handle and adds to the pleasure of the game. The price of a genuine Chinese set is high, but the 136 tiles are beautifully made with bamboo backs dovetailed into ivory or bone faces engraved and coloured. There are also 128 bone counters, two pairs of dice, a tong box, markers, and four stands for the pieces. See Plate VII opposite.

The Tiles

There are four of each kind of tile and the tiles are grouped into:

CARDINAL TILES	The Red, White, and Green Dragons.
WINDS	The East, South, West, and North Winds.
HONOUR TILES	The Ones and Nines of the three suits are honour tiles. The One of Bamboos is often represented by a rice bird.
MINOR TILES	These are the 2, 3, 4, 5, 6, 7, 8, of each of the three suits.

Many sets have eight additional tiles known as FLOWERS and SEASONS, but these are obsolete and rarely used today. See the tailpiece, p. 172. Four blank tiles serve as replacements for any lost pieces.

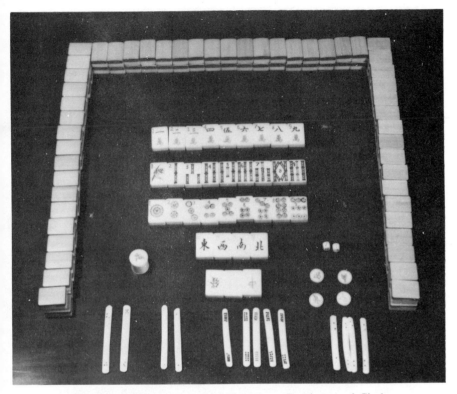

Ma-Jong set with one to nine of Characters, Bamboos and Circles,
four Winds and three Dragons exposed; also Tong, markers, pair of
dice, and a few bone counters (author's collection)

Lorry drivers playing Chinese Chess outside a co-operative store in Peking, 1958 (taken by Mr. R. S. Dawson)

The Deal

As this is a vicious gambling game among the Chinese, elaborate precautions were developed to make cheating almost impossible.

1. The four players stand round the table and one of them, usually a guest, takes the two dice and throws them once. The sum of the pips is noted and the player, starting with himself, counts each player round the table and stops at the player where the count ends and puts the small round box, or tong, in front of him (fig. 129).

Fig. 129. Tong in the centre surrounded by Wind discs (from set in author's collection)

The thrower's own numbers are 1, 5, 9. After placing the tong the thrower shuffles the four round discs representing the four winds face downwards on the table and then piles them one on top of the other. He then throws the dice again, and counts out the number on the four persons standing round the table, beginning with himself. The player at the end of the count draws the top disc from the pile, and the other players take a disc in turn, beginning with the player on the right of the one who has drawn the top disc. This is in an anti-clockwise direction.

2. The person drawing East Wind takes the seat in front of the tong and drops his disc into it, device downwards. The other players then take their places from him, and each replaces his disc in the tong in the following order: South, West, and North.

$$\begin{array}{c} W \\ N \quad S \\ E \end{array}$$

This is different from the familiar geographical arrangement of the compass points.

3. The tiles are then shuffled, face downwards, by East and West. The clinking of the ivory pieces is picturesquely known as the 'Twittering of the Sparrows'. Each player then builds a wall seventeen tiles long and two high in front of himself; the completed walls, representing the walls of a city, are then pushed towards each other until they make a perfect square. Any space left at the corners is said to let in the devils of ill-luck. More realistically, it allows a possibility of cheating.

4. East then takes the dice and throws them once. The total is counted out on the walls starting with the right hand end of the wall in front of East, and where the count stops the wall is broken by lifting the two tiles up and the underneath tile is placed on top of the right hand side of the opening and the uppermost tile is placed three tiles along from the opening. These two tiles, standing up like turrets, are known as the LOOSE TILES and form with the six pairs of tiles beneath them the DEAD WALL (fig. 130).

FIG. 130. The tiles of the Dead Wall are shaded and are separated from the other tiles by moving them half a space

5. East takes the first four pieces to the left of the breach, South takes the next four, West the next four, North the next four, East the next four, and this continues until all the players have drawn twelve tiles. Each player then lifts one more tile, making thirteen in his hand except for East who takes an extra one and holds fourteen. When the end of a wall is reached pieces are lifted from the next wall, moving in a clockwise direction. Each player turns his tiles up on end or places them in a rack, and sorts his hand into the suits and special tiles.

Method of Play

If East holds nine different Honour and Cardinal tiles without a pair in his original hand he may demand a new deal. The other players, after drawing their first tile, are allowed the same privilege. East begins by discarding a piece face up in the middle of the table, and calls it out: 'Four characters' or 'Six of circles' etc. In games with advanced players the pieces are placed face downwards. The turn of play passes anti-clockwise, South following East, etc.

After East discards, and provided there are no pungs, quongs, or chows (see below), South takes a tile from the open end of the wall and adds it to his hand; and then discards a tile from his hand, etc. In drawing from the wall the end piece must always be taken, and the top piece before the bottom.

PUNG. If any of the other three players holds two tiles identical with one just discarded, he may call 'Pung!' and take it out of the pool and place it down in front of his tiles, adding the two tiles from his hand to it, to make an exposed pung or three of a kind. If the player who makes a pung is not next in turn to play, any player who has been passed loses his turn, and play continues in an anti-clockwise direction. Only the last discarded piece may be punged, quonged, or chowed, and it is available only until the next discard is placed on the table. All the other pieces lying in the middle of the table are dead and out of the game. If a player has taken a piece from the wall, and has not yet discarded and another player pungs or chows the last discard, the piece must be returned to the wall and the player misses his turn.

QUONG. Should any player have three pieces in his hand similar to a piece just discarded by another player, he may call 'Quong!' and take it from the pool, and put it in front of his tiles, face upwards, and add the three tiles from his hand to it, making an exposed quong.

If a player has an exposed pung on the table, and he picks the fourth tile off the wall, he may add it to the pung, making an exposed quong.

If a player has a pung in his hand and draws the fourth tile, he declares a concealed quong and puts the four tiles, with the first and fourth tiles face downwards, upon the table in front of himself.

If a player has a concealed quong in his hand which he has not declared, and another player goes MA-JONG before he has put his quong on the table, it only counts as a concealed pung and an odd tile. Usually it is best to put a concealed quong down as soon as it is formed, unless the player wishes to prevent his opponents knowing what suit he is collecting. Until he has drawn a loose tile to compensate for the extra tile of the quong he cannot go ma-jong.

When a player puts a quong down on the table, either exposed or concealed, he takes the loose tile from the wall furthest from the breach, and adds it to his hand, and then he discards a tile in the ordinary way. When both loose tiles have been used to provide extra pieces for quongs, the next two tiles are lifted and put on the wall to form two more loose tiles and a pair of tiles from the live wall are moved to maintain the number of tiles in the dead wall at fourteen.

ROBBING A QUONG. A player needing a tile to go ma-jong may steal the fourth tile of an exposed quong from another player to do so. He may not rob a concealed quong.

CHOW. When a player discards a piece, the player next in turn may call 'Chow!' and use it to make a sequence of three consecutive numbers with two held in his hand. The three pieces are placed face up on the table before the player. A chow is a non-scoring combination, but helps towards going ma-jong. Only the player next due to play may chow a discard; and after chowing he discards in the usual way.

If two players want the same discarded tile, a player needing it to go ma-jong takes precedence; then a player requiring it for a pung or a quong; and lastly a player requiring it for a chow. If two players need it to go ma-jong the player whose turn to play comes first wins the tile and the game.

FISHING. If a player needs only one tile to go ma-jong he may declare that he is FISHING. Should any other player go ma-jong before him, his hand counts the full score of a ma-jong hand, less the bonus for going ma-jong; but having stated that he is fishing he cannot discard from his hand and begin to collect some other set or pair, even if he finds that the tile he wants is dead, or held in some other player's hand.

STANDING HAND. Should a player be fishing after his first discard in a game he may declare that he is STANDING. He must not touch or change his hand; but on completing it either with a tile drawn from the wall, or with a discard, he gets a bonus of 100 points.

DRAWN GAME. The last fourteen tiles in the wall, excluding the loose tiles, are never used, and if no one has completed his hand when this section of the wall is reached the game is drawn, and no scores are made. The tiles are re-shuffled, a fresh hand started, and the same player remains East.

THE PREVAILING WIND. Each wind, in turn, becomes the WIND OF THE ROUND. The first round is East Wind's, and continues until each player in turn has been East. South Wind's round then begins and continues until each player has been East a second time. The third round is West Wind's round and the fourth and last round is North Wind's round. A player holding a pung or quong of the prevailing wind has his score doubled.

EAST WIND. If the player who is East in the first hand goes ma-jong he remains East in the second and any subsequent hand until he loses. Then the player who was South becomes East, and the other players change their directions also (fig. 131).

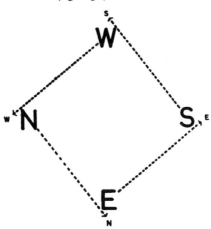

FIG. 131. Change of direction when East loses the first hand. The player who was East becomes North. The player who was South becomes the new East, etc. The players do not change their seats, but become different winds

THE COUNTERS (see Plate VII, facing p. 154). Little bone sticks marked with red or black dots are used to keep the score. The number provided varies with the set, but usually each player starts with about 2,000 points, made up of:

2 markers with 10 red dots	..	value 1,000 each	2,000
2 markers with 2 red dots	..	value 200 ,,	400
10 markers with 20 black dots	..	value 20 ,,	200
10 markers with 4 black dots	..	value 4 ,,	40
			2,640

SETTLEMENT OF SCORES. At the end of each hand the player going ma-jong receives the value of his score from two of the other players and double from East. If East is the winner the other three players each pay him double his score. The three losers then settle their payments between themselves. The one with the lower score paying the one with the higher the difference between their scores; but East pays, or receives, double the difference. A loser may have a higher score than the player who went ma-jong but the winner never pays a loser.

A LIMIT. As it is possible to score a over a hundred thousand points in a single hand, it is usual to make a limit, often 1,000 points, as the maximum a player can win on a single hand from each of his opponents. East pays or receives up to double the limit.

MA-JONG or GAME. A complete hand consists of any four sets of tiles and a pair. The sets may consist of THREE OF A KIND (pungs), FOUR OF A KIND (quongs), or RUNS OF THREE (chows). The pair may be any two similar tiles. The player who goes ma-jong does not discard a piece, and thus has 14 tiles in his hand, unless he has a quong when there will be 15.

Calculation of Scores

MINOR TILES 2, 3, 4, 5, 6, 7, 8, of any suit
MAJOR TILES 1, 9, of any suit and all winds and dragons

Combination	Exposed	Concealed
A chow	0	0
A pung of minor tiles	2	4
A pung of major tiles	4	8
A quong of minor tiles	8	16
A quong of major tiles	16	32
A pair of dragons	—	2
A pair of the player's own wind	—	2

Bonus Scores applying to the winner's hand only

For going ma-jong	20
Winning piece drawn from the wall	2
Winning with the only possible piece	2
Winning with a standing hand	100

Each player works out the basic score in his hand and then this score may be doubled as below:

Doubles applying to winner's hand only

Once for hand of all chows and a non-scoring pair.
Once for winning with a loose tile.
Once for robbing a quong to go ma-jong.
Once for winning with the last tile before the hand is dead.

Doubles applying to all hands

Once for a hand of only one suit and winds or dragons (cleared).
Once for a hand of 1's and 9's with winds and/or dragons.
Once for a hand free from chows.
Three times for a hand entirely of one suit.

SPECIAL HANDS

The standard ma-jong hand is four sets and a pair as already described; but there are ten special hands which score a limit, irrespective of their ordinary scoring values.

1. A hand of all WINDS AND DRAGONS.
2. The FOUR WINDS HAND. This contains a pair of one wind, three pungs or quongs of the other winds, and any chow, pung, or quong to make ma-jong. An incomplete hand containing the four winds as described pays the winner as usual, but is paid as a limit hand by the other losers.
3. Hand of all ONES AND NINES.
4. The THREE SCHOLARS. This hand must contain at least three of each kind of dragon. An incomplete hand with these combinations also scores the limit against the other losers.
5. Concealed hand going ma-jong with no chows.
6. The THIRTEEN ODD MAJORS consisting of a one and a nine from each suit, one of each wind, one of each dragon, and a pair to any one of these thirteen tiles.
7. The CALLING NINE TILE HAND. This is made up of a pung of the ones and the nines of any suit, with a sequence of 2, 3, 4, 5, 6, 7, 8 of the same suit, and any single tile of the same suit.
8. The HAND FROM HEAVEN. This is a hand dealt to East which is complete for ma-jong.
9. EARTH'S GRACE. This is a hand going ma-jong using East's first discard.
10. EAST'S thirteenth consecutive ma-jong.

MISTAKES AND PENALTIES

If the wall is broken in the wrong place, or the tiles are drawn in the wrong order, the tiles should be reshuffled and a fresh start made.

If a player puts down an incorrect combination as a chow, pung, or quong, he must correct it before the next player discards, or his hand becomes dead.

If a player calls ma-jong incorrectly and exposes his hand completely, the hand is dead and he must pay each of the other three players double the limit; but if he finds out his mistake before exposing the whole hand he may pick up his pieces again and play on.

If a player has three sets of three exposed tiles of one suit on the table, and another player discards a piece in the same suit which enables the first player to go ma-jong, the second player must pay the winner for the other two players as well as for himself.

If a player is making a special hand, e.g. a three dragon hand, and has two sets of dragons on the table, or a hand of Ones and Nines and has three sets of Ones and Nines on the table, and another player makes a discard allowing him to go ma-jong, the latter must pay the winner for the other players as well as for himself.

When ma-jong reached America many additional rules were made and the Western game differs considerably from the Chinese form described here.

EUROPEAN DOMINOES

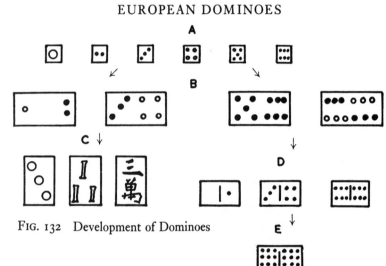

FIG. 132 Development of Dominoes

A, Chinese dice
B, Chinese dominoes
C, Ma-jong tiles
D, European double-six set
E, European double-nine set

The earliest report of Dominoes in Europe comes from Italy in the eighteenth century. They may have been introduced much earlier from China by Marco Polo or some other traveller. From Italy they were taken to France, and later still to England. Strutt, writing in 1801, damned the game with faint praise: 'This is a very childish sport, imported from France a few years back, and could have nothing but the novelty to recommend it to the notice of grown persons in this country.' A hundred and sixty years later dominoes are played over most of the world, even reaching the Eskimo!

The standard Western domino set is the DOUBLE-SIX, with twenty-eight tiles. The best sets are of ivory; others are made of bone backed with ebony, plastic materials, or stained wood. The duplication of some of the tiles in the Chinese sets has disappeared and is replaced in part by the introduction of BLANK tiles. The development of dominoes is shown diagrammatically in fig. 132.

An edition of Hoyle of 1812 describes a DOUBLE-TWELVE set which is still popular in the U.S.A. today. The larger sets are essential for some of the round games, and are also used when there are more than four players. Dominoes are shuffled by mixing them face downwards on the table:

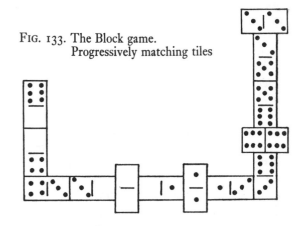

FIG. 133. The Block game.
Progressively matching tiles

GAMES USING A DOUBLE-SIX SET

THE BLOCK GAME

1. After shuffling each player draws a domino. The player with the highest double becomes the leader and the others follow in turn in a clockwise direction. If no double is drawn, the player with the domino with the most pips starts.

2. The dominoes are returned to the pool and reshuffled. If two are playing each draws seven dominoes; if there are more than two each draws five dominoes.

3. The leader plays a domino and the next player matches one end of it if possible. If he cannot do so he forfeits his turn and the next player tries. If no one can play, the game is BLOCKED and each

player counts the spots on the tiles still held in his hand. The player with the lowest number of spots scores the total number of spots in his opponents' hands in addition to those in his own.

4. A cribbage board (fig. 16, p. 22) is useful for scoring and the first player to reach 121 wins the game.

THE BERGEN GAME

1. The dominoes are shuffled face downwards. If there are two or three players each draws six tiles, if there are four players each draws five tiles.

2. The player holding the lowest double leads it, or if no one holds a double the lowest tile is led. Leading the lowest double is called DOUBLE HEADING and counts two points to the player. The players then match tiles, the turn moving in a clockwise direction. If a player cannot match a tile he draws one from the pool. If he is still unable to match, the turn passes to the next player. This process continues until someone can match, or there are only two dominoes left in the pool.

3. The object of the game is to make as many double headers or TRIPLE HEADERS as possible. A double header is made by matching the tile at one end of the line, so that the exposed number is the same at both ends. This counts two points.

A triple header is made by adding a double tile matching the other end of the queue, or, if there is a double tile at one end, the player plays a piece at the other end making the three exposed ends the same. A triple header counts three points.

4. A player within three points of the game only scores 2 points for a triple header, and when he is within two points of game, double or triple headers only count one point.

5. When there are three or four players game is ten points, and when there are two players it is fifteen.

6. The first player to put down his last tile calls 'DOMINO' and wins the hand, scoring two points.

7. If there are only two tiles left in the pool, and no one can match either end of the queue, the game is BLOCKED and the player with no doubles in his hand wins. If no doubles remain in any hand, the player with the lowest number of spots wins. If there is more than one double in each hand the player with the least number of double tiles wins regardless of the spot count. The winner of a blocked game scores two points.

Players tend to retain doubles as long as possible to make triple headers.

FORTY-TWO

Any number up to seven can play, though a four-handed partnership game is best. The object of the game is to win tricks, and to capture COUNTING TILES in the tricks. Each trick is worth one point; while every tile whose pips total 5 or 10 is a scoring tile and is worth the total of its pips.

1. The tiles are shuffled face down and each player draws seven. The player holding the 1-0 bids first. Each player in turn may make one bid and no more. A player may pass instead of bidding. The lowest allowable bid is 30, and each bid must be more than the previous one.

2. The highest bidder leads a tile and specifies which end is the trump suit. There are eight suits. Blanks, Doubles, and One to Six. Each player must follow suit to the lead if possible, and the tile of the suit led having the highest count wins the trick, unless a trump tile has been played. The winner of a trick leads for the next trick. When a trump is not led, the higher end of the tile determines its suit. Doubles take any trick of their kind.

3. At the end of the game one point is allowed for each trick, and the 5-5 and 6-4 tiles are worth 10 points each; the 5-0, 4-1, and 3-2 tiles are worth 5 points each, adding up to 35, and with the seven points for the tricks, the maximum score is 42.

4. If the bidding side makes more in tricks and counters than its bid, it scores the bid plus the amount of its score. If the bid, however, was 37 and the opponents make ten points, the opponents would score the bid (37) + 10 = 47 points.

BINGO

The object of this two-handed game is to win seven sets, each set consisting of 70 points.

Method of Scoring

1. All doubles score their spot value. The double blank counts 14 and is known as BINGO.

2. The 6-4 and the 3-0 score ten.

3. All tiles of the trump suit score their spot value, except the double which counts 28: e.g. when sixes are trumps the double six

is worth 28; but when sixes are not trumps the double six is only worth 12.

4. No other tiles score. The total score of a round varies according to the trump suit.

Trumps	Total Score
Blanks	143
Ones	135
Twos	138
Threes	131
Fours	134
Fives	147
Sixes	140

Method of Play

1. After shuffling the tiles one player takes a domino from the stock and the other must guess whether it is odd or even. If he guesses correctly he becomes the leader for the first trick. The domino is then returned to the stock which is reshuffled and each player draws seven pieces.

2. The second player then turns up one of the dominoes in the stock, and the higher figure becomes trumps. This tile is left face upwards. A blank counts seven.

3. The leader then plays any domino. The second player replies and he need not follow suit: the two tiles form a trick which is taken by the player of the higher domino. A trump takes anything except a higher trump or the Bingo.

4. The winner takes the trick and scores any points it may contain and then after drawing a tile from the stock he leads a domino for the next trick. His opponent also draws from the stock and then replies. The game proceeds in this way until all the dominoes have been drawn; the turned-up trump being taken by the player who has the last draw.

5. If a player has two doubles in his hand, on playing one of them he should show the other and announce DOUBLE. If he wins the trick he adds 20 to his score.

In the same way if he has three doubles in his hand, on playing one of them he calls TRIPLETS, and scores 40 if he wins the trick.

If he holds four doubles he calls DOUBLE DOUBLET and adds 50 if he wins the trick.

If he holds five doubles he calls KING, and if he wins the trick takes 60.

If he holds six doubles he calls EMPEROR and wins 70 points if the trick is won. This is one complete set towards game.

If he holds seven doubles, he calls INVINCIBLE and scores 210 points or three complete sets towards the game if he wins the trick. These combinations must be announced immediately the first double is played, otherwise they do not count.

6. When the last draw has been made the method of play changes, for the second player must follow suit if he can; if he cannot, he must play a trump if he has one; and if he can do neither he is forced to discard.

7. At any stage of the game after winning a trick a player may turn the trump on the table face down. This stops all further drawing from stock and the second player has to follow suit, or play a trump, or throw away as described above. The player who stopped the drawing contracts to score 70 points from that moment, and if he succeeds it counts one set towards game; while if his opponent has scored less than 20 points he gains two sets; and if the opponent has not taken a single trick he scores three sets.

8. If a contracting player fails to make 70 points, his opponent scores 140 points, or two sets towards game; and if the opponent had not taken a single trick before the trump was turned he wins 210 points or three sets.

9. The double blank, Bingo, takes any other piece, including a trump, and if it takes the double of trumps the one who played it scores a point. All points must be claimed as they are won, otherwise they cannot be scored. A cribbage board makes scoring easier.

DOMINO CRIB

Two, three, or four players can enjoy this game which was popular in the R.C.A.F. during the 1939–45 war. A cribbage board is used for scoring and a game consists of one circuit of 61 points or two circuits of 121 points. If the winner reaches 61 before his opponent reaches 31 in a single-circuit game, or 121 before his opponent reaches 91 in a double-circuit game, the opponent is LURCHED and the winner is credited with winning two games instead of one.

Method of Play

1. The tiles are shuffled face downwards and then each player takes six tiles.

2. After examining his tiles each player discards two from his hand, placing them face downwards on the table on the left of the dealer. These tiles form the crib.

3. After the crib has been formed, the dealer lifts a tile from the stock and turns it face upwards. This is the STARTER and it is not used during the play of the hands, but is counted with each hand, and with the crib in the final count. If the starter is a double the dealer scores two points which must be pegged before the opponent plays a tile, or the opportunity is lost.

4. The opponent places any tile from his hand face up on the table in front of himself calling its pip value. The dealer replies by playing a tile from his hand and calls the sum of the two tiles on the table. The play continues alternately, the pip value of each tile being added to the sum last called.

5. If a player can make a pip value of 15 he gains two points; the total of the tiles played must not exceed 31.

6. If, at his turn of play, a player hasn't a tile which will bring the sum to 31 or below, he calls 'GO'.

7. After GO has been called the other player plays as many tiles as he is able, announcing the sums as before, until he reaches 31, or can go no further.

8. If a player makes exactly 31 he wins two points.

9. If the score is still below 31 and neither player can play, the last to put a tile down scores one point. The other player then begins a new lap towards 31, the rules being the same as in the first lap. The players must play alternately except when one player has called GO and the other can still play one or more tiles.

10. The player playing the last tile of the hand scores one point.

11. After the tiles are played out, each player picks up his hand and counts all the points it contains, *in combination with the starter*. The dealer's opponent counts first. At the end of a close game this order is important, when first count may enable him to win before the dealer has a chance to add up his score and the crib.

12. After the dealer has pegged all the points in his hand, he turns up the crib and scores the points in it *in combination with the starter*.

Scoring Table

Any double turned up as the starter	1
Fifteen reached exactly in play	2
Playing a tile to make a pair with the previous tile played	2
Playing a third tile of the same denomination immediately after a pair, without a 31 or a pegged GO intervening	6
Playing a fourth tile of the same value after a triplet ..	12
Three or more tiles played in numerical rotation, though not necessarily in the sequence order, with no 31 or pegged GO intervening. For each tile of the sequence	1
Reaching exactly 31 in play	2
Being nearest to 31	1
Reaching fifteen with the last tile played	3

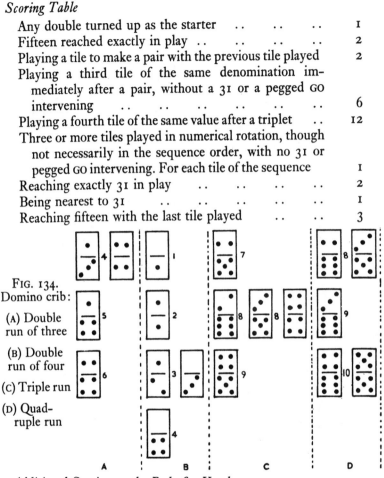

FIG. 134.
Domino crib:

(A) Double run of three

(B) Double run of four

(C) Triple run

(D) Quadruple run

A   B   C   D

Additional Scoring at the End of a Hand

Any combination adding up to fifteen	2
Double run of three: a three-tile sequence with a pair to any one of the three tiles (fig. 134A)	8
Double run of four: a four-tile sequence with a pair to any one of the four tiles (fig. 134B)	10
Triple run: a triplet with two other tiles in sequence with it (fig. 134C)	15
Quadruple run: two pairs and a tile in sequence with both (fig. 134D)	16

GAMES USING A DOUBLE-NINE SET

THE MATADOR GAME

In this game the tiles are added to the domino queue to form sums of ten instead of in matching pairs: the sum of the two approximating tile-ends must add up to ten unless one of the special MATADOR tiles is used. A 1 is added to a 9, a 2 to an 8, etc. Only a matador may be played on to a blank and there are six of these, 9–1, 8–2, 7–3, 6–4, 5–5, and the 0–0. A matador may be played at any time (fig. 135).

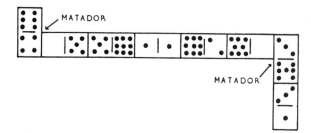

FIG. 135. Matador game. Progression by forming tens or using a matador tile

Method of Play

1. After shuffling, each player draws a domino; the player with the highest double, or failing a double, the tile with the greatest number of pips, becomes the leader.

2. The dominoes are returned to the pool and reshuffled. If there are three to six players each draws seven dominoes. If there are more, then each player only draws five.

3. The leader plays a double if he has one, if not then his highest domino. If a double 9 is led, it must be joined at either side by a 1 by the next player. If he hasn't a 1 he must play a matador or draw from the pool until he obtains a 1. If he played a 1–6, the end spots would then be 9 or 6. The next player must play a 1 to the 9, or a 4 to the 6. Play proceeds in a clockwise direction.

4. When a player cannot make the required TEN and does not wish to play a matador, or hasn't one, he must draw until he can play or until only two dominoes are left in the pool, and then if he has failed to draw a playable domino, he must play a matador if he has one.

5. When one player has drawn all but the last two dominoes from the pool, and can neither make a TEN, nor play a matador, he says,

'PASS'. If no other player can play, the game is BLOCKED and the player holding the lowest number of spots scores the spots held in his opponents' hands.

6. A player who plays his last domino cries 'OUT', and scores all the spots held in his opponents' hands.

7. A game is usually for two hundred points.

CYPRUS

The dominoes are shuffled face downwards and then the players draw their tiles.

No. of Players	No. of Dominoes
4	13
5	11
6	9
7	7
8 or 9	6
10	5

The remaining dominoes are left face downwards on the table and are not used.

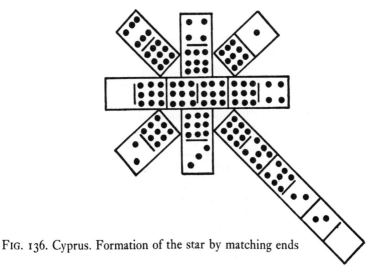

FIG. 136. Cyprus. Formation of the star by matching ends

Method of Play

1. The holder of the double 9 puts it face up on the table. If no one has the double 9 the dominoes are reshuffled and redrawn.

2. In clockwise rotation the players may play 9's to form a star, or match the ends of 9's already played (fig. 136).

3. The first player to play his last tile calls 'DOMINO' and wins the hand. He scores one point for each spot held in his opponents' hands.

4. If no player can play a 9, or match an end, the game is BLOCKED and the player with the least number of spots wins and scores the spots held in his opponents' hands. If two players have the same low count the game is drawn and no one scores.

TIDDLE-A-WINK

1. After shuffling the double-nine set the dominoes are dealt equally to all the players. Any remainder is left face down on the table and is not used.

2. The dealer then calls for the double 9 and the player holding it puts it face up on the table. If no player has it then the double 8 is called for and is played by its owner-holder.

3. A player playing a double either when leading or during the game, earns a second turn of play. Play continues in a clockwise direction, the players matching one of the open ends.

4. When a player is unable to make a match he calls 'PASS', and the next player tries.

5. The first player to play his last tile calls 'TIDDLE-A-WINK' and receives one point for each spot in his opponents' hands.

6. If no one is able to match an open end the game is BLOCKED and the player holding the lowest number of spots in his hand, or in the case of a tie, the least number of tiles, wins the game and scores a point for each spot in his opponents' hands.

7. A game is usually two hundred points.

Ma-jong Flower tile
(author's collection)

CHAPTER SEVEN

Making Boards and Pieces

One of the pleasures of collecting games is making the boards and pieces. The photographs following this chapter show results of some of the methods available. All the games in this book can be made by the average man or woman, and many are unobtainable in the shops.

The hobby can be adapted to any length of purse: superb pieces made by the world's craftsmen are available for the wealthy connoisseur; while the handyman in his workshop can produce in formica, perspex, bone, copper, wood, or other inexpensive materials reproductions of boards only to be found in great museums; and even there often in damaged and fragmentary condition.

The ancient craftsmen inlaid wood with faience, ivory, ebony, metals, and pieces of shell or glass. Formica, acrylic sheeting, perspex, and wood veneers provide effective substitutes. If the original boards were simple, crude techniques provide satisfying reproductions; if they were elaborate, sophisticated materials and methods are readily available.

Original pieces can be obtained from friends living abroad, or from antique and curio shops: the unexpected lies just around the corner.

Collectors will find the pastime gives an insight into national character: the superstitious West Indian playing Awari and anxiously watching the evening shadows lengthen while unwelcome Djombies wait to join the game, contrasts with the blasé cosmopolitan air-traveller killing time with a game of dominoes.

METHODS OF CONSTRUCTION

POKER WORK. This is suitable for simple native boards. Lines are drawn on wood with a red-hot poker or soldering iron. The photograph (fig. 137, facing p. 178) shows a Fighting Serpent board made in this way with beach pebbles as counters, which could have been made by any Amerindian.

WOOD CARVING. The fine Wari board in fig. 138 (facing p. 178) was carved from one piece of Osese wood by a professional carver in Old Hsuoyah, Ghana. Although made in 1957 it is in the traditional style. The stem is hollow and when the game is finished the bung is removed, the seeds popped into the cavity, and the bung replaced.

The holes for mancala boards are easily made by taking a round tin lid of a suitable size and using it as a marker for the outline of the cups; then four holes are bored sloping inwards and each cup is hollowed out with a gouge and a mallet (fig. 139 on Plate X).

CHIP CARVING. A Ludus Latrunculorum board cut into the top of a teak coffee table is shown in fig. 140 (on Plate X). A board for Saxon Hnefatafl made in the same way is shown in fig. 155 (on Plate XVIII).

INLAID WOODS. Hundreds of different woods are now imported into England and attractive boards can be made with inlays. This is an old technique which was much used in the Middle Ages, and is suitable for reproductions of this period. Fig. 141 (on Plate XI) shows a copy of fourteenth-century Tables. The background is 1 in. thick mahogany, inlaid with ranin for the light points, and with agba for the dark. The bar was of English oak with a wild grain. Recesses of the correct size and shape were chopped out of the background with a chisel and mallet, and the inlay pieces, some $\frac{3}{16}$ in. thick, were fitted into them, leaving an excess standing proud. When all the pieces had been glued in position with Britfix (which is clean and easy to use) the surface was planed and rubbed down with flourpaper. Two or three rubbers of white French polish followed by beeswax and turpentine completed it.

MARQUETRY. A wide range of veneers is available and several boards have been made by gluing shaped pieces of veneer to an underboard of plywood at least $\frac{1}{2}$ in. thick (fig. 142 on Plate XI). A solid underboard tends to warp a few weeks after the veneer has been applied unless it is very thick. The application of formica is even more likely to cause warping.

PAINT AND ENAMEL. The antique compendium of games from western India (fig. 143 on Plate XII) is a fine example of paint-work on wood. The upper surface is marked for Tablan, inside is a

Pallanguli board, and underneath is a Nine Men's Morris. The under surface of the lid is painted for Cows and Leopards, and two other games not mentioned in this book, Lau Kata Kati and Kaooa.

PAINTING ON MATS. The copy of an Aztec Patolli mat in fig. 144 (on Plate XII) was made by painting a bamboo mat from Hong Kong with poster paints. Costume-jewellery stones were used as counters. The originals were precious and semi-precious gems.

FORMICA. The Cows and Leopards board in fig. 145 (on Plate XIII) was made of yellow formica fastened to $\frac{3}{4}$ in. plywood with Evostick, and then grooved with a high-speed electric drill. Formica is also useful for making mosaic patterns. Many colours and designs are available. There is a tendency for small pieces to curl.

POTTERY. Games from Assyria, Ancient Egypt, Palestine, and Rome were scratched on tablets of clay and baked. Copies can be made at evening classes in pottery. The boards should be allowed to dry out slowly and require turning daily to prevent warping or distortion: in about three weeks they are ready for the first baking in a kiln; then they are coloured, glazed, and rebaked. If the clay is not dried out thoroughly before baking it may shatter into little pieces in the kiln.

Pottery was also used to reproduce the sandstone board found at Palenque (fig. 146 on Plate XIII).

LEATHERWORK. Some Oriental gaming boards are made of decorated leather, utilizing blind tooling, gilding, and inlay.

Method of Gilding

1. The leather is dampened.

2. The design is pressed into the leather with appropriate tools which are heated until they just hiss when touched with a damp piece of cotton wool. If they are too hot the leather is charred; if too cold the impression is unsatisfactory.

3. The blind-tooling pattern is carefully painted with a gold size made of white of egg.

4. When the size is dry, pieces of gold leaf (which is only 1/250,000 of an inch thick) are placed over the design and pressed lightly into the blind-tooling with a cotton wool pad.

5. The gilding tools are re-heated and the pattern is pressed again, the heat fixing the albumen and cementing the gold leaf to the leather.

6. The excess gold leaf is removed by rolling a ball of crude rubber over it. Rexine is a cheaper substitute for leather.

The Nine Men's Morris in fig. 147 (on Plate XIV) was made by cutting a piece of heavy cardboard into a square of 18 in., and gluing red rexine on to it. The pattern was marked out on th:n tissue paper, and then pieces of gold leaf mounted on waxed paper, which is obtainable at most stationers or leather merchants, were slipped underneath and the pattern was stamped with suitable gilding tools. These should be a little cooler than when working with leather which is damp, since the rexine is dry and more liable to scorch.

BEAD WORK. The Amerindians marked buffalo or elk hide with beads, coloured dyes, or porcupine quills. Fig. 148 (on Plate XIV) shows a Zohn Ahl track of beads on leather.

EMBROIDERY. The cloth Pachisi board in fig. 149 (on Plate XV) was made in India, but it could be duplicated with coloured scraps and a little embroidery by any housewife. More ambitious projects might interest expert needlewomen.

PAPER. Chinese paper boards are fragile and are best put behind glass or perspex for protection. Copies can be made by ruling lines in Indian ink on Bristol Board or heavy paper (fig. 150 on Plate XV).

PAPER BACKED WITH LINEN. Many of the Georgian and early Victorian race games were made of paper mounted in sections on linen. Fig. 151 (on Plate XVI) shows a Royal Game of Goose made by drawing the design on a piece of paper, cutting it up and fixing it to linen with thin glue. Protective covers were made of cardboard.

METALWORK. The Pallanguli board from Travancore (1957) (fig. 152 on Plate XVII) was beaten out of a malleable white metal and chromium-plated. The metal worker may like to try his hand at tapping out a similar series of depressions in a sheet of copper, heating it occasionally to restore its ductility.

PERSPEX. Perspex sheet is excellent for inlay work and takes a high polish if buffed with jeweller's rouge. Fig. 153 (on Plate XVII) shows a reproduction of a Tau board found in Cyprus; the pieces are originals from the author's collection and were found in Egyptian tombs of the eighteenth to twenty-sixth dynasties (1570–1349 B.C. to 663–525 B.C.) by Professor Flinders Petrie.

MAKING PIECES

A lathe is a great asset though not essential. The Bridges, Black and Decker, or Wolf Cub $\frac{1}{4}$ in. drill attachments are ideal.

WOODEN PIECES. These can be made of contrasting woods: teak polished with raw linseed oil, mahogany, or ebony, are excellent for dark pieces; while sycamore, boxwood, pear, or ranin are nearly white and turn well. Old lawyers'-rulers form a cheap source of ebony, while discarded bowling woods are often of lignum vitæ and are treasure trove to the turner.

Wooden pieces can be coloured most attractively with inexpensive lacquer enamels which are sold in convenient small tins. Humbrol art oil enamel manufactured by The Humber Oil Co. Ltd., Hull, can be recommended. It is sold in most model shops.

IVORY. Used billiard balls are sold for as little as $25p$. each and are delightful for turning gaming pieces, or making dice, etc. A set of reproduction mediaeval chessmen in ivory and ebony is shown in fig. 154 (on Plate XVIII) on an unchequered board of formica.

BONE. The Vikings and Saxons used bone for their pieces and the reproduction set for Hnefatafl in fig. 155 (on Plate XVIII) was made of mutton bones. They were boiled to get rid of the tags of meat and gristle and then bleached with Domestos. The Black pieces were dyed by boiling with Black Drummer dye.

The domino casket containing a set of miniature double-six dominos in fig. 156 (on Plate XIX) is an example of fine craftsmanship in bone. French prisoner-of-war work, early XIX century.

PERSPEX. The set of dominoes in fig. 157C (on Plate XX), made in 1958 by an old gentleman of 83, were of $\frac{1}{8}$ in. white perspex fused to $\frac{1}{4}$ in. black perspex with Tenuit adhesive. The fused sheet was then cut into the shapes, and the pips were made by filling drill-holes with cobbler's black heelball.

Six dominoes from a set made about 1850 are shown for comparison. The bone faces are fastened to the ebony backs with small brass sprigs (fig. 157D on Plate XX).

POTTERY. The beautiful reproductions in pottery of Lion and Jackal pieces for the Egyptian game of Senat were made in evening classes by a friend (fig. 158 on Plate XXI). John Flaxman designed a chess set for Wedgwood in blue and white stoneware, c. 1780.

STONES. It is surprisingly difficult to collect thirty stones of approximately the same size, shape, and colour, even on a pebble beach. A penny for every suitable stone gives great joy to the younger members of the family!

SEA-SHELLS. Cowries, used in many Indian games, can be bought quite cheaply from florists who used them for flower arrangements in bowls. Some of the sea-shells from our own shores may also be pressed into service.

SEEDS. Friends abroad may be able to send seeds used in native games; but beans, acorns, hazel nuts, and cherry stones form acceptable substitutes. The last-named are very attractive and can be stained any colour.

MARBLES. Coloured clay marbles cost about £1 per thousand and are useful for mancala counters, Solitaire, Seega, etc.

LOTS

GAMBLING STICKS. Copies of those used by the Kiowa Indians (fig. 159 on Plate XXI) were made from ⅜ in. diameter beech dowel rod, split lengthways. Clear copal varnish was applied and when dry they were enamelled. If enamel is applied to unvarnished wood the colour edges become blurred and ragged.

The Pam-nyout were made from an old ebony ruler which was sawn lengthways and then polished.

DICE (fig. 160 on Plate XXII). These were made from ivory billiard balls. A hacksaw was used to cut them out roughly and a Bridges' sanding disc completed the shaping. The pyramidal die from Ur was reproduced in ivory with two of the points tipped with red perspex. Tenuit was used as an adhesive.

'Chinese' dice can be made from western ones by drilling larger cavities on the 1 and 4 faces and colouring them with red enamel, or filling the depression with red sealing wax.

Fig. 161 (on Plate XXIII) shows a reproduction set of equipment for the game of All-tes teg-enuk. The dice were cut with a coping saw out of a large beef bone, grooved with a high-speed drill, and painted with blue enamel. The bowl was turned from a piece of sycamore; the large tallies were made of teak, and the small tallies of a pink Brazilian hardwood.

Bell and Hammer mallet, dice and cup, *c*. 1850 (author's collection)

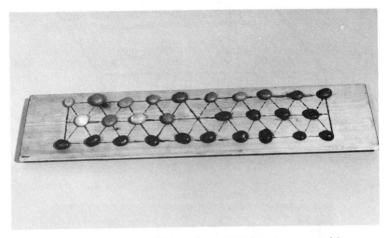

FIG. 137. *Poker work.* Board for Fighting Serpents with beach pebbles for counters

FIG. 138. *Wood carving.* A Wari board from old Hsuoyah, Ghana (author's collection)

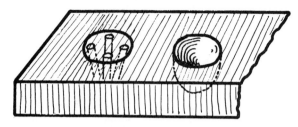

FIG. 139. Making a mancala cup

FIG. 140. *Chip carving.* A Ludus Latrunculorum board
cut into the top of a low table. The pieces of one side
are red and the other green though this does not show
in the photograph

FIG. 141. *Inlaying.* A reproduction of a fourteenth-century Tables board. Tablemen of boxwood and ebony, *c.* A.D. 1850

FIG. 142. *Marquetry.* A board for Continental draughts made with blackwood and zebrano on ¾″ plywood

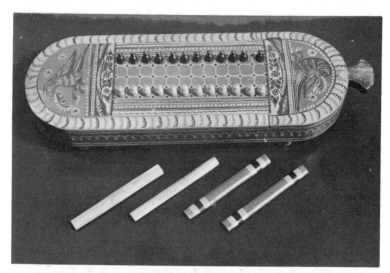

Fig. 143. *Paint work on white wood.* Antique Tablan board from western India (author's collection)

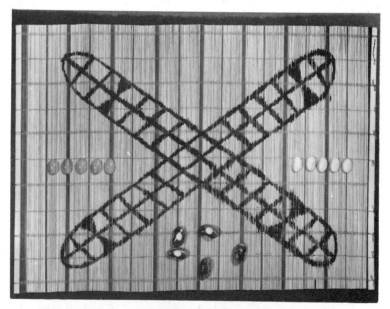

Fig. 144. *Paint on matting.* Copy of an Aztec Patolli board with pieces and beans

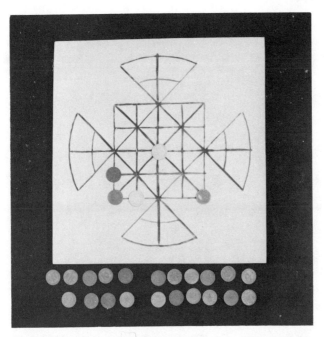

FIG. 145. *Formica on plywood*. Board for Cows and
Leopards; the cows are copper coins and the
leopards silver

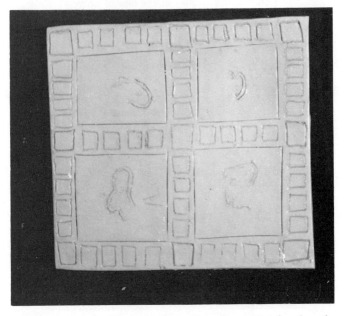

FIG. 146. *Pottery*. Reproduction of sandstone gaming board
from Palenque, Central America

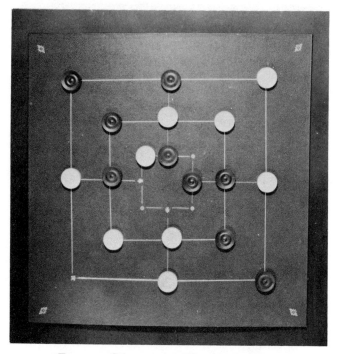

FIG. 147. *Gilt on rexine.* Nine Men's Morris
(An example of play at the end of Stage 1)

FIG. 148. *Beadwork on leather.* Zohn-ahl track
with dice-sticks and mutton-bone pieces

XV

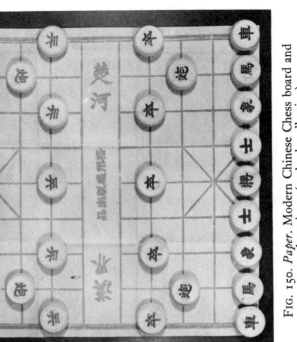

FIG. 150. *Paper*. Modern Chinese Chess board and wooden pieces (author's collection)

FIG. 149. *Embroidery*. An Indian Pachisi board with long dice and cowrie shells (author's collection)

XVI

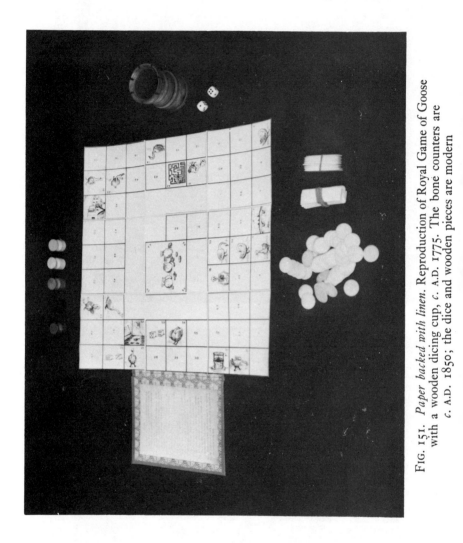

Fig. 151. *Paper backed with linen.* Reproduction of Royal Game of Goose with a wooden dicing cup, *c.* A.D. 1775. The bone counters are *c.* A.D. 1859; the dice and wooden pieces are modern

FIG. 152. *Metal work*. Modern Pallanguli board in white metal from Travancore (author's collection)

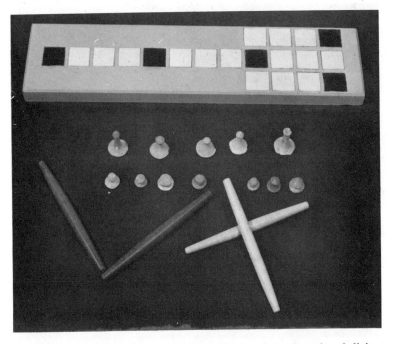

FIG. 153. *Perspex inlaid into wood*. Reproduction Senat board and dicing sticks. Original gaming pieces, *c.* 1570–525 B.C. (author's collection)

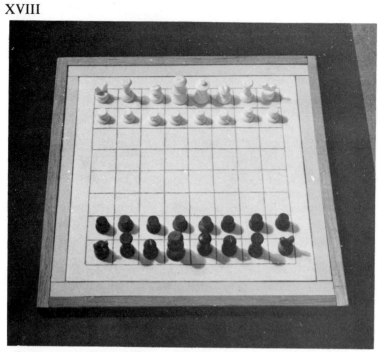

FIG. 154. *Ivory*. Reproduction Shatranj chessmen in ivory and ebony

FIG. 155. *Bone*. A reproduction Hnefatafl board of wood with
pieces made from mutton bones

FIG. 156. Bone casket containing a set of miniature double-six dominos. Lined with blue paper. French prisoner-of-war work, early XIX century

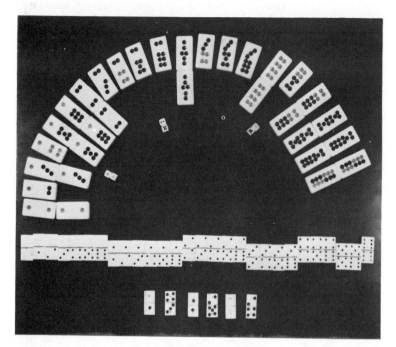

FIG. 157. Dominoes. *From top :*

(*a*) A modern set of Chinese dominoes of synthetic ivory arranged in an arc (from Hong Kong)

(*b*) Six Chinese dice arranged as if they were dominoes

(*c*) European double-six domino set made of black and white perspex

(*d*) Six pieces from an English set of bone and ebony dominoes, *c.* 1850

(Author's collection)

Fig. 158. *Pottery*. A reproduction board of the Game of Thirty
Squares (Senat). Teak inlaid with formica; long die of ivory, and ten
green jackals and ten blue lions of pottery

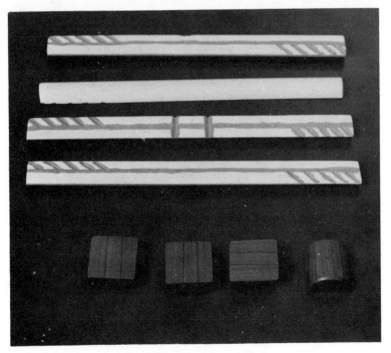

Fig. 159. Gambling sticks
Above, copies of those used by the Kiowa Indians for Zohn-ahl
Below, copies of pam-nyout for the Korean game of Nyout

FIG. 160. *Ivory.* Reproduction dice made from billiard balls. *From top:*

(*a*) English teetotum, *c.* A.D. 1800

(*b*) Large Roman fourteen-sided die, *c.* A.D. 200

(*c*) Sumerian pyramidal die, *c.* 3500 B.C.

(*d*) Long die for Shaturanga, *c.* A.D. 500

(*e*) Three long dice with pointed ends (Lucknow), *c.* A.D. 1850

(*f*) A pair of debased dice from the Gran Chaco, *c.* A.D. 1900

(*g*) Five dice from Qustul, *c.* A.D. 300

FIG. 161. *Turned wooden bowl* and equipment for All-tes teg-enuk

FIG. 162. Stone overdoor of Charles Cotton's fishing-lodge, 1674
(re-drawn from the *Complete Angler*, 1823 edition)

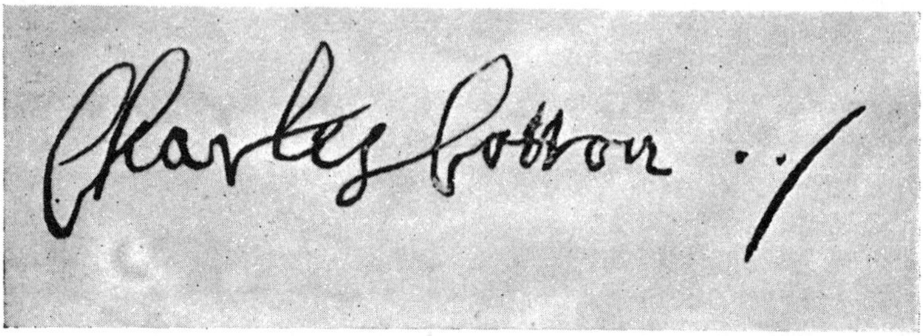

FIG. 163. Facsimile of Charles Cotton's signature in a letter to
Isaac Walton, 1675 (from the *Complete Angler*, 1823 edition)

FIG. 164. Facsimile of Edmond Hoyle's signature, 1769,
when he was over ninety (author's collection)
(A. H. Morehead suggests this is not Hoyle's own hand)

Biographies

Date	Book	Author
A.D.		
c. 920	*Kitab Ash-Shatranj*	as-Suli
1674	*The Compleat Gamester*	Charles Cotton
1689	*De Historia Shahiludii* ⎫	
1694	*De Historia Nerdiludii* ⎭	Thomas Hyde
1743	*Short Treatise on the game of Backgammon*	Edmond Hoyle
1801	*Sports and Pastimes of the People of England*	Joseph Strutt
1860	*History of Chess*	Duncan Forbes
1892	*Games Ancient and Oriental*	Edward Falkener
1895	*Korean Games* ⎫	
1895	*Chinese Games with Dice and Dominoes* ⎬	Stewart Culin
1896	*Chess and Playing Cards* ⎭	
1905	*Chess in Iceland*	Willard Fiske
1913	*History of Chess* ⎫	
1952	*History of Board Games other than Chess* ⎭	H. J. R. Murray

Tabulated above are the books which earned their authors a place in this Appendix. Several are rare as they were 'off subject'—a term used by bibliographers for works outside a writer's usual field. Such books tend to be published in small editions, or even privately, and they are in demand both for their merit in their own subject, and also by bibliophiles collecting entire works: a small manual on seaweed, perhaps, completing the writings of a famous novelist.

AS-SULI

Abu-Bakr Muhammad ben Yahya as-Suli was descended from a Turkish prince of Jurjan, whose ancestral home was on the banks of the river Atrek at the south-eastern corner of the Caspian Sea. During the reign of al-Muktafi, Caliph of Baghdad from A.D. 902 to 908, a chess tournament was arranged between the court champion, al-Mawardi, and as-Suli. The Caliph was present and he openly favoured al-Mawardi and encouraged him during the game. At first this embarrassed and confused as-Suli, but he soon recovered his composure and defeated his opponent so conclusively that there was no doubt who was the better player. The Caliph then transferred his favour from the old champion, al-Mawardi, dismissing him with a bitter pun: 'Your rose-water [maward] has turned to urine!'

The new champion's powers of improvising verse, and his attractive personality, maintained him in favour at court for three reigns. After the death of al-Muktafi, his successors, al-Muqtadir, followed by ar-Radi, gave him high positions. Ar-Radi was especially fond of him as as-Suli had been one of his tutors.

A contemporary historian, al-Mas'udi, relates that ar-Radi was once walking in the grounds of his country residence at Thurayya, and remarked on the beauty of the garden with its lawns and flowers: 'Have you ever seen anything more lovely?' The sycophants immediately began to dilate on the wonders of the garden, praising its beauty and placing it above the wonders of the world. 'You are wrong, gentlemen, the chess-skill of as-Suli is finer than all of these.'

As-Suli's reputation remained unchallenged among the Arabs for over six hundred years. His biographer ben Khalliken, who died in 1282, wrote:

'In chess he stood alone among the men of his generation. None were his equal and his play has passed into a proverb. When men wish to praise a player for his skill they say, "He plays like the Maestro as-Suli".'

Enough of his work survives in ancient manuscripts for us to assess his status as a master of Shatranj. We can see him criticizing his predecessors in a kindly fashion, though with the condescension of superior knowledge; his favourite openings are preserved, and they are based on definite principles. End games which occurred in actual play have been recorded, and there are comments on his skill in blindfold play; while occasional anecdotes underline his immense prestige.

He was the first player to try to discover the science of the game and to enunciate the underlying principles of play. His book, *Kitab Ash-Shatranj* (Book of Chess), is laid out in orderly fashion with ten standard openings; common problems in middle play; and a collection of end plays with comments. In the preface to his book he displays interest and skill in solving problems. Finally, he left behind him a pupil of outstanding merit, al-Lajlaj (the stammerer), whose memory is still respected among the Persians, Turks, and the Moghul Hindus.

As-Suli's other literary works include a history of the viziers; an unfinished history of the 'Abbasid House; an anthology of poems written by the descendants of Caliph 'Ali ben abi Talib; a history of Arabian poetry and monographs on several of the more noted poets. Many of these works are preserved in European or Istanbul libraries.

After ar-Radi's death in A.D. 940, as-Suli fell from favour through his sympathies for the 'Alids, later the Shi'ites, and he was forced to flee from Baghdad and go into hiding at Basra. He died there in poverty in A.D. 946.

CHARLES COTTON 1630–87

Cotton's story begins with the elopement of his father, Mr. Charles Cotton of Beresford Hall with Olive, the daughter of Sir John Stanhope of Elvaston in Derbyshire. Later the young swain made a reconciliatory statement saying that he did not know Sir John's daughter was under sixteen, nor that she was heiress to a considerable fortune, and that he had not carried her off at the point of a pistol.

Their only child, Charles Cotton the poet, was born on 28 April 1630 at Beresford Hall on the borders of Staffordshire and Derbyshire. The hasty, romantic marriage gradually became most unhappy and in 1647 Olive petitioned the House of Lords to enforce her husband to give her £300 a year on which to live.

Young Charles appears to have attended either Oxford or Cambridge University, but did not take a degree. He was a pupil of Ralph Rawson of Brasenose College, Oxford, and acquired a thorough knowledge of Greek, Latin, French, and Italian. As a young man he travelled in France, and probably Italy. He wrote many poems which were circulated among friends but not published until after his death.

In the summer of 1656 he married his cousin Isabella, the daughter of Sir Thomas Hutchinson of Owthorpe in Nottinghamshire. Before the marriage Cotton's father was forced to sell part of the family property to satisfy debtors, the rest was held in trust for the younger Cotton and his heirs.

Cotton was an ardent royalist and wrote several bitter satirical verses against the Roundheads. At the Restoration he published a panegyric in prose on Charles II and in 1664 his burlesque poem

'Scarronides, or the First Book of Virgil Travestie' appeared anonymously. Six editions of this work appeared during the author's lifetime, each more gross than the last.

In 1665 Cotton was empowered by an Act of Parliament to sell part of his estates to pay his debts. About this time he was granted a Captain's commission in the Army and was posted to Ireland. The ship was nearly wrecked and the incident was described in 'The Storm', one of the poems published after his death. Some of his adventures are also recorded in 'A Voyage to Ireland in Burlesque'. In a letter from Ireland to a friend he wrote that 'He had grown something swab [clumsy] with drinking good ale for he loved to toss the can merrily around.' He also complained of being besieged by duns. After his return to England he became a Justice of the Peace for Staffordshire and continued living as a country squire and writing and translating.

In 1674 *The Compleat Gamester* was published anonymously and it was not until 1734 in the fifth edition of the book that it was acknowledged that 'the Second and Third Parts were originally written by Charles Cotton, Esq., some Years since'.

Cotton's interests were those of an educated country gentleman. He was an authority on horticulture and his cousin Cokayne comments on his taste in planting the grounds at Beresford. His treatise *The Planter's Manual*, 'being instruction for the raising, planting, and cultivating all sorts of fruit-trees, whether stone-fruits or pepin-fruits, with their natures and seasons' (1675), gives practical information in a plain and simple fashion.

Cotton's wife died about 1670 leaving three sons and five daughters. Some time before 1675 Cotton married Mary, the dowager countess of Ardglass, and the eldest daughter of Sir William Russell, Bt., of Strensham in Worcestershire. She had a jointure of £1,500 a year but even this addition to his income was not enough to balance Cotton's expenditure, and in 1675 he was again allowed by an Act of Parliament to sell part of his estates to settle his debts.

Cotton was an ardent angler and he contributed a treatise on fly-fishing for the second part of the fifth edition (1676) of the *Compleat Angler*, a book written by his friend, Isaac Walton. Cotton's contribution was written in ten days. In 1674 Cotton built a fishing-lodge on the banks of the river Dove. Above the door he placed a stone carved with Isaac Walton's initials 'Twisted in Cypher' with his own (fig. 162 on Plate XXIII).

In 1681 he published a descriptive poem 'The Wonders of the Peak' dedicated to the countess of Devonshire. One of the wonders was Chatsworth. The last work published in his lifetime was his translation of Montaigne's *Essays* in three volumes in 1685. This is among the masterpieces of translation into the English language and has been frequently reprinted. He started translating 'Memoirs of the Sieur de Pontis' but died of a fever before it was finished. He was buried at St. James's Picadilly on 16 February 1687. An unauthorized collection of his poems was published without his family's permission in 1689. More than two hundred years passed before they were reprinted again in 1923 by John Beresford, a member of the Beresford family.

Cotton was brilliant, but cursed with the Curse of Versatility. His poetry is good, but not the best; his prose is easy, clear, and full of energy, but even as the co-author of a work which has gone through more editions than any other in the English language, apart from Shakespeare's plays or *Pilgrim's Progress*, he is overshadowed by his friend Isaac Walton; his achievements in horticulture were notable but not outstanding; while his extravagance caused ever-recurring financial embarrassment. There is a tradition that he used to hide from creditors in a cave overlooking the Dove, in the grounds of Beresford Hall, and that one of his maidservants brought him food in his humiliating retreat.

His love of good company is perpetuated in *The Compleat Gamester* which gives a picture of the manners, habits, and pastimes of an English gentleman during the last days of the House of Stuart.

COTTON'S CHIEF WORKS

1660 Panegyric to the King's Most Excellent Majesty.
1663 The Valiant Knight or The Legend of St. Perigrine (anonymously.
1664 Scarronides, or the First Book of Virgil Travestie.
1670 A Voyage to Ireland in Burlesque.
1670 A translation of Gerard's *History of the Life of the Duke of Esperon*.
1674 A translation of *The Commentaries of De Montluc, Marshal of France*, with a dedication to his relative the Earl of Chesterfield.
*1674 *The Compleat Gamester* (anon.).
1674 *The Fair One of Tunis, or the Generous Mistress* (anon.).
1675 Burlesque upon Burlesque, or the Scoffer Scoft, being some of Lucian's dialogues, newly put into English Fustian (anon.).

1675   *The Planter's Manual.*
1676   The Second Half of the *Compleat Angler.*
1679   The Confinement. A Poem (anon.).
1681   The Wonders of the Peak. A Descriptive Poem.
1685   Translation of Montaigne's *Essays.*

Posthumously

1689   Unauthorized collection of poems.

*This work was reprinted coupled with the *Lives of the Gamesters* by Theophilus Lucas (1714) in The English Library, Routledge and Sons (1930), under the title *Games and Gamesters of the Restoration.*

THOMAS HYDE 1636–1702

Thomas Hyde was born on 29 June 1636 at Billingsley, near Bridgnorth in Shropshire. His father, Ralph, was the vicar of the parish, and gave young Thomas his first instruction in oriental languages. When he was sixteen he went to King's College, Cambridge, and became a pupil of Wheelock, the professor of Arabic. Hyde concentrated on Persian, and assisted Walton in the publication of the Persian and Syriac versions of the Polyglot Bible, transcribing the Persian translation of the Pentateuch which had been published in Hebrew characters at Constantinople into its proper alphabet. He added a Latin translation.

In 1658 when he was twenty-two he went to Queen's College, Oxford, to become a reader of Hebrew. After reading one lecture on Oriental Languages he was awarded an M.A. by order of the Chancellor of the University. In 1659 he became underkeeper of the Bodleian Library, and in 1665 was elected the chief librarian. He was made a prebendary of Salisbury Cathedral in 1666, Archdeacon of Gloucester in 1673, and a Doctor of Divinity in 1682. He succeeded Pocock as Laudian Professor of Arabic in 1691, and was Regius Professor of Arabic in 1697. In 1701 he resigned the librarianship of the Bodleian, saying that he was tired of the drudgery of a daily attendance and was also anxious to complete his work on *Difficult Places in the Scriptures.*

During the reigns of Charles II, James II, and William III, he was interpreter in oriental languages to the Court, meeting most of the envoys from those countries, which gave him an unrivalled opportunity for collecting information on oriental games without ever leaving the shores of England. This information is contained in two volumes, *De Historia Shahiludii* in 1689, and *De Historia*

Nerdiludii in 1694. In the Newcastle University copy the two books are bound together, and in the instructions to the binders and printers are orders to colour the fore edge of the first book and to leave the fore edge of the second book plain. This has been done.

The first 72 pages of the first book are unnumbered and contain a dedicatory Epistle to Sydney Godolphin; then a page of instructions to the publishers and bookbinders in English. Next comes a digression called 'De Shahiludo Prolegomena Curiosa' containing puzzles and diagrams, written in a curious mixture of Latin, Hebrew, and Greek, verse and prose.

The reproduction of a double page gives an idea of the extraordinary mixture of languages employed by the writer (see Plate VI, facing p. 81).

The second part of Book One is titled 'Historia Shahiludii'. In this portion he describes chess, and has a diagram of an Ashtapada board; there is also a folding chart of the layout of the Great Chess (Tamberlane's) showing the initial positions of the 28 men on each side.

The third part of 71 pages is 'Historiae Shaduludii in Tribus Scriptis Hebraicis' (Chess among the Jews). The page numbering starts again at 1; the left-hand pages contain the original Hebrew texts, and the right-hand pages Hyde's translations into Latin. The three primary works are those of R. Abraham Abenezrae; R. Bons Aben-Jachiae; and an anonymous writing called 'Deliciae Regis'.

The second Book is separated from the first by a further page in English of instructions to the printers and binders, followed by a dedication to Johannes Hampden and an introduction. These pages are unnumbered. The rest of the book of 278 pages is paginated. Pages 1 to 70 deal with backgammon, its history, pieces, and boards; the game in antiquity and the Chinese form; 70 to 101 with De Ludo Promotionis Mandarinorum—The Promotion game of the Mandarins. Next follow three sections on Alea to page 129, then Talorum to 172, Latrunculorum to 195 and Wei-ch'i to 201.

The third section of the book, headed 'Historia Triodii', contains several of the games described in the present volume; indeed any work on the subject must owe a great debt to Hyde, the first English writer on oriental games. The last three pages of the book contain a bibliography, and mentioned there is the *Compleat Gamester* (1674).

Hyde died on 18 February 1702 at his rooms in Christ Church and was buried in the church of Handborough, near Oxford. His reputation as a scholar was very high in Germany and Holland, though he was not truly appreciated in Oxford. Some idea of his energy and output is indicated by the report that at his death he was engaged on no less than thirty-one works at the same time and they were all in various stages of completion. Some sixty years later Dr. Gregory Sharp, Master of the Temple, collected and published some of them under the title *Syntagma Dissertationum et Opuscula*, in two volumes.

Hyde's *Historia Religionis Veterum Persarum* (Oxford, 1700) was his most important and celebrated work. It was the first attempt to treat the subject in a scholarly fashion, and abounds in oriental learning.

Hyde was a friend and tutor of Sir Robert Boyle, the physicist— known to every schoolboy as the inventor of Boyle's Law concerning the proportional relations between elasticity and pressure in a gas. Boyle, however, was also a generous supporter of projects for the propagation of the scriptures and he financed, partly or wholly, the printing of Indian, Irish, and Welsh Bibles, the Turkish New Testament, and the Malayan version of the Gospels and Acts—the last publication being the work of his friend, Dr. Thomas Hyde. Hyde also helped Boyle in his studies in Hebrew, Greek, Chaldee, and Syriac.

HYDE'S MAJOR PUBLICATIONS

1665   Text and Latin translation of a Persian version of an astrono-
mical treatise, *Tabulae Stellarum Fixarum ex Observatione Ujugh Beoghi*, originally written in Arabic.

1674   Catalogus impressorum librorum Bibliothecae Bodleianae, Oxford.

1677   Malayan version of the Gospels and Acts.

1688   An account of the system of weights and measures of the Chinese in a treatise on weights and measures of the ancients by Edward Bernard.

1689   *De Historia Shahiludii*   } Published together as 'De Ludis
1694   *De Historia Nerdiludii*   } Orientalibus libri duo'.

1691   *Itinera Mundi*, a Latin translation, with notes, of a work by Abraham Peritsol, son of Mordecai Peritsol. This was a supplement to Abulfeda's *Geography*.

1692   An account of the famous Prince Giolo.

1700   *Historia Religionis Veterum Persarum*.

1702   *Abdollatiphi Historiae Aegypti Compendium*.

Posthumously

1712 A Treatise of Bobovius on the liturgy etc. of the Turks.
1767 Syntagma Dissertationum quas olim Hyde separatim edidit.
2 vols. 4to. This includes 'De Ludis Orientalibus'.

EDMOND HOYLE 1679–1769

'According to Hoyle' has become synonymous with the standard method of playing games. Over three hundred editions of his book have been published. Hoyle was born about 1679 and probably studied as a barrister. He became interested in the game of Whisk which in the eighteenth century was the game of the tavern and the servants' hall. About 1736 a set of gentlemen, including the first Lord Folkestone, frequented the Crown Coffee House in Bedford Row and began to study the game seriously. The vulgar 'Whisk' became the genteel 'Whist' and they formulated four fundamental rules:

1. Play from the strongest suit.
2. Study your partner's hand as much as your own.
3. Never force your partner unnecessarily.
4. Attend to the score.

Hoyle may have belonged to this coterie. It is certain that he became fascinated with the mathematics of the game about this time and in 1741 when he was over 60 began to give lessons on whist, as masters taught music or fencing. About 1743 each pupil received a set of manuscript notes; pirate copies soon appeared and to secure the copyright Hoyle published his notes in book form. The small book had a long title:

'A short treatise on the Game of Whist, containing the Laws of the Game; and also some Rules whereby a Beginner may, with due attention to them, attain to the Playing it well. Calculations for those who will Bet the Odds on any point of the score of the Game then playing and depending. Cases stated, to shew what may be effected by a good player in Critical Parts of the Game. References to cases viz. at the End of the Rule you are directed how to find them. Calculations directing with moral Certainty, how to play well any Hand or Game, by Shewing the Chances of your Partner's having 1 2 or 3 certain cards. With Variety of Cases added in the Appendix.' Printed by John Watts for the Author, London 1742.

There is only one known copy of this first edition which is now in the Bodleian Library; several of the other early editions are also preserved only in single copies. The price of the book, one guinea, encouraged piracies, the first appearing in 1743. Hoyle countered by lowering the price of his second edition (1743) to two shillings and he also certified every genuine copy with his autograph. The last edition with his signature is the fourteenth (fig. 164, facing p. 179); in the next it was replaced by a wood-block stamp.

In the earlier editions Hoyle offered to disclose the secrets of his 'Artificial Memory which does not take off your attention from your game' for a guinea. The success of his first book encouraged Hoyle to publish similar manuals on Backgammon, Piquet, Quadrille, Brag, and Chess.

An amusing skit entitled 'The Humours of Whist—A dramatic satire, as acted every day at White's and the Other Coffee-houses and Assemblies' lampooned the teacher and his pupils. The principal characters in the short comedy were Professor Whiston (Hoyle) who gave lessons on the game, and Sir Calculation Puzzle, an enthusiastic player who muddled his head with Hoyle's mathematics and always lost; together with other pupils, sharpers, and their dupes. Hoyle's many years of studying whist was dismissed with:

> Who will believe that man could e'er exist,
> Who spent near half an age in studying whist?
> Grew grey with calculation, labour hard,
> As if life's business center'd in a card?

Hoyle lived to enjoy the reward of his labours, but in the fifteenth edition of his book the well-known signature was replaced by an impression from a wood block, and in the seventeenth it was announced that 'Mr. Hoyle was dead'.

The popularity of Hoyle's teaching of Whist among ladies is referred to as early as 1743 in a Ladies' Journal; in 1753 he is called 'The Great Mr. Hoyle', but by 1755 the old maestro, then about seventy-six, had given up personal teaching. In 1769 the newspapers gave accounts of the death of the well-known public character Mr. Hoyle. A writer shortly afterwards quotes from the Parish Register of Marylebone: 'Edmund [*sic*] Hoyle, buried August 3rd 1769', adding that 'He was ninety years of age at the time of his decease.' No register or tombstone exists today. His will, dated 26 September 1761, was proved in London on 6 September 1769. No authentic portrait is known; the picture by Hogarth exhibited in 1870 at the Crystal Palace represents a Yorkshire Hoyle. Little more is known about Edmond Hoyle, Esq.

Hoyle was the first to write scientifically on whist, or indeed on any card game. His 'Short Treatise' soon became an accepted standard. His other works were:

1. *Short Treatise on the Game of Backgammon.* London, 1743.
2. *Short Treatise on the Game of Piquet, to which are added some Rules and Observations for playing well at Chess.* London, 1744.
3. *Short Treatise on the Game of Quadrille, to which is added the laws of the Game.* London, 1745.
4. *Short Treatise on the Game of Brag, containing the Laws of the Game, also Calculations, shewing the odds of winning or losing certain hands dealt.* London, 1751.
5. *An Essay towards making the Doctrine of Chances Easy to those who understand vulgar arithmetic only, to which is added, some useful tables on Annuities for Lives.* London, 1745. The book explains the method of calculating various problems in piquet, all-fours, whist, dice, lotteries and annuities.
6. *An Essay towards making the Game of Chess easily learned by those who know the moves only, without the assistance of a master.* London, 1761.

JOSEPH STRUTT 1749–1802

Joseph Strutt was born on 27 October 1749 at Springfield Mill, Chelmsford, the younger son of Thomas Strutt, a wealthy miller. A year later Thomas Strutt died leaving his widow to bring up Joseph and his elder brother, John, who later became a fashionable physician in Westminster. Joseph was educated at King Edward's School, Chelmsford, and when he was fourteen was apprenticed to the engraver, William Wynne Ryland.

In 1770, when he was twenty, he attended the Royal Academy and when he had been there only a few months was awarded one of the first silver medals. The following year he won a gold medal. In 1771 he became a student in the reading room of the British Museum —the source of most of his information for his antiquarian works. His first book was *The Regal and Ecclesiastical Antiquities of England* (1773). It contained engravings of illustrations from ancient manuscripts of kings, costumes, armour, seals, and other interesting objects.

On 16 August 1774 he married Anne, the daughter of Barwell Blower, a dyer, of Bocking, Essex, and took a house in Duke Street, Portland Place. Between 1774 and 1776 he published the three volumes of his *Manners, Customs, Arms, Habits Etc. of the People of England*; and in 1777–8 the two large quarto volumes of his *Chronicle of England*, which was profusely illustrated, and contained material from extensive original research.

In 1778 his wife died and he spent the next seven years painting pictures, nine of which were exhibited in the Royal Academy. Several of his best engravings were made during these years, using the stippled style which had been introduced from the Continent by his master Ryland.[1]

In 1785 Strutt returned to his antiquarian and literary researches, and published his *Biographical Dictionary of Engravers* in two volumes (1785–6) which has formed the basis of all succeeding works in the same field.

In 1790 he lost most of his wealth through the dishonesty of a relative; his health also failed and he left London to live very quietly at Bacon's Farm, Bramfield, in Hertfordshire. He returned to engraving and produced several of exceptional quality, including those in Bradford's edition of *Pilgrim's Progress* (1792) after designs by Stothard.

By 1795 his debts were paid and his health had improved and he returned to London and continued his researches. The *Dresses and Habits of the English People* was published in two volumes in 1796 and 1799. This was followed by *The Sports and Pastimes of the People of England* (1801), which has been frequently reprinted. Strutt was then fifty-two, and started a romance, *Queenhoo Hall*, based on an ancient manor house at Tewin, near his home at Bramfield. He planned to portray the lives and customs of fifteenth-century England, but he died at his house in Charles Street, Hatton

[1] Strutt's tutor, William Wynne Ryland, was born in 1732. He was apprenticed to Ravenet, and then to Boucher in France. Ryland introduced a stippled style of engraving from the Continent into England which imitated drawings in red chalk. Many of his engravings were of sentimental subjects based on classical themes: for example, the Judgement of Paris, printed in red. He was appointed engraver to George III at £200 a year. Eventually, he had his own print business in the Strand with a stock valued at some £10,000.
In 1783 he forged a bank bill worth several thousand pounds which was accepted and honoured by the Bank of England. Later, when suspicions arose, he disappeared. He was betrayed by a cobbler's wife who had noted the name RYLAND in a pair of boots which had been handed in for repair. He was apprehended in his hide-out in Stepney while attempting suicide with a razor. He was tried on the capital charge, found guilty, and was the last criminal to be hanged at Tyburn.

Garden, on 16 October 1802, before it was finished. He was buried in St. Andrew's Churchyard, Holborn.

The manuscript of *Queenhoo Hall* was given to Sir Walter Scott, who added an unsatisfactory ending. The book was published in 1808 in four small volumes. Two unfinished poems, 'The Test of Guilt' and 'The Bumpkin's Disaster', were published together in the same year. There is a portrait of Strutt in the National Portrait Gallery by Ozias Humphrey R.A. in crayon (No. 323).

Strutt was a pioneer in his branch of archaeology, his engravings were of high quality, and Sir Walter Scott admitted in the general preface to the later editions of the Waverley Novels that they had been inspired by Strutt's *Queenhoo Hall*.

DUNCAN FORBES 1798–1868

Duncan Forbes was born at Kinnaird in Perthshire on 28 April 1798. His parents were working-class people and emigrated to America in the spring of 1801, taking only their youngest child with them. Duncan was left behind with his grandfather in Glenfernate. He had very little schooling, and did not learn English until he was thirteen. Nevertheless, when he was seventeen he was chosen as the village schoolmaster of Stralock. Shortly afterwards he attended Kirkmichael school as a student. He entered Perth Grammar School in 1818 when he was twenty, and matriculated to the University of St. Andrews in two years, obtaining an M.A. degree in 1823. In the same year he accepted an appointment in the Calcutta Academy, but he resigned in 1826 through ill-health and returned to England, becoming an assistant to Dr. John Borthwick Gilchrist, a teacher of Hindustani.

In 1837 he was appointed Professor of Oriental Languages at King's College, London, and proved to be a successful teacher. When he retired in 1861 he was elected an honorary fellow of the college.

He was also employed from 1849 to 1855 by the Trustees of the British Museum to make a catalogue of the collection of Persian manuscripts which at that time numbered just over a thousand. While he was working on it new material was added, equalling the original collection, and Forbes's work was obsolete before it was finished, but it formed the basis for the later 'Catalogue of Persian Manuscripts'.

His tastes were very simple, even spartan. His main relaxation was playing chess. He was a member of the Royal Asiatic Society and was created an honorary LL.D. of St. Andrews University in 1847. He died on 17 August 1868.

He covered so wide a field of oriental study that his knowledge of some of the languages was rather limited, and his books contained little original thought or research, but they were clear and convenient to use and his elementary manuals were often more useful to beginners than more pretentious volumes.

Under the nom de plume of 'Fior Ghael' he opened a warm controversy in the *Gentlemen's Magazine* for May 1836 on Celtic dialects, maintaining that Welsh should not be included among them.

FORBES'S PUBLICATIONS

1828 *A New Persian Grammar* (with Sandford Arnot).

1828 *An Essay on the Origin and structure of the Hindostanne Tongue with an account of the principal elementary works on the subject.*

1830 Translation of the Persian romance, *The Adventure of Hātim Taī.*

1844 New edition of Arnot's *Grammar of the Hindustani Tongue.*

1845 *The Hindustani Manual, a pocket companion for those who visit India.*

1846 *A Grammar of the Hindustani Language in the Oriental and Roman Character.*

1846 New edition, with vocabulary, of the *Bāgh o Bahār.*

1848 *A Dictionary : Hindustani and English, to which is added a reversed Part, English and Hindustani.*

1849 *Oriental Penmanship, an Essay for facilitating the reading and writing of the Talik character.*

1852 His edition of *Tota Kahāni* in Hindustani.

1857 His edition of *Baitāl-Pachisi* in Hindi.

1860 *A History of Chess.*

1861 *A Grammar of the Bengali Language.*

1862 *The Bengali Reader . . . A New Edition.*

1863 *A Grammar of the Arabic Language.*

1864 *Arabic Reading Lessons.*

1866 *Catalogue of Oriental Manuscripts, chiefly Persian, collected within the last five-and-thirty years.*

EDWARD FALKENER 1814-96

Edward Falkener, the son of Lyon Falkener, head of the ordnance department of the Tower of London, was born in London on 18 February 1814. He was educated at a private school in Kent and then was articled to John Newman, an architect. In 1836 he became a student at the Royal Academy and in 1839 won its gold medal for a plan of a cathedral church.

In 1842 he visited all the countries of Europe except Spain and Portugal; and then continued on through Asia Minor, Syria, Palestine, Egypt, and the Greek islands. He studied the architectural remains in the places he visited, many being well off the beaten track. While in Denmark he made drawings of Fredericksberg Palace, and in 1859 when it was burned down, the King used Falkener's drawings in the restoration, and created him a Knight of the Order of Dannebrog for his services.

In 1847 Falkener was permitted to excavate the house of Marcus Lucretius at Pompeii at his own expense. A plan and a description of the house is given in his *Museum of Classical Antiquities*. Falkener practised as an architect for a few years, building some offices on St. Dunstan's Hill, London, but he spent most of his time in literary work and making drawings of restorations. Those he exhibited at the Exposition Universelle in Paris in 1855 won the Grande Médaille d'Honneur, and in 1861 the King of Prussia presented him with a gold medal for his work on classical archaeology.

In 1866, when he was fifty-two, he married Blanche Golding, gave up his private practice and retired to Wales, where he continued his studies and restorations for many years and was engaged on a treatise on the Greek houses at Pompeii when he died on 17 December 1896, leaving a widow, son, and three daughters.

Falkener had a sound knowledge of every branch of architecture and classical archaeology, and wrote on the lighting of museums and the artificial illumination of mosques and churches. Some of his illustrations appear in Fergusson's *History of Architecture* and many of his sketches were published in the Architectural Publication Society's Dictionary. He was a member of the Academy of Bologna, of the Architectural Institutes of Berlin and Rome, and was elected an honorary fellow of the Royal Institute of British Architects on 2 December 1895.

OTHER WORKS

1851– He edited the *Museum of Classical Antiquities.*

1860 *Daedalus; or the causes and principles of the excellence of Greek Sculpture.*

1862 *Ephesus and the Temple of Diana.*
Frequent contributions to the proceedings of the Royal Institute of British Architects.

1884 *Does the 'Revised Version' affect the Doctrine of the New Testament?*
Under the pseudonym of E. F. O. Thurcastle (Edward Falkener of Thurcastle).

1892 *Games, Ancient and Oriental.* This rare book is unreliable but contains interesting information. A paperback republication of the second edition by Dover Publications, Inc., appeared in 1961.

STEWART CULIN 1858–1929

Robert Stewart Culin was born in Philadelphia on 13 July 1858, the son of John Culin. He was educated at Nazareth Hall, Pennsylvania, and then studied archaeology until 1890. In 1892 when he was thirty-four he became director of the Archaeological Museum of the University of Pennsylvania; and in 1903 he was appointed the curator in Ethnology at the Museum of the Brooklyn Institute of Arts and Sciences, a position he held until his death.

Culin was an able scientist, and a man of wide knowledge; outspoken and unorthodox in speech and habits. He was a good judge of men, pictures, books, bronzes, fans and lace, and had a flair for appreciating the valuable even when it was surrounded by rubbish. His outstanding work at the Brooklyn Institute was achieved with an outlay which would hardly have bought the equipment for a standard museum expedition.

He founded the Oriental Club in Philadelphia and was its secretary for fourteen years, and had a profound knowledge of Chinese customs and psychology; once, when he was a witness in a case involving members of a secret Chinese society, his knowledge was so extraordinary that he was thought to have been a member at some time. His friendships with young Chinese students, men who later became the leaders in the New Republic, enabled him to prophesy the overthrow of the Chinese Empire at a time when the forecast appeared absurd.

He went on several field expeditions to Japan, China, Korea, and India, setting out with his fare: a lead pencil, a set of ideas, and a smile. He came back with the same smile, more ideas, and many packing cases whose contents were used to reconstruct the very air of the visited country in the exhibition hall of the Brooklyn Museum. When he was fifty-nine, on 11 April 1917, he married a widow, Mrs. Alice Roberts, née Mumford. She was a well-known artist who had studied in France and Spain and exhibited in salons in Paris, London, and cities of the U.S.A. Culin died on 8 April 1929.

PRINCIPAL WORKS

1887 'The Religious Ceremonies of the Chinese in the Eastern Cities of the United States' (An Essay).Privately printed, Philadelphia.

1887 'The Practice of Medicine by the Chinese of America.' *Medical and Surgical Reporter*, Philadelphia.

1891 *The Gambling Games of the Chinese in America.* Pennsylvania Univ.

1893 Exhibit of Games in the Columbian Exposition. *Journal of American Folklore*, Boston.

1894 Retrospect of the Folklore of the Columbian Exposition. *Journal of American Folklore.*

1895 *Chinese Games with Dice and Dominoes.* Smithsonian Inst., Washington.

1895 *Korean Games* (With Notes on the corresponding games of China and Japan). Pennsylvania Univ.

1896 *Mancala, the National Game of Africa.* Washington.

1896? *East Indian Fortune Telling with Dice; Syrian games with dice, tip cats etc.*

1898 *Chess and Plàying Cards.* Washington. Report U.S. Nat. Museum 1896, pt.2.

1899? 'Archaeological Application of the Roentgen rays.' *Scientific American Supplement*, New York.

1899 'Hawaiian Games.' *American Anthropologist*, n.s., i. 1899.

1903 'America the Cradle of Asia?' *Harper's Monthly*, New York, March 1903.

1907 *Games of the North American Indians.* Smithsonian Inst.

On the eve of forwarding the manuscript of this book to the publishers the Department of Primitive Art of the Brooklyn Museum kindly provided the additional list of Culin's works given below. They were unknown to the author and have not been consulted.

1916 'Bibliography of Japan.' *Brooklyn Museum Quarterly.*

1918 'Christian Relics in Japan.' *B.M.Q.*

1919 'Ceremonial Diversions in Japan.' *Asia.*

1920 'Japanese Game of Sugoroku.' *B.M.Q.*

1920 'Across Siberia in the Dragon Year of 1796.' *Asia.*

1924 'Beiderwand.' *B.M.Q.*

1924 'Creation in Art.' *B.M.Q.*
1924 'Game of Ma-jong, its origin and significance.' *B.M.Q.*
1924 'Amir Hamzah.' *B.M.Q.*
1925 'Japanese Game of Battle Dore and Shuttlecock.' *B.M.Q.*
1925 'Burri-burri Gitcho—Japanese swinging bat game.' *B.M.Q.*
1925 'The Art of the Chinese.' *International Studio.*

WILLARD FISKE 1831–1904

Daniel Willard Fiske, of puritan stock, was born on 11 November 1831 at Ellisburg, New York. He went to school at Cazenovia Seminary, and then to Hamilton College, but he left in his second year to study Scandinavian languages in Copenhagen and at the University of Uppsala in Sweden. When he returned to New York in 1852 he spoke fluent French, German, Danish, Swedish, and Icelandic, and could read classical Icelandic and interpret runic characters. He joined the staff of the Astor Library until 1859. In 1860 he became the General Secretary of the American Geographical Society. From 1857 to 1860 he was also co-editor with Paul Morphy of the newly-founded *American Chess Monthly*. In 1861 he was appointed attaché to the United States Legation in Vienna for two years, and while there he learned Russian, Italian, and Roumanian. In spite of his excellent ear for languages he had no musical appreciation, to his own considerable regret. When he returned to America he joined the 'Syracuse Daily Journal' for two years and then became a bookseller in Syracuse. In 1868 he was appointed professor and librarian of North-European Languages at Cornell University.

In 1880 after several years' friendship, Professor Fiske married, in Berlin, Miss Jennie McGraw, the wealthy daughter of a lumberman millionaire, and they began a protracted honeymoon travelling through Europe and Egypt in search of better health for the bride. Unfortunately, they were unsuccessful and she died the following year. At Fiske's direction flowers were placed on her tomb for the next twenty-three years on the fourteenth day of every month in commemoration of their wedding.

Jennie left a large part of her fortune to Cornell University for extensions to the library, but when it appeared that the money was to be misappropriated for other purposes, Fiske brought a legal action against the University Trustees and won his case, the legacy becoming part of his estate.

Two years after his wife's death he left Cornell and settled in Italy. In 1883 he rented the villa Forini in the eastern quarter of Florence. Mark Twain (Samuel Clemens) and his wife were near neighbours and friends. In 1892 Fiske bought the villa Landor, between Florence and Fiesole, and carried out extensive alterations. The villa dated back to the days of Boccaccio, and it is claimed that it was the scene of the famous Decameron.

Fiske spent his time in study and writing and he had his own private printing press. He was an ardent bibliophile and made no less than four separate great collections of books. His libraries of Dante, Petrarch, Icelandic literature, and the Rhaeto-Romance languages were each among the finest in the world. Two examples of his collecting methods give an insight into his character.

When visiting a village church in Iceland he noted an early Icelandic bible and offered to buy it from the elders. They were perturbed at the thought of exchanging a holy book for money and Fiske fell in with their scruples. He offered to exchange the book for a church organ, and the offer was accepted until one member asked who would play it. Fiske then offered to provide the organ, and to send the vicar's son to Reykjavik for lessons. The bible was added to Fiske's collection!

Late in the summer of 1891 Fiske was unwell and went to the baths of Tarasp in the lower Engadine. One afternoon he walked to the village of Schulz and saw some books written in Rhaeto-Romance. This language is a survival of the speech used by Roman settlers in 16 B.C. who were later entirely cut off from Italy by German-speaking tribes, and their language developed independently of the romance languages elsewhere. It is confined to the higher recesses of the valley of the Inn and along the steeply-sloping sides of the upper Rhine. Fiske entered the shop and bought twenty small volumes, mainly school books; the same evening he wrote to Leipzig for a Rhaeto-Romance bibliography and a dictionary. For the next few weeks he attended the baths in the morning and in the afternoons slipped off with a friend into the surrounding villages and went from door to door buying Rhaeto-Romance books. Women came with dusty volumes in their aprons, boys and girls lugged baskets and satchels full of books. The two Americans sat at a table and checked off the volumes against their bibliography, Dr. Boehmer's *Verzeichniss Rätoromanischer Litteratur*, and then bought what they required. They spent the evenings in collating and cataloguing the purchases and packing them up to send to London for binding.

They wrote to the booksellers of Innsbrück, Trento, Udine, and Gorizia and bought the cream of their Rhaeto-Romance literature. Later they went to St. Moritz and explored the villages of the upper Engadine in the same way and then to Chur to repeat the process once again.

Fiske was a man of boundless enthusiasm. He campaigned for the reformation of the Egyptian alphabet, worked for the advancement of Icelandic culture, and belonged to many learned societies including the American National Institute of Arts and Letters; he was an honorary member of the National Icelandic Literary Society, and a corresponding member of the Royal Society of Northern Antiquities, Copenhagen. He was honoured by King Humbert I of Italy in 1892, and by King Christian X of Denmark in 1902, for his literary achievements. His writings were varied and numerous, and included some excellent verse.

He died in Germany in 1904, when seventy-two, and in spite of his quarrel with the trustees of Cornell, left more than half a million dollars to the University library, thus fulfilling his wife's wishes, together with three of his magnificent collections of books; the fourth, of Icelandic literature, was given to the people of Iceland. His will was long and complicated, but he provided for his adopted son, once a destitute Italian lad, and left a sum of money to be spent annually on books and literature for one of the outlying Icelandic communities. He was buried by his wife's side in a memorial chapel built by the trustees of Cornell in the grounds of the University.

Chess in Iceland was published in Florence a year after his death. It is an extraordinary book, full of information on many subjects, including chess. It is disjointed and repetitive. Fiske apologizes for this confusion in his introduction: '. . . but I am too tired to sort things out—I will leave it to others to do that for me. . . .'

H. J. R. MURRAY 1868-1955

The greatest of the chess historians was born on 24 June 1868 in Peckham Rye, London, the eldest of eleven children. His father was Sir James A. H. Murray, the editor-in-chief of the Oxford English Dictionary. Harold went to school at Mill Hill and won an exhibition in mathematics to Balliol College, Oxford. He graduated in

1890 with a First in mathematics and became an assistant master at Queen's College, Taunton, and then at the Carlisle Grammar School. He became headmaster of Ormskirk Grammar School, Lancashire, in 1896, and on 4 January 1897 he married Miss Kate Maitland Crosthwaite, the eldest daughter of his former headmaster at Carlisle.

In 1901 he was appointed by the Board of Education as an Inspector of Schools and in 1916 he became a Divisional Inspector. On retirement in 1928 he was made a member of the Consultative Committee of the Board of Education. He was responsible for drafting large sections of the reports on The Primary School (1931); Infant Nursery Schools (1933); and the Spens Report on Secondary Education (1938). He also served as a member of the War Graves Education Committee (1929–37) which was concerned with the education of children of gardeners and other English staff in the cemeteries in France. He was a member of the Midhurst Rural District Council from 1931–55 and Chairman of the Housing Committee, 1938–48.

In 1897, with the encouragement of Baron von der Lasa, Murray began a monumental research into the development of chess from its obscure Indian origin to the modern European game. He collected and collated material from hundreds of sources, sifting the wheat from the chaff. He obtained help from scholars of living and dead languages, and himself learned Arabic which enabled him to unravel the chess writings of al-Lajlaj, a Mohammedan chess player of the tenth century A.D. J. C. White of Cleveland, Ohio, and J. W. Rimington Wilson in England put their magnificent collections of manuscripts and rare books at his disposal and in 1913 Murray published his incomparable 900-page *History of Chess*, well illustrated and with scores of diagrams. It received world-wide appreciation.

In 1952 when he was eighty-four his second book, *A History of Board Games other than Chess*, was published. It was full of scholarship and learning and formed a valuable check-list for future works, but it lacked popular appeal and brought only a moderate reward to its distinguished creator.

Murray loved young children and played delightful imaginative games with them. He was also interested in string games (cat's cradles) and, when bored in company, he had the disconcerting habit of practising them by going through the motions, sometimes to the consternation of strangers! He wrote poetry and studied the psychology of dreams, writing down some of his own which were highly entertaining. He was a shy and modest man and avoided the limelight. His outstanding trait was his tremendous power of concentration: he would sit sunk in some mathematical problem throughout a beautiful summer's day, oblivious of the weather. His wife declared that he wrote the *History of Chess* with his three children playing round his study and quite unaware of their noise. Cooking, too, was wasted on him. He would become absorbed in *The Times* crossword, a daily pleasure, and never notice what he was eating.

When he died in 1955 at the age of eighty-six he was working on a history of Heyshott, the village of his retirement.

MURRAY'S WORKS

1913   *History of Chess.*
1952   *History of Board Games other than Chess.*
1954   An article on chess in *Things* edited by Geoffrey Grigson.
1963   *A Short History of Chess.*

UNPUBLISHED

The Dilaram Arrangement.
The Dilaram Position in European Chess.
A History of Draughts (two versions).
A History of Heyshott (unfinished).
The Early History of the Knight's Tour (bibliographical).
The Knight's Problem (1942).
Magic Knight's Tours. A Mathematical Recreation (1951).
The Classification of Knight's Tours.

Rajah from
Indian chess set
(from Hyde's
*De Ludis
Orientalibus*)

Shah.

Index

Games described in detail in the text, and the main reference to them, are in bold type; references to illustrations are in italics

Abenezrae, A., Rabbi, 185
Aben-Jachiae, B., Rabbi, 185
Ace Negative, 145
Aces, 139–40
Aces in the Pot, 130
Ad Elta Stelpur, 37
Adhesives: Britfix, 174; Evo-stick, 175; Tenuit, 177
Adindan, 28
Agathias, 34
Agra, 9
Ahl stone, 4
Akbar, Mogul emperor, 9
Ak-hor, 26, 27, *fig. 21*
Akkad, 22
al-Beruni, 54, 58
Alea, 35, 185
Alexanderplatz, 64
Alfonso X, 36, *fig. 48*
Allahabad, 9
al-Lajlaj, 180, 199
All-tes teg-enuk, 127–9, *figs. 111,112,161*
al-Mas'udi, 180
al-Mawardi, 179, 180
al-Muktafi, 179, 180
al-Muqtadir, 180
Alquerque, 36, 47–8, 71, *figs. 38, 39*
America, 3,.43, 64, 65, 72, 89, 132, 135, 152, 154, 162, 163, 191, 194, 196
American 90th Infantry Division, 64
Amerindian games, 3, 4, 7, 48, 50, 89, 125, 127–9, 174, 176
Andalusia, 58
Angle (Chinese chess), 68
Arabia, 115
Arabs, 12, 27, 43, 47, 125
Army, Gen. Patton's Third, 64
ar-Radi, 180, 181
Aschaffenburg, 36
Ashanti, 117
Ashtapada, 51, 185, *figs. 43, 45*
as-Sarakhsi, 58
as-Suli, 58, 179–81
Assyria, 22
Aswan, 28
Athelstan, King, 80
Austin, R. G., 31, 34, 84
Automatic doubling (Backgammon), 46
Awari, 121–3
Axon, W. E. A., 61
Ayubite dynasty, 58
Aztecs, 6, 175

Babylon, 22, 42
Backgammon, 23, 37, 38, 42–6, 95, 188, *figs. 36, 37, 141, tailpiece p. 46*
Baganda, 123
Baggara, 12
Baghdad, 58, 81
Ba-Ila peoples, 123
Ball, billiard, 178, *fig. 160*
Ballana, 28
Balliol College, Oxford, 198
Bambra-ka-thul, 58, *fig. 47*
Baqt, 26
Bar, the (Backgammon), 43, 45
Barbudi, 130–1
Bare King, 60
Basra, 58, 181
Bassus, S., 84
Beadwork, 176, *fig. 148*
Bear off (Backgammon), 44
Becq de Fourquière, L., 34, 85
Bell and Hammer, 140–2, *fig. 114, tailpiece p. 178*
Bellasis, A. F., 58
Benihasan, 26, 27, *fig. 22*
ben Khalliken, 180
Beresford Hall, Staffordshire, 181, 183
Beresford, John, 183
Bergen Game, 164–5
Berlin, 64
Bhavishya Purana, 52
Bible, Polyglot, 184
Bingo, 165–7
Bishop, 63
Bland, N., 61
Blemyes people, 28
Blocked game, 163, 164, 171, 172
Block Game, 163–4, *fig. 133*
Blot, 41, 45
Boccaccio, 197
Boehmer, Dr., 197
Bone, 70, 177
Bowl Game, 127–9, *figs. 111, 112*
Bowles and Son, booksellers, 15
Boyle, Sir Robert, 186
Brag, 188
Bramfield, 190
Brandenburg, Elector-Prince Frederick William of, 62
Bray, 93
Britain, games in, 35, 43, 76, 80, 84, 92, 93, 96, 125, 126, 127, 140, 154
Bruges, 60

Buck Dice, 136
Buck: big, 136; little, 136
Building an Empire, 55
Burma, 65
Bush Negroes, 122
Bustamente, C. M., 7
Buzurjmihr, 57
Byzantine court, 57, 58

Cairo, 27
Calcutta Academy, 191
Calling Nine Hand, 161
Camp (Halma), 98
Cannon, 66–8
Canterbury, 92
Canton, 154
Capita aut Navim, 127
Cardinal tiles, 154, 156
Carnarvon, Lord, 20
Carter, H., 20
Carving, 174, figs. 138, 140, 155
Caspian Sea, 179
Caster, 94, 132, 133
Cat, 69
Caxton, Wm., 60, 61
Cessolis, Jacobus de, 60
Ceylon, 47, 51, 81, 93, 115, fig. 69
Chak t'in kau, 146–8
Chance point, 132
Chariots, 66, 67
Char-koni, 9, 11
Charlemagne, emperor, 58
Charles II, King, 184
Chasing the Girls, 37–8, fig. 31
Chaucer, G., 132
Chausar, 12
Check, 68; Perpetual, 60
Checkers, 72
Checkmate, 60, 68
Chelmsford, 189
Chess, 95, 185, 188; Circular, 61, 62, fig. 49; Chinese, 66–8, figs. 54, 55, 150, Pl. VIII; Courier, 62–5, figs. 50, 51; Great Chess, 61, 185; International, 65, Pl. IV; Medieval, 43, fig. 154; Shatranj, 57–60, fig. 154; Shaturanga, 51–7
Chess Players, The, 64–5, Pl. III
Chester, 86
Chesters, 84, fig. 73
Chichen Itza, 3
China, 42, 65, 92, 99, 149, 153, 154, 194
Chinese Chess, 66–8, figs. 54, 55, 150, Pl. VIII
Chisolo, 123–4, fig. 108
Chow, 158, 160
Christian X, king of Denmark, 198
Chosroes I, king of Persia, 57
Cicero, M. T., 32, 35
Circular Chess, 61, 62, fig. 49

Citadels, 62
Civil series, 146–7, 149, figs. 124, 126
Claudius, emperor, 33
Codex, see Manuscripts
Collecting Tens, 152–3, fig. 128
Commodus, emperor, 32
Comparetti, D., 30
Concourse of Shipping, 55
Confucius, 92, 153
Corner-rattler, 38
Cotton, Charles, 40, 179, 181–3, figs. 162, 163
Cotton manuscript, 59, fig. 48
Counters, 159
Courier Chess, 62–5
Cow, 81, 115
Cows and Leopards, 51, 81–2, 175, figs. 69, 145
Crabs, 132
Craps, 132, 135
Cr Bri Chualann, 93
Crib, 168
Cribbage, 22, 164, 167, fig. 16
Crockford, Wm., 133–5
Cross and Circle games, 1, 3, 4, 6, 8, 12
Crown and Anchor, 142–3, figs. 115, 116, 117
Crown Coffee House, 187
Crowning, 71
Crusades, 58
Culin, R. Stewart, 1, 4, 5, 49, 50, 98, 125, 128, 145, 146, 147, 153, 179, 194–6
Cunliffe, Lord, 61
Custodian capture, 78, 81, 82, 83, 97, figs. 65, 71, 85
Cyprus, 25, 176, fig. 19
Cyprus, 171–2, fig. 136

Dahomey, 121
Dakarkari people, 95
Damascus, 57
Dame, 71
Dancing Dragon, 145, fig. 123
Dara, 95–6, fig. 82
Dead Wall, 156, fig. 130
Decimal pair, 153
Decision: one shot, 131; two shot, 131
'Deliciae Regis', 185
Denbighshire, 31, fig. 26
Denmark, 79, 193, 196, 198, fig. 66
Dice, 125–7:
  Bell and Hammer, 141; Chinese, 144, 178, tailpiece p. 148, fig. 157; cowrie shells, 9, 18, 177, fig. 9; Crown and Anchor, 142, figs. 115, 116, 117; cubic, 12, 29, 94, 149, figs. 23, 47, 109, 160; Dodecahedron, fig. 160; Egyptian, 125; Etruscan, 125; grotesque German and Roman, 126, fig. 110; Liar, 143, figs. 118, 119; long, 10, 25, figs. 9, 13, 19, 45,

158, 160; Maiden Castle, 125, pyramidal, 23-4, 125, *figs. 17, 160*; Rome, 125; seeds, 17, 89, 178, *figs. 7, 75, 144*; sticks, 2, 4, 5, 12, 87, 178, *figs. 2, 6, 74, 143, 153, 159*; Sumer, 23-4, 125; Teetotum, *fig. 160*; to make, 178
Dice-box, 29, *tailpiece, p. 90*
Disputing Tens, 151-3.
Dog, 69
Dominicans, 61
Domino Crib, 167-9, *fig. 134*
Dominoes, Chinese, 149-62, *figs. 126, 127, 128, 132, 157*; European, 162-72, *figs. 132, 133, 134, 156*
Dönhoffstrasse, 64
Double Doublet, 166
Double Heading, 164
Double Twelve, 163
Doubles, 46, 160, 166
Doublet, 39, 45
Dragons, 154, 161
Draughtsman, 72, *fig. 58*
Drawn game, 56, 60, 158
Draughts:
    Continental or Polish, 75, *figs. 61, 142*; Diagonal, 73, *fig. 59*; English, 71-2, 75, *figs. 57, 58*; Italian, 73; Losing Game, 72-3; Turkish, 73, *fig. 60*
Drop Dead, 137
Duran, D., 6, 7
Du Chaillu, 79, *figs. 66, 81*
Durai, Mrs. H. G., 124
Dux, 86

Earth's Grace, 161
East's Thirteenth Consecutive Ma-jong, 161
Edward II, King, 127
Edward IV, King, 76
Egypt: Ancient, 20, 21, 22, 25, 26, 28, 29, 47, 57, 58, 86, 87, 92, 114, 125; modern, 28, 82, 87, 113
Elephant, 52, 54, 56, 59, 66, 67, 69, 70
El-quirkat, 47
Embroidery, 176, *fig. 149*
Emery, W. B., 28, 29
Emperor, 167
England, *see* Britain
Enkomi, Cyprus, 25, *fig. 19*
En prise, 48
Ernakulam, 115
Esharhaddon, king of Assyria, 22
Eskimo, 163
Etruscan die, 125, *fig. 109*
Exoniensis, Codex, 35

Fader, 130-2
Falkener, E., 27, 179, **193-4**
Fallas, 41
Faro, 133, 135

Fayles, 41, *fig. 35*
Fellaheen, 82, 86, 125
Fences, 106-7, *fig. 98*
Fers, 71
Fierges, 71
Fighting Serpents, 50, 174, *figs. 41, 137*
Final Three, 147
Firdausi, 57
Fish, Large, 151
Fishing, 150-1
Fishing, 158
Fiske, D. W., 42, 77, 92, 179, **196-8**
Five Field Kono, 98, *fig. 86*
Fitzgerald, R. T. D., 95, *fig. 82*
Flaxman, J., 177
Flowers, 154
Flush: Royal, 144; Low, 142
Forbes, D., 52, 57, 61, 179, **191-2**
Formica, 175, *fig. 145*
Fortification, 107, 108
Fortress, 66
Forty-two, 165
Four Winds Hand, 161
Fox, 76
Fox and Geese, 76-7, 111, *figs. 62, 63, 103*
France, 38, 43, 58, 64, 71, 75, 92, 162
Frederick William, Elector-Prince of Brandenburg, 62
Freystafl, 77
Fritillus, 29, 32, *fig. 24*
Full-house, 137
Fuchau, 153
Fyn, 79

Gambia, 121
Gammon, 46
Geese, 76
Gemara (Babylonian Talmud), 42
General (Chinese chess), 66, 67, 68, *fig. 55*
Gentlemen's Magazine, 192
George IV, King, 133
Germani, 125
Germany, 43, 62, 63, 64, 126, 140
Ghana, 116, 174
Ghazna, 54
Gilding, 175-6
Gloucester, 92
Go, 166
Go, 96, 100-11
Go-moku, 96, *fig. 83*
Gokstad ship, 93-4, *fig. 81*
Goldsmith, O., 16
Gomara, 6
Goose, Royal Game of, 14-16, *Pl. I*
Grand Forçat, Le, 75
Grande Acedrez, 36
Gravenburg, W., 63
Greece, 57
Gronow, Capt. R. H., 133

Guiana, 121
Gusman, P., 33
Gye, 132

Hadrian's Wall, 84
Haidarabad, 58
Hala-tafl, 76
Halberstadt, 62
Halma, 98–9, *fig. 87*
Hand from Heaven, 161
Handicap (Wei-ch'i), 110–11, *fig. 102*
Hasami Shogi, 97–8, *figs. 84, 85*
Hatshepsut, Queen, 26, *fig. 20*
Haus der Kunst, Munich, 65
Hazard, 126, 132–5
Heads and Tails, 127
Heaven, 147
Herskovits, M. J., 122, *fig. 107*
Hesy, tomb of, 14
Heyshott, 200
High Jump, 83, 84, 86, *figs. 71, 72*
Hillelson, S., 13
Himly, K., 42
Hising, 126
Hitler, Adolf, 64
Hnefatafl, 77, 79–81, 94, 174, 177, *figs. 66, 67, 68, 155, Pl. XVIII*
Hnefi, 80, *fig. 67A*
Hogarth, Wm., 189
Holt, Denbighshire, 31, *fig. 26*
Honan, 99
Honour tiles, 154, 156
Hornaskella, 38
Horse, 53, 67, *fig. 55*
Horsemen, 67
Hoyle, E., 133, 163, 179, 187–9, *fig. 164*
Huff, 48, 72
Humphrey, O., 191
Hun Tsun Sii, 42
Hunns, 80, *fig. 67B*
Hyde, Thomas, 51, 92, 179, 184–7, *tailpiece p. 200, Pl. VI*
Hyena, 12–14, 125, *fig. 11*
Hyrcania, 54

Iceland, 37, 76, 80, 197, 198
I-go, 97, *fig. 83; see* Wei-ch'i
'Il più col più, 73
Impasse, 105, *fig. 95*
Inciti, 35
India, 9, 17, 42, 51, 54, 57, 58, 65, 87, 115, 149, 191, 194
Indian Dice, 137–8
Inlay, 174
Inn, 142
Invincible, 167
Ireland, *see* Britain
Irene, empress, 58
Iron Age, 79
Isidore of Seville, 35

Italy, 43, 73, 92, 94, 125, 162, 197, 198
Ivory, 29, 177, *fig. 154*

James II, King, 184
Japan, 42, 66, 96, 97, 99, 100, 111, 194
Jester, 63
Jeu Forcé, 71, 75; Plaisant, 71
Jito, empress, 42
Jobson, R., 121
Jonson, Ben, 41
Jonsson, Finnur, 76
Joseki, 111
Joy-leap, 63
Jump, short, 71
Jungle Game, 68–70, *fig. 56*

Kaooa, 175
K'ap t'ai shap, 152–3
Karnak, 114
Kekchi Indians, 89
Khiva, 54
Khusru Parviz, king of Persia, 57
Khwarizm, 54
Kill, 81
King, 59, 62, 70, 71, 72, 75, 77, 78, 167; bare, 60
Kiowa Indians, 4, 178
Knight, 63
Ko, 103
Kolowis Awithlaknannai, 49–50
Konakis, 77, 78
Konungahella, 126
Korea, 1, 125, 194
Kramer, Agnes, 89
Kurna, 47, 92, 93, 114, *figs. 38, 78, 80*
Kwat p'ai, 150

Ladies' Journal, 188
Lake dwellings, 93
Lampridius, A., 32
Lanciani, R., 31, 127
Lane, E. W., 82, 87, 113
Lansquenet, 134
Lapland, 77, 79, *figs. 64, 65*
Lasa, T. von der, 94, 199
Lathe, 176, *fig. 161*
Latrunculi, 33
Lau kata kati, 175
Laws of Manu, 56
Leatherwork, 175, *fig. 148*
Lebanon, 43
Leipzig, 63
Leofric, 35
Leopards, 81
Leyden, Lucas v., 64, *fig. 50, Pl. III*
Liar Dice, 143–4, *figs. 118, 119*
Li'b el Merafib, 12
Libraries: St. Lorenzo del Escorial, Madrid, 36; King's College, Newcastle on Tyne, 185; Astor, New York, 196;

Bodleian, Oxford, 184, 188; Victor Emmanuel, Rome, 94
Limit, 160
Linnaeus, C., 77, 79, *figs. 64, 65*
Lion, 69, 70
Londesborough, Lord, 127
London, 61, 92, 133–5, 188, 190, 191, 193, 198
Loose tiles, 156
Lucretius, M., 193
Ludo, 12, *fig. 10*
Ludus Duodecim Scriptorum, 30–4, *figs. 25, 26, 27*
Ludus Latrunculorum, 82, 84–7, 174, 185, *figs. 73, 140*
Luk tsut k'i, 92
Lurched, 167
Luxor, 115

Macao, 134
Macrobius, A. T., 86
Macuilxochitl, 6
Madrid, 36
Mahadathika Maha-Naga, 93
Maharajah and the Sepoys, 65, *fig. 53*
Maiden Castle, 125
Main point, 132
Maine, 127
Maize Highway, 89
Ma-Jong, 153–62, *tailpiece p. 172, figs. 129, 130, 131, 132, Pl. VII*
Major tiles, 160
Making a point, 45
Mancala games:
    Awari, 121–3, *fig. 107*
    Chisolo, 123–4, *fig. 108*
    Mankala'h, 113–15, *figs. 104, 105*
    Pallanguli, 115–16, *tailpiece p. 124, fig. 152*
    Wari, 116–21, *fig. 106*
    making a cup, 174, *fig. 139*
Mandarin, 66, 67
Mankala'h, 113–15, *figs. 104, 105*
Mansura, 58
Manuscripts: Alfonsine, 39, 41, 43, 47, 94, *fig. 48*; Athelstan, 80; *Civis Bononiae*, 94; Codex Exoniensis, 35; Cotton, 59; North Italian Academies, 94; Persian, 61
Marelles, 77
Marin, G., 82
Marquetry, 174, *fig. 142*
Martial, M. V. M., 92
Martinetti, 136, *fig. 113*
Marylebone, 188
Matador, 170–1, *fig. 135*
Matching pair, 153
Maurice, emperor, 57
Mayas, 3, 89, *figs. 3, 4*
Mecca, 57

Medina, 57
Megiddo, 20, 21, *fig. 14*
Memphis, 114
Merels, *see* Morris
Mesopotamia, 23
Metal-work, 176, *fig. 152*
Mexico, 6, 7, 130
Mihintale, Ceylon, 93
Military series, 146–7, 149, *figs. 124, 126*
Mill, 94
Mine Host, 141
Minnows, 151
Minor tiles, 154, 160
Mississippi, 135
Montezuma, 6
Moors, 47
Morphy, P., 196
Morris, *see* Three, Six and Nine Men's Morris
Mouskat, P., 71
Muhammad, 115
Munich: Art Exposition, 36; Haus der Kunst, 65
Murray, H. J. R., 22, 62, 80, 179, 198–200
Muscovite, 77, 78
Museums: Black Gate, Newcastle on Tyne, 84; British, 26, 57, 58, 189, 191, *fig. 20*; Brooklyn Institute, 194, 195; Cairo, 27, *fig. 21*; Chesters, Northumberland, 84; Kaiser Friedrich, Berlin, 64; Nat. Museum of Wales, 31, *fig. 26*; University of Pennsylvania, 194
Myrine, 34
Mysore, 87

Nard, 27, 42, 43
Nathan ben Jechiel, 42
National Gallery of Art, Washington, 65
Naushirawan, 57
Negro's Game, 135
Nerdshir, 42
Nero, emperor, 32, 127
Neutralization (Wei-ch'i), 108
New Mexico, 48
New Orleans, 135
Newgate Prison, 15
Nicks, 132
Nigeria, 95, 121
Nine Men's Morris, 93–5, 175, 176, *figs. 80, 81, 147*
Nines, 147
Ningpo, 153
Noddy, 22
Norway, 93, 126.
Norwich, 92
Notabae people, 28
Noughts and Crosses, 91, *fig. 76*
Nubia, 28, 29
Nui Seng-ju, 68
Nyout, 1–3, 125, *figs. 1, 2, 159*

Oklahoma, 4
Olaf, king of Norway, 126
Olaf, king of Sweden, 126
Old Hsuoyah, 174
On the Parish, 144
Ones and Nines (Ma-jong), 161
Ordinarii, 35
Oriental Club, 194
Ormskirk, 197
Osese wood, 116, 174
Over the Top, 129
Ovid, P. O. N., 33, 84, 92
Oxford, 184

Pachisi, 9–12, 176, *figs. 8, 9, 149*
Paint work, 174, 175, 177, *figs. 143, 144*
Palenque, 3, *figs. 3, 146*
Palestine, 20, 21
Palestrina, 30, *fig. 25*
Palm Tree Game, 20–2, *figs. 13, 14, 15*
Pallanguli, 115–16, 175, 176, *tailpiece p. 124, fig. 152*
Pam-nyout, 2
Panther, 69
Paper boards, 176, *figs. 150, 151*
Paris, 75, 193
Parker, H., 47, 81
Pass, 171, 172
Passamaquoddy Indians, 127
Patolli, 6–8, *figs. 7, 144*
Pawn, 53, 59, 63; privileged, 56; promotion of, 55
Perpetual attack, 103, *fig. 94*; check, 60; positions, 103
Persia, 42, 57
Perspex, 176, 177, *figs. 153, 157*
Petrie, F., 14, 113, 114, *fig. 105*
Pieces: bone, 177, *figs. 155, 156, 157*; cowrie shells, 177, *fig. 149*; ebony, 177, *fig. 154*; faience, *fig. 153*; ivory, 177, *fig. 154*; marbles, 178; perspex, 177, *fig. 157*; pottery, 177, *fig. 158*; sea-shells, 177; seeds, 178, *figs. 138, 152*; wood, 176–7, *figs. 52, 140, 141, 142, 143, 147, 149, 150, 151, Pl. IIb*
Pig, 130
Piquet, 188
Plaisant, 71
Playing Heavens and Nines, 153
Point Number, 136
Points, 43; making, 45; game, 46
Poker work, 173, *fig. 137*
Poland, 74, 75
Polo, Marco, 162
Pompeii, 33, 86, 193, *afterpiece p. 201, figs. 28, 29*
Pottery, 175, 177, *figs. 146, 158*
Prevailing Wind, 158
Priest of the Bow, 49
Prime Minister, 59

Pryle, 144
Puff, 43
Puluc, 89–90, *fig. 75*
Pung, 157, 160
Put and Take, 148, *fig. 125*
Pyrgus, 32, *fig. 24*

Quadrille, 188
Queen, 63
Quinn, J. P., 135
Quirkat, 47
Quong, 157, 160; robbing a, 158
Qustul, 28, 29, 31, *fig. 23*

Raichi, 78
Rajah, 51, 52, 54, 55
Rashepses, 26
Rat, 69, 70
Rattray, R. S., 117, *fig. 106*
Red Mallet Six, 147
Regaining a throne, 54
Reversi, 74–5
Rexine, 175, *fig. 147*
Rhodesia, Northern, 123
Richborough, 84
Rimington-Wilson, J. W., 199
River (Chinese chess), 66
Robinson, J. A., 80, *Pl. V*
Roka, 56
Roman soldiers, 28, 29, 31, *fig. 160*
Rome, 15, 32, 92, 94, 125, *fig. 27*
Rook, 63
Royal Academy, 189, 190, 193
Royal Asiatic Society, 192
Rubbish Holes, 116
Ruhk, 59
Ruiz, A., 3
Ruppert, K., 3
Ryland, W. W., 189, 190 n.

Sagas, 77, 80
Sage, 63
Sahagun, Fr. Bernardino de, 6
Sahe, 5
St. Kitts, 122, *fig. 107*
St. Lorenzo del Escorial, Madrid, 36
Sakkarah, 26
Saladin, 58
Salisbury, 92
Sanskrit, 56
Sapper, K. von, 89
Saracens, 58
Saramacca, 121, *fig. 107*
Sargon, king of Assyria, 22
Saturnalia, 35
Scandinavia, 75, 77
Scarne, J., 136, *fig. 113*
Schimmel, 140–2
Scotland, *see* Britain
Scott, Sir W., 191

Screen (Chinese chess), 68
Seasons, 154
Seega, 82–4, 85, 86, *fig. 70*
Seizing a throne, 54
Seki, 105
Senat, 26–7, *figs. 20, 21, 158*
Sente, 107
Selenus, G., 63
Sennacherib, king of Assyria, 22
Sequences, 138–9
Seville, 35
Shanghai, 153, 154
Sharp, Dr. G., 186
Shatranj, 57–60, 62, 65, 66, 180, *figs. 47, 48, Pl. IIb*
Shaturanga, 51–7, *figs. 44, 45, 46, Pl. IIa*
Shepherd, J., 14–15
Ship, 53, 55, 56, *fig. 46*
Ship, Captain, Mate and Crew, 138
Shipping, concourse of, 55
Shooter, 130–1
Short jump, 71
Siang K'i, 66–8
Sicily, 43
Six Men's Morris, 92, *fig. 79*
Sixe-Ace, 39–41, *figs. 33, 34*
Sixteen Soldiers, 50–1, *fig. 42*
Slain (Puluc), 90
Soldiers (Chinese chess), 68
Solitaire, 111–12, *fig. 103*
Somali people, 82, 84, 86, *figs. 71, 72*
Spain, 35, 43, 47, 58
Spoil Five, 96
Stack, 90, 150
Stalemate, 68; strangled, 60
Standing hand, 158
Starter, 168
Strangled stalemate, 60
Ströbeck, 62, 63
Stone Warriors, 48–9, *fig. 40*
Stones, 101, *tailpiece p. 112*
Strung Flowers, 145–6, *figs. 120, 121, 122, 123*
Strutt, J., 61, 162, 179, 189–91
Suckling, Sir J., 22
Sudan, 12, 28
Suetonius, G., 33
Sumer, 22, 125, *frontispiece, figs. 15, 17, 18, 160*
Sumerian Game, 23–5
Sung period, 42
Sugoroko, 42
Supreme pair, 150, 151
Swahili, 123
Swedes, 77, 78
Syria, 57, 58
Sz'ng luk, 145–6

Tab, 87, 125
Taba, 13

Ta'biyat, 60
Tablan, 87–9, 174, *figs. 74, 143*
Tablas de Alcedrez, 36
Tablas reales, 43
Table, inner, 43, 45; outer, 43
Tablemen, 71, *tailpiece p. 46, fig. 141*
Tables, 36, 37, 43, *figs. 36, 141*
Tablut, 77–9, *figs. 64, 65*
Tabula, 33, 34–5, 86, *fig. 30*
Tacitus, C., 125
Tafl, 75–81
Talmud, 42
Talorum, 185
Tamberlane, 61, 185
Tamil, 20, 115
Tau, 25, 26, 176, *figs. 19, 153*
Tavole reale, 43
Teetotum, 148, *figs. 125, 160*
Thaayam, 17–20, 51, *fig. 12*
Thebes, 20, 21, 22, 114, *fig. 13*
Thillai-nayagam, Dr., 20
Thirteen Odd Majors, 161
Thirty-Six, 129
Thirty Squares, Game of, 26–8, *figs. 20, 158*
Three Men's Morris, 91–2, *figs. 77, 78*
Three Scholars, 161
Throne, 54
Throwing Heaven and Nine, 146–8, *fig. 124*
Thurayya, 180
Tiger, 69, 70
Tiles, blank, 163; cardinal, 154, 156; counting, 165; flower, 154, *tailpiece p. 170*; honour, 154, 156, loose, 156; major, 160; minor, 154, 160
Timgad, 32, *fig. 27*
Tiu ü, 150–1
Todas Tablas, 43
Togoland, 121
Tong, 155, *fig. 129*
Torquemada, Juan de, 6
Tourne-case, 38–9, *fig. 32*
Trajan, emperor, 86
Trap, 69, 70
Travancore-Cochin, 115, 176, *fig. 152*
Tric-trac, 43
Trimalchio, 92
Triple Heading, 164
Triplets, 166
Troy, 93
T'shu-p'u, 42
Tsung shap, 151–2
Tuichi, 78
Turkey, 73
Tutankhamen, 26
Twenty-six, 139
Twittering of the Sparrows, 156

Universities: Cornell, 196, 198; Newcastle, 185; Oxford, 184, 188, Pennsylvania, 194; St. Andrews, 191, 192
Uppsala, 196
Ur, 21, 23, 25, *frontispiece, figs. 15, 17, 18*

Vagi, 35
Varnish, 178
Varro, M. T., 84
Vesuvius, 33
Victim, 60
Viking, 79, 93
Voluntary Doubling, 46

Wadi es Sebua, 28
Wales, *see* Britain
Walton, I., 182, *fig. 162*
War Horse, 59
Wari, 116–21, 174, *figs. 106, 138*
Watari, 110
Wei-ch'i, 68, 96, 97, 99–111, 185, *tailpiece p. 112, figs. 83, 84, 88, 89, 90, 91, 92, 93, 94, 95, 96, 97, 98, 99, 100, 101, 102*
Wei dynasty, 42

West Indies, 121
Westminster Abbey, 92
White, A. S., 91
— J. C., 199
White Horse, 141
Whitehouse, F. R. B., 15
Whisk, 187
Whist, 187
Wild, J., 15
William III, King, 184
Wimose, 79, 80, *fig. 66*
Wind discs, 155, *fig. 129*
Wind of the Round, 158
Winds, 154, 155, 158–9, 161, *fig. 131*
Wolf, 69
Woolley, Sir Leonard, 21, 23
Woodperry, Oxfordshire, 80, *fig. 67*
Woodpile, 150, 151, *figs. 127, 128*
Wright, T., 126, *fig. 110*

Yucatan, 3

Zeno, emperor, 33, 34, 35, *fig. 30*
Zohn Ahl, 4–5, 176, *figs. 5, 6, 148, 159*
Zuni Indians, 48, 49

BOARD and TABLE
GAMES
From Many Civilizations

BOARD and TABLE GAMES
From Many Civilizations

by
R. C. BELL

Volume Two

Dover Publications, Inc.
New York

Chinese ladies playing Wei-ch'i. (Eighteenth-century painting on glass in the author's collection.)

INTRODUCTION

This second volume of Board and Table Games supplements the earlier work, but is also designed to be an entity in itself. The same structure of presentation has been used, and when necessary references are made to games described in the first volume. The material has been arranged in ten chapters:

RACE GAMES

WAR GAMES

POSITIONAL GAMES

MANCALA GAMES

DICE GAMES

DOMINO GAMES

GAMES OF WORDS AND NUMBERS

CARD GAMES REQUIRING BOARDS

GAMES OF MANUAL DEXTERITY

and a final chapter devoted to a brief description of gaming counters. To save space the bibliography also serves as a table of contents.

ACKNOWLEDGEMENTS

The author is once more indebted to the writers of all the publications listed in the bibliography, and to the staff of the Newcastle-upon-Tyne University Library for their help in obtaining obscure articles for reference; while Mr Raymond S. Dawson and Mr. A. C. Barnes, of the School of Oriental Studies, the University of Durham, helped with the translation of Chinese writings.

Many readers of Volume I have written to the author describing games unknown to him; several are now included in this volume, and acknowledgements are made in the bibliography. More than fifty letters have been received from all parts of the world, and the author is very grateful for the interest shown by these correspondents.

The staff of the Oxford University Press have again been most courteous and helpful; and last, but not least, my thanks are due to my wife for her patience and support in bringing this work to completion.

Newcastle upon Tyne   RCB
January 1969

CONTENTS AND BIBLIOGRAPHY

INTRODUCTION   v

ACKNOWLEDGEMENTS   vi

LIST OF ILLUSTRATIONS   xiv–xviii

Chapter One: RACE GAMES

GAME   REFERENCES

1. CROSS AND CIRCLE RACE GAMES

PANCHA KELIYA   Parker, H., *Ancient Ceylon*, London,   1
                       1909, p. 609.
                       Marin, G., 'An Ancestor of the Game
                       of Ludo', *Man*, XLII 1942, p. 114.
EDRIS A JIN   Culin, S., *Chess and Playing Cards*,   2
                       Washington, 1898, p. 857.

KERALA   Commonwealth houseman; identity   3
                       lost.

TOTOLOSPI (I)   Culin, S., *Games of the North American* 5
                       Indians, Washington, 1907, pp.
                       160–1.

2. SPIRAL RACE GAMES

JUBILEE   Author's collection   6

3. SQUARE RACE GAMES

AN ECCENTRIC EXCURSION
   TO THE CHINESE EMPIRE Author's collection   8
SNAKES AND LADDERS   Author's collection.   10

4. OVAL AND ROUND RACE GAMES

THE GAME OF THE RACE   Author's collection,   11

5. THE BACKGAMMON GROUP

THE BOTTLE GAME   Hyde, T., *De Ludis Orientalibus*, Ox-   12
                       ford, 1694, p. 65.

GAME	REFERENCES	
THE ENGLISH GAME	Fiske, W., *Chess in Iceland*, Florence, 1905, p. 166.	15
THE LOMBARD GAME	Fiske, W., *Chess in Iceland*, pp. 166–7.	16
THE IMPERIAL GAME	Fiske, W., *Chess in Iceland*, p. 166.	16
THE PROVINCIAL GAME	Fiske,W., *Chess in Iceland*, p. 167.	17
THE QUEEN'S GAME	Fiske, W., *Chess in Iceland*, pp. 299, 353.	17
MYLIS	Fiske, W., *Chess in Iceland*, p. 167.	18
ICELANDIC BACKGAMMON	Fiske, W., *Chess in Iceland*, pp. 346–53.	19

Chapter Two: WAR GAMES

1. THE ALQUERQUE GROUP

| FANORONA | Montgomery, W., 'The Malagasy Game of Fanorona', in *Antananarivo Annual*, iii (1896), quoted by Murray, H.J.R., *History of Board-Games other than Chess*, Oxford, 1952, pp. 87–9. | 24 |

2. THE CHESS GROUP

BURMESE CHESS	Murray, H.J.R., *History of Chess*, Oxford, 1913, pp. 109–13.	28
SIAMESE CHESS	Murray, H.J.R., *History of Chess*, pp. 113–17.	31
JAPANESE CHESS	Falkener, E., *Games Ancient and Oriental*, London, 1892, pp. 155–76. Murray, H.J.R., *History of Chess*, pp. 138–45. Leggett, T., *Shogi, Japan's Game of Strategy*, Rutland, Vermont, 1966.	33
KRIEGSPIEL	Rengger, H.D., personal communication, October, 1960.	39

3. THE DRAUGHTS GROUP

TURKISH DRAUGHTS	Hoolim, H., personal communication, September 1967.	41
FOUR FIELD KONO	Culin, S., *Games of the Orient*, Tokyo, 1958, p. 101.	42
TIGERS AND OXEN	Culin, S., *Chess and Playing Cards*, p. 876. Stewart, D., personal communication, December, 1963.	42

GAME   REFERENCES

4. THE TAFL GROUP

THROW-BOARD   Murray, H.J.R., *A History of Board-*   43
                         Games other than Chess, p. 63.

FITHCHEALL   Murray, H.J.R., *A History of Board-*   45
                         Games other than Chess, pp. 59–60.

ASALTO   Duff, D.I., personal communication,   46
                         May 1961.
                         Murray, H.J.R., *A History of Board-*
                         Games other than Chess, pp. 104–5.

THE TIGER GAME   Murray, H.J.R. *A History of Board-*   47
                         Games other than Chess, pp. 107-12

5. THE LATRUNCULORUM GROUP

SIXTEEN SOLDIERS   Culin, S., *Chess and Playing-cards*, pp. 48
                         874–5.

6. RUNNING-FIGHT GAMES

TAB .   Lane, E.W., *Manners and Customs of*   49
                         the Modern Egyptians, 2nd Ed. Lon-
                         don, 1890, pp. 317-20.

7. LOST GAMES

CHUKI   Culin, S., *Chess and Playing-cards*,   52
                         pp. 871-3.

TOTOLOSPI (2)   Culin, S., *Chess and Playing-cards*,   53
                         pp. 879–80.

Chapter Three: GAMES OF POSITION

1. MORRIS GAMES

ACHI   Appia, Dr. (one time resident, Durham   55
                         County Hospital), personal commu-
                         nication.

2. BLOCKING GAMES

PONG HAU K'I   Culin, S., *Games of the Orient*, p. 101. 56

MU TORERE   Gould, W.B., personal communica-   56
                         tion, 1968.
                         Murray, H.J.R., *A History of Board-*
                         Games other than Chess, p. 93.

3. FIVE IN A ROW GAMES

MULINELLO QUADRUPLO   Fiske, W., *Chess in Iceland* pp. 107-10. 57

4. REPLACEMENT GAMES

PYRAMID   Hindman, D.A., *Handbook of Indoor*   57
                         Games and Conquests, English Edn.
                         1957, p. 167.

SALTA   *British Chess Magazine*, 1901, p. 241.   58
                         Scott, Eileen, personal communication.

GAME   REFERENCES

5. GAMES OF TERRITORIAL POSSESSION

WEI CH'I   Anonymous painting in the author's   59
                    possession. (See Frontispiece)
AGON   Cassell's Book of Sports and Pastimes, 61
                    London, undated, c. 1890, pp. 382-3

6. PATIENCE GAMES

FRENCH SOLITAIRE   Berkeley, 'Dominoes and Solitaire,'   63
                    Bohn's Library Handbook of Games,
                    London, 1890, pp. 30-2.
SEVEN-PIECE TANGRAM Bell, R.C. Tangram Teasers, New-   66
                    castle upon Tyne, 1965.
FIFTEEN-PIECE TANGRAM Rare Chinese Work, Title page missing, 68

Chapter Four: MANCALA GAMES

1. TWO RANK MANCALA

BA-AWA   Afoakwa, S., personal communication,   72
                    1957.
LONTU-HOLO   Herskovits, M.J., 'Wari in the New   73
                    World', Journal of the Royal Anthro-
                    pological Institute, lxii (1932), p. 25.
                    Quoted by Murray, H.J.R., A History
                    of Board-Games other than Chess,
                    pp. 203-4.

2. FOUR RANK MANCALA

HUS   Wagner, P.A., 'A Contribution to our   76
                    Knowledge of the National Game
                    of Skill of Africa', Trans. Royal Soc-
                    iety of South Africa, Vol. VI, 1917-18,
                    pp. 47-68, and Plates XIII-XVII.

Chapter Five: DICE GAMES

1. TWO-SIDED DICE

LU-LU   Culin, S., 'Hawaiian Games', American 78
                    Anthropology, Vol. I, 1899, p. 243.
MON SHI MO UT   Culin, S., Chess and Playing-cards, pp. 78
                    691-4.
THE WALNUT GAME   Culin, S., Chess and Playing-cards, p. 80
                    737.
PITCH AND TOSS   Mine Host at the Bay Horse, West   80
                    Woodburn, personal communica-
                    ation.
DITTAR PRADESH   Mehra, S.K., personal communica-   81
                    tion, 1964.
SIXTEEN COWRIES   Mehra, S.K., personal communica-   82
                    tion, 1964.

GAME	REFERENCES	
2. SIX-SIDED DICE		
FIFTY	Wood & Goddard, *The Complete Book of Games*, 1940, p. 363.	83
ROTATION	Scarne, J., *Scarne on Dice*, 2nd Ed. Harrisburg, Pa., 1946, p. 376.	83
FOUR-FIVE-SIX	Scarne, J.,*Scarne on Dice*, p. 352.	84
GRAND HAZARD	Scarne, J., *Scarne on Dice*, p. 342.	84
BIDOU	Campbell, J.H., personal communication, 1961.	86
PAR	Scarne, J., *Scarne on Dice*, p. 389.	91
COCKFIGHTING	Dobree, C.T,. *Gambling Games of Malaya*, Kuala Lumpur, 1955, pp. 98–9.	92
GRASPING EIGHT	Culin, S., *Chinese Games with Dice and Dominoes*, p. 496. Report of the National Museum 1893.	93
THE GAME OF EDUCATION	Culin, S., *Chinese Games with Dice and Dominoes*, pp. 496–8, and plate 3. Report of the National Museum, 1893.	94
3. GAMES WITH SPECIAL DICE		
SPINNING TREASURE	Dobree, C.T., *Gambling Games of Malaya*, pp. 121–4.	97
FISH, PRAWN, KING CRAB	Dobree, C.T., *Gambling Games of Malaya*, p. 109.	99
HEARTS	Hindman, D.A., *Handbook of Indoor Games and Conquests*, English Ed. 1957, p. 175.	100

Chapter Six: DOMINO GAMES

1. GAMES USING CHINESE DOMINOES		
PAI KOW	Dobree, C. T., *Gambling Games of Malaya*, pp. 85–7.	102
BULLFIGHTING	Dobree, C. T., *Gambling Games of Malaya*, pp. 88–9.	104
TIEN KOW	Dobree, C. T., *Gambling Games of Malaya*, pp. 90–1.	105
2. GAMES USING MA-JONG TILES		
TEN AND A HALF	Dobree, C.T., *Gambling Games of Malaya*, pp. 79–80.	106

GAME   REFERENCES
3. GAMES USING WESTERN DOMINOES (Double-six set)

BLIND HUGHIE   Mine Host, The Bay Horse, West   108
                    Woodburn, personal communica-
                    tion, 1960.
ENDS   Mine Host, The Bay Horse, West   108
                    Woodburn, personal communica-
                    tion, 1960.
DOMINO WHIST   Berkeley, 'Dominoes and Solitaire', 110
                    p. 9, Handbook of Games, Vol. I.
DOMINO POOL   Cassell's Book of Sports and Pastimes, 111
                    p. 389.
DOMINO LOO   Berkeley, 'Dominoes and Solitaire', p. 111
                    23, Handbook of Games, Vol. I.

        Chapter Seven: GAMES WITH NUMBERS
LOTO   G.H.N. Esq., Hoyle's Games, London,   114
                    1853, p. 74.
BINGO   115

        Chapter Eight: CARD GAMES REQUIRING BOARDS
CRIBBAGE   Cassell's Book of Sports and Pastimes, 117
                    p. 867.
POPE JOAN   Cassell's Book of Sports and Pastimes, 120
                    p. 883

        Chapter Nine: GAMES REQUIRING MANUAL
                       DEXTERITY
SHOVE HA'PENNY   Inn Games, p. 25–8. 'Know the Game'   123
                    series. London undated
CROKINOLE   Frank, K., personal communication.   124
CARUMS   de Costa, G.I.B., personal communi-   127
                    cation.
SQUAILS   Cassell's Book of Sports and Pastimes, 129
                    p. 830.
SHOVEL BOARD   Foster's Encyclopedia of Indoor Games, 130
                    London, 1901, p. 573.
BROTHER JONATHAN   Cassell's Book of Sports and Pastimes, 131
                    p. 799.
NINE-PINS   Cassell's Book of Sports and Pastimes, 132
                    p. 812.
SPELLICANS   Anonymous rules in cheap Chinese   133
                    Spellican set. (Author's collection).

GAME	REFERENCES	
STRING GAMES	Fidler, V., 'String Figures,' *The Beaver, Winter Number*, Winnipeg, 1963, pp. 18–21.	134
	Haddon, K., *String Games for Beginners*, Cambridge, 2nd Ed. 1967.	

Chapter Ten: GAMING-COUNTERS

PORCELAIN	Author's collection.	137
MOTHER-OF-PEARL	Author's collection.	137
METAL	Hawkins, R.N.P., 'Minor Products of British Nineteenth-Century Die-sinking', *British Numismatic Journal*, Vol. XXX, pp. 174–87, 1960.	138
	Hawkins, R.N.P., Catalogue of the Advertisement Imitations of 'Spade' Guineas and their halves, *British Numismatic Journal*, Vol. XXXII, pp. 174–219, 1964.	
	Hawkins, R.N.P., Supplement I to Catalogue of the Advertisement Imitations of 'Spade' Guineas and their halves, *British Numismatic Journal*, Vol. XXXIV, pp. 149–61, 1966.	
	Hawkins, R.N.P., personal communication.	
APPENDIX A	The Eight Immortals.	144
APPENDIX B	Method of constructing an Agon board.	147
ADDENDUM		149
INDEX		153

TEXT FIGURES

Chapter One: RACE GAMES

Figure   1.   Pancha Keliya board and markers   I

          2.   Board for 'Edris a jin'   3

          3.   Board and pieces for 'Kerala'   4

          4.   Hopi Indian games cut into sandstone slabs   5

          5.   Jubilee track and eight sided teetotum   6

          6.   Diagram of track, markers and totum of 'An Eccentric Excursion to the Chinese Empire'   8

          7.   Diagram of 'Snakes and Ladders'   10

          8.   Diagram of 'The Game of the Race'   11

          9.   Diagram of 'The Bottle Game'   12

        10.   Diagram of backgammon board   14

        11.   Initial position of pieces for 'The English Game'   15

        12.   Initial position of pieces for 'The Lombard Game'   16

        13.   Initial position of pieces for 'The Imperial Game'   16

        14.   Initial position of pieces for 'The Provincial Game'   17

      15a   Initial position of pieces in 'The Queen's Game'   17

      15b   Position of Black's pieces when they have been unstacked   18

        16.   Initial position of the pieces for 'Mylis'   18

        17.   Initial position of pieces in 'Icelandic Backgammon'   19

Tailpiece: Lead horse and jockey from 'The Game of the Race'   23

Chapter Two: WAR GAMES

        18.   Initial position of pieces in 'Fanorona', and notation key   27

        19.   Chess notation when played on the squares   27

        20.   Chess notation when played on the points of intersection   28

        21.   Initial placing of soldiers in 'Burmese chess'   24

      21a   A chariot from a Burmese chess set   28

        22.   Initial opening position of pieces in 'Burmese chess'   30

        23.   Initial position of pieces in 'Siamese chess'   31

        24.   Japanese chessboard   33

        25.   Pieces in 'Japanese Chess'   34

        26.   Initial position of pieces in Japanese Chess   34

        27.   Japanese Chess: Jewelled King's moves   35

        28.   Japanese Chess: Gold General's moves   35

        29.   Japanese Chess: Silver General's moves   36

        30.   Japanese Chess: Honourable Horse's moves   36

        31.   Japanese Chess: Flying Chariot's moves   36

        32.   Japanese Chess: Angle-going's moves   37

        33.   Japanese Chess: Lance's moves   37

Figure 34. Japanese Chess: Soldier's moves 37
35. Arrangement of boards and players in 'Kriegspiel' 39
36. Initial position of pieces in 'Four Field Kono' 42
37. Board and pieces for 'Tigers and Oxen' 42
38. Reconstruction of possible initial position of pieces in Tawlbwrdd 43
39. Drawing of wooden gaming-board found in lake-dwelling at Ballinderry 45
40. Initial position of pieces in 'Asalto' 46
41. Board and pieces for 'The Tiger Game' 47
42. Initial position of pieces for 'Sixteen Soldiers' 48
43. Initial position of pieces in 'Tab' 49
44. Notation and direction of movement of the pieces 50
45. Opening position of pieces in 'Chuki' 52
46. Opening position of pieces in Totolospi 53
Tailpiece: Eighteenth century Turkish draughtsmen 54

Chapter Three: GAMES OF POSITION

47. Board and pieces for 'Achi' 55
48. Initial position of pieces in 'Pong hau k'i' 56
49. Board for Mulinello Quadruplo 57
50. Initial position of pieces in 'Pyramid' 58
51. Initial position of pieces in 'Salta' 58
Tailpiece: A Chariot from a Burmese chess set 59
52. Initial position of pieces in 'Agon' 61
53. End of game in 'Agon' 62
54. Notation for French Solitaire board 63
55. Final position of pieces in 'Le Lecteur au milieu de ses amis' 64
56. Final position of pieces in 'Le croix de St. Andrew' 64
57. Final position of pieces in 'Le tricolet' 65
58. Final position in 'Problem four' 65
59. Tangram pieces converted into square and triangle 67
60. Typical tangram puzzles 67
61. Solution to puzzle Fig. 59 67
62. Solution to puzzles in Fig. 60 68
63. Pieces of the fifteen-piece tangram 68
64. Three typical fifteen-piece geometric shapes 68
65. Outline of household items 69
66. Two fifteen-piece tangram pictures 69
67. Solutions of Fig. 64 69
68. Solutions of Fig. 65 70
69. Solutions of Fig. 66 70
Tailpiece: Ivory tangram box 70

Chapter Four: MANCALA GAMES

Figure 70. Woodcut by Thomas Bewick of negroes playing mancala 71
71. Diagram of board and pieces at the beginning of 'Ba-awa' 72
72. Notation of lontu-holo board 73
73. Patients playing Choro on the steps of a mission hospital in Uganda 75
74. Initial position of stones in 'Hus' 76
Tailpiece: Central piece of Ivory Solitaire set 77

Chapter Five: DICE GAMES

75. Dice used in 'Lu-Lu' 78
76. Basket, dice and counters for 'Mon shi mo ut' 78
77. Walnut-shell dice used for 'The Walnut Game' 80
78. George V penny piece 80
79. A score of 8 in 'Dittar Pradesh' 81
80. Diagram to show the players' numbers in 'Sixteen Cowries' 82
81. Modern western dice 83
82. Diagram showing a throw of 'four-five-six' 84
83. Layout for Grand Hazard 85
84. Dice combination in 'Bidou' 87
85. Dice bowl and Chinese dice for 'Cockfighting' 92
86. Layout for 'Grasping eight' 93
87. Tallies used in 'The Game of Education' 94
88. Poh Kam, Poh, stake counters and staking-board for 'Spinning Treasure' 97
89. Dice and layout for 'Fish, Prawn, King Crab' 99
90. Diagram of special dice used in 'Hearts' 100
Tailpiece: Knights from a Siamese chess set 100

Chapter Six: DOMINO GAMES

91. Set of Chinese dominoes 101
92. Chinese Domino pairs in descending order for 'Pai Kow' and 'Tien Kow' 102
93. Dominoes ready for a five-handed game of 'Blind Hughie' 108
94. Showing method of forming a fifth tail in five-handed 'Ends' 109
95. Dominoes at the start of a game of 'Domino Whist' 110
Tailpiece: Chess King made of Dyed Bone 113

Chapter Seven: GAMES WITH NUMBERS

Figure 96. Loto card, reel and counters   114
       97. A bingo card   116
       97b A Keno card   116
Tailpiece: Mother-of-pearl fish counter   116

Chapter Eight: CARD GAMES REQUIRING BOARDS

       98. A cribbage board   117
Tailpiece: Cribbage board of walrus ivory from Baffin Land   122

Chapter Nine: GAMES REQUIRING MANUAL DEXTERITY

       99. Diagram of a 'Shove Ha'penny' board   123
       99a Groat of Edward IV   124
      100. Diagram of a 'Crokinole' board   125
      101. Diagram of a 'Carums' board   127
      102. Initial arrangement of Carums pieces within the
            central circle   128
      103. Diagram of a game of 'Squails'; and an elevation
            of a squail   129
      104. Shovel Board and discs   130
      105. Board for 'Brother Jonathan'   131
      105a American cent 1795   132
      106. Arrangement of pins for 'Nine-pins'   132
      107. Part of a Chinese set of ivory spellicans   133
      108. String figures   135
Tailpiece: Nineteenth century Chinese mother-of-pearl gaming
            counter   136

Chapter Ten: GAMING COUNTERS

      109. A counting-board with counters arranged to record the
            number 2,540,027   138
      110. From Reisch's *Margarita Philosophica*, 1503   139
Tailpiece: Siamese porcelain gaming-counters   143

            APPENDIX

      111. Method of constructing an Agon board   147
      112. Board for Mu Torere   149
      113. Crucial positions in Mu Torere   151

PLATES

Chinese ladies playing on Wei-ch'i.

Frontispiece

facing page

1 *The Jubilee*   12
2 Title page of book of rules for the game of Jubilee.   12
3 *An Eccentric Excursion to the Chinese Empire.*   13
4 *The Game of the Race,* c. 1850.   28
5 Reproduction board and pieces of *The Bottle Game.*   29
6 Chinese lacquered backgammon board; and tablemen and   29
   dicing-cups of ivory; all c. 1830.
7 Burmese chessboard of teak, and pieces of pinkadoe.   44
8 Siamese chessboard and pieces.   44
9 Reproduction Japanese chessboard and pieces, arranged for   45
   the start of a game.
10 Modern Indian draughtsboard, with eighteenth century   45
   Turkish ivory draughtsmen coloured red and green.
11 Victorian Asalto board and marbles, c. 1850.   60
12 Chinese tangram box and puzzle in ivory; c. 1860.   60
13 Eighteenth century ivory solitaire board and pieces, probably   61
   French.
14 Modern Whyo board; Ibibio tribe, Nigeria.   76
15 Spinning Treasure board, Poh (die), and Poh Kam (cover).   76
16 Ma-jong tiles of the three suits; Winds and Dragons, with the   77
   extra eight Flower and Season tiles.
17 Early nineteenth century compendium of games in bone.   92
18 Loto reels, bag, cards, markers, and bone counters, c. 1880.   92
19 A three-handed cribbage board and markers, c. 1890.   93
20 Pope Joan board, cards and counters.   93
21 Squails and lead target.   108
22 Ivory tenpins and tops, c. 1820.   108
23 Chinese spellicans and hooks of ivory, c. 1880.   109
24 Chinese lacquered box containing four sets of cards, and three   109
   shapes of mother-of-pearl gaming counters.
25 Two views of a Chinese dicing cup in ivory, c. 1750.   124
26 Victorian card holder of china.   125
   Gaming Counters   *between pp.* 140 *and* 141

CHAPTER ONE

Race Games

1. CROSS AND CIRCLE GAMES

PANCHA KELIYA

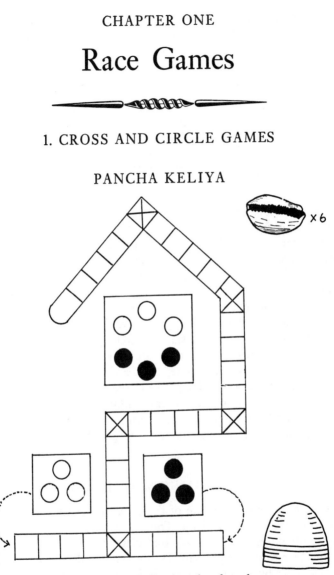

FIG. 1. Pancha Keliya board and markers

Pancha Keliya (The Five Game) of Ceylon belongs to the cross and circle group of games, but only half the original track remains. (See Volume I, figs. 1 and 3.)

Two, four, six, or eight players may take part, and each side has three dome-shaped pieces made of painted wood. The track may be marked out on the ground, or embroidered on a cloth. Six yellow cowries shaken in half a coconut shell are used as dice and score:

6 mouths up	=	6
5	,,	,,	=	5
4	,,	,,	=	4
3	,,	,,	=	3
2	,,	,,	=	2
1	,,	,,	=	1
0	,,	,,	=	0

The opposing pieces are entered at the opposite ends of the horizontal part of the track, and can only enter on a throw of 6, 5, or 1. After each of these numbers the player has an additional throw, which is repeated as long as he continues to throw any one of them. The piece moves along the line of squares by the total amount thrown; or the score of each individual throw may be used to move a different piece, but cannot be divided between two pieces. If a piece lands on a square occupied by an enemy piece, the latter is sent back to the starting circle and has to begin again; but a piece on a marked square is safe from attack. Only one piece may rest on any square at a time, and if a player cannot use a throw, it is lost and the turn of play passes to the opponent.

Exactly one more than the number required to land on the last square is needed for a piece to escape from the track into the home square, and the first player (or team) to get all his pieces into the finishing square is the winner.

EDRIS A JIN (The Genii's Game)

This is the most elaborate of the cross and circle games and is played by the Druses of Syria. The board is marked out on a large square of cotton as a parti-coloured diagram with four arms, each having four rows of eight squares; the outer ends being connected to each other by a diagonal row of eight squares; the whole forming an octagonal figure. The inner area, composed of sixteen squares, is called the *Serai*. The moves are controlled by the throws of four cowries, and each of the four players has three men, made of shells with coloured paper pasted to them; the colours being red, green,

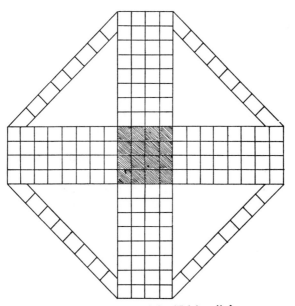

FIG. 2. Board for 'Edris a jin'

yellow, and black. One of each force is called the 'chief', and is filled with red wax. The other two are 'soldiers'. All the pieces move in the same way.

Culin remarked that the game seemed to have developed a little way in the direction of chess, but not in the direct line. Unfortunately his account is incomplete, and efforts to obtain details elsewhere have been unsuccessful.

KERALA

(This game was described by a Commonwealth houseman, and unfortunately his identity, and the country of the game's origin has been lost. It appears to be a considerably modified cross and circle game.)

Kerala is usually played by two or three players, the game becoming overlong with more. The board shown in fig. 3 is marked out in the sand, and each player has five distinctive stones. The moves are controlled by throwing five cowrie shells, and when the stones are awaiting entry on the board there are special starting scores:

5 backs up = 5 points
4 backs up = 1 point

When a stone is on the board the moves depend upon the number of mouths up:

> 5 mouths up = 10 points
> 4 mouths up = 4 points
> 3 mouths up = 3 points
> 2 mouths up = 2 points
> 1 mouth up = 1 point
> 0 mouths up = 5 points

Only one stone can move on a throw; but if a 5 is scored the player has a second throw, and this can be used to advance the same stone, or a different one; if 5 is scored again, the player has another throw, with the possibility of a third stone being moved; and this choice continues as long as 5s are thrown.

If a player cannot make use of a throw it is lost. This includes a 5, when the player does not get a second throw.

All five of a player's stones must reach the centre before any can start on the return journey. If a stone is hit on its way to the centre,

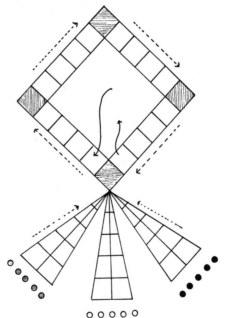

Fig. 3. Board and pieces for 'Kerala'

even by one of its own colour, it retires to the starting point and must begin again; but if it is hit while travelling from the centre it retires to this position.

A stone resting on a marked square is safe from attack, and each player may have one stone on a haven square at the same time. The first player to get all his stones off the board wins the game, and the other players continue for second and third places.

TOTOLOSPI (I)*

The most modified of the cross and circle games was played by the Hopi Indians of Oraibi, Arizona, and consisted of only one degenerate limb of the cross. The board described by Culin was marked out on a slab of sandstone (see fig. 4a). He did not give any details of the rules.

The same tribe played another game, Totolospi, using a more complex board which retained enough of the original shape to show

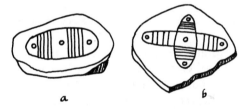

a   b

FIG. 4. Hopi Indian games cut into sandstone slabs. (After Culin)

its origin. Two or four players took part, each having one stone, and the moves were directed by the throws of three staves, each having one face flat and plain, and the other curved and marked with a pattern of dots. The only scoring throws were when all the staves fell the same way, and the player's stone moved on one point. A scoring throw gave the player another throw, and this continued until he failed to score, when the turn passed to the next player (see fig. 4b). No further information is available.

* Not to be confused with a different game of the same name (see page 53).

2. SPIRAL RACE GAMES

JUBILEE

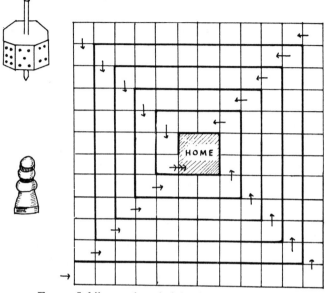

FIG. 5. Jubilee track and eight sided teetotum

Between 1750 and 1850 a multitude of spiral race games, inspired by the Royal Game of Goose, were invented. Some were for amusement only, but the majority were designed to teach children history, geography, scripture, architecture, etc.

The Game of JUBILEE (see plates 1, and 2) was published in 1810 by John Harris at the corner of St. Paul's Churchyard, and consisted of twelve sections of paper pasted onto a linen backing, in the same manner as maps are made. The sections formed an anticlockwise spiral of little pictures, numbered from 1 to 150. There were also six markers of different colours for six players (though more or less could play if desired), and an eight-sided teetotum with the faces marked from 1 to 8. Each player also started with about two dozen counters.

The players spun the teetotum in turn, and advanced their marker according to the number exposed on the uppermost face, this being added to that on which the marker stood. The player then referred to an accompanying booklet and paid any fines, or received any rewards as indicated.

If a marker landed on an occupied square, the resident piece moved one square forward, obeying any instructions of its new position. All fines were paid into the pool, and all rewards taken from it. The first player making exactly 150, or the JUBILEE, won the game; but any player spinning above this number retraced his steps by the number of squares he had overshot it. Players moving backwards were exempted from paying fines. (See plate 1.)

The title page of the book of rules is shown on plate 2, and three extracts are given of the rules, and of additional information contained in forty pages, designed to improve the minds of the young.

Picture 38 shows a gibbet. Rule 38: Jack the Painter hanged, March 10, 1776.—May the enemies of their country ever meet the same reward!

Enlargement: In 1776, Jack the Painter, alias James Aitken, was hanged on the 10th of March, for having wilfully set fire to the Rope-house in Portsmouth.

He had lately been in America, where he had imbibed an inveterate antipathy to England; and he resolved to vent it in setting fire to her dock-yards, and principal trading cities and towns. Previously to his execution, he confessed that he had informed an agent from America to Paris of his projects, and had been promised by him great rewards if he succeeded.

Picture 46 shows two men holding a banner labelled NO POPERY, with an inscription on a stone behind—RIOTS IN LONDON. Rule 46: Riots in London, 1780.—Go back to 38.

Enlargement: The year 1780 was disgraced by the RIOTS IN LONDON.

On this occasion a mob, supposed to consist of 50,000 persons, and headed by Lord George Gordon, marched to the House of Commons, and insulted many of the members; the chapels of the Sardinian and Bavarian ambassadors were demolished; the prisons of Newgate, the King's Bench, the Fleet and New Bridewell, were destroyed, and the prisoners liberated; the Bank of England was attempted; and a great number of houses were wrapped in flames, whilst another party of the rebels marched to cut off the pipes of the New River, and render abortive all attempts to extinguish the conflagration. For some time the Ministry remained inactive, and seemed to have been affected with no less terror than the citizens. But at length the military power was brought forward; Lord George Gordon was apprehended, and order and tranquillity were restored. On the subsequent meeting of Parliament, his Majesty lamented the necessity he had been under of employing force to suppress the riots; and an address of thanks was unanimously voted.

Picture 3 shows a Bank of England dollar. Rule 3: Dollars issued, 1804.— Receive one counter from the Bank.

Enlargement: Dollars were issued by the Bank of England as five shilling tokens, after being stamped with suitable impressions, at Mr. Bolton's (sic) mint, in Birmingham.

3. SQUARE BOARD RACE GAMES

AN ECCENTRIC EXCURSION TO THE CHINESE EMPIRE

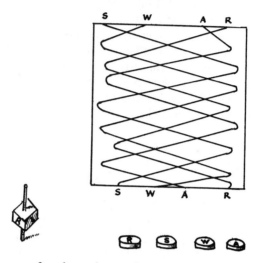

FIG. 6. Diagram of track, markers and totum of 'An Eccentric Excursion to the Chinese Empire' (Author's collection) see also plate 3.

The earlier tracks were spiral and mostly anticlockwise; (see *Jubilee, p.* 6, and the *Royal Game of Goose,* Volume I, p. 14); but under the influence of William Spooner, who had a business in London between 1836 and 1854, new styles of track were invented. His *Eccentric Excursion to the Chinese Empire,* published on 1 December 1843, is typical of many early Victorian games with multiple starting and finishing posts. (See plate 3.)

Equipment

1 A lithograph map of a fantastic countryside marked with four routes: a river traversed by a steamboat; a footpath; a railway track; and the course of an aerial machine. (This game was published sixty years before the momentous flight of the Wright brothers on 17 December 1903.)

2. A four-sided teetotum with a letter on each face, either A or S or R or W.

3. A marker for each player.

4. A number of counters. Mother-of-pearl 'fish' are excellent.

Each route is marked with a series of circles onto which the players move their pieces during the game. These circles bear letters of the mode of transport; and where one route crosses another, the circle contains both letters.

> S represents Steamboat
> W Walker
> A Aerial machine
> R Railway

It is important to realize that the players may switch from one mode of transport to another in their journey to the Celestial Empire.

Rules

1. Each player contributes three counters into a pool.

2. The starting point of each player is decided by spinning the teetotum; and if the route indicated has already been allotted to another player, another spin is made. If there are more than four players, they may be designated first walker, second walker, etc.

3. The steamboat traveller begins by spinning the teetotum, and moves from his starting place, marked S to the next circle if he turns up an S or an A, otherwise he remains stationary and passes the teetotum to walker, who spins and on a W can advance to the circle figured 1, on 'Muddy Island'; if S he moves to the circle figured 2, but he has to pay four counters into the pool. If A or R is uppermost he does not move, and the teetotum passes to the aviator. The railway passenger spins last. After either of the walker's opening moves he continues according to the ordinary rules of play.

4. Assuming that the steamboat traveller has moved to the first circle on his route, on his next spin he moves forward to the next circle on either of the letters R or S, but if he spins one of the other letters, he must move backwards down either route until he reaches a point bearing the letter that has been spun. In this instance it would be along the aerial to the next circle which is marked A/W. If this circle were occupied the two players would transpose their markers, but a player who is removed neither pays any fines nor wins any rewards which may be designated at his new position.

The other players spin in turn and move in the same way, forwards if possible, and if not then backwards to the nearest circle marked with the letter thrown. (Note. The markers do *not* have to remain on the route they set out upon.)

5. Players are not allowed to move over a circle, except for the walker on his first spin; nor onto a route unconnected with the circle upon which his marker stands.

'6. When a player reaches a circle with the single letter of his starting point, he *receives two counters* from the pool; but if the circle bears a single letter of any other method of transport, he must *pay two counters* into the pool. This payment is in addition to any fines or rewards mentioned on the map.

7. A player cannot move another's marker from a circle, if any other circle is available to him.

8. The player first reaching one of the circles marked GAME wins, and takes all the counters remaining in the pool.

SNAKES AND LADDERS

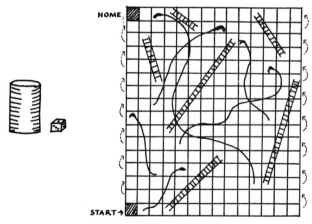

FIG. 7. Diagram of 'Snakes and Ladders'.

Success in this simple race game with a die is governed by luck, and children meet their elders on equal terms. Any number may play, each player having his own distinctive marker, which can only be entered on the board with a throw of 6. A player throwing a 6 has another turn, otherwise the die passes from player to player in a clockwise direction, The markers move on the number of squares indicated by the throw, and if a marker lands on the base of a ladder it moves to the top rung; while a marker landing on the head of a snake travels down to the tip of its tail. If a marker lands on a square occupied by a rival marker, the latter is sent back to the START.

The first player to reach HOME wins the game, and the other players continue for places.

4. OVAL AND ROUND RACE GAMES
THE GAME OF THE RACE

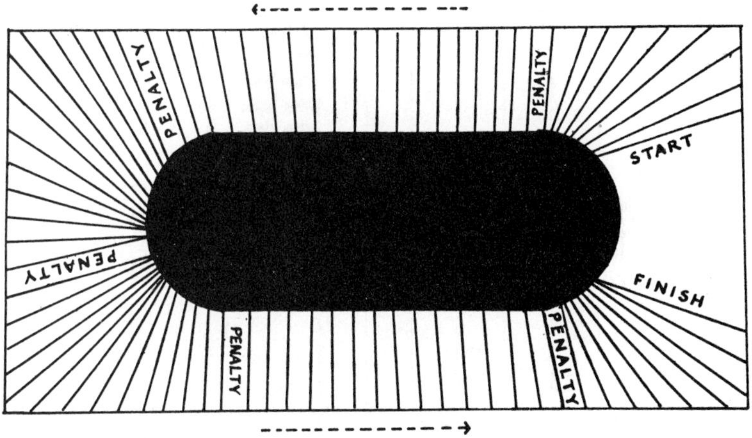

FIG. 8. Diagram of 'The Game of the Race'. (Author's collection).

The Game of the Race appeared about 1850. (See plate 4.) Each player had a little lead horse and jockey, the latter wearing well-known racing colours. The rider's progress in a steeplechase was controlled by the throw of a six-sided die. Along the course were hazards: at 11 the horse bolted; at 24 he fell into a stream; at

38 the horse balked at a high wall; at 54 the rider was thrown; at 67 the horse fell; and at 88 horse and rider lost their way.

The little horses are now collector's items, sought by followers of the turf; the colours worn by the jockeys recalling famous stables of the past. The tailpiece on page 23 shows one of these pieces from a set in the author's possession. Note the jockey sitting in the middle of the horse's back, and riding with a straight leg; instead of the more forward position and bent leg of the modern steeplechaser.*

*The horses were made galloping in a 'rocking-horse' action. The true motion of a galloping horse was only realized with the advent of high speed photography.

5. THE BACKGAMMON GROUP

THE BOTTLE GAME (Çoan ki)

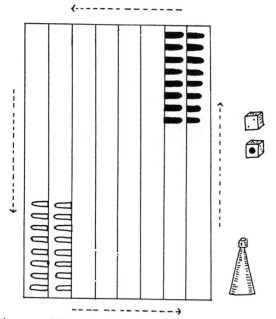

FIG. 9. Diagram of 'The Bottle Game'. (Adapted from T. Hyde's *De Ludis Orientalibus*, 1694.) Also see plate 5.

1. *The Jubilee.* Published by John Harris in 1810. (Author's collection.)

2. Title page of book of rules for the game of Jubilee.

3. *An Eccentric Excursion to the Chinese Empire*. Published by
William Spooner in 1843. (Author's collection.)

In *De Ludis Orientalibus*, 1694, p. 65, Dr. Thomas Hyde described the Chinese game of *Çoan ki*. Each player had sixteen bottle-shaped pieces two to three inches high of distinctive colour which were arranged on a board of eight lines as shown in fig. 9. The moves of the bottles were controlled by the throws of two six-sided dice: anticlockwise from left to right across the spaces; along the eighth space to the opponent's side of the board (this counted as one space); back across the board to the player's left side; and then down the board to take up the original position of the pieces at the start of the game. The first to accomplish this was the winner.

Rules

(Dr. Hyde's work is written in a vulgar Latin, and his meaning is not always clear. The following interpretation gives a playable game, which has some affinities to modern forms of Oriental backgammon.)

1. The dice are thrown alternately, and the scores are used to move bottles the directed number of spaces. This can be one bottle by the total score of the two dice, or two bottles each by the score of one die; and may be bottles which have already moved, or bottles which are still in their initial position.

2. Certain throws of the dice have special significance:

(*a*) On a throw of 1:1 a player must remove one of his bottles from the board, and pay a tenth part of his stake (*to his opponent?*).

(*b*) If doublets are thrown the player has a choice of either moving one bottle half the number thrown, or two bottles the whole number thrown: i.e. on a throw of 4:4, one bottle could be moved four spaces, or two bottles each eight spaces.

(*c*) If the throw forms a run, e.g. 5:6, making 11, the player may move one bottle five spaces and another eleven; or move two bottles at the same time ten spaces on, and then one of them to the next space which is the eleventh.

Hyde's description is incomplete. He does not mention what happens to throws which the player cannot utilize. Probably they were wasted. Nor does he describe the opening of the game; it is suggested that each player throws both dice, and the highest score counts, and the caster starts the game with this score.

The account does not relate what happens to a player who has lost a bottle on a throw of 1:1. It seems reasonable that he should continue with a slight advantage for which he has paid his opponent one tenth of his stake. He would only have to obtain fifteen bottles in their initial position to win the game. The mention of the word stake indicates that wagers were placed on the game.

BACKGAMMON

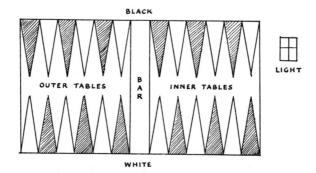

FIG. 10. Diagram of backgammon board

Several rules are common to most games of the backgammon group. To avoid repetition they are listed below:

1. The board consists of four sets of six elongated triangles known as points; each player has an INNER TABLE of six points, and an OUTER TABLE of six points, the two being separated by the BAR. By custom the inner tables are considered to be those nearer the source of light.(See fig. 10, and plate 6.)

2. The initial positions of the players' pieces vary from game to game. Moves are controlled by the throws of three dice (in some games two); each player tries to assemble all his pieces on his own inner table, and then bears them off the board with exact throws of the dice.

3. The scores on the dice may be used separately to move different pieces; or together to move one piece the total score, but in stages corresponding to the numbers on each die.

4. In most games a player cannot place more than five pieces on any one point, and is not allowed to place a piece on a point occupied by two or more opposing pieces.

5. If a player has a singleton, known as a BLOT, on a point, and his opponent moves a piece onto this point, even temporarily as a stage in a double move, the blot is HIT and put on the bar; it then has to enter the game again in the opponent's inner table.

6. While a player has a piece on the bar he is not allowed to move any other of his pieces.

7. The first player to bear all his pieces off the board wins the game.

There are many games played 'within the tables'; five were described in Volume I; five more will now be added to them.

THE ENGLISH GAME

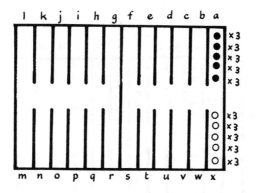

FIG. 11. Initial position of pieces for 'The English Game'

Three dice were used, or two and a constant imaginary throw of 6. White placed his fifteen men at x, and Black his fifteen men at a. White's pieces moved through the tables x–s, r–m, l–g, into f–a, where they were borne off. Black moved in the opposite direction. The player first bearing all his men off the board won the game. (See fig. 11.)

THE LOMBARD GAME

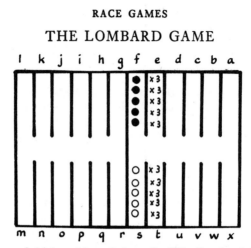

FIG. 12. Initial position of pieces for 'The Lombard Game'

The Lombard game was similar to the English Game except that Black started with fifteen men on f, while White's fifteen men started on s. This made the game a little shorter. (See fig. 12.)

THE IMPERIAL GAME

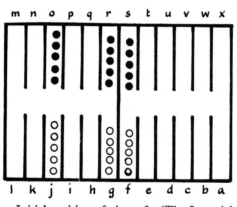

FIG. 13. Initial position of pieces for 'The Imperial Game'

Three dice were used. Black began with five men on o, five on r, and five on s. White's pieces were placed on j, g, and f. If Black brought all his men to x, before White's pieces reached, a, Black won, and *vice versa*. In this game each player remained on his own side of the board and there was no hitting of blots. (See fig. 13.)

THE PROVINCIAL GAME

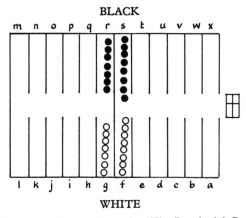

FIG. 14. Initial position of pieces for 'The Provincial Game'

Seven of White's men started on g, and eight on f. Black had seven men on r, and eight on s; otherwise the game was the same as Imperial. (See fig. 14.)

THE QUEEN'S GAME

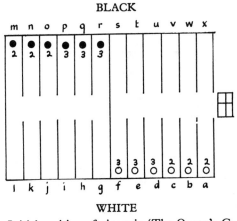

FIG. 15a. Initial position of pieces in 'The Queen's Game'

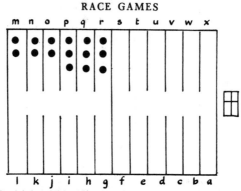

FIG. 15b. Position of Black's pieces when they have been unstacked,

Two dice are used in this simple game of luck. The players stack their pieces as in fig. 15a, and then unpile them in accordance with the throws of the dice: i.e. if Black throws 6:4 the top piece of stack r3 is lifted down onto r, and the top piece of stack p3 is lifted down onto p. When *all* the pieces are unstacked, they are stacked back into the original piles as they were at the beginning of the game.

When the piles have been reconstructed the pieces are borne off the board according to the throws of the dice, the black pieces travelling towards x, and the white towards l. Exact throws are required to bear pieces off the board, and the player emptying his side of the board first wins the game. Any throw which a player cannot use may be used by his opponent. If neither player can use a throw it is ignored and the game continues by alternate throws of the dice.

MYLIS

BLACK

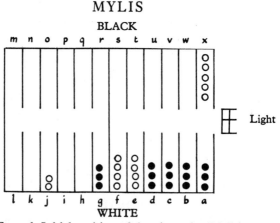

WHITE

FIG. 16. Initial position of the pieces for 'Mylis'

This was a variant of backgammon with the same rules (see Volume I, pages 44–6), but with a different initial position of the pieces. (See fig 16.)

White began with
$\begin{cases} 2 \text{ men on j.} \\ 4 \text{ men on f.} \\ 4 \text{ men on e.} \\ 5 \text{ men on x.} \end{cases}$

Black began with
$\begin{cases} 3 \text{ men on g.} \\ 3 \text{ men on d.} \\ 3 \text{ men on c.} \\ 3 \text{ men on b.} \\ 3 \text{ men on a.} \end{cases}$

At the end of each game the players exchanged colours. This is one of the very few examples in the series of the players starting from positions which were not symmetrically arranged; hence the need for the players to change pieces.

ICELANDIC BACKGAMMON (Kotra)

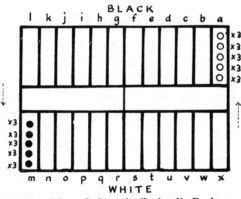

FIG. 17. Initial position of pieces in 'Icelandic Backgammon'

Kotra or Icelandic backgammon is similar to, but not identical with the Swedish game of Svenskt brädspel. They are both survivals of earlier forms of Tables played in Europe towards the end of the Middle Ages, and belong to a group of elaborate games which culminated in the Grand Tric-trac of France which was fashionable in aristocratic society.

Magical formulae were used in Iceland to obtain victory at chess, and others for kotra. One of these taken from a manuscript preserved in the archives of the Icelandic Literary Society, and once highly prized, runs:

'If thou wisheth to win at backgammon take a raven's heart, dry it in a spot on which the sun doth not shine, crush it and then rub it on the dice.'

Alternatively, others suggested:

'Take the tongue of a wagtail, and dry it in the sun; crush, and mix it afterwards with communion-wine, and apply it to the points of the dice, when you are sure to win.'

In an edition of the *Bualog* written about 1500 A.D. the fee for teaching kotra is given as eight ells of cloth, or about five crowns in Danish money.

Rules

1. Each player places his fifteen men on his opening point as shown in fig. 17, and then casts a single die. LOW plays first.

2. The opening player throws two dice and the scores may be used separately to move two pieces, or combined to move one: i.e. if Black makes a cast of 5:3, one piece may be moved to point r, another to point p; or one piece may be moved to one of these points, and then on to u. He cannot add the two scores together and move the piece in one step. The count is made from the point on which the piece stands. Black's pieces move in the direction from m to x, and a to l; and White's from a to l, and m to x.

3. If either player throws a double at his first cast only one piece can be moved, unless 6:6 is thrown when a special rule operates and four pieces are moved to g (White), or to s (Black).

4. While these four pieces remain together on g or s, they are vulnerable as if they were a single 'blot', and if they are hit all are sent off the board and must be re-entered in the usual way. Once one of these pieces has been moved, the other three are safe from attack except according to rule 7.

5. A player may not move a piece from the opponent's side of the board until he has moved five men from his starting point. (Except under rule 4.)

6. A player may not place more than one man on a point (except under rule 4), until he has a man on the furthest point of the opposite side of the board (l for White, or x for Black), then he may pile two or more pieces on any point on the far side of the board, or on his own.

7. A player may not place a piece on a point which contains two

or more enemy pieces unless it is impossible to pass a block of hostile pieces, when he can land on a point and capture the pieces on it, e.g. if White had men on s, t, u, v, w, x, Black could not pass even with a throw of 6, and therefore he can land on any point in accordance with the throw of his dice. It is therefore unwise to have two or more pieces on six consecutive points.

8. If it is possible a player throwing doublets must play the indicated number four times. (See modification in rule 3.)

9. A player may move a piece onto a point occupied by an opposing piece (blot), if the dice throw permits, and the captured piece must then be re-entered from the bar into the opponent's opening table.

10. A piece which has been sent off the board must be re-entered before any other of the player's pieces can be moved. This may mean a long wait, since the player cannot re-enter captured pieces on points which are already occupied by his own pieces, nor on points which are held by two or more enemy men.

11. The game may end in several ways:

(a) *By bearing the men off the board* Scores 2 points
When all a player's pieces have reached the bearing-off quarter of the board (e.g. Black's men are on the points g to l, or White's are on s to x), he may bear them off or move them up. In bearing off, doublets are most useful, for four men can be borne off at one turn of play. If a player throws a higher number than he can play when he is bearing off, he must bear off from his rear point. This may leave a blot and allow his opponent to capture it. If this happens the captured man must be re-entered in the player's entering quarter, and the player cannot bear off any more pieces until it has arrived back in the bearing-off table. The first player to bear off all his men scores 2.

(b) *Winning by a Jan* Scores 15 points
When a player has more men captured than there are empty points in his entry quarter, the points being filled with his own pieces, he is *Jan*, or blocked; e.g. if Black has five blots in the Black opening quarter, and White hits two more men and sends them off the board, Black can only re-enter one of them and then he is *Jan* or blocked. This ends the game and White scores 15.

(c) *Winning by Janstork* Scores 15 points

If a player has one or more men hit and there is no vacant point on which to enter them because all the points in the re-entering quarter are occupied by a mixture of his own blots and double points of his opponent, it is impossible to re-enter them and therefore the game is finished and the player becomes *Janstork*. His opponent scores 15 points.

SPECIAL METHODS OF WINNING

(*d*) *The Master's win* Scores 13 points
This is achieved if a player places all his men on his opponent's exit point, when the game is finished; e.g. if all Black's pieces are on l, or all White's pieces are on x. The winner scores 13 points.

(*e*) *The Little Monk* Scores 7 points
This is achieved by White having five men each on v, w, x, or Black having five men each on j, k, l. The winner scores 7 points.

(*f*) *The Big Monk* Scores 5 points
White must place three men each on the points t, u, v, w, x; or Black three men each on the points h, i, j, k, l. The winner scores 5 points.

(*g*) *A half Monk* A player gains half a Monk if he can get his men into a Monk position, either Little or Big, by using only half his throw; i.e. if White were playing for a Little Monk and had five men on x, five on w, four on v, and one on s. If he threw 6:3 he would only need the 3 to move the single piece from s to v, to score a Little Monk, but as he had not made use of the 6 which was also thrown, he would only score half the full score for a Little Monk, namely $3\frac{1}{2}$ points.

(*h*) *The Big Black* Scores 3 points
This is obtained by White getting three men on each of the points s, t, u, v, w, or Black three men on each of the points g, h, i, j, k. This scores 3 points.

(*i*) *The Little Master's win* Scores 3 points
This is achieved by White placing eight men on x, and seven men on w; or Black having eight men on l, and seven men on k. This mode of winning is only recognized by some players. It scores 3 points.

EXTRA POINTS

If a player hits and sends one of his opponent's men off the board in the throw which brings victory, the opponent is said to be *Mar*, and two extra points are added to the winner's score.

AFTER THROWS

If one player has borne off all his men before his opponent has borne off any, he scores 2 points for 'bearing off', but his opponent is then granted five, seven, or thirteen 'after throws' (the number varies in different parts of the island) to try to make a Big Monk, a Little Monk, or a Master, and if he succeeds he scores the full amount of the ending. Some players do not permit 'after throws', when Monks are very rare.

ADDITIONAL THROW

Some players allow the second player at the beginning of the game to have one more throw if his opponent has borne off all his pieces, and if he also manages to bear his off in the extra throw the game is declared drawn and both score 2 points.

If more than one game is played the player *bearing off*, or obtaining a *jan* plays first in the next game. Special Winnings do not count in this respect.

Lead horse and jockey from 'The Game of the Race' (page 11)

CHAPTER TWO

War Games

1. THE ALQUERQUE GROUP

FANORONA

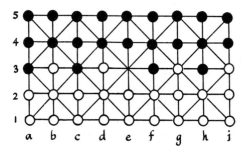

FIG. 18. Initial position of pieces in 'Fanorona', and notation key.

This Madagascan game was used in divinatory rituals; and during the storming of the capital by the French in 1895 the Queen and her advisers placed more faith for victory on the result of an official game between designated professionals than they did on their army.

Fanorona developed from Alquerque about 1680 by doubling the board, increasing the numbers of pieces to forty-four, and changing the method of capture. The board is shown in fig. 18, and may be inscribed on a flat stone or marked out on the ground. The central point is left empty, the other points being covered with pieces.

Rules

1. White starts and moves along any line to an adjacent empty point.

2. If a move ends on a point in contact with a point or points beyond *in the line of movement* occupied by enemy pieces in unbroken sequence, these are captured and removed. This is capture by APPROACH.

3. Capture may also be by WITHDRAWAL. If a player's piece moves away from a point contiguous with a point or points occupied by enemy pieces in *the line of movement*, these pieces are removed from the board.

4. Captures are compulsory, but on the first move by each player only one sequence can be taken.

5. On the second and later moves a player may make several captures, either by approach or withdrawal, but each move must be along a *different marked line;* i.e. the piece must change direction to make each capture.

6. If a move places enemy pieces in two directions *en prise*, the player can choose to remove the pieces in either direction, but not in both. He is not compelled to capture the larger number.

Readers may like to work through the following game played by two Malagasks and reported by Montgomery in 1896. The = sign is used to indicate the number of men captured by each move.

White			Black			White			Black		
1. e2–e3	=	2	f4–e5	=	3	11. h2–g2			a5–b5		
2. h1–h2	=	3	f3–f4	=	2	12. g2–f2			b2–c2		
			f4–g3	=	1	13. i3–h4			a3–b3		
			g3–f2	=	1	14. d3–c3	=	1	c4–c5	=	1
			f2–e2	=	4				c5–d5	=	1
			e2–e1	=	1	15. h4–g3			c1–d1		
			e1–f1	=	4	16. g3–f4			b5–b4		
3. g2–g3	=	2				17. f2–g2			c2–d2		
g3–h4	=	1				18. f4–e3	=	1	b4–c5		
h4–g4	=	1	f1–e1	=	1	19. e4–d4	=	1	a4–a3		
4. d3–e3	=	1				20. d4–d3	=	1	d1–d2	=	1
e3–f2	=	2				21. g2–g3			a3–b3		
f2–g3	=	1				22. g3–f3			b3–c3		
g3–f4	=	1				23. f3–g3			c3–d4		
f4–f3	=	1	a3–b2			24. g3–h4			d4–e3		
5. f3–e3			b2–b1	=	1	25. h4–h3			e3–f4		
6. e3–d4			b4–a3			26. h3–i3			d2–e3		
7. d4–d3	=	1	a3–b2			27. i3–h3			e3–f2		
8. g4–f4			b1–c1			28. h3–i3			f2–f3		
9. i2–h2			b5–b4			29. i3–i2			f4–g3 and wins		
10. f4–e5			b4–a3								

The second game is played differently. The defeated player starts, and the previous winner sacrifices piece after piece until he has lost seventeen. During this *vela* play the winner refrains from making any captures, and his opponent may only take one man at each move. Montgomery gave the following example of a *vela* game.

White			Black	White			Black	
1. d3–e3	=	1	c3–d3	18. i2–i3	=	1	h3–h4	= 2
2. e3–f3	=	1	d4–c3				h4–h3	= 1
3. d2–e3	=	1	g5–f4				g3–h2	= 1
4. e3–d4	=	1	h5–g5				h2–g1	= 1
5. e2–e3	=	1	b5–c5				g1–f2	= 1
6. e1–d2	=	1	i5–h5				f2–f3	= 1
7. b3–c3	=	1	c5–b5	19. f4–f5	=	1	g4–f4	= 1
8. b2–b3	=	1	a4–b4	20. f5–g5	=	1	f4–e3	= 1
9. d4–e4	=	1	d5–c5				e3–d3	= 1
10. c3–c4	=	1	b5–c5				d3–d2	= 1
11. d2–c3	=	1	c5–b5				d2–c3	= 1
12. b3–b4	=	1	h5–i5				c3–b2	= 1
13. e4–d4	=	1	e5–f4				b2–a3	= 1
14. d4–e4	=	1	g5–f4				a3–a4	= 1
15. e4–d4	=	1	g4–f4				a4–b4	= 1
16. d4–e4	=	1	i5–h5	21. c2–c3			a5–b5	
17. f3–f4	=	1	h4–g5	= 1	22. c3–d2	=	1	b5–c5
			g5–g4	= 3*	23. b1–b2			c5–c4	
				24. b2–a3 and wins.				

*There is a mistake here and black should continue:
g4–h4=2
h4–g3=1
g3–f4=2
f4–g5=1   R.C.B.

2. THE CHESS GROUP

Games of Chess may be recorded by using grid references (see fig. 19); and in forms of chess where the pieces are placed on the points, the lines instead of the areas are lettered and numbered (fig. 20).

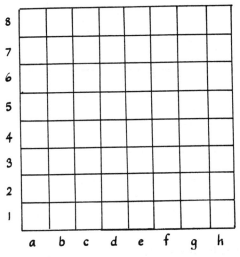

FIG. 19. Chess notation when played on the squares.

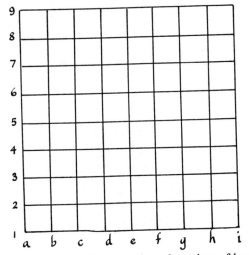

FIG. 20. Chess notation when played on the points of intersection.

BURMESE CHESS (Sittuyin)

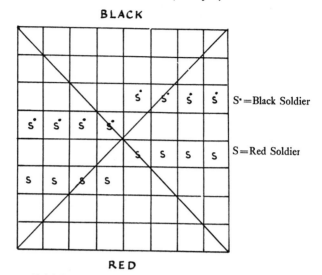

BLACK

S˙ = Black Soldier

S = Red Soldier

RED

FIG. 21. Initial placing of soldiers in 'Burmese chess'

Burmese chessboards are large and made like a shallow box for the comfort of the players who squat on the ground. At either end is a drawer to hold the chessmen when not in use. The playing surface may be chequered but is more commonly plain with the squares on the long diagonals marked in some way. See plate 7.

The chessmen are always carved figures, though the workmanship may be crude and stylized. They are usually made of wood and stained red and black. Ivory pieces are extremely rare.

FIG. 21a. A chariot from a Burmese chess set (Author's collection)

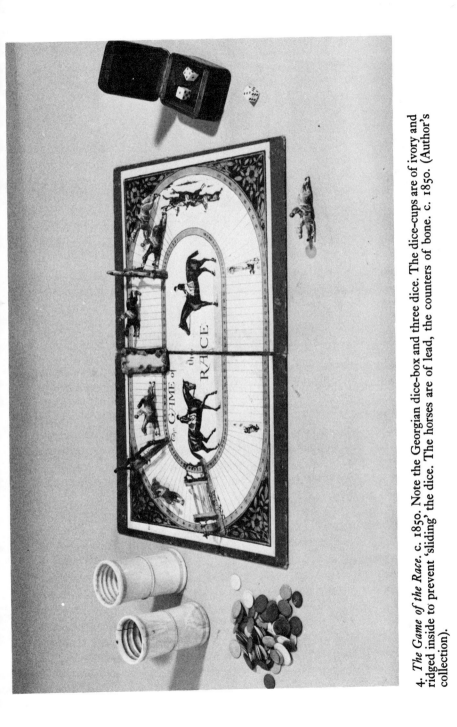

4. *The Game of the Race.* c. 1850. Note the Georgian dice-box and three dice. The dice-cups are of ivory and ridged inside to prevent 'sliding' the dice. The horses are of lead, the counters of bone. c. 1850. (Author's collection).

5. Reproduction board and pieces of *The Bottle Game*. (Made by the Author.) The dicing-cup is Chinese, c. 1850.

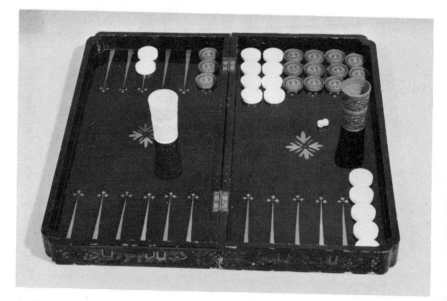

6. Chinese lacquered backgammon board; and tablemen and dicing-cups of ivory; all c. 1830. The pieces are arranged for the start of *Mylis*, see page 18. (Author's collection.)

Each player starts with:

Number	Piece	Equivalent	Power of move
8	soldiers	pawn	One square forwards, but captures one square diagonally forwards.
2	elephants	bishops	One square backwards or forwards along a diagonal, or one square orthogonally forwards.
2	horsemen	knights	The knight's leap of European chess.
2	carriages	castle	Orthogonally any number of unoccupied squares.
1	commander	queen	One square diagonally, backwards or forwards.
1	king	king	One square in any direction.

At the beginning of the game the soldiers are placed as in fig. 21, and then the players place their major pieces alternately on any vacant square on their own half of the board. Usually the kings stand on g2 and b7; the horsemen support each other; one elephant is placed next to the king; and the carriages on files that are comparatively empty of pieces, ready to break through as soon as possible. A major piece may be placed on a square occupied by a soldier, the latter then being placed elsewhere behind the row of soldiers.

When all the pieces are on the board the players may continue to rearrange their major pieces by abnormal moves, moving one piece in each turn of play, until a soldier is moved, when both players must continue only with legal moves of the chessmen. Most Burmese have favourite arrangements of their pieces; though these formations may require modification to meet the opponent's disposition.

Any soldier moving onto a square on either of the long diagonals can be promoted to a commander, provided that the player has no commander on the board. In promotion the new commander may occupy the square of the soldier, or any adjacent square not commanded by an opponent's piece. Promotion of a soldier is only to commander; no other captured piece may return to the board.

If a player whose turn it is to play has a soldier standing on a marked square, and no commander on the board, he can if he wishes, promote the soldier without moving. This may be a valuable privilege when to move could be disastrous. If a soldier passes beyond the marked square it can no longer be promoted.

Stalemate is unknown in Burmese chess as a player is not permitted to place his opponent in this position; he must leave room for play.

Comments The shorter moves of the pieces brings them into close contact, giving rise to a mêlée of battle absent in European chess with the abstract development of power upon specific squares by pieces at a distance. The feeling of physical conflict in Burmese chess is heightened by the realistic shape of the pieces. See plate 7.

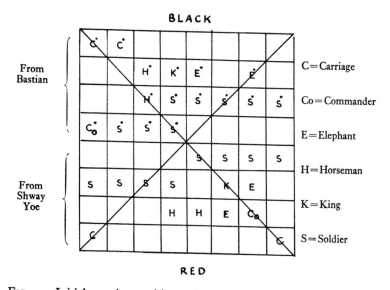

FIG. 22. Initial opening positions of pieces in 'Burmese chess.' Black after Bastian; Red, from Shway Yoe.

SIAMESE CHESS (Mak-ruk)

BLACK

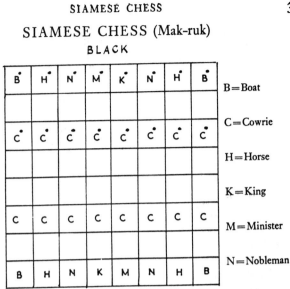

B = Boat

C = Cowrie

H = Horse

K = King

M = Minister

N = Nobleman

WHITE

FIG. 23. Initial position of pieces in 'Siamese chess'

Siamese chessboards are unchequered. See plate 8. The chessmen are of conventional shape, their names and moves being:

Number	Piece	Equivalent	Power of move
8	cowrie shells*	pawn	One square vertically forward; capture one square diagonally forward.
2	nobleman	bishop	One square vertically forward, or diagonally one square backwards or forwards.
2	horse	knight	The knight's leap of European chess.
2	boat	rook	Orthogonally any number of empty squares.

*Real cowrie shells are often used, mouth down before promotion, and mouth up afterwards.

Number	Piece	Equivalent	Power of move
1	minister	queen	One square diagonally forwards or backwards; and two squares vertically forwards on its first move only, if desired.
1	king	king	One square in every direction. On its first move it may use the knight's leap.

At the beginning of the game the pieces are arranged as in fig. 23. Note that the kings are placed crosswise, and the minister stands at the king's right. The cowries are on the third rank. Promotion occurs when a cowrie reaches the opposing initial cowrie rank, the player's sixth row. A cowrie reaching this row becomes a minister, and there is no limit to the number of ministers a player may have at one time. Promotion is indicated by turning the piece upsidedown.

The end game tends to be tedious. To reduce this, there are special rules relating to a solitary king. When only the opponent's king remains, a player must secure checkmate within a prescribed number of moves, which are calculated by subtracting the number of pieces left on the board from a basic number, the latter depending upon the strength of the pieces remaining in play.

Pieces in play	Basic number	Pieces on board	Moves allowed
Two boats	8	4	4
One boat	16	3	13
Two noblemen	22	4	18
One nobleman	44	3	41
Two horses	33	4	29
One horse	66	3	63
One minister	—	3	Drawn game
Minister and 2 Cowries	88	5	83
Minister, nobleman, horse and boat	16	6	10

If a player does not achieve checkmate in the moves allowed the game is drawn. Stalemate is also a drawn game.

JAPANESE CHESS (Sho-gi)

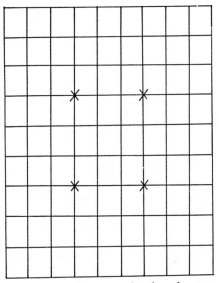

FIG. 24. Japanese chessboard

Japanese chess or the Generals' Game is played on a little table with its upper surface marked into a rectangle which is divided into 9 × 9 = 81 smaller rectangles. At one end of the table is a drawer to hold the pieces when not in use. The pieces are placed on the spaces and not on the points as in the Chinese and Korean chess from which it was probably derived. Paper boards are also used. At the four corners of the central block of nine spaces are small dots or crosses, to mark the three rows at each end of the board, the respective territories of the players, upon which they place their pieces at the beginning of the game. When a piece passes into enemy territory it may be promoted if the player wishes.

FIG. 25. Pieces in Japanese Chess. The original rank on the left, and after promotion on the right.

The chessmen are shaped like little coffins and made of wood or ivory. They are thicker at the base than at the point, and differ slightly in size, the soldiers and pikemen being narrower than the

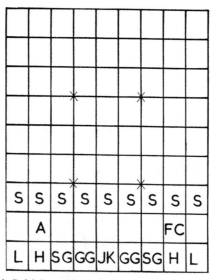

FIG. 26. Initial position of pieces in 'Japanese Chess'.

other pieces. Each chessman bears its rank on the upper surface; and its promoted rank beneath. Most pieces become a gold general on promotion; but the original rank is indicated without turning the piece over by the manner in which the word 'gold' is written. The original rank may decide which piece to capture when there is a choice.

The pieces of both players are alike; but each places his forces with the point towards his opponent. When a player promotes a piece he merely turns it over to show its new rank. Each player starts with twenty pieces:

Number	Japanese name	Translation	Promotion
1	O-sho	Jewelled king	—
2	Kin-sho	Gold general	—
2	Gin-sho	Silver general	Kin-sho
2	Kei-ma	Honourable horse	Kin-sho
1	Hisha	Flying chariot	Ryo-wo*
1	Kakko	Angle-going	Ryo-ma†
2	Yari	Lance	Kin-sho
9	Fu-hyo	Soldiers	Kin-sho

*Ryo-wo is a Dragon King with the move of O–sho+Hisha
†Ryo-ma is a Dragon Horse with the move of O–sho+Kakko

MOVES OF THE PIECES

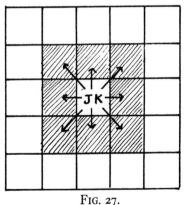

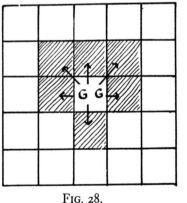

FIG. 27.
Jewelled King one space
in every direction

FIG. 28.
Gold General one space orthogonally
or one space diagonally forwards

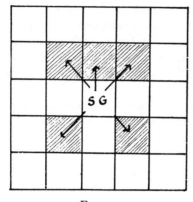

FIG. 29.
Silver General one space diagonally,
or one space forward

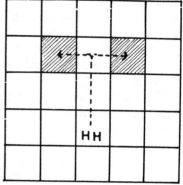

FIG. 30.
Honourable Horse
(only the two most forward
of the Western Knight's leaps)

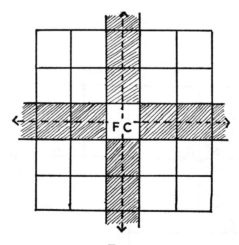

FIG. 31.
Flying Chariot any distance orthogonally

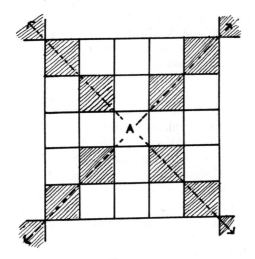

FIG. 32.
Angle-going any distance diagonally

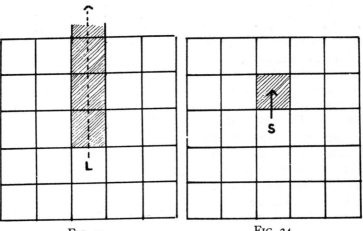

FIG. 33.
Lance any distance vertically
forwards

FIG. 34.
Soldier one space vertically
forwards

When a piece enters enemy territory it may be turned over and promoted. This is done in the same move as its entry onto the qualifying space, but promotion may be delayed to a later turn if the player wishes; an honourable horse with its power of leaping may be preferable to the more powerful gold general, since the check of the honourable horse cannot be covered.

The unique feature of Japanese chess is the reintroduction of captured pieces into the player's own forces. Instead of moving one of his men a player may enter a prisoner onto any unoccupied space. This addition of strength makes capturing doubly valuable —the enemy is weakened by the loss of the piece, and it becomes available for inclusion in one's own forces at an opportune moment. Reintroduction is controlled by rules:

1. A second soldier cannot be entered on a file containing one of the player's unpromoted soldiers. If a player accidentally does so, the piece is huffed and his opponent continues his own move.

2. A soldier cannot be entered upon the opponent's back row, nor an honourable horse on his two back rows, since these pieces could not move, and could not be promoted.

3. A re-entered piece only possesses its original value even if it is entered within the opponent's territory; but in the latter event it qualifies for promotion on making its first move.

4. Checkmate cannot be given by a 'dropped' soldier, but it may be dropped to give check followed by forced mate on the next move.

First move in the opening game is usually decided by tossing up a soldier; the other player calling 'soldier' or 'general'. The winner of a game begins the next; and in tournaments the match is decided on the best of three games. The 'touch and move' rule is strictly observed. The game is drawn if a king penetrates enemy territory.

There are about ten million Sho-gi players in Japan, and the leading hundred are classed as professionals. The Meijin-sen, or match between the title holder and the leading contender, is held annually; and the winner bears the title 'Meijin'. The best Sho-gi boards and men are used in the Meijin-sen matches, the boards being of Japanese torreya wood, the pieces of boxwood, and small piece boards to hold captures, of wood from the mulberry tree. Such sets may cost nearly £500.

Readers who wish to study Japanese chess in more detail should consult Trevor Leggett's excellent book (see Bibliography).

KRIEGSPIEL

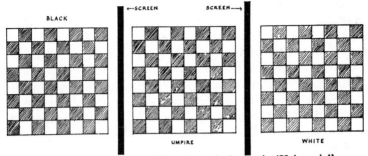

BLACK   ←---SCREEN   SCREEN---→

UMPIRE   WHITE

FIG. 35. Arrangement of boards and players in 'Kriegspiel'

Kriegspiel is often regarded as a variant of chess by those who have never played it; and as a game in its own right by those who have; but a good knowledge of chess is required to play success-fully. There are three chess boards and sets of chessmen; two screens; two players; and an umpire. The boards and players are arranged as in fig. 35, with the players on opposite sides of their respective boards, and separated by the screens and the umpire and his board. The umpire can look at all three boards, but the players only their own. Each board is set up for a game of chess. The choice of black or white is decided by one of the players taking a white pawn and a black pawn, shuffling them behind his back, and then holding out both closed fists to his opponent who chooses one, and when it is opened the chooser plays the colour of the pawn exposed.

White starts, and each move is duplicated by the umpire on his master-board. As the game proceeds each player will have his own men correctly placed, but has to guess the positions of his oppon-ent's pieces; and will be continually modifying his assessment. Only the umpire's board shows the true state of the game.

Rules

(a) The umpire

The game starts by the umpire calling on White to move; and at the completion of each move throughout the game he announces, 'Played', and the move passes to the opponent.

He is responsible for preventing illegal or impossible moves by stating, 'Not a move', but gives no reason, and the player must then try some other move.

The players are not allowed to address the umpire, except when a player with the move wishes to try for pawn captures. He is entitled to try each pawn diagonally in turn until he either makes a capture or realizes that there are none to make. This would produce a series of 'Not a move', from the umpire, and to save time the player may ask, 'Have I any pawn captures?' and the umpire replies, 'No pawn captures', or 'Try'. These calls are usually abbreviated to 'Pawns?'—'No pawns'—'Try'.

If the umpire says 'Try', the player *must* make at least one try but need not proceed any further. The only exception to this is that if there is only one possible capture on the umpire's board, and this is also obvious to the player, i.e. only one pawn is in a position to capture, the others being blocked by his own men, the umpire will not answer 'Try', but will announce the capture.

Captures are announced by the umpire naming the square concerned—e.g. 'Capture king 4'. The square relates to the player whose piece has been captured. (If White played onto his own queen 6th with a capture, the umpire would announce, 'Capture queen 3rd', addressing Black.)

Checks are announced together with the direction: e.g. 'Check rank', 'Check file', or with a diagonal check, by the long or short diagonal relative to the checked king, 'Check long', or 'Check short'. Checks by a knight are given as such, i.e. 'Check knight'.

The object of the game is to mate the opposing king.

(*b*) The players

If chess clocks are used to limit the time taken on moves, each player is responsible for the *whole* manipulation of his 'double' clock. The umpire's clock is the final arbiter.

Comments

Players usually take it in turns to be umpire, but the umpire must be an experienced player with a very clear mind. He must carry a mental picture of the true state of the game as given on his board and apply it instantly to the more or less garbled forms shown on the players' boards. The umpire requires an above average chess ability, and the players the wit to interpret the curt announcements of the umpire, and to estimate possibilities and probabilities by deductive and intuitive reasoning. A player must be able to carry several lines of possible enemy development in his mind for several moves until some confirmation is received one way or the other.

The game develops on a different plane from international chess and calls for quicker and more retentive thought. The king comes into his own as a valuable fighting piece, probing the enemy lines, and in an expert's hands is a joy to watch.

Although the game is normally only played by very experienced chess players of match class, it can be enjoyed by any competent chess player *provided* that the *umpire* is experienced (this is essential), and the players are reasonably matched.

(The author is indebted to Mr. H.D. Rengger for the above account. Mr. Rengger belonged for many years to the 'Gambit'; a luncheon and chess club in the City of London which unfortunately was demolished for a new office block. Some of the finest chess and kriegspiel players in the country used to gather there, and the standard of play was very high.)

3. THE DRAUGHTS GROUP

TURKISH DRAUGHTS

This game was described in Volume I, pages 73–4. A few months ago the author obtained a Turkish draughts set in London which was said to be eighteenth century—a statement easy to make and difficult to prove. The pieces are of ivory, one side being green and white, and the other red and white. The bases are hollowed out to accept the spires of the piece underneath when a king is formed. (See the tailpiece, page 54, and also plate 10.) The set is standing on a modern Indian chess board bought at the same time.

Haar Hoolim, writing from Israel on 27 September 1967 says:

'Last week I was again in old walled Jerusalem and saw another Turkish checker game with the same rules as yours. (As described in Volume I.) The board was a low table, a sort of bench but raised around the border so the pieces won't ever roll off; square, each square being nearly 2″ by 2″, or 16″ by 16″ for the board. The board was dirty from much use and the pieces were a surprise; huge pawns bigger than any chess piece including the king. They were kept in a drawer under the board, were red and some other colour.'

The next two games are not forms of draughts; but have some similarities to this group and therefore, for want of a better place, are included here.

FOUR FIELD KONO (Nei-pat-ko-no)

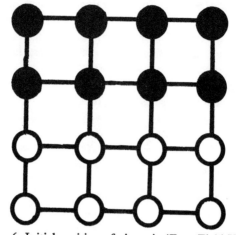

FIG. 36. Initial position of pieces in 'Four Field Kono'

In this Korean game each player has eight pieces arranged on a
board as in fig. 36. Black moves first. The pieces capture by jumping
over one of their own pieces onto an enemy piece on the point
immediately beyond. When not capturing the pieces move orthogonally one point at a time. The object of the game is to capture or
block the opposing force.

TIGERS AND OXEN (Sua ghin gnua)

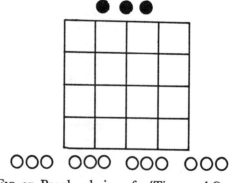

FIG. 37. Board and pieces for 'Tigers and Oxen'

This Siamese game is played on a board of twenty-five points. One player has three tigers and the other twelve oxen. The pieces are introduced onto the points by alternate moves of play; when the three tigers are in position they can move along a line to the nearest point, or jump over an ox by a short leap, when the latter is removed from the board. When all the oxen are in position, and only then, they may also move to any adjacent point along a line.

The oxen try to hem in and corner the tigers to prevent them moving; while the tigers endeavour to destroy the oxen.

4. THE TAFL GROUP

THROW-BOARD (Tawlbwrdd)

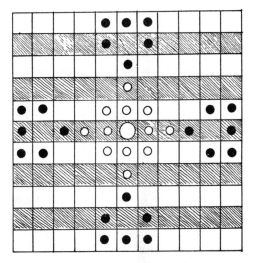

White 12 men and a king.   Black 24 men.

FIG. 38. Reconstruction of possible initial position of pieces in Tawlbwrdd

This ancient Welsh game appears to have been introduced by the Norsemen, though records are tantalisingly incomplete. The Laws of Howel Dha were drawn up between A.D. 914 and 943, and mention is made of a Tawl-bwrdd or 'Throw-board' being one of the gifts given to a judge on taking office.

In appendix E of Forbes' *History of Chess* is a quotation from the Dimetian Code b.2,c.35 5–20:

The king's throwboard is six score pence in value; a throwboard of the bone of a sea animal [? a whale] is three score pence in value; a throwboard of any other bone is thirty pence in value; a throwboard of a hart's antler is twenty-four pence; a throwboard of a bullock's horn twelve pence; a throwboard of wood four legal pence. (At this time a silver penny had a purchasing power about equal to a modern pound note).

In Welsh *tawl* is a throw, and a *tawlbwrdd* in its literal sense is a throw-board. This may indicate that some form of dice were employed in the game.

A manuscript in the Welsh National Library written by Robert ap Ifan in 1587 contains a description of tawlbwrdd and a drawing of the board. The latter consists of 11 × 11 squares, and the second, fourth, sixth, and eight columns are shaded. (Possibly the tenth column should also have been shaded as shown in fig. 38 above.) A translation of Ifan's account runs:

The above board must be played with a king in the centre and twelve men in the places next to him; and twenty-four lie in wait to capture him. These are placed, six in the centre of every end of the board and in the six central places. Two players move the pieces, and if one belonging to the king comes between the attackers, he is dead and is thrown out of the play; and if one of the attackers comes between two of the king's men, the same.

If the king himself comes between two of the attackers and if you say 'Watch your king' before he moves onto that space, and he is unable to escape, you catch him. If the other says gwrheill [?] and goes between two, there is no harm. If the king can go along the ——*line that side wins the game.

*indecipherable.

There is a mistake in the original description or the translation. Six in the centre of every end of the board, and six in the central places makes a total of thirty attacking pieces. Only twenty-four 'Lie in wait to capture him'.

The arrangement in fig. 38 nearly satisfies the account, and makes a playable game. The —— may refer to the periphery.

Suggested rules

1. The pieces are placed on the board as in fig. 38.

2. Each player has a six-sided die, and the players throw alternately.

3. If a player throws an odd number, he may move one of his pieces; if he throws an even number he misses a move.

7. Burmese chessboard of teak, and pieces of pinkadoe. Modern, but traditional forms. (Author's collection.) Opening positions advised by Bastian, and Shway Yoe.

8. Siamese chessboard and pieces. Modern, but traditional forms. (Author's collection.)

9. Reproduction Japanese chessboard and pieces, arranged for the start of a game. (Made by the author.)

10. Modern Indian draughtsboard, with eighteenth century Turkish ivory draughtsmen coloured red and green; see Vol. I, pps. 73–4. Note there are only twelve pieces instead of the usual sixteen. (Author's collection.)

4. Any piece can move orthogonally any number of vacant squares. (The rook's move in chess.)

5. A capture is made by trapping an enemy piece, including the king, between two of the player's pieces on rank or file, but not diagonally.

6. Only the king may move onto the square between two enemy pieces, without being captured, and then only after declaring his intention by calling 'Resting'.

7. All pieces may pass safely between two enemy pieces without stopping on the intervening square.

8. White wins if his king reaches any square on the periphery of the board, and loses if the monarch is captured.

FITHCHEALL

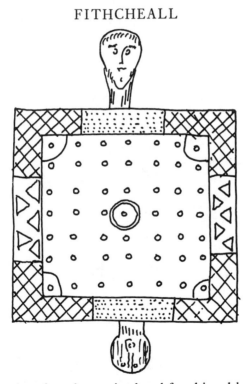

FIG. 39. Drawing of wooden gaming-board found in a lake-dwelling at Ballinderry.

On 7 October 1932 *The Times* published an account of a wooden board 9½" square, with 7×7 holes for pegs, which had been found in a crannog or lake-dwelling at Ballinderry, near Moate, Co. Westmeath, Ireland. The central hole was surrounded by a circle, and the four corner holes by quadrants. The board was framed with tenth-century patterns suggestive of manufacture in the Isle of Man. The board had two handles carved as heads, though one seems small to hold, unless it were for a child. See fig. 39.

In the appendix of Forbes' *History of Chess* is a description of a Fithcheall board, taken from *The Book of Rights* by John O'Donovan, which was published about 1847.

It was a board of silver and pure gold, and every angle was illuminated with precious stones, and a man-bag of woven brass wire. Midir than arranged the fithcheall. 'Play', said Midir. 'I will not except for a wager,' replied Eochaidh.... The rest of the mystical description of the encounter of the two men is irrelevant.

Those with taste for puzzles may like to ponder: could this little wooden board be for fithcheall? How was the game played? The period (tenth century) and the source (Isle of Man) suggests that it was probably some form of tafl.

ASALTO (Officers and Sepoys)

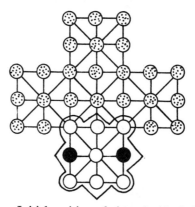

FIG. 40. Initial position of pieces in 'Asalto'

Asalto is a late form of Fox and Geese (see Volume I, page 76). The pieces can move along the marked lines orthogonally or diagonally. During the Indian Mutiny the game was renamed Officers

and Sepoys, and a fine board in the possession of Mr. D.I. Duff
probably belongs to this period. He writes in a letter:

The board is about 7½″ square, and seems to have been made in India where I probably picked it up at a house sale; but there were no 'men' to fit the peg holes. though
any pegs of the correct size would do. It is attractively inlaid with ivory, and the cross
lines in the squares are also inlaid. Four of the large squares are white, and the fifth
green. . . .

The green square represents a fort, and one player places two
officers on any two points within its walls. His opponent controls
the moves of twenty-four sepoys who occupy all the points in the
neighbouring countryside. All pieces move one point along any
marked line, but the sepoys must always move towards the fort.
The officers capture by a short leap, but are subject to *huffing*. If a
capture is possible an officer is removed from the board if he fails
to take a sepoy. The sepoys win if they occupy every point in the
fort, or if they trap the officers and render them unable to move;
but if they are depleted until this becomes impossible, the officers
are victorious. (See plate 11).

THE TIGER GAME (*Pulijudam* from India)

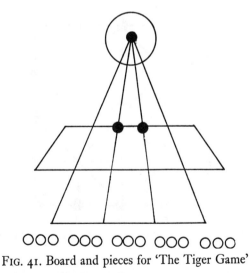

FIG. 41. Board and pieces for 'The Tiger Game'

This game appears to be a modification of Fox and Geese (see
Volume, I, p. 76).

Three tigers are placed on the board at the points shown in fig. 41. The other player has fifteen lambs which are placed one at a time on any point of intersection; alternating with the moves of a tiger. The tigers try to jump over a lamb in a short leap, and when one does so the lamb is 'Killed' and removed from the board. The lambs cannot move until they are all on the board, and then they move along a line to the next point.

If the lambs can immobilize the tigers they win the game, but if they become too weak to do so the tigers triumph.

5. THE LATRUNCULORUM GROUP

SIXTEEN SOLDIERS (Shap luk kon tsu tseung kwan)

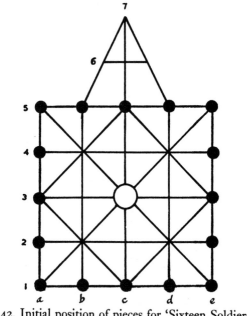

FIG. 42. Initial position of pieces for 'Sixteen Soldiers'

This game is popular with Chinese children and labourers; the board often being found marked out in the dust of quiet roads.

One player has sixteen rebel soldiers, and the other their loyal

TAB 49

general. The pieces are placed as in fig. 42. All the pieces move one point along any marked line, but only the general may enter the triangular sanctuary, referred to as 'the privy'. If he is confined there and is unable to make an exit, however, his player loses the game.

The methods of capturing by the general and the rebels are different: the former captures by occupying the point immediately between two rebels on the same marked line when he takes them both by *intervention;* while the latter capture by occupying the points immediately on both side of the general, all three being on the same marked line, known as *custodian* capture.

The rebels make the first move.

An example of play

Black moves e2 to d2. White replies c3 to b2, capturing the rebels on a3 and c1 by intervention; but his triumph is short lived. Black moves d2 to c2 and takes the general by custodian capture, and wins the game.

6. RUNNING-FIGHT GAMES

TAB

This game for two players is popular among the lower classes in Egypt. The board is often scratched on the ground and consists of four rows of nine squares (see fig. 43). Each player has nine pieces of his own colour called 'dogs'. These may be pieces of pot, brick, or stones and are placed on his home squares. Four split sticks about

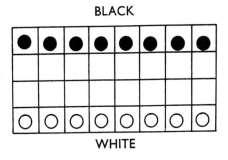

FIG. 43. Initial position of pieces in 'Tab'

eight inches long are thrown against a wall or upright stick driven into the ground. The throws score:

One flat side up = 1 (called TAB)
Two flat sides up = 2
Three flat sides up = 3
Four flat sides up = 4
Four round sides up = 6

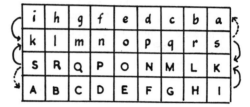

FIG. 44. Notation and direction of movement of the pieces

On scoring 1, 4, or 6, a player throws again; but on a throw of 2 or 3, the turn passes to his opponent. One player owns the squares marked A, B, C, D, E, F, G, H, I, and the other a, b, c, d, e, f, g, h, i; the two central rows being neutral with pieces circulating along them in the direction of the arrows.

Rules

1. At the beginning of the game the players throw the sticks alternately until one throws *tab*, and then he continues to throw until he obtains a 2 or a 3. Suppose the opening player threw tab and 4 and 2. He would lift the dog from square I and place it in the seventh square from I in the nearest neutral row, which is Q. He must always start with the dog in square I, and then square H, then square G, etc. His opponent starts from square i.

2. No dog can be moved from its original square except on a throw of tab. While dogs are in their initial position they are known as 'Christians'; but on moving they become 'Muslims' and are privileged to fight. Each time a player throws tab he usually converts

TAB 51

a christian into a muslim, until all are true believers and able to circulate.

3. Each player may have any number of dogs in circulation at the same time.

4. When a dog reaches the end of the neutral squares he may either repeat the same round, or enter his adversary's row, as long as there is an enemy dog remaining in that row: but the intruder does not continue to circulate except under rule 9.

5. Whenever a throw, or any of two or more throws enables a player to move a dog onto a square occupied by an opponent's dog, the latter is captured and removed from the board. If one player had a dog on m, and the other has one on o, and another on s, and the first player threw tab, 4 and 2, then by the throw of 2 the dog in o is captured; the throw of 4 captures the dog in s; and by the throw of tab he could pass into a, and take a third dog if the square contained one.

6. A player may move one of his dogs onto a square already occupied by one of his own, and these may be added to a third or more. Such harnessed dogs circulate together as if they were one; but the player cannot divide them again and move them separately except on the throw of tab.

7. If harnessed dogs are made to pass back into a row through which they have already passed either separately or together, they become reduced to a single dog; but the player need not use such a throw; he may wait until he throws tab. Harnessing dogs speeds their progress to safety; but they can be captured, or make captures, as if they were a single piece.

8. A dog entering the opponent's row is safe since the latter's dogs cannot return to their home row.

9. A dog cannot circulate through the opponent's row until the player has no dog remaining in his own row; or has only harnessed dogs in this row, and does not throw tab, which allows him to divide them.

10. In circulating through an opponent's row a dog moves in order of the letters on the diagram.

11. Once a dog has passed through the opponent's row it cannot return; but must circulate only through the two middle rows.

12. The player who losses all his dogs loses the game.

7. LOST GAMES

Two games will be described under this heading in the hope that some reader will be able to supply the missing rules. Both original descriptions are so incomplete that it is not even possible to determine the group to which they belong.

CHUKI

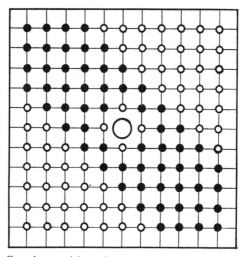

Fig. 45. Opening position of pieces in 'Chuki'. (After S. Culin)

Stewart Culin's account in *Chess and Playing-cards*, pp. 872-4, contains a diagram of the board, reproduced above in fig. 45, and the description:

> . . . Chuki is a game played upon a board in the form of a small table, marked with squares, ten* on a side. The four squares in the centre of the board are in part occupied with a small raised square 'place of the bowl'; leaving one hundred and twenty points of intersection exposed, on which sixty white and sixty black stones are arranged. Two persons play alternately, letting three dice fall in a bowl, which is set on the raised square in the middle, and taking off the board the pieces of the thrower, according to the casts.

Culin also gives a drawing of a chuki table, which was 6½″ high and 16″ square, from Johore, Straits Settlements. Three dictionaries are quite unhelpful and contradictory:

1852, Crawford, *Malay and English Dictionary*, pp. 39, 62. *Chuke*, name of a game resembling draughts.

*The drawing shows twelve.

1875, Favre, *Dict. malais-français*, 1:491. *Xuki*, sorte de jeu d'échecs.

1880, Von Wall and Van der Tuuk, *Maleisch-Nederlandsch woordenboek*, 2:46. *Tjoeki*, a sort of backgammon, with two dice and fifty-two pieces of two different colours on opposite sides, which are usually of Chinese porcelain.

TOTOLOSPI (2)*

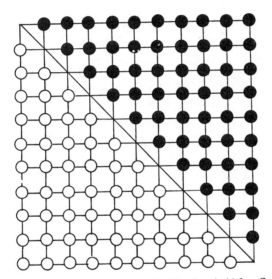

FIG. 46. Opening position of pieces in Totolospi. (After S. Culin)

In *Chess and Playing Cards*, pp. 879-80, Culin reports a game played by the Moki Indians of New Mexico, and gives a drawing of of the board reproduced in fig. 46. Apparently figures of this game were cut into the rocks near the village of Walpi.

Totolospi can be played by two or more parties. A rectangular figure divided into a large number of squares, is drawn upon the rock, either by scratching or by using a different coloured stone as a crayon. A diagonal line, *tuh-ki-o-ta*, is drawn across the rectangle from northwest to southeast and the players station themselves at each end of this line. When two parties play, a single person acts as player and the other members of the party act as advisers.

*Not to be confused with a different game of the same name, see page 5.

The first play is won by tossing a leaf or corn husk with one side blackened. The pieces which are used are bean or corn kernels, stones and wood, or small fragments of any substance of marked colour. The players were stationed at each end of the diagonal line. They move their pieces upon this line, but never across it. (On this line the game is fought.) The moves are intricate, and the player may move one or more pieces successively. Certain positions entitle him to this privilege. He may capture, or as he terms it, kill one or more of his opponents at one play. In this respect the game is not unlike checkers, and to capture the pieces of the opponent seems to be the main object of the game. The checkers, however, must be concentrated and always moved toward the southeast corner.

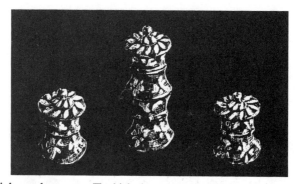

Eighteenth century Turkish draughtsmen (Author's collection)

CHAPTER THREE

Games of Position

MORRIS GAMES

ACHI

FIG. 47. Board and pieces for 'Achi'

Achi is played by Ghanese school children; the board being marked out on the ground, and each player has four little sticks, one player's having the bark left on, and the other's being peeled. Alternatively, coloured stones may be used. In the first phase the markers are entered onto the points of the board in alternate turns of play; and when the eight pieces are in position, the second phase begins, when each player moves one marker one point along a line at each turn of play, attempting to obtain three markers in a row. The first player to achieve this is the winner. (See fig. 47.)

Achi is better known in the West as Tic-Tac-Toe, and was played by Roman soldiers throughout their empire. Recently a stone marked for the game has been recovered at the Roman Station of Corstopitum (Corbridge) in Northumberland, and dates from the third or fourth century A.D.

2. BLOCKING GAMES

PONG HAU K'I

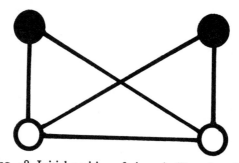

FIG. 48. Initial position of pieces in 'Pong hau k'i'

In Korea this game is known as Ou-moul-ko-no; Pong hau k'i being its name in Canton, China. Each player has two stones of his own colour which are placed as in fig. 48, and they move one stone at a time in alternate turns of play along any line to the next empty point; their object being to block the opponent's stones.

Instead of starting from a set position, some players place their stones at the beginning of the game on any point in alternate turns of play, and then continue as described.

MU TORERE

(See Addendum, p. 149-51)

3. FIVE IN A ROW GAMES

MULINELLO QUADRUPLO

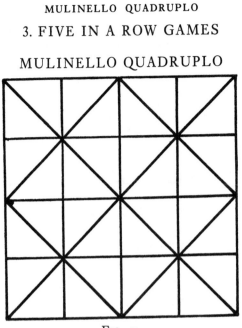

FIG. 49.

There is some doubt if this game was ever played, or if it was an invention of J. Gelli, who described it in his *Come posso divertirmi?* (Milan, 1900). According to this author the game was played on the alquerque board (see fig. 49), and each player had five men, which were entered on the points, one at a time in alternate turns of play. When all were positioned, they acquired the power of moving one step along any marked line to a contiguous point. The aim was to align five men on a marked line.

4. REPLACEMENT GAMES

PYRAMID

Each player places ten draughtsmen on a draughtsboard as in fig. 50. The men move one square diagonally as in draughts, and jump over enemy pieces by a *short leap*, being allowed to make more than one jump with the same piece in a single turn of play, as in draughts; but the pieces passed over are not removed, and at the end of the game there are still twenty men on the board. The player who first occupies his opponent's initial squares wins the game.

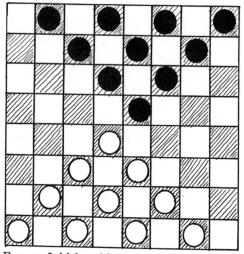

FIG. 50. Initial position of pieces in 'Pyramid'

SALTA

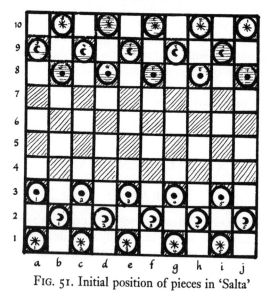

FIG. 51. Initial position of pieces in 'Salta'

Salta was invented about 1900, and is played on the black squares of a continental draughtsboard of 10 × 10 squares. Each player has fifteen men arranged on his first three rows as in fig. 51. The pieces on the first row are stars, the second row are moons, and the third row are suns. In each row the pieces are numbered 1 to 5 from left to right. Each piece moves one square diagonally, forwards or backwards. If a piece can jump forward over a hostile piece onto a vacant square beyond it must do so, though pieces are not removed from the board. If a player omits to jump when possible, his opponent calls 'Salta' (leap). Only one piece can be passed at each turn of play, and an opponent's piece cannot be passed over in a backward direction. If it is possible to jump an opponent's piece in more than one place on the board, the player has the choice of move.

The object of the game is to occupy all the opponent's squares, placing on each square one's own piece of the same emblem and number; thus the white lone star starting on a1 must finish on j10, the initial position of the black lone star.

The winning player counts as many points as his opponent requires moves to achieve his final formation.

5. GAMES OF TERRITORIAL POSSESSION

WEI-CH'I

The eighteenth-century Chinese painting on glass reproduced as the frontispiece, shows two ladies playing Wei-ch'i on an antique form of board of 13 × 11 squares. This picture was painted when Chinese art was under Western influence (c.f. the Chinese influence on the West about the same time: Chinese Chippendale furniture, Willow pattern earthenware, etc.); the artist tried, and failed, to use Western perspective to convey the impression of distance, instead of relying on 'atmosphere' of the Chinese school.

Most Chinese pictures of the period were either religious or poetical; fortunately this also illustrates a secular subject. The tablets on the wall behind the players read:

'Under the pine-tree I asked for the master; he had gone gathering herbs among the hills.'*

'Since you went away, why have I no longer bothered with the abandoned board? When I think of you, I am like the full moon whose clear brilliance wanes night after night.—Your mate.'

Unfortunately the picture has been exposed to damp, and the colours have run; but this curious hybrid of Oriental and Occidental art is sufficiently rare to be of interest to the growing body of Go players in the West.

Draughts was introduced into America to become checkers; Wei-ch'i was taken to Japan in the eighth century A.D., becoming *I-go*, or *Go*. The Japanese have outshone their tutors, and are now the undisputed masters of the game.

When the account of Wei-ch'i in Volume I was written in 1958, there were few Go players or clubs in Britain, and no authoritative account of the game was readily available. Fortunately this is no longer true; most of the larger towns have Go clubs, and the following books can be ordered through any stationer:

Takagawa, Kaku. *How to play Go,* Japan, 1956. Imported by Charles E. Tuttle Co.

Takagawa, Kaku. *The Vital Points of Go,* Japan, 1958.

These two books by the then reigning Japanese champion, and printed under the auspices of the Japanese Go Association, are extremely helpful to beginners and intermediate players.

Two older books which have been reprinted recently are of more limited value, but worth attention:

Lasker, E. *Go, and Go-Moku,* Dover Publications, New York, 1960. (First published, 1934.)

Smith, A. *The Game of Go,* Charles E. Tuttle Co., Rutland, Vermont, 1958. (First published 1908.)

The first and second International Go Tournaments were held in Tokyo in 1963 and 1964. More than fifty Go players from the United States, Britain, Germany, Czechoslovakia, Hungary, Holland, China and other countries participated.

*These lines are based on a quotation from a poem by Sun Ke: 'Under the pine-tree I asked your servant lad; he said the master had gone gathering herbs.' The words, 'under the pine-tree' are also an allusion to a line in a poem by Wen T'ing-yiin: 'The unfinished game of Wei-ch'i under the pine-tree wishes you godspeed on your return journey.' Note the game is being played beneath a pine-tree.

11. Victorian Asalto board and marbles, c. 1850. The marbles are flecked with metallic particles. (Author's collection.)

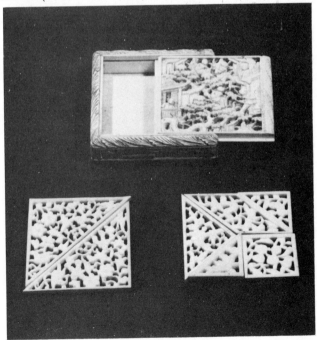

12. Chinese tangram box and puzzle in ivory; c. 1860. (Author's collection.)

13. Eighteenth century ivory solitaire board and pieces, probably French. *Le Tricolet*; see page 65. (Author's collection.)

Championship Go boards are made from a solid block of wood about 18″ long, 16″ wide and some 5″ thick. The best boards are made of a species of yew, called 'Kaya' (*Torreya nucifera*). They are also made of 'Gingko' (*Salisburia adiantifolia*) and 'Hinoki' (*Thuya obtusa*). Another beautiful wood for the board is 'Katsura' (cinnamon tree) or the Japanese Judas tree (*Cercidiphyllum japonicum*).

AGON or THE QUEEN'S GUARD

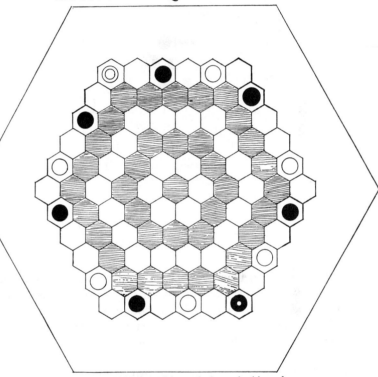

FIG. 52. Initial position of pieces in 'Agon'

In this game for two players each has a queen and six guards of their own colour, arranged on the hexagonal board as shown in fig. 52. (See Appendix B, p. 147 for construction.)

Rules

1. The choice of first move is decided by the throw of a die.

2. The players move their pieces alternately, one space forwards or sideways. They cannot move backwards except in accordance with rules 3 and 4.

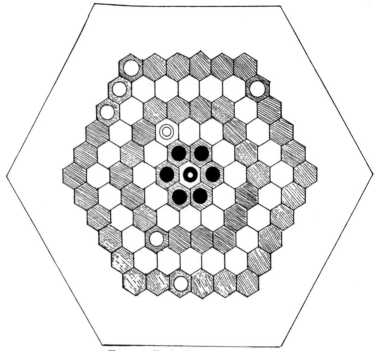

FIG. 53. End of game in 'Agon'

3. If a piece other than the queen has enemy pieces on the contiguous spaces on either side of it, on the player's next move it must be lifted and placed on a space in the outermost row.

4. If the queen is sandwiched between enemy pieces she also, at the next move, must be lifted, but can be placed on any vacant space on the board.

5. No piece can be moved between two enemy pieces.

6. The object of the game is to place the queen on the central hexagon with her guards posted around her on the six adjacent spaces. (See fig. 53.)

7. Only a queen may move onto the central space.

8. If two or more pieces are liable to be moved backwards at the same time, and one is the queen, she is moved first; and the others are removed one at each move; the order being optional.

9. If a piece is touched, it must, if possible, be moved.

10. If a player's six guards occupy the inner circle surrounding

an empty central space, the player loses the game, as neither player can achieve the game's object.

Hints on play

(*a*) It is usually unwise to throw back only one enemy piece; this often allows it to be placed in a better section of the board than that from which it was removed.

(*b*) It is wiser to try for a position from which in successive moves a player can throw back several enemy pieces, and so be able to advance his own towards the centre before he can be overtaken.

(*c*) It is unwise to push the queen too far forward ahead of her guards.

(*d*) It is often helpful to hold one piece back in the early stages of the game, but to keep it in a position to reach the centre quickly when the game reaches a crises.

An interesting variant of this game begins by placing the queens on opposite corners of the board, and then the players place their pieces alternately on any space. When all the pieces are in position the game continues as already described. The variety of situations attained in play precludes monotony.

6. PATIENCE GAMES
FRENCH SOLITAIRE

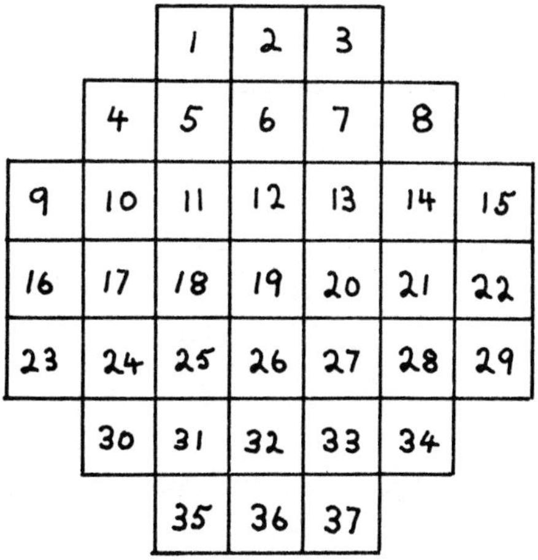

			1	2	3			
		4	5	6	7	8		
	9	10	11	12	13	14	15	
	16	17	18	19	20	21	22	
	23	24	25	26	27	28	29	
		30	31	32	33	34		
			35	36	37			

FIG. 54. Notation for French Solitaire board.

The early French solitaire boards were marked with thirty-seven holes instead of the modern board's thirty-three; and the problems were more difficult. It seems to be impossible to leave the last piece in the hole from which the first was lifted. Some of the problems, however, are very pretty. Four with solutions are given below:

LE LECTEUR AU MILIEU DE SES AMIS. Lift a piece at 19, and leave the central piece surrounded by sixteen pieces. (See fig. 55.)

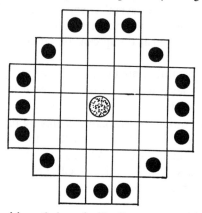

FIG. 55. Final position of pieces in 'Le Lecteur au milieu de ses amis'

LE CROIX DE ST. ANDREW. Lift a piece at 19, and leave five pieces in a saltire cross. (See fig. 56.)

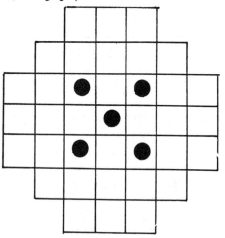

FIG. 56. Final position of pieces in 'Le croix de St. Andrew'

LE TRICOLET. Lift a piece at 19, and leave a cross moline.

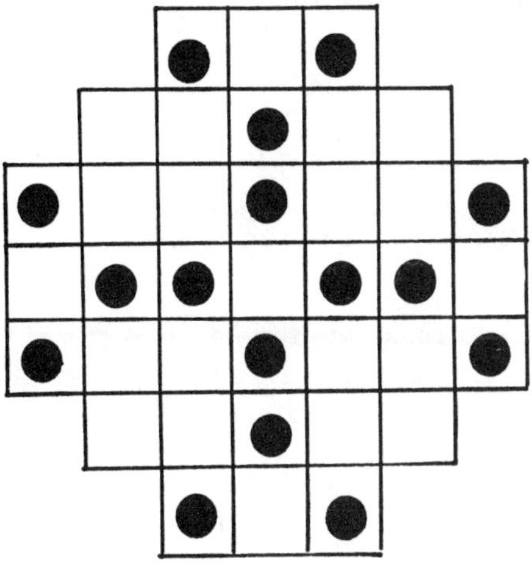

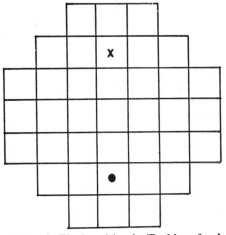

FIG. 57. Final position of pieces in 'Le tricolet'

PROBLEM FOUR. Lift a piece at 6, and leave a piece at 32. (See fig. 58)

FIG. 58. Final position in 'Problem four'

OTHER PROBLEMS

(a) Lift from 1 and leave a piece in 15, or 22, or 35.

(b) Lift from 26, and leave a piece in 28, or 36.

(c) Lift from 3, and leave a piece in 37.

(d) Lift from 19, and leave a piece in 6.

(*e*) Lift from 32, and leave a piece in 2.

(*f*) Lift from 6, and leave a piece in 3.

Method

Problem I.

6 to 19, 4 to 6, 18 to 5, 6 to 4, 9 to 11, 24 to 10, 11 to 9, 26 to 24, 35 to 25, 24 to 26, 33 to 31, 27 to 25, 25 to 35, 29 to 27, 14 to 28, 27 to 29, 19 to 21, 7 to 20, 21 to 19.

Problem II.

6 to 19, 8 to 6, 2 to 12, 4 to 6, 18 to 5, 20 to 7, 1 to 11, 3 to 13, 16 to 18, 22 to 20, 30 to 17, 34 to 21, 26 to 24, 12 to 26, 26 to 28, 21 to 19, 18 to 5, 5 to 7, 7 to 20, 20 to 18, 17 to 19, 23 to 25, 36 to 26, 26 to 24, 35 to 25, 24 to 26, 29 to 27, 27 to 25, 9 to 11, 15 to 13, 37 to 27.

Problem III.

6 to 19, 10 to 12, 19 to 6, 2 to 12, 4 to 6, 17 to 19, 31 to 18, 19 to 17, 16 to 18, 30 to 17, 21 to 19, 7 to 20, 19 to 21, 22 to 20, 8 to 21, 32 to 19, 28 to 26, 19 to 32, 36 to 26, 34 to 32.

Problem IV.

19 to 6, 10 to 12, 1 to 11, 12 to 10, 14 to 12, 3 to 13, 12 to 14, 9 to 11, 15 to 13, 2 to 12, 12 to 10, 17 to 19, 4 to 17, 20 to 18, 32 to 19, 18 to 20, 31 to 18, 23 to 25, 18 to 31, 35 to 25, 16 to 18, 18 to 31, 30 to 32, 28 to 26, 37 to 27, 26 to 28, 21 to 19, 36 to 26, 26 to 12, 12 to 14, 29 to 27, 8 to 21, 22 to 20, 20 to 33, 34 to 32.

The lovely ivory solitaire board and pieces shown on plate 13 were made about 1780, probably in France; and may have been brought to Britain by a refugee from the French Revolution. They belonged to a very old lady who had an antique shop in Penrith; and during her lifetime she refused many offers for them; but with her death their history has been lost. For a drawing of the exquisitely carved central piece, see the tailpiece, page 77.

SEVEN-PIECE TANGRAM

Occasionally small flat ivory boxes may be found in antique shops (see tailpiece page 70). They are usually empty, but on a lucky day may contain a *Chi'i shiso pan*, or Wisdom Puzzle—seven small shapes of pierced ivory. The pieces form two squares to fit into the box, see fig. 59. In England the puzzle is better known as a

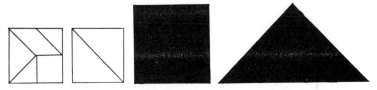

FIG. 59. Convert the pieces of the two small squares into the large square or the triangle (solution below)

tangram, and forms a link between games and puzzles. Various geometric shapes can be constructed with the seven pieces, and two typical puzzles are given above; but hundreds of fascinating silhouettes can be formed, puzzles merging imperceptibly into artistic games. Three outlines from a rare Chinese book printed on rice paper in 1826 are reproduced below. More puzzles and pictures will be found in the author's *Tangram Teasers,* listed in the bibliography. (Also see plate 12.)

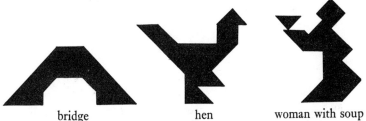

bridge   hen   woman with soup

FIG. 60. Typical tangram puzzles (solution on page 68)

Tangrams can be made from cardboard, plywood, or plastic sheeting, a handy size being three inches square, marked out as in fig. 61. White perspex forms an attractive substitute for ivory. (Recently a reproduction in plastic of an antique Chinese ivory box and tangram has been manufactured by Palitoy.)

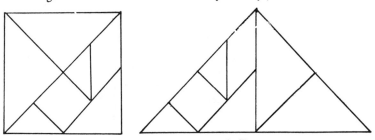

FIG. 61. Solution to puzzle FIG. 59

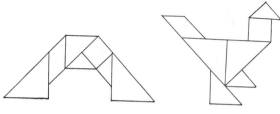

FIG. 62. Solution to puzzles in FIG. 60

FIFTEEN-PIECE TANGRAM

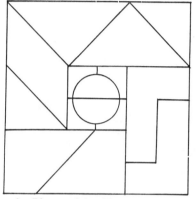

FIG. 63. Pieces of the fifteen-piece tangram

The fifteen-piece tangram shown in fig. 63 is much rarer than the seven piece. Three puzzles, and four picture problems from another early nineteenth century Chinese book, are given below:

Parallelogram   Cross   Swastika

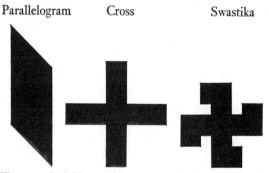

FIG. 64. Three typical fifteen-piece geometric shapes. (Solutions on page 69)

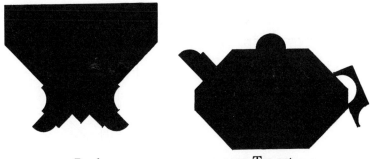

Bowl   Tea pot

FIG. 65. Outline of household items (solution on page 70)

The shrine of his ancestors   Vigil on the bridge

FIG. 66. Two fifteen-piece tangram pictures. (solution on page 70)

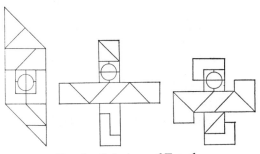

FIG. 67. Solutions of FIG. 64

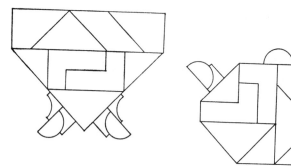

FIG. 68. Solutions of FIG. 65.

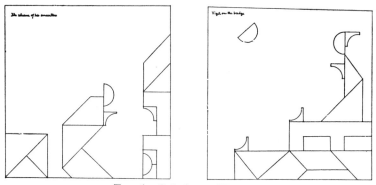

FIG. 69. Solutions of FIG. 66.

Ivory tangram box. (Author's collection)

CHAPTER FOUR

Mancala Games

FIG. 70. Woodcut by Thomas Bewick of negroes playing mancala

Thomas Bewick's woodcut, c. 1790 (fig. 70), shows two Africans with a mancala board of two rows of six holes and a storage hole at each end. Similar boards are still in use; one which folds down the middle from Nigeria is shown in Plate 14.

1. TWO RANK MANCALA

BA-AWA

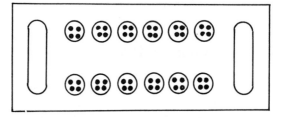

FIG. 71. Diagram of board and pieces at the beginning of 'Ba-awa'

Ba-awa played by the Twi people of Ghana, is one of the simpler forms of mancala and appears to be extremely ancient. The board consists of two rows of six holes dug in the ground; or carved out of a piece of wood. The two players sit facing each other across the board; and start with four seeds in each of their holes. (See fig. 71.)

Rules

1. The opening player lifts all the seeds from any of the holes on his own side of the board, and sows one into each contiguous hole in an anti-clockwise direction around the board. When the last seed has been sown, he lifts all the seeds from the last hole, including that just placed in it, and continues sowing. This process is repeated until the last seed of a lap falls into an empty hole when the turn ceases. (The opening turn always consists of five lifts unless a mistake has occurred.)

2. When the first player has finished his turn, the second player lifts the seeds or seed from any hole on his side of the board, and sows in an anticlockwise direction around the board.

3. After the opening play, when any hole contains four seeds the owner of the hole lifts them, regardless of whether he or his opponent is playing, and puts them into his store.

4. If a player makes four seeds in a hole with his last seed of a lift on his own side of the board, he wins the four seeds but his turn ceases; if it happens on the opponent's side of the board the latter wins the seeds, and the turn of play ceases.

5. When there are only eight seeds left on the board, the game is over and these eight seeds belong to the opening player.

6. For the next game each player fills as many holes as he can with four seeds, and these become 'his holes'.

7. The player who started in the opening game plays second in the following game, and the privilege of beginning alternates with each game.

8. The contest finishes when one player is unable to fill even one hole at the beginning of a game with four seeds.

9. Three players may take part, each starting with four holes, and the game develops into a struggle between the two surviving players when the third has been eliminated.

LONTU-HOLO

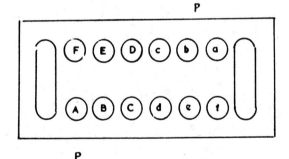

FIG. 72. Notation of lontu-holo board

This game is played by the Djuka tribe of Bush negroes in Dutch Guiana, and appears to be unrelated to any form of mancala found in the old world. The board has two rows of six holes with a store hole at either end, but each player owns half of each row. See fig. 72.)

Rules

1. Four beans are placed in each hole, and the player's beans circulate anti-clockwise round his own holes.

2. Each player tries to get rid of his beans by passing them into his opponent's holes.

3. Beans can only be transferred to loaded holes.

4. There are several opening moves, but Herskovits only reported four. The opening player chooses an opening, and his opponent repeats it on his own half of the board.

Openings

i. P transfers all the beans in D,E, and F to B. He then sows C4 and next B16 ending in F. He then picks up the four beans in each of D,E, and F and holds them in hand, while p repeats these openings on his half of the board. P's position is now A7, B2, C3, D0, E0, F0. P then enters the beans he holds in hand, four in each of a, b, and c; p does the same in A, B, and C.

When the opening play is finished, the players play in turn, lifting and sowing the beans from one of their holes and omitting this hole during the sowing. If the sowing ends in making the contents of a hole four beans, these, and those of an unbroken sequence of fours, are placed in any one of the opponent's loaded holes; and if the opponent has only singletons he transfers one singleton to another, making a hole with two beans, and transfers his beans to this hole.

The other openings recorded by Herskovits were:

ii. P transfers D2 and F2 to E, and A2 and C2 to B; sows B8 and the position becomes A3, B1, C4, D4, E9, F3. He picks up C4 and D4 and holds them in his hand while p repeats the move on his side of the board. P then puts four of the beans in hand in each of two of p's loaded holes. p repeats this.

iii. P transfers A2, B2, D2 and E2 to C, and F4 to A, B, D, and E (one bean in each), making three beans in each of these holes; next E3 to A, B, D, and the position becomes: A4, B4, C12, D4, E0, and F0. He then picks up the contents of A, B, and D, holding these twelve beans in hand while p makes the same moves on his side of the board. P then transfers C2 to one of his own empty holes. p does the same, and first P and then p puts the twelve beans in hand into one of the opponent's loaded holes.

iv. P transfers D3 and A1 to B; C3 and D1 to E; B1 to A, and C1 to F, and picks up A4 and D4 and holds them in hand while p makes the same moves. P then puts four beans in hand into two of p's loaded holes, and p does likewise.

2. FOUR RANK MANCALA

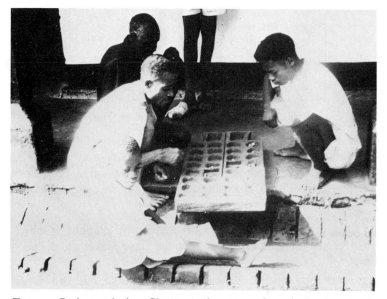

FIG. 73. Patients playing Choro on the steps of a mission hospital in Uganda

The most complex of the mancala games with four rows of holes are mainly found in eastern and southern Africa. A few years ago an English nurse arrived at a small mission hospital in Uganda, and set about isolating patients suffering from various infectious diseases. A day or two later she was horrified to find her 'isolation cases' huddled together in a dusty yard 'dropping nasty little bits of rubbish into rows of horrid little holes'!

HUS

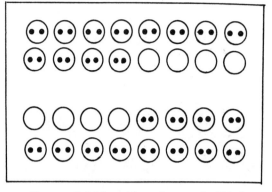

FIG. 74. Initial position of stones in 'Hus'

The Hottentot game of Hus is played on a four-rank board, and unlike most forms of mancala, all the pieces remain in play; there are no stores. (In most of the games played in Zaire, the pieces remain in play [Philip Townshend, 1974].)

Rules

1. The privilege of playing first is decided by lots, but in subsequent games the winner of the previous game makes the opening move.

2. Four rows of eight holes are dug in the sand, and two stones are placed in each player's back row, and two in each of the holes in the right half of his front row.

3. All moves are made in a clockwise direction, and are confined to the player's own side of the board.

4. The opening player lifts the stones from any hole on his side of the board and sows them one at a time in successive holes. If the last stone falls into an empty hole the turn ceases.

5. If the last stone is sown into a loaded hole all the stones, including that just placed in it, are lifted and the sowing continues.

6. If a sowing ends in a loaded front row hole, and the opponent's corresponding front hole is loaded, the player lifts these stones instead of those in his own hole, and sows on. He may make several captures in a single turn of play.

7. When a player makes a capture from an enemy front hole, and the corresponding enemy back hole is also loaded, the player wins

14. Modern Whyo board; Ibibio tribe, Nigeria. This game is similar to Ba-awa, see p. 72 (Author's collection.)

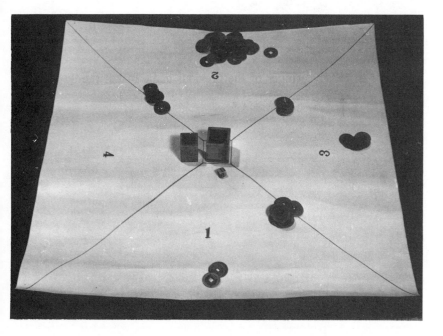

15. Spinning Treasure board, Poh (die), and Poh Kam (cover), seized by police in a gambling house in Malaya twenty years ago. (Author's collection.)

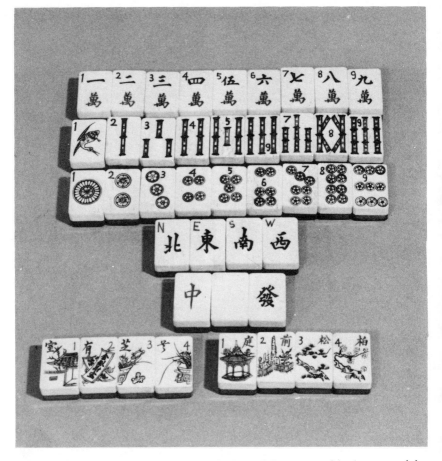

16. Ma-jong tiles of the three suits; Winds and Dragons, with the extra eight Flower and Season tiles. (Author's Collection.)

the contents of both holes plus a bonus of robbing any hole on the enemy side of the board, all the captures being sown in consecutive holes on the player's side of the board starting in the next beyond that from which the capture was made.

8. A move must begin from a hole containing two or more stones, and if there are only singletons left on a player's side of the board he cannot move and loses the game.

9. If a player captures all the enemy pieces it counts as a double win.

10. A contest is the best of seven games, and Hus is remarkable for rapid changes of fortune.

Fragments of four-rank mancala boards of stone have been found in and around the ruins of Zimbabwe in Southern Rhodesia, the spectacular remains of an African civilization which flourished from about 1450 A.D. to 1800 A.D.

Central piece of Ivory Solitaire set. (Author's collection)

CHAPTER FIVE

Dice Games

I. GAMES WITH TWO-SIDED DICE

LU-LU

FIG. 75. Dice used in 'Lu-Lu'

This Hawaiian game for any number of players is played with four discs of volcanic stone about an inch in diameter. One surface of each disc is painted with dots and a cross in red; the other is left plain. (See fig. 75.)

The discs are shaken in both hands and then thrown onto the ground. Each player throws the dice in turn, and if any stone has its unmarked surface uppermost, it is lifted by the next player and thrown again. The spots are counted, and the player throwing the highest number in a round wins; alternately the first player to reach an agreed number, usually a hundred, wins. If a player throws all marked faces up it counts ten and he has another throw.

MON SHI MO UT

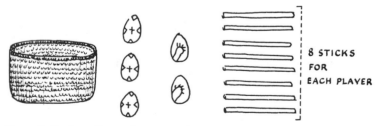

FIG. 76. Basket, dice and counters for 'Mon shi mo ut'. (After S. Culin)

This gambling game was played by the squaws of the Cheyenne Indians for small stakes, amid constant chatter and joking.

Equipment

(*a*) A grass basket eight inches across and about four inches deep with flat bottom.

(*b*) Five plum-stones, plain on one side, but marked on the other with a hot iron: three having the paint pattern worn by young girls of the tribe; this being a cross on the bridge of the nose, and a V mark on the cheeks, chin, and forehead. These plum-stones represented maidens. The other two stones bore the mark of a bear's paw.

(*c*) Eight tally-sticks for each player, who arranged bets with the player sitting opposite.

Method of play

The players sat opposite each other, or if several were playing, in two opposing rows. The five dice were placed in the basket which was lifted up by the first caster, and then brought down smartly onto the ground, the stones jumping a few inches into the air on the impact.

Scoring

There were seven scoring combinations, and these also entitled the caster to another turn. If the throw did not score, the basket and stones were passed to the player on the right who threw, and so to each member of the team. At the end of the line of players the basket was passed to the player opposite, and it travelled back along the opposing team in the same way. All the players of a team won or lost according to the caster's score, the whole team winning or losing together; each player, however, would have previously arranged her particular stake with the player sitting opposite.

If a stone fell out of the basket, the throw was spoiled and the turn passed to the next player.

Winning combinations and another turn:

5 blanks. Each player in the caster's team won a stick.
3 blanks and 2 bears. Won one stick.
1 blank, 2 bears, and 2 maidens. Won one stick.
2 blanks and 3 maidens. Won three sticks.
2 bears and 3 maidens. Won eight sticks and the game.

Losing combinations, but with another turn for the caster:
2 blanks, 2 bears, and a maiden. Each member of the team lost one stick.

4 blanks and a bear. Lost one stick.

No other throw scored.

When a team secured all their opponent's sticks, they won the agreed stakes, and the game was over.

THE WALNUT GAME

FIG. 77. Walnut-shell dice used for 'The walnut game'

The women of the Yokut tribe of Amerindians living near Fort Tejon in California, played this game using eight half walnut-shells filled with pitch and powdered charcoal, and inlaid with small red and white glass beads or bits of shell. (See fig. 77.)

Four squaws sat round a large, nearly flat grass basket, and a fifth kept tally with fifteen sticks. Each player threw in turn, scooping up the eight dice in her hands and casting them into the basket. When two or five flat surfaces were uppermost the player scored one, and took a tally. When all the tallies were taken, the game was over and the player with the greatest number of tallies had won.

PITCH AND TOSS

FIG. 78. George V penny piece

This was a favourite game of the miners in Fyfeshire. Any number formed themselves into a *school*, stuck a knife into the ground, and from a distance each player threw a penny at it, the nearest having first toss. If there were six players in the school he took a penny from each and tossed the six coins into the air, calling 'Heads' or 'Tails' before they struck the ground. For each correct call he won a stake from each player, and the winning pennies were withdrawn. The player next nearest to the knife with his throw then took the remaining pennies, tossed them, and called when they were in the air, being paid by every player for each correct coin. These winning pennies were withdrawn, and the round continued with the third nearest having his turn, etc.

When all the pennies had been withdrawn, the whole school again threw their pennies at the upright knife to start a second round. Players could drop out or enter the game at the beginning of every round. The stakes were often a pound for each correct call, and in the words of my informant, 'fivers floated around like toilet paper'.

DITTAR PRADESH

FIG. 79. A score of 8 in 'Dittar Pradesh'

Any number of players, sitting in a circle, may play this very simple game from Pakistan. Sixteen cowrie shells are used as dice. Each player puts a stake into a central pool, and then tries to guess the number of shells which will fall mouth upwards on the next throw. A player with the correct guess wins the pool. If two or more players are correct they share the pool. If no one is correct, new stakes are added to the pool; the players repeat their former calls, and the shells are thrown again. The pool may be increased several times before a winning number is thrown.

The cowries are cast by the winner of the last pool until there is a new winner, who becomes the new caster.

SIXTEEN COWRIES (Sulahai)

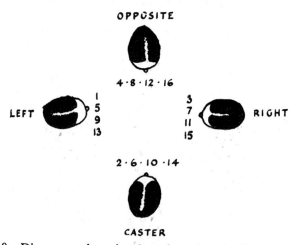

Fig. 80. Diagram to show the players' numbers in 'Sixteen Cowries'

This game from Pakistan is played with sixteen cowries. Four players sit at the cardinal points of the compass, and each has his own numbers shown in fig. 80. The caster forecasts the number of shells that will fall mouth uppermost, and then makes his throw. If he calls correctly, he wins a stake from each player and a double stake from the owner of the number. If his call is incorrect he has to pay a stake to each player, and a double stake to the owner of the winning number. If one of his own numbers is thrown, the other players each pay him a double stake.

When a caster wins, he casts for the next round; but if he loses, the player owning the winning number becomes the new caster.

If no mouths are uppermost the game ceases, since to continue would be to invite Fortune's displeasure.

2. GAMES WITH SIX-SIDED DICE

FIFTY

This very simple game for two or more players is played with two dice and a dicing cup. Each player in turn has one throw with the two dice. Only doubles count, any double being worth five

FIG. 81. Modern western dice

points, except double six which is worth twenty-five and double three which cancels the player's complete score. The first to reach fifty wins the game.

ROTATION

Two dice are used and any number of players may participate. The order of throwing is immaterial. In the first round, each player throws once and tries to score two. If successful he scores two points, and if not, nothing.

In the second round the target is three points, successful player scoring three, and unsuccessful nothing. In all, there are eleven rounds in which the numbers from two to twelve are required, and at the end of the eleventh round the player with the highest score wins.

FOUR-FIVE-SIX

FIG. 82. Diagram showing a throw of 'four-five-six'

Any number of players may take part in this game from the north-west of the United States of America and western Canada using three dice thrown from a cup. Each player puts his wager on the table in front of him, and the banker, who covers all bets, plays against each player in turn. After the first round the player on the banker's left becomes the new banker.

When either banker or player throws 4:5:6, any pair and a six, or three of a kind, it is a winning decision; while 1:2:3, or any pair and an ace, is a losing decision.

When any pair is thrown and the third die is 2, 3, 4, or 5, the number on the third die becomes the shooter's point. If his opponent fails to score a winning or a losing decision, and also throws a pair and a point, the player with the higher point wins. If a player throws a neutral roll, he must continue throwing until he wins, loses, or throws a point.

The banker always rolls first, and this gives him a slight advantage of about $2\frac{1}{2}\%$, or $2\frac{1}{2}p$. in the £1.

GRAND HAZARD

This game is played with three dice and a layout; and has nothing to do with the hazard of Chaucer or the Reformation gamesters. (See Volume I, pp. 130–3.) The bar running across the top of the layout is divided into spaces marked 1 2 3 4 5 6 . The bets are the same as in Crown and Anchor. If one ace appears when the three

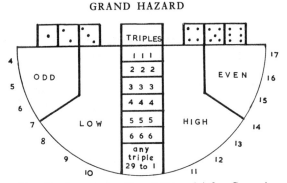

FIG. 83. Layout for Grand Hazard (after Scarne)

dice are thrown, the bank pays the players who have bet on the first space at even money; if two aces appear, at two to one; if three aces appear, at three to one. The other numbers in the bar are paid in the same way. The bank has an advantage of nearly 8%.

High and low bets

Money placed on the space marked HIGH wins if the sum of the spots on all three dice totals eleven or more, *excluding three of a kind*, when the bank wins. Money on the LOW space wins when the total is ten or less, *excluding three of a kind*. This exclusion gives the bank its advantage which is nearly 3%.

Odd and even bets

Money on the ODD space wins when the sum of the spots is odd, *excluding three alike*. Money on the EVEN space wins when the sum of the dice is even, *excluding three alike*. The bank's advantage is again nearly 3%.

Specific Triple

A bet on any specific triple wins 179 to 1 from the bank. The true odds are 215 to 1, and therefore the bank has an advantage of nearly 17%.

Any Triple

The wager is that the next throw will be one of any triplet. The bank pays 29 to 1, when the correct odds are 35 to 1. This gives the bank an advantage of nearly 17%.

Specific Numbers

The numbers at the bottom of the layout are from 4 to 17, and money on one of these wins when the sum of the three dice is the same as the number. In every case the odds given by the bank are lower than they should be. In the table below the bank's odds are given in column two; the true odds in column three; and the bank's advantage in column four.

Number	Banker's odds	Real odds	Banker's advantage
4 17 }	60 to 1	71 to 1	15 5/18%
5 16 }	30 to 1	35 to 1	13 8/9%
6 15 }	18 to 1	29 3/5 to 1	12 1/27%
7 14 }	12 to 1	13 2/5 to 1	9 13/18%
8 13 }	8 to 1	9 2/7 to 1	12 1/2%
9 12 }	6 to 1	7 16/25 to 1	18 53/54%
10 11 }	6 to 1	7 to 1	12 1/2%

This table is from *Scarne on Dice*, p. 342.

BIDOU

This game was brought to the author's notice by Mr. James H. Campbell of Jackson, Michigan, U.S.A., who learnt it on a fishing trip in the interior of Quebec Province, Canada.

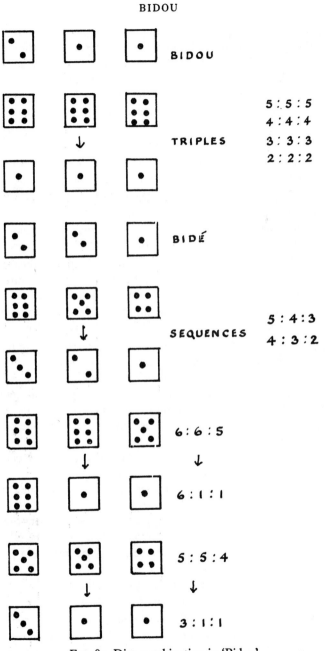

FIG. 84. Dice combination in 'Bidou'

The relative values in descending order of the dice combinations in Bidou are shown in fig. 84; except that 1:1:1 exceeds Bidou when they meet, as it does any other three of a kind when Bidou is thrown, but not otherwise. Below three of a kind, the value of a combination depends on the numerical value of the throw and not the sum of the points: a throw of 6:5:1 (651), ranks above 6:4:4 (644).

Bidou for two Players

1. Nine counters are placed in the centre of the table, and the player who acquires them during the game is the loser.

2. Each player has a cup and three dice, and on the opening throw the player with the highest numerical value becomes the leader for the round. (*Note:* In the opening throw, the special Bidou values do not apply: 6:5:1 (651), is higher than 5:5:5 (555).

3. Both players make a concealed throw; and if either is dissatisfied he may take up his dice and throw a second or a third time if his score is low. Alternatively he may decide to bet on a bluff. If both players stop on the same throw, the leader bets or passes first; otherwise the player who stops first has this privilege.

4. The opening caller may stake as many counters as he desires. The other players may then pass, call, or raise the bet.

(*a*) If both players pass, neither takes any counters.

(*b*) If the bet is called, the loser takes the number of counters staked from the central pool into his own cache.

(*c*) If a player refuses to call or raise the bet, he takes one counter as a *penalty*.

(*b*) If the bet is called, the loser takes the number of counters staked from the central pool into his own cache.

(*c*) If a player refuses to call or raise the bet, he takes one counter as a *penalty*.

(*d*) If a player bets and his opponent raises the bet, the first player may raise the bet again, or retire. If he retires he takes the number of counters he originally bet, plus one more as a penalty for passing.

(*e*) The winner of a round is the leader in the next.

(*f*) If both players pass, the leader changes for the next round.

5. Players may bet from the counters in the central pool until these have all passed into the player's caches, or make mixed bets from the pool and their own cache. When all the counters have

been taken from the pool, betting is from each player's cache, the loser receiving counters from his opponent.

6. If one player has eight counters in his cache, and the other only one, the losing player is granted the privilege of an 'open throw'. The player with one counter must throw his dice *exposed*, once, twice, or three times, at his discretion.

Then the player with the eight counters may throw up to three times, and if he exceeds his opponent's throw he passes one of his counters to him, and the game continues as before the open throw; but if he loses he takes his opponent's remaining counter and he has lost the game.

Extra rules for three or more players

7. Instead of a central pool of nine counters, each player starts with a personal cache of six counters in front of him.

8. Each player throws his three dice and the numerically highest score becomes the leader for the first round.

9. They throw again but this time concealing their dice. The leader starts the betting; the other players following in clockwise order round the table. The winner of a round becomes the leader of the next. If all the players pass, the new leader is the player on the old leader's left.

10. If all the players take three throws, the leader bets or passes first; if several players stop short, the player with the least number of throws and nearest on the leader's left opens the bidding. A player stopping short must inform the others immediately, and he may not throw again during the round. Beginning with the leader, and passing clockwise round the table, any player may bet, pass, call, or raise.

Examples of play

i. Leader A bets two counters; B passes; C calls; D and E pass. A or C, whichever is the loser, receives the four counters wagered.

ii. Leader A bets two counters; B passes; C calls; D raises two more counters; E passes. If A wishes to call (not raise) D, he adds two additional counters to his stake. Alternatively, if A thinks it wise to retire, he must take up seven counters: his own two, C's two, two of D's, and a third of D's, as a penalty for passing. One counter remains in play. C in turn is forced to call (if he does not wish to raise) this lone counter.

iii. Leader A bets two counters; B passes; C calls; D raises three counters; E passes. A then passes, taking up his own two counters, two for C's call, two for D's raise (which was not accepted), and one as a penalty for retiring. D takes back the last counter.

iv. Leader A bets two counters; B passes; C calls; D raises four counters. A passes and takes up seven counters. C passes and takes up one counter as a penalty; D takes back the other two. (A player receiving the benefit of a penalty cannot discard counters.)

v. Leader A has three counters in his cache, B two; C four; D and E none.

A lays three counters; B calls for the two he has; C passes. If A wins the bet, B takes four counters (his own two and two from A's cache), and A takes back his remaining one. (A player cannot discard his last counter when he is called by a player with less counters; nor can two or more players with one counter each, go out on a tie.)

vi. Leader A has two counters in his cache; B has one, C four; D and E none.

A lays two counters; B calls for the one he has; C passes. A and B have tie throws. A takes back one of the counters he wagered, and discards the other into a discard pile of dead counters. B takes back his counter as he cannot go out on a tie.

vii. If one player bets, and all the others pass, he discards a counter, even though it is his last.

viii. All players tying, discard a counter unless it be their last.

ix. When only two players are left with counters in their caches, these two continue until one has lost the game. If they have more than nine counters between them, each discards a counter each time a bet is made and not called, until the total of counters becomes nine, and then play continues as in the two-handed variety.

A player can only bet, call, or raise for the number of counters he has in his cache; his interest in the play is only related to the number of counters he posseses.

When a player completes a throw of his dice he must not expose or lift them until all the players have finished betting.

Once a player has passed, he takes no further part in the round.

There are 216 possible combinations with three dice, and the odds against throwing the following combinations are:

Bidou	3:216 (1:72)
Three of a kind	6:216 (1:36)
Bidé	3:216 (1:72)
A sequence	24:216 (1:9)

36 out of 216 throws average sequences or better (1:6)

6:6:5 to 6:6:1	15:216
6:5:5 to 6:5:1	21:216
6:4:4 to 6:4:1	21:216
6:3:3 to 6:3:1	15:216

A throw of 6:3:1 is just within the upper 108 combinations, and therefore represents a better than average throw.

PAR

Each player starts with an equal number of counters. They all throw five dice in turn, and, with the ace counting as seven, the highest scorer becomes the first caster; the second highest sits on his left and casts second, etc; while the lowest scorer has the last turn. Tying players throw again.

The first caster throws all five dice on his first roll. He must then leave at least one die on the table, and can throw as many of the others as he wishes, and he may continue throwing, but always after each throw he leaves at least one additional die on the table, or he may stop throwing on any throw.

The object of the game is to score twenty-four or more. If after rolling the last die a player has less than twenty-four, e.g. if he scored twenty, he would have to pay each player four counters. A score of twenty-four breaks even; while if he scores more than twenty-four, the difference becomes his *point;* e.g. if he scored twenty-eight, his point is 4, and he then throws all five dice once, and for every 4 thrown, he collects four counters from each player. On a score of twenty-six, the player's point is 2, and for each 2 thrown he collects two counters from each player.

After the counters are paid, the dice are passed to the next player. Any player with no counters drops out of the game.

COCKFIGHTING (Ta Kai)

FIG. 85. Dice bowl and Chinese dice for 'Cockfighting'

Cockfighting is played with six standard Chinese dice, and a flat-bottomed bowl into which they are cast. The bowl may be embedded in plaster to increase the bounce of the dice. Any number of players can participate, one being the banker. This office passes in rotation anti-clockwise to each player.

To begin, all the players except the banker place their stakes on the table. The banker may impose a limit on the size of the stakes. The banker then takes the six dice and casts them into the bowl. There are winning, losing and neutral combinations, as recorded below. After the banker throws, he settles the stakes between himself and each player; and then the player on his right takes up the dice and casts into the bowl.

If the banker throws a winning combination, all the players pay him, if a losing combination he pays them; if a neutral throw there is no exchange. When a player throws a scoring combination he wins or loses to the banker alone. As soon as the banker throws a scoring combination, win or lose, the player on the right becomes the new banker.

Scoring

In all scoring combinations an additional stake is paid for each 4 or 6 thrown.

Winning combinations

1. Six of a kind   stake × 7
2. Five of a kind   stake × 7
3. 4:4:5:5:6:6   stake × 7
4. Four of a kind with the other two dice adding to the same as one of the four, e.g. 3:3:3:3:2:1   stake × 7

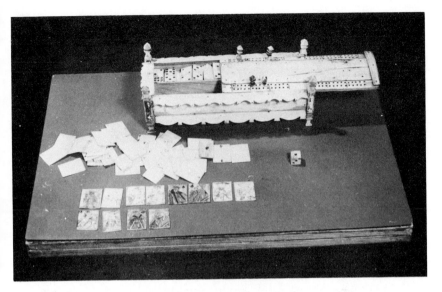

17. Early nineteenth century compendium of games in bone, possibly made by prisoners of war, containing a die, set of double-six dominoes, cribbage board and markers, and a pack of bone cards 1″ by 1¼″. (Author's collection.)

18. Loto reels, bag, cards, markers, and bone counters, c. 1880. The cards are reproduction. (Author's collection.)

19. A three-handed cribbage board and markers, c. 1890. The cards are a little later. (Author's collection.)

20. Pope Joan board, c. 1830, cards, c. 1810 and counters, c. 1870. (Author's collection.)

5. 1:2:3:4:5:6   stake × 3
6. 2:2:3:3:6:6   stake × 3
7. Three of a kind with the other three dice adding to 5, or 14 and upwards, e.g. 3:3:3:5:5:5   stake × 1

Losing combinations
8. 1:1:2:2:3:3   lose stake × 7
9. Three of a kind with the other three dice adding to 4 or 6 or 7, e.g. 3:3:3:2:1:1   lose stake × 1

All other throws are neutral

Examples of bonus scoring for 4s and 6s

Combination	Example	Scoring
1.	4:4:4:4:4:4	stake × (7+6) = stake × 13
2.	5:5:5:5:5:4	stake × (7+1) = stake × 8
4.	6:6:6:6:5:1	stake × (7+4) = stake × 11
7.	4:4:4:3:5:6	stake × (1+4) = stake × 5

Example of increased loss for 4s and 6s

9.   4:4:4:3:2:1   lose stake × (1+3) = stake × 4

A player may retire at any time after settling a score.

GRASPING EIGHT (Pát chá)

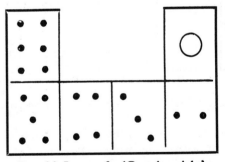

FIG. 86. Layout for 'Grasping eight'

In this Chinese gambling game the banker has a board with squares marked from one to six (see fig. 86). The players place their stakes on the numbers of their fancy.

One of the players throws eight dice. The banker pays eight times the stake on any number with three or more dice of the same value, and sixteen times the stake on any number with six or more dice of the same value. He wins the stakes on all the other squares.

THE GAME OF EDUCATION (Chong ün ch'au)

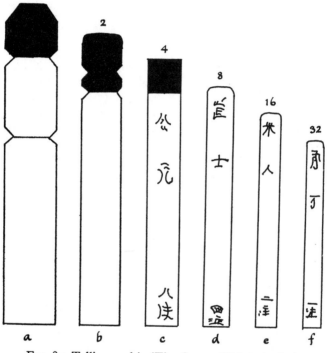

FIG. 87. Tallies used in 'The Game of Education'

According to Stewart Culin, this Chinese game for two or more players was only played by women and children. Six dice and sixty-three bamboo tallies with special names are required:

(*a*) A professor: about six inches long and worth 32 points.

(*b*) Two lecturers: about 5½″ long and worth 16 points each.

(*c*) Four honours graduates: about 5″ long and worth 8 points each.

(*d*) Eight graduates: about 4½" long and worth 4 points each.
(*e*) Sixteen students: about 4" long and worth 2 points each.
(*f*) Thirty-two schoolboys: about 3½" long and worth 1 point each.

The professor, lecturer, and honours graduates bear crude pictures and names, but the others are usually distinguished only by their size. The players throw the six dice in turn from right to left, and after throwing each draws the tallies to which he is entitled, according to their values. If a tally indicated by a throw has been drawn, its value may be made up by taking the equivalent number of smaller ones, but the holder of the professor must surrender him without recompense if another player makes a higher throw than that made by its present holder.

When all the tallies are taken the game is finished, and the player with the 'school' containing the greatest number of points is the winner. The scoring is complicated, and is listed below:

Method of scoring

Six identical dice are known as *Ts'unshik,* and the lucky player takes all the tallies. Should two players throw a Ts'unshik in the same round, the higher denomination takes precedence. On Chinese dice the fours are marked in red, and a Ts'unshik of six 4s is the highest possible score. The order of priority of the Ts'unshik are:

> Fours
> Sixes
> Fives
> Threes
> Twos
> Ones

> 32 points

Any of the following throws arranged in descending order of priority, is worth thirty-two and wins the professor.

> Five 4s and 6, or 5, or 3 or 2 or 1
> Five 6s and 4, or 6 or 5 or 2 or 1
> Five 3s and 4, or 6 or 5 or 2 or 1

Five 2s and 4, or 6 or 5 or 3 or 2
Five 1s and 4, or 6 or 5 or 3 or 2
Four 4s and 3 and 1
Four 4s and 2 and 2
Four 6s and 4 and 2
Four 6s and 5 and 1
Four 6s and 3 and 3
Four 5s and 4 and 1
Four 5s and 3 and 2
Four 3s and 2 and 1
Four 2s and 1 and 1
Four 4s and 6 and 6
Four 4s and 6 and 5
Four 4s and 5 and 5
Four 4s and 6 and 3, or 6 and 1
Four 4s and 5 and 3, or 6 and 2
Four 4s and 5 and 2, or 5 and 1
Four 4s and 3 and 3, or 3 and 2
Four 4s and 2 and 1, or 1 and 1

16 points

Any of the following throws is worth sixteen and wins a lecturer:
Two 4s two 5s and two 6s
Two 1s two 2s and two 3s
Three 4s and three 6s, or three 5s, three 3s, three 2s, or three 1s
Three 6s and three 5s, or three 3s, three 2s or three 1s
Three 5s and three 3s, or three 2s, or three 1s
Three 3s and three 2s, or three 1s
The sequence from one to six, 1:2:3:4:5:6.

8 points

Three 4s with any combination except those already mentioned
count as eight and win an honours graduate.

4 points

Four 6s, or 5s, or 3s, or 2s, or 1s, with any combination of dice
except those already mentioned, count as four, and win one of the
graduates.

2 points

Two 4s count as two and win one of the students

1 point

One 4 counts as one, and wins a schoolboy.

Scoring in this game is easier with Chinese dice, having red 4s and large red 1s.

3. GAMES WITH SPECIAL DICE

SPINNING TREASURE (Lien poh)

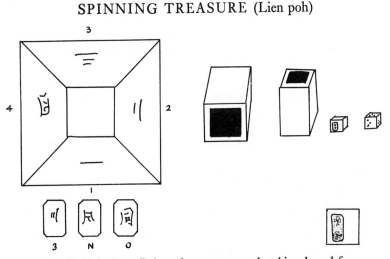

FIG. 88. Poh Kam, Poh, stake counters and staking-board for 'Spinning Treasure'.

This simple game is played in Malayan clubs and gambling dens, or often in the open air. The equipment shown on plate 15 was confiscated by the Malayan police a few years ago, and is now in the author's possession.

Equipment

1. A staking-board of wood or paper; see fig, 88, and plate 15.
2. Six tallies marked 1, 2, 3, 4, *opposite* and *neighbours*. (These are in Chinese characters, see fig. 88.)

3. A special die or *poh* is used; each face being marked with the same design which is restricted to one half of the surface, the other half being blank; see fig. 88.

4. The die fits loosely into a box of thick brass, and this in turn fits into a larger box of the same metal. These boxes are known as the *poh kam* or dice cover.

Method of play

Any number of players can take part. The banker sits at one end of a table, and the players around the other three sides. At the beginning of each round, the banker drops the die into the larger brass box, shakes it, and then inserts the smaller box into it and pushes it home while shaking the die so that it falls into the recess in the inner box. He then places the *poh kam* upright in the centre of the staking-board and spins it round on its slightly convex base.

The players try to decide which quadrant of the board will be nearest to the marked side of the die when the cover is removed, and place their stakes on it. The outer box is then raised by the banker to expose the die, and he pays dividends to the successful players, collects the stakes of the losers, and begins another round as before.

There are six ways of placing a stake in a quadrant. Using quadrant ONE as an example:

1. If the stake is placed in the centre of this quadrant, and 1 is declared the winner, a dividend of 3 × the stake is paid to any player with a stake in this position. If 2, 3, or 4 is called, the stake is lost.

2. If the stake is placed on the dividing line between quadrants ONE and TWO, and either 1 or 2 is announced as the winner, the player receives a dividend equal to the stake, and loses his stake if 3 or 4 is announced.

3. If the stake is placed in quadrant ONE, but near the line between ONE and TWO, if 1 is called, the player wins twice the stake, if 2 is called the stake is returned to him; but if 3 or 4 is announced he loses his stake.

4. If the stake is placed in the centre of ONE together with the tally marked 3, if 1 or 3 is announced as winner, the player receives a dividend equal to his stake. The stake is lost if 2 or 4 is called.

5. If the stake is placed in the centre of ONE together with the tally marked OPPOSITE, and 1 is announced the player receives 2 ×

stake; if 3 is called his stake is returned; and it is lost if 2 or 4 is announced.

6. If the stake is placed in the centre of ONE together with the NEIGHBOUR tally, and 1 is announced as winner, a dividend equal to the stake is paid to the player. The stake is returned to him if 2 or 4 is called, and lost if 3 is announced.

These six methods of laying stakes apply equally to the other three quadrants.

In gambling houses the management deducts 10% from the winning dividends as commission.

FISH, PRAWN, KING CRAB (Hoo, Hey, How)

FIG. 89. Dice and layout for 'Fish, Prawn, King Crab'

Hoo, Hey, How, is the Kokkien Chinese name for this simple game of pure luck, played with three six-sided dice whose faces are inscribed with a fish, prawn, king crab, flower, butterfly, and beautiful lady, respectively. A board bearing six spaces each marked with one of these symbols is used for placing stakes. (See fig. 89.) When the stakes are laid, the banker shakes the dice, and throws them into a bowl.

The banker pays players with a stake on a space corresponding to the design on one die the equivalent of the stake, twice the stake if two dice correspond, and three times the stake for three dice. The stake itself is always returned to winning players; and the stakes of losing players pass to the banker.

In gambling houses 10% is deducted from all winnings as the management's commission.

HEARTS

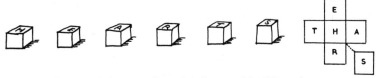

FIG. 90. Diagram of special dice used in 'Hearts'

Six special dice with H.E.A.R.T.S. on the six faces are required for this game. The players throw in turn, and H=5 points, H.E.=10 points, H.E.A.=15 points, H.E.A.R.=20 points, H.E.A.R.T.=25 points, and H.E.A.R.T.S.=35 points. If three H's are thrown the player loses all his score. The first player to reach 100 points wins the game.

Examples of Scoring

> H.H.A.R.T.S.=5
> H.E.A.T.T.S. =15
> E.A.R.T.T.S. =0
> H.H.H.T.S.S.=Loss of all the player's score

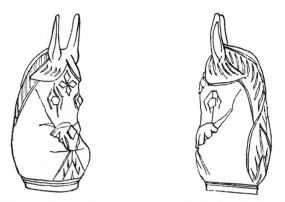

Knights from a Siamese chess set (Author's collection)

CHAPTER 6

Domino Games

1. GAMES USING CHINESE DOMINOES

There are no blanks in a set of Chinese dominoes; but eleven of the pieces are duplicated, making a total of thirty-two tiles. The eleven paired tiles form the 'civil' series; and the unpaired tiles the 'military' series. (See fig. 91.)

The identical tiles of the civil series pair together, while those of the military series pair in total counts; the exception being the 2–4 and 1–2 tiles which form the SUPREME pair, which is the highest of all, though separately these tiles are the lowest.

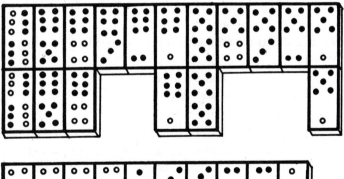

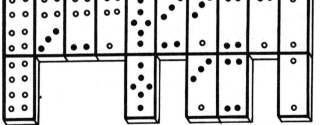

FIG. 91. Set of Chinese dominoes. The duplicate pieces form the civil series (Author's collection)

PAI KOW

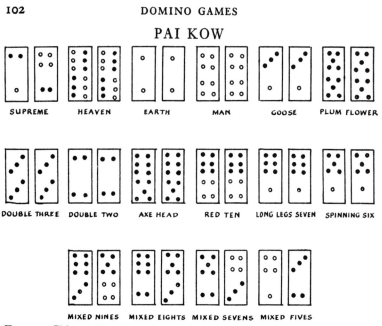

FIG. 92. Chinese Domino pairs in descending order for 'Pai Kow' and 'Tien Kow'

Below mixed fives are four other pairs, arranged in descending order of value:

> 6–6 and a nine
> 1–1 and an eight
> 4–4 and a seven
> 3–1 and a five

The pairs 2 to 12 are made up of civil dominoes (two alike in a set); the remainder are military dominoes (only one in a set).

All other combinations rate according to the total of their pips; but if these amount to double figures, only the last figure counts: e.g. a total of 12 becomes 2; 15 becomes 5, etc.

Pai Kow is played with a full set of Chinese dominoes, and the rating of the pairs is shown in fig. 92, in descending order from left to right.

Four players take their places at a table and the dominoes are shuffled face downwards. They are then stacked face downwards in two piles, each pile containing four rows of four dominoes.

Three dice are thrown and the aggregate score counted anticlockwise round the table, ending with the player who becomes the first banker; the latter throws the dice again to indicate in the same way where the deal begins. The dominoes are dealt anticlockwise by the banker, each player receiving four dominoes.

The players examine their tiles without exposing them; and then place them face downwards on the table in two pairs designed to beat the two pairs held by the banker. When the three players have placed their dominoes on the table, they put their stake alongside. The banker may impose a limit if he wishes. Any onlooker may participate in the game by placing a stake alongside the dominoes of a chosen player.

When all the stakes have been placed, the three players expose their first pair, the banker exposing last. They then expose their second pair.

To win a round, the same player or the banker must win both exposures by holding at each exposure a pair of dominoes of higher standing than his companions. If two different players win one exposure each, the round is drawn, and the stakes are lifted from the table, and may be staked again after the next deal. If the banker wins both exposures, he takes all the stakes on the table. If a player wins both exposures, the banker pays him his stake, and also those of any onlooker who may have laid a stake with him. The banker also pays the other players (and participating onlookers), if their pairs rate higher than both of his; but if their pairs are lower, then the banker wins their stakes. There is no exchange between banker and a player unless the value of each pair is higher (or lower) on both exposures.

When the gains and losses have been settled, the banker deals the second pile of sixteen dominoes, and the second round is played in the same way. When both rounds are finished, all the dominoes are reshuffled and stacked in two piles of sixteen dominoes each. The player on the banker's right becomes the new banker, and the game continues. Players may drop out at the end of any round and their place be taken by an onlooker.

Chips of varying shapes denoting different denominations are usually used for staking, and then accounts are settled at the end of the game. These chips may be of pottery, porcelain, ivory, mother-of-pearl, or other substances. See tailpieces, pp. 116 and 136.

BULLFIGHTING (Tau ngau)

This game is played with a full set of thirty-two Chinese dominoes, and three to six players take part. Any number of onlookers may place stakes alongside those of a player of their choice.

Dice are thrown to determine the banker, and then the dominoes are shuffled face downwards; each player, including the banker, draws five dominoes. Before looking at their pieces the players place their stakes in front of them to any limit which may be imposed by the banker. When the stakes have been placed, the players look at their dominoes. The value of each piece depends upon its number of pips, except that the 2–1 may count as three points or six points, and the 4–2 as six points or three points.

Every player must discard three dominoes forming ten points, or a multiple of ten:

Examples

3–1 + 2–2 + 1–1 = 10
6–6 + 3–3 + 1–1 = 20 (a multiple of ten)
2–1 + 6–5 + 3–3 = 20 (the 2–1 counting as three points)
2–1 + 4–4 + 3–3 = 20 (the 2–1 counting as six points)

After discarding three dominoes, the remaining two are exposed and score the total of their pips, but if these reach double figures, the first figure is ignored: e.g. fifteen pips would count as 5.

If a player's scoring points are less than the banker's, he loses his stake to him, if his scoring points are more than the banker's, the latter pays him the equivalent of his stake; if a player and the banker have equal scores there is no exchange between them.

If a player cannot discard three dominoes to form ten, or a multiple of ten, he is 'stuck'; and the banker takes his stake. If the banker is 'stuck', he pays the equivalent stake to all the players who are able to discard three dominoes, but there is no exchange between players who are 'stuck' and a banker similarly afflicted.

If a banker has scoring points, the player on his right becomes the new banker for the next round; but if the banker is 'stuck' he remains banker. After each round all thirty-two dominoes are shuffled together; and then each player draws five dominoes and the game continues as before.

TIEN KOW

This popular Hokkien game for four players is played with a set of thirty-two Chinese dominoes. A banker is chosen by throwing dice, then the dominoes are shuffled face downwards, stacked and eight dealt to each player by the banker. They examine their tiles, and then the banker leads by placing a domino face upwards on the table. The three players follow in turn anticlockwise, each player trying to take the trick with a domino of higher value than the others. If a civil domino is led, the other players must follow with the same suit; and if a player has none, he must discard a military domino. Similarily if a military domino is led, the trick can only be taken by a military domino. A civil discard cannot win.

The player taking the trick stacks it in front of himself; then he leads with a domino from his own hand; and the other players try to win the trick as before. The game continues until all eight tricks have been won; and the player winning the final trick becomes the new banker, and responsible for dealing the next hand. If the banker wins the last trick he remains banker; but the scoring of the new hand will be different as described below. After the last trick of each hand, the points are adjusted, usually by the exchange of counters, and then the dominoes are shuffled face downwards, stacked, and dealt by the new banker.

Instead of leading one domino, a player may lead one of the sixteen named pairs or couples, see page 102, or one of the eight couples comprised of:

> 6–6 and a mixed nine (6–3 or 5–4)
> 1–1 and a mixed eight (6–2 or 5–3)
> 4–4 and a mixed seven (5–2 or 4–3)
> 3–1 and a mixed five (4–1 or 3–2)

and the round can only be won by a pair or couple of higher value. The SUPREME couple (2–1 and 4–2) only scores highest in this game when it is led; otherwise it is the *lowest* of the couples. The tiles of the SUPREME couple are very lowly on their own, 2–1 being the least domino in the set, and the 4–2 is twenty-ninth out of thirty-two!

If a player wishes he may lead two pairs or couples at a turn of play. These can only be captured by two pairs or couples in the same suit, civil or military, and one of the pairs or couples being of a higher value than either of those led.

Scoring

This is on a basic four point system.

A player with no tricks loses 4 points to the winner of the last trick, who also becomes the new banker.

A player with less than four tricks deducts this number from 4, and pays the difference to the winner of the last trick.

A player winning four tricks neither wins nor loses any points.

A player winning more than four tricks deducts 4 from the number, and claims the difference from the winner of the last trick.

If a banker becomes the new banker, the basic figure in the second hand becomes 8 instead of 4, at a third deal 12, at a fourth 16, etc. There is no limit to the number of times a banker may deal. There is usually an indicator on the table to show how many times the banker has dealt. When there is a new banker the basic figure reverts to 4.

Extra points

If the banker leads the SUPREME couple, he claims a bonus of 4 from each player.

If a player leads the SUPREME couple, he claims a bonus of 4 points from the banker, and 2 points from each of the other players.

Similarily if the banker led any two of the following couples:

> 6–6 and a mixed nine
> 1–1 and a mixed eight
> 4–4 and a mixed seven
> 3–1 and a mixed five

he claims a bonus score of 8 points from each player; while a player making the same lead wins 8 points from the banker, and 4 points from each of the other players.

A game may finish at a set time, or by mutual consent.

2. GAMES USING MA-JONG TILES

TEN AND A HALF (Sap tim pun)

This Cantonese gambling game is played with a set of Ma-jong tiles (see plate 16), and up to forty players can take part. The 144 tiles are shuffled, and then built into four walls two tiles high and eighteen long (see Volume I, fig. 130). Each player, including the banker, draws one tile from the wall, which is placed face down on the table and the player lays his stake beside it. The 108 suit tiles—bamboos, characters, and circles—are each valued according to their number, i.e. the six of circles is worth six points. The sixteen Wind tiles, the twelve Honour tiles, and the eight Flower tiles, are each worth ½ a point.

When the stakes have been placed, the players turn their tile over, and if the banker has drawn an East Wind, he takes all the stakes on the table. If a player has drawn an East Wind the banker pays him his stake. The East Wind tile is then discarded and another drawn in its place, and the game proceeds.

If a player's tile is worth 5 points or less, he must draw another tile from the wall; if it is worth 6 points or more, further drawing is optional. Only two extra tiles can be drawn from the wall, making a maximum of three tiles in any player's hand. The drawing of extra tiles begins with the player on the banker's right, and passes anticlockwise around the table. Each player tries to bring the value of the tiles in his hand to 10½, or as near this figure as possible.

If 10½ is exceeded the hand is ruined; it is laid face up on the table, and the player's stake passes to the banker.

When all the players have finished drawing, the banker turns his tile face up on the table, and if it is a 5 or below, he must draw a tile from the wall, otherwise he has the choice of standing, or drawing a tile to bring his score as near to 10½ as possible. If he exceeds this figure he pays all the players still in the game their stakes. If the banker holds tiles worth exactly 10½ points, he wins all the stakes on the table; but if his score is less than 10½, he pays the players with higher scores, but receives the stakes of players with lower scores, and there is no exchange with players with the same score.

After each round of play the player on the banker's right becomes the new banker, who declares the maximum stake for the round.

3. GAMES USING A DOUBLE-SIX SET OF WESTERN DOMINOES

BLIND HUGHIE

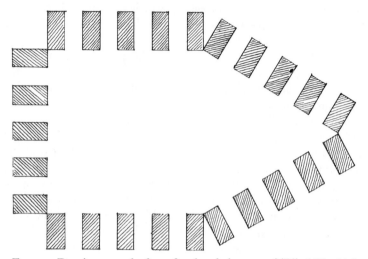

FIG. 93. Dominoes ready for a five-handed game of 'Blind Hughie'

This game of luck is popular with Fifeshire miners. Two to five may participate, and each player starts with five tiles dealt face downwards. Play is always with the tile on the left. The players draw for starting, high tiles taking precedence. The leader plays his left-hand tile into the centre; the next player turns up his left-hand tile and if he can follow either end of the exposed tile he does so, otherwise the tile is placed face up at the right end of his pile.

The first player to dispose of his pile wins, and is paid the pip value by each player of the tiles left in his hand. If no one can play all his tiles, the player with the lowest hand is paid the difference between his hand and each opponent's by the opponent.

ENDS

This account was provided by the publican of a country Inn in Northumberland.

A double-six set of dominoes is used for this game for four players. After the dominoes have been shuffled face downwards on

21. Squails and lead target.
(Author's collection.)

22. Ivory tenpins and
tops, c. 1820.
(Author's collection.)

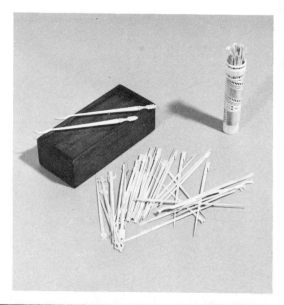

23. Two sets of Chinese spellicans. The one in the filigree ivory casket, c. 1820; the other with ivory hooks and mahogany box, c. 1880.

'24. Chinese lacquered box containing four sets of cards, and three shapes of mother-of-pearl gaming-counters. (Author's collection.)

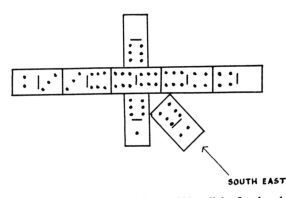

SOUTH EAST

FIG. 94. Showing method of forming a fifth tail in five-handed 'Ends'

the centre of the table, each player draws seven and examines them, The player with the 6–6 places it face upwards on the centre of the table. If no one has the 6–6, then the 5–5, or 4–4 etc., is used instead.

The next player on the left follows on if he can, making a tail; and if he is unable to do so he asks for a suitable tile from his neighbour on the left; if he in turn cannot provide one then play passes to the player next on the left, and so round the table. If no one can help, the next player on the left joins on any tile in his hand and makes a new tail.

The first player to get rid of all his dominoes is the winner of the game, and each of the other players pays him the value of the pips on the tiles left in their own hands. (In this pub the stakes were ½d a pip).

In the second game the double next below the 'opener' in the previous game is used: e.g. if it were 6–6, then 5–5, or if the first game had started with 4–4, then the second would open with 3–3 etc.

If no player holds a double, the highest of 6–5, 6–4, 6–3, 6–2, 6–1, is used instead.

The game can be played by five players, when each draws five dominoes instead of seven. The fifth end is made to grow out at the south-east. See fig. 94.

After 1–1 has been used as the 'opener', the 'opener' of the next game returns to 6-6, or 5-5, etc.

DOMINO WHIST

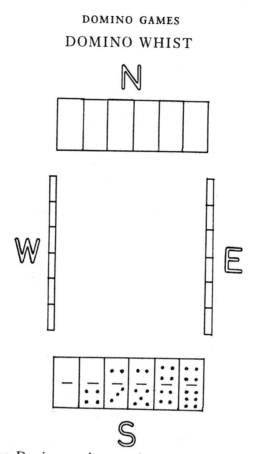

FIG. 95. Dominoes at the start of a game of 'Domino Whist'

North and South play against East and West; each player being dealt six dominoes face downwards, and the four remaining tiles are put into reserve.

In the first game North leads a tile; East matches one end if he can, and passes if he cannot; South then matches or passes, followed by West, etc. The first team to play all its dominoes wins the round, and scores the total number of pips remaining in the opponent's hands; or if there is a block and neither side can play, the round is won by the players with the lowest number of pips, and they score the total of pips held by their opponents. A game consists of 100 points, and a rubber is the best of three games.

It is usually wise to play high dominoes as soon as possible.

DOMINO POOL

A pool is created by subscriptions from the four players, each being on his own. The dominoes are then shuffled face-downwards on the centre of the table, and the players take five dominoes each. The holder of the highest domino leads, and the player on his left tries to follow, but if he fails to do so the turn passes clockwise round the table.

Method of scoring

1. When a player has no dominoes left in his hand, the other players' pips are counted on their remaining tiles, and each player's total is scored against his name.

2. If all the players are blocked, the scores are recorded in the same way.

3. When a player has 100 points he is *out*. The player surviving his opponents wins the game and the pool.

4. By prior agreement, *starring* may be allowed. If a player is out, he may star by paying again into the pool the original stake. He then re-enters the game with the same score against him as the player in the worst position.

5. Players are not compelled to star, and are only allowed to star once. The last two players in the game are not allowed to star, though they may have done so before they reached this position.

Tactics

If a player is in a much better position than his opponents, it is often advisable for them to concentrate on opposing him, and thus make the game more even. Combination against a player must not be by open agreement, but as a principle of play. There should be silence during a game.

The leading player usually tries to block the player immediately behind him rather than the others.

DOMINO LOO
For two players

The dealer deals two hands of five dominoes, and then turns one tile face uppermost, the highest number on this tile becoming the trump suit. The value of the tiles in descending order is:

(*a*) The double of the trump suit.

(*b*) The rest of the trump suit in descending order; trump-six ranking above trump-five, etc.

(*c*) The plain suits. The double is the highest tile in each suit, and double blank ranks above blank-six.

The opening player may discard his whole hand before leading, and take six more tiles from the stock. This is called taking a *miss*. One of the six tiles is then discarded face upwards. The dealer who plays second may pick up this discard, or he may also take a miss, but he cannot do both. He then replies to the lead.

Rules

1. If a player holds two or more trumps, he must lead one; and on winning a trick he must play a trump if possible.

2. The second player must follow suit if he can, but he need not take the trick if he can follow suit without doing so. (See, however, rule 5.)

3. Any tile, other than a double or a trump, may be one of two suits. The player must declare which, the first number called being that of the suit. The 5-1 tile can be called five-one, or one-five. As five-one any other five tile except 5-0 would take it; but one-five would only be taken by 1-6, 1-1, or a trump.

4. Each trick counts one point, and the game is fifteen points.

5. A player who fails to take a trick when he is able to do so is *looed*, and loses five points from his score, or if he has no points then he owes five, and will require 20 points to win the game.

Three or four players

Domino Loo can be played by three players, when only two of them can take a miss; or by four players when only one of them can take a miss, and he lifts all seven tiles, and discards two.

A pool is formed; the dealer paying three counters into it for the privilege, and then distributes the tiles as follows:

1. The tiles are shuffled on the table, and one tile is turned face up. He then deals one tile face up to each player.

2. If a player has a higher tile of the same suit as the tile exposed, he wins the pool. The other players are looed, and pay a counter into the pool.

3. If more than one higher tile appears, the owner of the highest wins the pool, and the others are looed as under rule 2.

4. If no one receives a higher tile of the same suit as that exposed, all are looed and pay one counter each into the pool.

5. The tiles are then gathered up, shuffled again, and five tiles dealt face downwards to each player, a spare miss being left in the middle of the table.

6. The remaining three tiles are placed face downwards on the table, and one is turned up by the dealer to decide which suit is trumps, this being the higher number on the tile.

7. Every player then examines his tiles and decides whether:

(*a*) To stand, when he retains the five tiles and says, 'I play'.

(*b*) To retire, by placing his tiles face downwards on the table; he is then out of the rest of the hand, neither paying nor receiving any counters.

(*c*) To take the miss, and return his original five tiles to the table. He is then compelled to stand.

8. The player on the left of the dealer has the first choice of the alternatives under rule 7; then the player on his left, etc. The dealer is last, but he, too, may take the miss if it is still available.

9. If all the players retire, the dealer wins the pool; and then a new pool is started with a new dealer.

10. The game usually ceases when one player wins fifteen counters.

Chess King made of Dyed Bone, from a Spanish 'Pulpit' set

CHAPTER SEVEN

Games with Numbers

LOTO

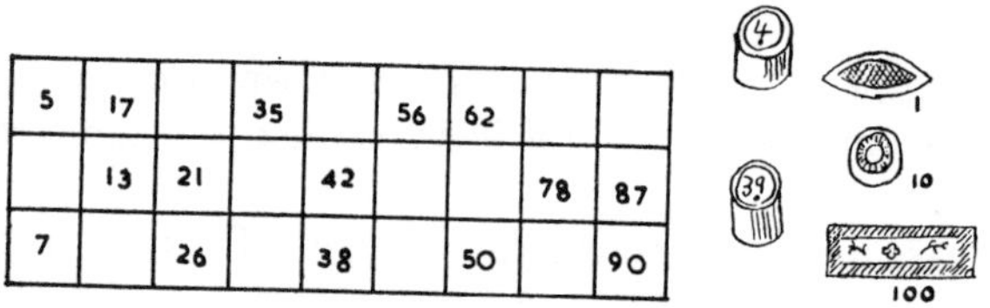

FIG. 96. Loto card, reel, and counters (Author's collection)

Loto was popular in England a century ago. Any number of players took part. The equipment consisted of a hundred counters, each worth 1 unit; 14 of another colour or shape, each worth 10 units; and 12 of a third colour or shape worth 100 units. The TENS were often fish shaped, and the HUNDREDS rectangular. Frequently these counters were made of mother-of-pearl. There was also a bag of 90 wooden reels or balls, numbered from 1 to 90, and a pack of eighteen or twenty-four large cards, each marked with three rows of five numbers from 1 to 90 inclusive. See fig. 96 and plate 18.

Rules

1. Each player drew two cards and deposited the agreed stake in the pool.

2. A sufficient number of discs was placed in the middle of the table to cover all the the numbers on the cards in use.

3. Each player threw two dice, the highest throw indicated the leader, who placed the ninety reels in the bag and shook them up, and then drew ten out, one at a time, calling the numbers aloud, and placing them on the table.

4. Any player having a number called on one or both his cards, took up a disc or discs and covered the number with them.

5. When ten reels had been taken out of the bag:

(*a*) A player with one disc on a horizontal line won a counter.

(*b*) If he had two discs on a horizontal line, he won two counters, plus a bonus of five more.

(*c*) Three discs on a horizontal line won three plus a bonus of twenty-five counters.

(*d*) Four 'discs on a horizontal line won four plus one hundred counters.

(*e*) Five discs on a horizontal line won five plus two hundred and fifty counters.

6. The highest scorer was paid out of the cache first; the next highest second, etc. When all had been paid, the reels were returned to the bag, shaken, and passed clockwise to the next player, and a new draw of ten reels was made.

7. When all the counters were distributed, any player awaiting payment was unlucky. The players then shared out the pool in proportion to the number of counters each held.

8. The cards were handed in, reshuffled, and dealt out again: a new pool of stakes was formed, and a new game started.

In the Victorian nursery Loto was played with pictures, flowers, and letters, instead of numbers; and the games were known as Botanical Loto, Spelling Loto, Geographical Loto, Historical Loto, etc. They were designed to have educational value.

Loto was derived from the Italian game Tumbule, which was taken to France to become Tombola, and thence to England and the southern states of the U.S.A. The Latin Americans play a related game, Bolito. The Americans invented numerous variations of Loto. In Keno the cards became a 5 × 5 grid; and the reels were drawn out of the bag until one player had five counters in a row, either horizontally, vertically, or on a long diagonal.

Recently Keno has been adapted to become a popular game in the casinos of Nevada. Each player has a card marked from 1 to 80 (see fig. 97b), and crosses out eight numbers. The card is handed to the operator with a stake of $1.00. When all players' cards have been received, 20 numbers out of 80 are ejected from an automatic blower, and these numbers are lit on the Keno flashboards throughout the casino. If the player has marked five or more of the numbers, he has a winning card and is paid the amounts tabled below (fig. 97b).

BINGO

A recent popular variant is Bingo. Only seventy-five balls are used, and the cards are 5 × 5 grids with the central square a free number. The first player to obtain five numbers in a row or column, or four plus the central square, cries 'Bingo', and wins the pool. (See fig. 97).

Some cinemas introduced Screeno; on 'bank' nights the patrons receive a free screeno card with their seat ticket. Valuable prizes are given to the winners.

1	24	6	57	3
14	19	69	30	17
27	61	■	73	52
4	8	36	7	44
13	56	75	42	9

FIG. 97. A bingo card

1	2	3	4	5	6	7	8	9	10
11	12	13	14	15	16	17	18	19	20
21	22	23	24	25	26	27	28	29	30
31	32	33	34	35	36	37	38	39	40

$1.00

41	42	43	44	45	46	47	48	49	50
51	52	53	54	55	56	57	58	59	60
61	62	63	64	65	66	67	68	69	70
71	72	73	74	75	76	77	78	79	80

8

FIG. 97 b. A Keno card

8 spots for $1.00.

Catch 5- win $9.00   Catch 7- win $1,650.00
Catch 6- win $90.00   Catch 8- win $18,000.00

Mother-of-pearl fish counter (Author's collection)

CHAPTER EIGHT

Card Games requiring Boards

CRIBBAGE

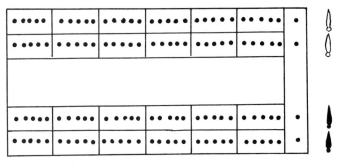

FIG. 98. A cribbage board

Two players

An ordinary pack of fifty-two cards and a cribbage board is required for this game. The players cut the pack; low becomes the dealer, and high card the non-dealer or *pone*. Each player has two pegs with which he records his score on the board. If a player's first score was 2, he would place a peg in the second hole on the outer row of his side of the board; if his next score was 7, he would place the second peg in the seventh hole beyond the first peg; and on his third score he would lift the first peg and place it the required number of holes beyond the second peg. The first player to traverse the sixty holes of the board twice, i.e. score 121 or more, wins the game. Usually the two players' pegs are of different colours, but this is not essential.

Method of play

1. The cards are shuffled and pone cuts, leaving the pack divided into two parts on the table, face downwards. The dealer lifts the undermost part and deals six cards to his opponent, and then six to himself. The remaining cards are placed on top of the other heap.

2. In the first hand of a new game, pone pegs three holes at the start as compensation for the dealer owning the crib.

3. The players examine their hands, and both discard two cards face downwards onto the table.

4. Pone again cuts the pack, and the dealer lifts the top card of the cards on the table and exposes it face upwards on the heap. Pone places the cut cards under the heap.

5. This exposed card and the four discarded cards form the *crib*, which belongs to the dealer. The exposed card is also used in making up the score of both players, as well as the crib.

6. If the exposed card is a Jack, the dealer gains a bonus of two points: 'Two for his heels'.

7. Pone leads the first card, calling out its value; court cards and tens count as 10, and the other cards according to the number of their pips. Aces count as one.

8. When the first card has been placed on the table and its value declared, e.g. SEVEN, the dealer will try to win points by either playing another seven to make a pair (2 points); or play an eight, to bring the score to *fifteen*, for which he would also gain 2 points. If he has neither of these cards, he would play something else, e.g. a three, and would call 'ten'.

9. Pone could then play a five to make fifteen (2 points); or another three to make a pair (2 points). Perhaps he could do neither and played a Queen calling 'twenty'.

10. The dealer might then play another Queen, calling 'thirty' and taking 2 points for a pair. If pone were unable to make *thirty-one*, and this could only be done with an Ace, the dealer would win a bonus point for playing the last card of a *stop*. If the stop is at exactly thirty-one the player wins a bonus of 2 points.

11. When the cards on the table approach thirty-one, and the player whose turn it is to play is unable to do so without overshooting thirty-one, he calls 'Go'. The other player then plays any other card or cards up to that limit, scoring 2 points if he reaches thirty-one exactly, and 1 point if he stops short of it.

12. When thirty-one or the nearest possible number to it has been reached, the player who played the last card leads in the next stop, and the scoring is the same.

To recapitulate: 2 points for *fifteen* and *thirty-one*; 2 points for making a pair; 6 points for making a pair royal 'three cards of a kind); 12 points for double pair royal (four cards of a kind); three or more cards in sequence, regardless of suit, peg the number of cards in the sequence; 1 point for playing the last card in a stop if the total is under thirty-one.

13. Three or more cards of any suit forming a sequence (2,3,4, etc.) count 1 point for each card in it for the last player. The cards need not be played in order: e.g. if a 5 and a 4 had been played, a 3 or a 6 would form a sequence and score 3 points for the player. If the opponent could then add to this to make a run of four, he would win 4 points. King, Queen, Jack, ten . . . is a sequence, but not Ace, King, Queen. In this game Ace counts low.

14. When all the cards have been played out, pone picks up his cards and counts the points in his hand:

Scoring

For a sequence of three, four, or five cards	3, 4, or 5 points
For every fifteen, e.g. 6 & 9; 10, 4, & 1	2 points
For every pair	2 points
For three of a kind, e.g. three 6s (pair royal)	6 points
Four of a kind (double pair royal)	12 points
For the Knave of the exposed card, 'his nobs'	1 point

15. The exposed card is counted as part of the hand, and if the player had a sequence of 5, 6, 7, and the exposed card was a 7, this would form two separate sequences and a pair, scoring $3+3+2=8$ points.

16. Although all court cards count 10, a pair must be the same card, e.g. two Kings. A King and a Queen are not a pair.

17. Pone always counts his score first, and at the end of the game it may be an important privilege, as he may reach 121 and win. The dealer may also have 121 or more, but his score is not counted if the game has already been won by his opponent.

18. In reckoning the value of a hand the fifteens in it are counted first; then the pairs, pair royal, or double pair royal; followed by the sequences; and if three cards are in sequence, and there is a duplicate of any one of them, this makes a double run scoring 6 points, and 2 points for the pair. If three are in sequence and the other two are duplicates of one of them, this constitutes a triple run of three (9 points) and a pair royal (6 points) totalling 15 points.

19. If all the cards in the hand are of the same suit the player scores a *flush*, worth 5 points, and if the exposed card is of the same suit, then 6 points. If the cards in the crib are all the same suit the

flush is worth 4 points, and if the exposed card is also the same suit, 5 points.

Three combinations are listed below to show how the scoring is calculated:

Four fives: four fifteens=8; a double pair royal=12; total=20.

Two sixes, a four and a five: two fifteens=4; a pair=2; and two runs of three=6; total 12.

A five and three court cards in sequence: three fifteens=6; a sequence of three=3: total 9.

Tactics

The dealer tries to put useful cards into the crib, and his opponent useless ones.

In play try to prevent the opponent scoring fifteen or thirty-one, and certainly avoid letting him score a pair or a sequence at the same time.

Three handed cribbage

When three play, each receives five cards, and places one card in the crib. The player on the dealer's left leads, and has first scoring hand. He deals in the following hand. The score is marked on a triangular board; see plate 19.

Four handed cribbage

When four play, North and South are partners against East and West. Each player receives five cards and puts one into the crib, which belongs to the dealer. The player on the dealer's left leads, and has first scoring hand. One partner scores on the board for both. Game is usually 121 points.

POPE JOAN

There are many variations of Pope Joan, but this is one of the best.

Any number of players may take part, and each starts with thirty counters. A fifty-two card pack is required, with the eight of diamonds removed; and a special board (see Plate 20) consisting of a circular tray revolving around a central pillar and divided into eight compartments marked:

POPE	KING
MATRIMONY	QUEEN
INTRIGUE	KNAVE
ACE	GAME

POPE is the nine of diamonds.

MATRIMONY the King and Queen of trumps in the same hand.

INTRIGUE the Knave and Queen of trumps in the same hand.

The dealer *Dresses* the board by placing 15 counters from his own store into the compartments on the board:

> POPE — 6 counters
>
> MATRIMONY — 2 counters
>
> INTRIGUE — 2 counters
>
> ACE, KING, QUEEN, KNAVE, and GAME — 1 counter each.

Hands are then dealt to each player, with an extra hand in the centre of the table, and any cards left over are added to this. The last card of the pack is turned up to decide the trump suit. If the turn-up is the nine of diamonds (Pope), or an Ace, King, Queen, or Jack, the dealer wins all the counters in the appropriate compartment of the board.

The player on the dealer's left leads, and names the card as he does so. The holder of the card in the same sequence immediately above it, follows; and this continues until the play comes to a halt by no one being able to continue; either the King of the suit has been reached, or the wanted card is in the extra hand, or the card has already been played, or it is the seven of diamonds. (The eight was removed to form a stop before Pope, the nine of diamonds.)

When the Jack, Queen, King, or Ace of trumps are led during the game, the player wins the counters in the appropriate compartment, and if he can play the Jack and Queen, or the Queen and King, he wins as a bonus the counters in INTRIGUE or MATRIMONY respectively.

The first player to be rid of all the cards in his hand wins the counters in GAME; and also one counter from each player for every card he holds in his hand. The holder of an unplayed Pope card, however, is exempt from this payment.

Tactics

When no one can follow a card led, the same player leads any other card he wishes; therefore players should remember the stop cards, and also the cards which cannot be led to, and these should be played as soon as possible.

Sequences are valuable as they enable a player to dispose of two, three, or more cards at a turn of play; alternate sequences are nearly as useful: e.g. a six, eight, and ten of a suit. The lowest is led, and whether a card proves a stop or not the leader can continue the sequence as long as some other player does not go 'out' on an intermediate card.

Pope can only be played when the holder has the lead; it is usually wise to play Pope at the first opportunity after playing any known 'stops'.

The unclaimed counters in each compartment are left to accumulate, and sometimes MATRIMONY and INTRIGUE may not be claimed in a whole evening. Any unclaimed counters at the end of the game may be disposed of by dealing a final round face uppermost without the surplus hand, and the holders of Pope, Ace, King, Queen, and Jack of diamonds receive the counters in the respective compartments; the holder of the Queen also taking half the counters in INTRIGUE and MATRIMONY, the other halves being taken by the holders of the Jack and King.

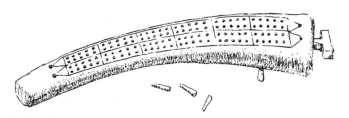

Cribbage board of walrus ivory from Baffin Land (Author's collection)

CHAPTER NINE

Games requiring Manual Dexterity

SHOVE HA'PENNY

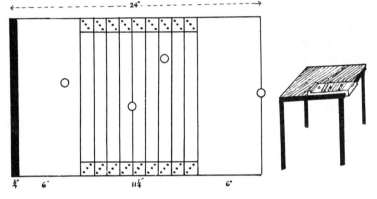

FIG. 99. Diagram of a 'Shove Ha'penny' board

This game for two players was played in English taverns at least as early as the sixteenth century, when the popular coin to use was the Edward IV groat, from which the game was known as Shoffe-grotte.

The board can be marked out on a table-top in chalk or pencil, but most modern boards are made of hardwood with the grain running lengthwise, and with a strip of wood under the near edge to prevent slipping. Ten narrow grooves cut across the board divide it into nine beds, each $1\frac{1}{4}''$ wide. Two lines $1\frac{1}{4}''$wide from the long edges limit the playing area, and three holes in each square receive pegs for keeping the score, one player using the right side and the other the left.

Five tuppenny pieces serve as counters, and are placed one at a time over the near edge of the board and then struck with the palm of the hand, being propelled along the board to come to rest within the playing area. Those lying on the beds score, but those cutting a line are 'dead', unless they are knocked by another counter clear of the line. The first player to score three times in each bed is the winner.

The players take turns to shoot the five coins; those passing beyond the beds are 'dead', and are immediately removed; those more than half over the side lines into the marker squares are also removed; those less than half over the line remain on the board, but cannot score unless they are knocked back into a bed. At the end of each turn the coins lying within a bed score, and corresponding pegs are inserted into the marker holes. The beds may be filled in any order; but once three of a player's coins have come to rest in a bed, any further score is credited to his opponent, if the latter still needs a score in this bed. The final point of a game, however, must be scored by the winning player.

Cannoning, and striking one coin with another, is allowed, and no points are scored until the last coin of the turn has been played. If a coin lies on top of another, neither scores. If a coin stops short of the first line, the shot is taken again; but if it touches the line it is in play and must be left. It may be tapped on by another coin, but if the latter thereby stops short of the line it may not be lifted. It in turn can be knocked on by another coin.

Skilled players usually fill the distant beds first.

FIG. 99a. Groat of Edward IV (Author's collection)

CROKINOLE (played on the coast of British Columbia)

A crokinole board is shown in fig. 100. The central depression is $1\frac{3}{8}''$ across, and $\frac{1}{8}''$ deep. The radii of the three circles are $3\frac{1}{2}''$, $7''$, and $10\frac{1}{2}''$, respectively; and the gutter is $1''$ beyond the outer circle.

The game is usually played by two or four persons—though three, six, or even eight may play—partners sitting opposite each other.

25. Two views of a Chinese dicing cup in ivory, c. 1750. See pps. 144–6. (Author's collection.)

26. Victorian card holder of china. (Author's collection.)

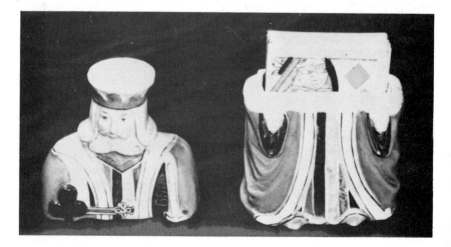

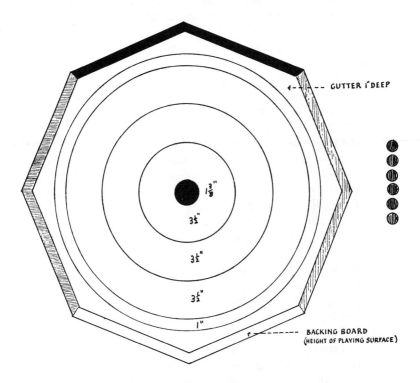

FIG. 100. Diagram of a 'Crokinole' board

When there are three players, one plays against the other two who are partners and shoot alternately. Six players arrange themselves as a double three, and eight players each have one face of the octagonal perimeter, and shoots his discs from the outermost circle within the angle of his 'side'. For simplicity the game for four players will be described.

Four-handed crokinole

1. Each player has six round discs of his own colour made of wood $1\frac{1}{4}''$ in diameter, and $\frac{5}{16}''$ thick with the edges bevelled.

2. The game begins by one of the players placing a disc on the inch wide outermost ring within his own quadrant of the board; and with a flick of the middle finger he tries to lodge it in the central recess.

3. The player on his left then places one of his discs on the outermost ring on his quadrant of the board, and shoots in the same manner, but he tries to knock his opponent's disc into the gutter.

4. Each player shoots in turn until all the discs have been used, and then the scores are counted.

5. The count is calculated thus:

(*a*) A disc in the central recess counts 20, and must be recorded at once, unless this score would finish the game, when it can only be counted at the end of the round; e.g. in playing a game of 100, if a player had scored 80 or more, and his disc entered the recess, it would not be counted until the end of the round, the opponents thus having an opportunity to dislodge it.

(*b*) At the end of the round each disc in the inner ring counts 15, the middle ring 10, and in the outer ring 5. Those outside the outer ring or in the gutter count nothing. Discs resting in the central depression which have already been counted do not score again.

(*c*) A disc resting on the line of any ring is counted as being outside that ring.

(*d*) Each side counts its points; and the *difference* is added to the successful team's total score.

6. The game may be for 100, 200, or 500 points.

7. Players must keep their discs and their hands off the board, except when it is their turn to play.

8. Neither the board, nor any player's chair may be moved during a round.

9. Any player may place his disc against any disc near the outermost ring within his quadrant, and thus send them both in any direction, and when a disc of his own colour lies so near the outermost ring as to prevent the disc being placed outside it, he may place the new disc inside in contact, and then shoot with the outer piece. This rule does not apply to a piece belonging to an opponent.

10. A player is obliged to shoot at an opponent's disc in the board and try to put it in the gutter. Only if there are none on the board may he aim directly at the central recess. If an opponent's disc is not touched, the player's disc is taken off the board and placed in the gutter.

11. A disc can only be played once during a round, except under rule 9.

12. If a disc is shot off the board it is placed in the gutter.

13. A disc lying tilted into the gutter is lifted and placed in it.

14. At the end of a round no discs are removed until the score has been agreed upon.

Tactics

Always try to force enemy pieces into the gutter. It may be possible to ditch two or three pieces at a single shot by clever planning of cannons. Beginners are apt to try to place as many of their discs as possible within the inner circle, but this is child's play. Do not concentrate on making high scores, but keep the opponent's score as low as possible.

CARUMS

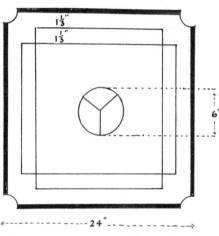

FIG. 101. Diagram of a 'Carums' board

This popular Burmese game is played on a board resembling a small billiard table with four netted pockets at the corners. The entrances to the pockets are $1\frac{1}{2} \times$ the diameter of the striker.

Equipment

The measurements of a Carums board are given in fig. 101. The board is highly polished, and the coefficient of friction is further reduced by powdered French chalk.

Each player has nine discs of his own colour, and there is one red queen disc. All are 1″ across and some $\frac{3}{16}$″ in thickness, made of hardwood; and a striker 1⅜" across, of bone or ivory. The discs are arranged within the central circle as shown in fig. 102. and then the opening player (White) places the striker anywhere within the rectangular box on his own side of the board, and flicks it with the middle finger of his right hand at the discs in the centre, trying to knock one of his own discs into a pocket.

FIG. 102. Initial arrangement of pieces within the central circle

Rules

1. White plays first, and the turn continues as long as a white disc is pocketed.

2. After each strike the striker is returned to the player's own box.

3. The striker may rebound from the walls and then strike a disc.

4. The striker must cross the front line of the box, but it can be directed at a side wall with spin to cause it to screw back over the line and hit a disc behind the striker's starting point.

5. A player may hit an opposing disc to use it to pocket one of his own.

6. If a player pockets one of his opponent's discs it remains in the pocket, and the turn ceases.

7. Pocketing the red disc promises 5 points, but it must be 'covered' by a player's disc in any pocket, otherwise it is returned to the centre point, together with any of the player's discs pocketed in the same turn of play.

8. If the striker enters a pocket with a disc, the disc is returned to the board and placed anywhere within the central ring by the *opponent*, and the turn ceases.

9. If the striker enters a pocket, the opponent takes one of the player's discs out of a pocket and places it within the central ring. If the player has not scored he is penalized by a score of –1 point.

10. When a player has pocketed all his discs he scores the number of his opponent's piece still on the board, plus 5 for the queen if she has been pocketed by him. The queen-score only counts for the winner of the set-up.

11. There may be several set-ups to a game; and a match consists of three games, each of 30 points.

Alternatives

There are two methods of scoring with the red queen:

i. The red may be pocketed at any time, but must be covered in the same turn of play with a player's disc in any pocket. (As described in rule 7.)

ii. The red must be pocketed *after* the player's last disc. This is the more skilful game.

On the 4th March, 1956, an All-India Carrom Federation was formed to control the size and shape of championship boards, and to draw up a code of rules. These are obtainable from the All-India Carrom Federation, Nehru Stadium, Madras-3. Price: Rs. 1.25.

SQUAILS

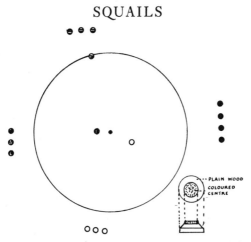

Fig. 103. Diagram of a game of 'Squails'; and an elevation of a squail

This game can be played on an ordinary table by two to eight players. Each has an equal number of coloured wooden discs called squails; and by alternate turns of play, the players place their squails half over the edge of the table, and then strike them with the open palm of the hand towards a small lead target placed at the centre of the table. (See fig. 103 and Plate 21.)

The players are divided into teams, and one from each side alternately strikes a squail towards the target. If the latter is moved more than six inches from its initial position, it is replaced. The object of the game is to obtain the greatest number of squails near to the target; and it is legitimate to knock opposing squails away from the target as well as trying to leave one's own close beside it. The squail furthest from the target scores 1, and the squail nearest 16. A tape measure is used to decide disputed positions.

The author has a diary written by an English emigrant to Australia in 1862, on board the clipper ship *Orient*. He remarks when mentioning the various recreations of the cabin passengers: '... our amusements grow stale and insipid; though the never failing cards, chess, backgammon, and draughts serve to while away the weary hours. Squails, in which the ladies join and are becoming dangerous rivals for the gentleman, have a large patronage.'

The movement of the ship must have introduced additional difficulties into the calculations!

SHOVEL BOARD

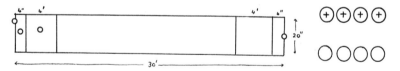

FIG. 104. Shovel Board and discs (not to scale)

Shovel board was originally played on the long low table that usually stood in the baronial hall of most country mansions. Later it was adapted to smaller tables and was a popular game in the coaching inns and taverns of Shakespeare's time. Master Slender refers to shovel board in the *Merry Wives of Windsor*, Act I, scene I, during an argument with Pistol.

The early boards were thirty feet long and twenty inches wide; but smaller tables provide an excellent game. At each end of the table a line is drawn four inches from the edge, and another at four feet. Each player has four flat metal discs distinctively marked, which he propels down the table in alternate turns of play, and tries to place in a scoring position, or uses to destroy his opponent's formation.

Scoring

1. A disc hanging over the far edge of the table, but not falling off, scores 3 points; between the edge and the distant line, 2 points; and beyond the near line, 1 point.

2. Discs stopping short of the near line do not score, unless they are knocked beyond it subsequently by either player. (See, however, rule 5.)

3. Discs falling off the table do not score.

4. A disc lying exactly on a line, counts as 'in'.

5. If there are no scoring discs at the end of a round, the nearest disc to the near line counts as 'in', and wins 1 point.

6. Game is usually 11 points.

Four players

7. The players divide themselves into two teams, and one partner of each team stands at either end of the table, to contest alternate rounds with their opposite number in the opposing team.

8. Game is usually 21 points.

BROTHER JONATHAN

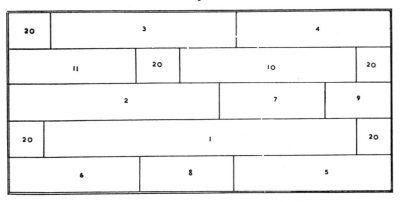

FIG. 105. Board for 'Brother Jonathan'.

This eighteenth century American game consisted of pitching copper cents at the spaces marked on a board (see fig. 105). The players stood at a set distance from the board and took turns to toss five coins. (Tuppenny pieces are a handy size.) The number marked on the compartment was scored towards game when a coin alighted upon it; but coins touching a line did not count. Note the larger the compartment the smaller the score, and *vice versa*. The total for game was decided by the players before play began.

The scores were calculated at the end of each player's turn of five throws.

FIG. 105a. American cent 1795. (Author's collection). Actual size

NINE-PINS

Nine small pins are arranged on the top of a table. The players in turn roll two balls towards them, and score one point for each pin knocked down. The winner is the player first reaching an agreed

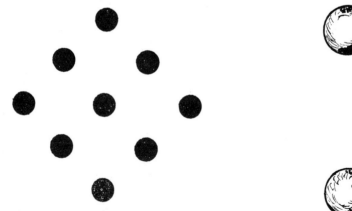

FIG. 106. Arrangement of pins for 'Nine-pins'

total. There are several modifications of this game, and the pins may be set up in a diamond formation as in fig. 106. or in a line, or a circle.

In a Georgian tenpins set belonging to the author, the pins are of ivory, and instead of balls, there are two small ivory tops with serrated edges. Considerable skill is required to spin the tops accurately down the table, which needs to be smooth and polished. See Plate 22.

SPELLICANS

Any number of players may take part in this game, which begins by the spellicans being thrown onto the table in a heap; then the players in turn hook them out one at a time without disturbing any other piece in the pile.

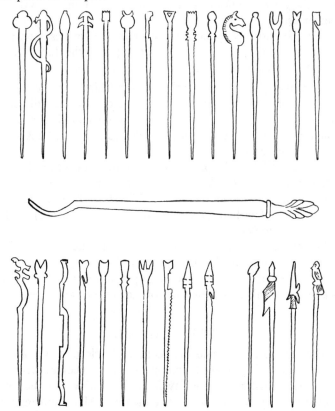

FIG. 107. Part of a Chinese set of ivory spellicans (Author's collection)

Rules

1. The seniority of the players is determined by throwing dice, or in other handy manner; the junior player throws down the spellicans, and after a piece has fallen from his hand it cannot be adjusted.

2. The senior player then takes the hook and tries to remove a piece from the pile without disturbing any of the other pieces. If successful he tries to remove another spellican, and continues until a piece not under attack is disturbed, when the hook is passed to the player on his left.

3. After a piece has been touched, the player cannot attack any other piece until it has been disengaged completely from the pile.

4. When the hook is passed to a player, he may continue to attack the same spellican as his predecessor, or may choose some other piece.

5. At the end of a game the holder of the smallest number of spellicans is the first player in the next; and the holder of the greatest number casts the spellicans upon the table.

This game appears to have originated in China. The best sets are made of ivory, and the higher scoring pieces are carefully fretted into familiar shapes: a spear, saw, snake on a staff, a bird on a branch, a trefoil, mitre, trident, horse's head, fork, a bucket yoke, etc. (See Plate 23.)

The more difficult the piece is to move by virtue of its shape, the more points are scored by extracting it from the pile, and every piece is marked with its own value. There are two of every kind (see fig. 107). The highest scoring piece is the saw (50), and the lowest a woman (5).

Cheaper Chinese sets are made of bone or cane, and the shapes are more roughly made. European Jerk-straws, gaily coloured straight sticks of wood, are even cheaper substitutes. Each colour has a different value, and the rules of play in the two games are the same.

STRING GAMES

String games are outside the scope and title of this book, but they are so widely played among primitive peoples, from the aboriginee of Australia to the Navaho in the southwest of the United States, that they warrant a passing mention. More information is available in Kathleen Haddon's excellent monograph, *String*

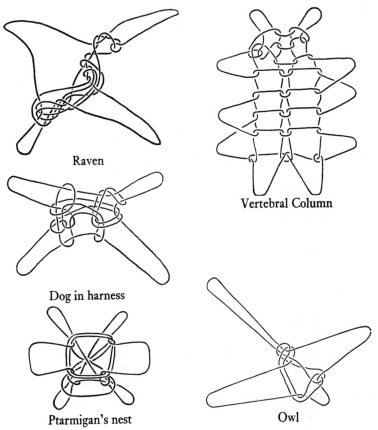

Raven

Vertebral Column

Dog in harness

Ptarmigan's nest

Owl

FIG. 108. String figures (From V. Fidler)

Games for Beginners, Heffer & Sons, Cambridge, 1934 (Fifth reprint, 1967).

Games related to our own 'cats' cradles' have been recorded from most parts of the world; very elaborate forms being found among the Eskimo, who use a long loop of sealskin thong placed around the thumbs and little fingers. By a series of manipulations, complicated figures are formed, the movements of the digits being accompanied by a song or poem describing the shapes that are being made, or the actions they are performing—perhaps a caribou running up a hill.

For centuries Eskimo parents have amused their children with these fanciful figures, and preserved legends and folk-lore that otherwise would have disappeared. Over the years innumerable intricate patterns have been evolved of birds, animals, people, sleighs, boats, and other familiar objects of the frozen north. Most settlements have stories associated with each thong figure, which are chanted as the patterns develop.

There are only three initial positions, but an infinite number of final forms. Many of the 'pictures' are extremely fanciful, and their interpretation requires the same degree of imagination as the appreciation of constellations in the sky, which antiquity saw as hunters, ploughs, bears, crabs, and goddesses. Primitive peoples appear to have a facility for converting dots and lines into concrete shapes.

In the western Arctic, thong games are only permitted when the sun is below the horizon: to play in summer brings ill-luck, and bad weather follows play while the sun is shining. The Eskimo of the eastern Arctic have no taboo against the time of playing; but thong games are forbidden to young boys lest when grown to manhood their fingers might tangle in a harpoon line.

The few forms illustrated above are but a minute fraction of a good player's repertoire; they may, however, serve to put on record a dying pastime. Thong games are fast disappearing, being replaced by packs of cards bought at the nearest trading post, or from an airforce canteen. The tailpiece on page 122. shows a cribbage board of walrus ivory made for the author thirty years ago by an Eskimo patient from Frobisher Bay in Baffin Land.

Nineteenth century Chinese mother-of-pearl gaming-counter. (Author's collection)

CHAPTER TEN

Gaming-Counters

Gaming-counters have been made of shell, stone, metal, ivory, bone, wood, glass, faience, pottery, leather, and in recent years, cardboard and plastic. A few of these materials merit further attention.

Porcelain

Porcelain counters were used in Siamese gambling houses, being redeemable in money at the end of a session. Eventually they became recognized as an unofficial currency and served as low denomination coins. They are included in most collections of strange and primitive monies. (See Plate 27, nos. 1–5. Also tailpiece on page 143.)

Mother-of-pearl

During the eighteenth century Canton developed a flourishing trade with Europe and America in mother-of-pearl gaming-counters. They ranged from simple shapes with trifling designs (Plate 27, nos. 6–9.) to beautiful pieces engraved on one side with scenes of Chinese life, and on the other ornamentation and a space for the owner's initials (Plate 27, nos. 10–13). Such sets were ordered two years before delivery. Instructions were sent by sea to an agent in Canton with details of the required cipher; these were duly cut, and then the pieces were shipped to the West—a round voyage of eighteen months from order to receipt in the days of East Indiamen.

The shapes represented different units: perhaps a shilling, ten shillings, and a pound, in the homes of the well-to-do, and much higher in the gambling establishments frequented by the Prince Regent and his coterie. In *Pride and Prejudice*, written in 1796–7, though published several years later, Jane Austen mentions Lydia talking '. . . incessantly of fish lost and fish won.' These were fish-shaped mother-of-pearl counters (see Plate 27, no. 14).

Metal*

In the Middle Ages when Roman numerals were used in Europe, addition and subtraction, multiplication and division, were performed on a counting-board (fig. 109, 110).

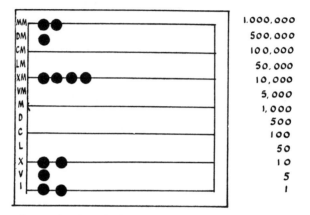

FIG. 109. A counting-board with counters arranged to record the number 2,540,027

Originally coins were used as markers; but the risk of loss, especially in open markets or windy streets, led to substitution by casting counters of brass. These were manufactured in considerable quantities at Tournay in France, in the Netherlands, and in Nürnberg in Germany (Plate 27, nos. 15-18). Few, if any, were made in England. Many of these casting-counters, or *jetons*, simulated coins, and cause difficulty to collectors of medieval money.

There is little doubt that on occasion jetons were used as gaming-counters; and the well-known 'Abbey pieces' probably served this double purpose. They are frequently found in medieval ecclesiastical graves (Plate 27, nos. 19-20).

Towards the end of the sixteenth century Arabic numerals began to be used in Europe, counting-boards became obsolete, and jeton manufacturers were faced with ruin. To recover lost trade they turned to gaming-counters. The last of the Nürnberg jetons were made about A.D. 1650, though for a few more years they made dual purpose pieces bearing the legend: GAMING AND RECKONING COUNTER

*This account has been considerably shortened to maintain a balance of contents, but it is hoped to publish detailed information on metal gaming counters at some future date.

(*Nürnberger speil und rechenpfennig*). Plate 27, nos. 21–2, shows an unusual piece which has the same design on the obverse and reverse. The Arms are intended for those of Maximilian I, Holy Roman Emperor (1459–1519).

FIG. 110. From Reisch's *Margarita Philosophica*, 1503

During the reign of George III several English button and token manufacturers entered into the profitable gaming-counter market, striking a number of semi-political pieces which were used for whist and other card games. Some of these imitation coins were passed in change by dishonest persons at fairs, race-courses, and taverns, and the dividing line between counterfeiting and reputable trade was ill-defined.

Between 1787 and 1817 there were two large issues of Trades-men's Tokens which supplemented the totally inadequate regal copper currency; and tokens, spurious pieces, political medalets, and gaming-counters have become intermingled, with borderline pieces of each class. A few examples of these gaming-counters are shown on Plates 27–8, nos. 23–30. Note nos. 29–30 with the mounted figure of Frederick William III, King of Prussia, on the obverse, and SPIEL MARKE (gaming counter) on the reverse. This piece indicates the true nature of many of the 'political medalets' of the period.

Plate 28, nos. 31–2 is an interesting piece showing the interior of a toyshop in the early nineteenth century. On the counter is a stuffed cat and a windmill, and on the shelves behind can be seen some birds. Unfortunately the piece is very worn, and the details are obscured. The reverse reads: DUTCH AND ENGLISH TOYS, FANS, &c SOLD BY I. KIRK IN ST. PAULS CHURCH YARD.

In the chaotic state of the country's copper currency at the end of the eighteenth century, many of these pieces circulated as farthings or halfpennies, and are considered by some token-collectors as non-local tokens, but they are better regarded as gaming-counters.

Close copies of British coins, especially the shillings and sixpences of Anne, and sixpences of Georges I and II, and guineas and half-guineas of George III, were manufactured over a period of at least a century (See Plate 28, nos. 33–4.) A fine guinea-sized piece dated 1798 was made by Henry Smith, Birmingham, in 1867. These pieces vary considerably in their workmanship.

Foreign coins were also imitated; Plate 28, nos. 35–6 shows a half-zecchino of Florence, one of the best known of the medieval Italian pieces; but this copy has as legend the name in Latin of the manufacturer: JOHANNES ILLE COQVVS SUI FILIQVE (John Cooke and Son).

When Queen Victoria ascended the British throne in 1837, she was barred by the Salic Law in force in Hanover from succeeding to William III's continental possessions, and the dukedom passed to her unpopular uncle, the Duke of Cumberland. Many satirical pieces were struck depicting the young queen on the obverse, and on the reverse the mounted figure of the duke riding past a dragon (a parody of St. George and the dragon on the current sovereign) with TO HANOVER in the legend; but with the unspoken sentiment TO HELL AND HANOVER. (See Plate 28, Nos. 37–8.)

The queen's bust was associated with a large number of reverses, three being shown on Plate 28, Nos. 39–41. Note the piece bearing the two-headed eagle of the Holy Roman Empire, suggesting that this was struck in Nürnberg; this is supported by Plate 28, Nos. 42–3 with the same eagle as an obverse, and SPIEL MARKE on the reverse. Another German piece of the time is shown, the obverse recording a stagecoach. (See Plate 28, Nos. 44–5.)

There was a revival in the production of gaming-counters in Birmingham in the second half of the nineteenth century, some twenty firms participating between 1850 and 1870. The obverse of these pieces bore the head of George III; and the reverse a crowned pointed shield, known as a 'spade' because of its resemblance to the prevalent shape of earth-digging spades of the period. Most of

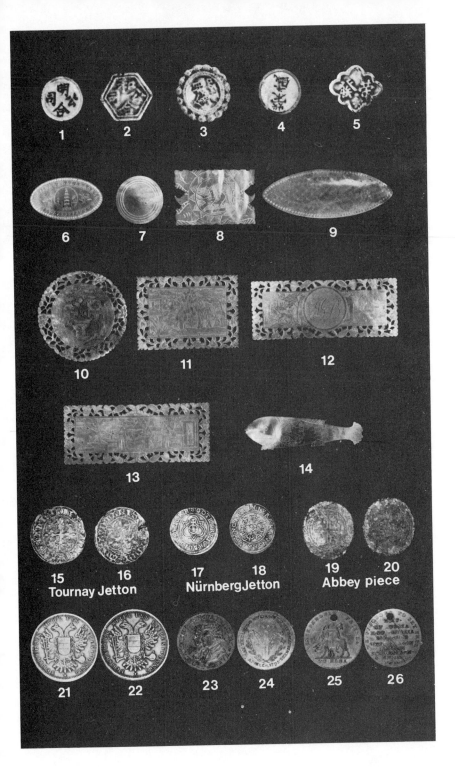

1

2

3

4

5

6

7

8

9

10

11

12

13

14

15   16
Tournay Jetton

17   18
Nürnberg Jetton

19   20
Abbey piece

21

22

23

24

25

26

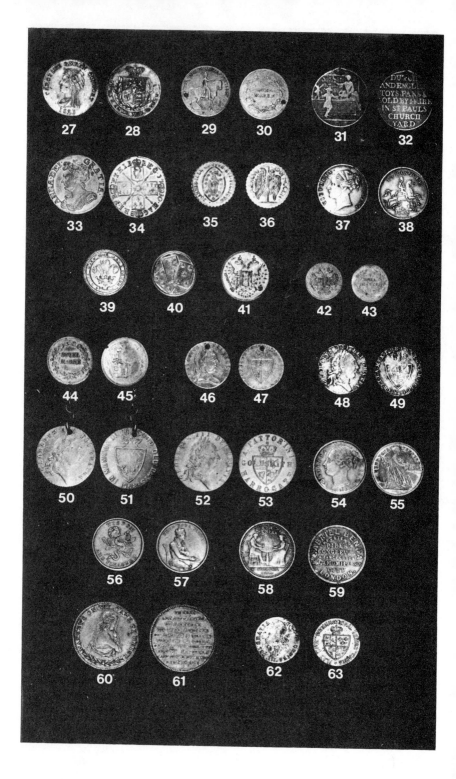

these pieces are signed with the names or initials of the firms striking them. (See Plate 28, Nos. 46–53.)

EXAMPLES OF TYPES

i. *Full name in the legends*

C.H.A.R.L.E.S.P.E.V.E.R.E.L.L.E.L.A.T.E.M.C.A.R.R.O.L.L.M.A.K.E.R.B.I.R. (Charles Peverelle set up as a hardwareman at 48 Edgbaston Street, Birmingham about 1866.) For his half guinea see plate 28, Nos. 46–7.

ii. *Initials only in the legends*

T.B.ET.T.A.REX.F.D.B.AR.S.T.DS.T.M.S.ET.C. (See Plate 28 Nos. 48–9) (Thomas Brookes & Thomas Adams (Rex, fidei defensor) Barr Street, die-sinkers, tool makers, stampers, etc.) Also half-guinea size. c. 1870.

In 1883 the Counterfeit Medals Act was passed; this may have influenced the choice of an incontrovertibly obsolete coin design; even so at least one advertiser was warned by the Royal Mint to stop its spade reproductions.

At this time it was fashionable to wear guineas as ornaments on brooches and watch-chains, and imitation guineas were used as cheap substitutes. Many of these gaming-counters have been holed for suspension. See Plate 28, Nos. 50–1.

iii. *Unsigned pieces*

These are of four types, with the legends:

T.H.E.O.L.D.E.N.T.I.M.E.S. (Guinea and half-guinea dated 1797)
I.N.M.E.M.O.R.Y.O.F.T.H.E.O.L.D.E.N.T.I.M.E.S. (Guinea, dated 1788)
IN MEMORY OF THE GOOD OLD TIMES (Guinea, dated 1788)
IN MEMORY OF THE GOOD OLD DAYS (Guineas dated 1768 and 1797, half-guineas dated 1768 and 1788). See Plate 28, Nos. 50–1.

The first three types were manufactured before 1875, but how much earlier is not known. The last type are mostly poorly struck, and probably were not made earlier than 1880, and extended at least up to 1925, and possibly later. These pieces were used for stage money, and the actress Vesta Tilley threw 'Good Old Days' guineas to her audiences as souvenirs. See Plate, 28 Nos. 50–1.

Between 1860 and 1950 a large series of advertisement pieces were struck bearing the names, trades, or addresses of the firms who

issued them, as circular legends, or in lines across the field. A few
of the legends and inscriptions are listed below.

iv. *Advertisement Pieces*

A.FATTORINI GOLDSMITH HARROGATE. This retail jewellery firm still
exists at 10 Parliament Street, Harrogate, Yorkshire. The last of
their 'guineas' was struck in the 1890s. (See Plate 28, Nos. 52–3).

PLAY WITH 'INTERNATIONAL SERIES' GAMES

The International Card Co, was founded in 1903 by Mr. H. P.
Gibson at No. 2 Bury Street, London. In 1919 it was converted into
a limited company as H. P. Gibson & Sons Ltd. Their Leadenhall
St. premises were destroyed during the Second World War. The
current brand-name is 'HPG Series'.

The firm marketed 'guineas' before the First World War; again
in the early 1920s. when they used the brand-name 'International
Series' until the beginning of the Second World War; and again for
a short time around 1947–51, until rising costs and reduced demand
made their production unprofitable. (See Plate 28, Nos. 62–3.)

Further information is available in Hawkins' excellent articles;
see the bibliography.

During the early Victorian period many gaming counters urged
the players to 'KEEP YOUR TEMPER'. Two varieties are shown on
Plate 28, Nos, 54–7; one bears the queen's head on the obverse, and
the other has a curious design of a rose entwined by a serpent.
Tradesmen also issued 'KEEP YOUR TEMPER' pieces for their client's
use; the queen's head being replaced by an advertising inscription.
See Plate 28, Nos. 58–9.

The author's collection contains four brass pieces which appear
to belong to an incomplete set. One is the size of a two-pound piece;
the obverse bearing the head and torso of a young woman* with the
legend: MATHEWS (*sic*) ON THE GAME OF WHIST; while the reverse is
an inscription in ten lines: THERE ARE 4 PENALTIES ON A REVOKE TO
TAKE 3 TRICKS OR DEDUCT 3 TRICKS FROM THEIR SCORE OR ADD 3 TO
THEIR OWN AND THE REVOKER CANNOT WIN BUT MUST REMAIN AT
NINE. (See plate 28, Nos. 60–1.)

The three one-pound size pieces have their faces numbered 1 to
6, and are inscribed with more rules of whist.

This chapter can only serve as a brief introduction to an extensive
* *Said to represent the female figure Silence (—whisht!—whist). Thomas Matthews
of Bath was a contemporary exponent of the game.

subject; but enough, perhaps, to encourage others to investigate further into the background of these curious pieces. Collectors will find *Batty's Catalogue of the Copper Coinage of Great Britain, Ireland, British Isles & Colonies,* useful. Many pieces are undated, but any listed in this work must have been struck before its date of publication, 1868.

Siamese porcelain gaming-counters (Author's collection)

The Chinese dicing cup shown on Plate 25 was found in an antique shop in Plymouth, and bought for a few shillings. A large cork had been rammed into the bottom, splitting the side and base. It was repaired with ivory from an old billiard ball.

The figures represent Eight Taoist Immortals, and from the type of carving, and the running hand script, which is an abbreviated form of writing using colloquial speech, the cup was dated between A.D. 1750 and A.D. 1800. The bottom character of each column is the signature of the carver; the other seven characters are arranged in a popular poetic form, and describe the feelings of an unsuccessful gambler who compares his unhappy lot with the ever-lasting delights of the Immortals:

> *The Immortals at dice in their Celestial Heaven,*
> *Have turned dry river into flooding stream:*
> *But I have wandered for years in the desert*
> *Alone with the stones, and the wind's wild scream.*

The Immortals often appear on tangram boxes (see Plate 12), and other pieces of Chinese carving. Their legends are not older than the Sung dynasty, A.D. 960–1280. The Immortals occupy eight grottos of the upper spheres, and each has a distinctive attribute:

Li T'ieh-küai is depicted with a crutch and a gourd filled with medicines. He left his body to go on a journey, asking a disciple to watch it for seven days; but the young man deserted it on the sixth to visit his sick mother, and when the spirit returned he found his body in ashes. The spirit entered the body of a beggar who had just died, but instead of being a handsome man as previously, he was a cripple; his head was long and pointed, his eyes huge—he was 'Li of the iron crutch'. He often returns to earth, sleeping at night in a bottle, and helps others in the transmigration of their souls. *Attribute* a crutch.

Chung-li Ch'üan was a Marshal of the Empire in 2496. In his old age he became a hermit, and during the great famine transmuted copper and pewter into silver with a mysterious drug. He gave this treasure to the poor, and saved thousands of lives. One day while he was meditating the wall of his cave in the mountain split open exposing a jade casket which contained secret information on how to become immortal. He studied it carefully; his room filled with coloured clouds, and to the sound of heavenly music the celestial stork bore him away to the regions of immortality. *Attribute* a feather fan.

Lans Ts'ai-ho, the strolling singer of the Immortals, was a hermaphrodite. On earth he played a flute or a pair of cymbals. He wore a tattered blue gown, held by a black wooden belt three inches wide; one foot was bare and the other shod; in summer he wore an undergarment of padded material; and in winter he slept on the snow, his breath rising like steam from a boiling cauldron. He earned his living by singing in the streets and reciting doggerel verses denouncing this fleeting life and its delusive pleasures. When given money he distributed it to the poor. One day he became drunk at an inn, and disappeared on a cloud, throwing back to earth his shoe, robe, belt, and castanets. *Attribute* a musical instrument.

Chang Kuo lived as a hermit in the hills. The Empress Wu (A.D. 684–705) ordered him to come to court; but on the way he died at the Gate of the Temple of the Jealous Woman. His body began to decay and was infested with worms, but he was seen again back in the mountains alive and well. He rode a white mule which carried him thousands of miles in a single day; and when the journey was over, Chang Kuo would fold him up like a piece of paper and place him in his wallet. When the mule's services were required again, he spat on the packet, and the animal resumed his proper shape. Finally Chang fell sick and died a second time. When his disciples opened his tomb it was empty.

He is usually depicted on a white mule, sometimes facing its head, sometimes its tail. He carries a phoenix feather, or a peach of immortality. His picture is often found in nuptial chambers, seated on a donkey and offering descendants to a bride and groom. *Attribute* a paper mule.

Ho Hsien Ku is the only woman among the Immortals. She holds a magic lotus-blossom—the flower of open heartedness—or the peach of immortality; and is seen drinking wine, or playing a reed organ.

At birth she had six hairs on her head and she never grew more.

She lived on a mountain and one day found a mother-of-pearl stone. In a dream she was ordered to powder it and eat the powder to gain agility and immortality. She obeyed the command, at the same time vowing eternal virginity; and thenceforth she floated from one mountain peak to the next gathering fruits for her aged mother. She gradually found that she required less and less food; and finally she floated upon a cloud to the abode of the Immortals. *Attribute* a lotus-flower.

Lü Tung-pin was five feet two inches tall; and when twenty years old made a journey on which he met the Fire-dragon who gave him a magic sword which enabled him to become invisible. Later he was exposed to ten temptations which he overcame successfully, and acquired supernatural powers and magic weapons.

He travelled the kingdom for four hundred years, slaying dragons and ridding men of divers evils; his skill at fencing was proverbial, and he is always represented with his magic sword Chan-yao Kuai, the Devil slaying sabre. In his other hand he holds a fly-whisk, the symbol of his power to fly through the air and walk on the clouds of heaven. *Attribute* a magic sword.

Han Hsiang Tzu is depicted with a bouquet of flowers, or a basket of peaches of immortality. He was educated by his uncle Han Yü, the great poet of the T'ang dynasty, but he soon outshone his teacher; and made verses which held the secret of the future. One day he climbed the supernatural peach tree of the genii, but fell from its branches, and during the fall attained the state of immortality. *Attribute* a flower basket.

Ts'ao Kuo-chiu was a member of the Imperial Sung family, and is shown with a tablet of admission to the Court in his hand. His younger brother committed murder; and Ts'ao retired as a hermit to the mountains, where he clothed himself in wild plants. He studied the Way to the Sky, and learned that the Heart is the Sky, and the Sky is the Way. Thus the origin of the Universe became clear, and he took his place among the Perfect Ones. *Attribute* a tablet of admission to Court.

APPENDIX B

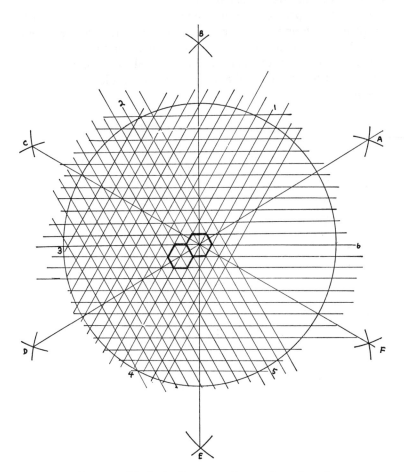

FIG. 111. Method of constructing an Agon board

1. Draw a circle, centre O, of radius 6″; and without altering the compasses describe arcs on the circumference at 1, 2, 3, 4, 5, and 6; thus dividing the circle into six equal parts. Join 1–4, 2–5, 3–6.

2. With a reduced radius, arcs are subtended from 1 and 2 at B; and similarily from 2 and 3 at C. Arcs D, E, F, and A are constructed in the same way and then lines BE, CF, DA are drawn.

3. Starting from the centre the lines OB and OE are marked off

in $\frac{1}{2}''$ lengths and then lines drawn through these points at right angles to the line BE (or parallel to the line 4–5).

4. Similarly, parallel lines at $\frac{1}{2}''$ intervals are drawn perpendicular to the lines CF and DA. The three sets of parallel lines produce a grid of small equilateral triangles, six forming a hexagon.

5. Alternate rings of hexagons are coloured, but it is immaterial which, and fig. 52 shows the outer ring plain while in fig. 53 it is coloured.

Addendum

MU TORERE

While this volume was in the press the author received the following account of Mu Torere, a game for two played by the Maori people, from Mr. W. B. Gould of Auckland, New Zealand.

Rules:

1. *Playing equipment:* The board consists of an 8-pointed star, with a circular area in the centre, called the *putahi.* Each player has four pieces of a distinctive colour. At the beginning of the game, one player's pieces are placed on four adjacent points, and the remaining points are the other player's.

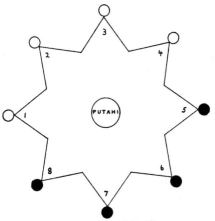

FIG. 112. Board for Mu Torere

2. *Object:* To block the opponent's pieces so that they cannot move.

3. *The play:* Black begins and players move alternately. Only one piece is allowed in each area. Jumping is not allowed. There are three varieties of move:

(a) a piece (*perepere*) may be moved from one of the arms (*kawai*) direct to an adjacent arm,

(b) or from the *putahi* to an arm,

(c) or from one of the arms to the *putahi*, providing that one or both of the adjacent arms are occupied by an enemy piece or pieces. *Variant:* the restriction on the movement of a piece from the arms to the *putahi* is sometimes observed only for the first two moves of each player.

Although the Maori culture is rich in action games and other amusements Mu Torere appears to be the only 'board game' played by them. The Maori board was made in three ways. The first was to mark it with charcoal on a hewn slab; the second was to mark it on the ground with a pointed stick; the third was to mark it on the inner bark of totara while green so that the design remained when the bark dried—two straight sticks being tied at each end to prevent curling. It appears to have been played mainly on the East Coast of the North Island of New Zealand, by the Ngati Porou tribe.

There has been some doubt as to whether it is a pre-European game, or not. 'Mu' is the word given by the Maoris to European Draughts, and is a transliteration of the English word 'move'. It is probable, however, that the game was originally called Torere, and Mu has been added as a prefix. Early colonists seem to have regarded it merely as a variation of Draughts, but this could be due to their tendency to explain the unfamiliar in the light of the familiar. There seems to be no basic similarity in the games: the objects are different—there is no capture in Mu Torere—movement is different—and of course the board and number of men are different. Mu Torere would seem to have more in common with Mill than with Draughts. Further, it is unlikely that this game was derived from European Draughts when the latter was so eagerly accepted by the Maoris.

There is only one trap to cause any difficulty. Once a player recognizes the situation and knows the correct move to escape it, he should never be beaten. Between two players who both know the trap, the game should (in the absence of error) result in a draw.

Diagram 1: White to move. He has the choice of 1–8 or 7–8. But the move 7–8 will be fatal, because Black will answer with 6–7. The chief characteristic of this situation is the V shape formed by Black's men at 5, 6, and P. This V must not be allowed to split open.

Diagram 2: The situation here is basically the same but not so obvious. It is White's move with the choice of 2–3 or 4–3. The move 2–3, however, will be followed by 1–2, 8–1, and 7–8, opening the V and winning again. There is an unavoidable circular movement round the edge of the board.

Diagram 3: If the variant rule in 3 (c) is played, it is a cardinal principle that if the opponent has three men in a line around the edge, you must either get possession or keep possession of the *putahi*. It is White's move, with a choice of 4–5 or P–5. If he moves P–5 Black will reply with 7–P. Possession of the *putahi* is essential to any victory.

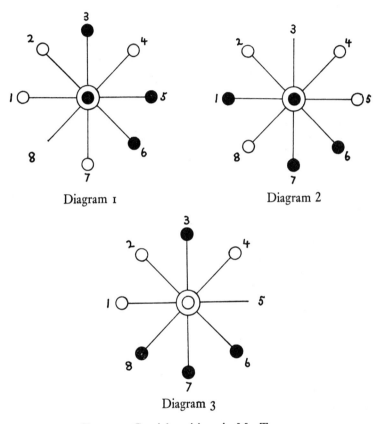

Diagram 1   Diagram 2

Diagram 3

FIG. 113. Crucial positions in Mu Torere

Index

Games described in detail in the text, and main references to them, are in bold type; references to illustrations are in italics.

Abacus, 138
Achi, 55–6, *fig. 47*
Agon, 61–3, 147–8, *figs. 52, 53, 111*
Alquerque, 24–6
Amerindians,
 Cheyenne, 79;
 Hopi, 5;
 Moki, 53;
 Yokut, 80
Arizona, 5
Asalto, 46–7, *fig. 40, plate 11*

Ba-awa, 72–3, *fig. 71*
Backgammon, 14–15, *fig. 10 plate 6.*
Backgammon group, 12–23
Baffin Land, 122, 136
Ballinderry, 45–6
Bastian, Dr. A., 30
Batty, D. T., 143
Bewick, T., 71, *fig. 70*
Bidou, 86–91, *fig. 84*
Bingo, 115–16, *fig. 97*
Blind Hughie, 108, *fig. 93*
Bolito, 115
Bottle game 12–14, *fig. 9, plate 5*
Brother Jonathan, 131–2, *fig. 105*
Bualog, 20
Bullfighting, 104, *fig. 91*
Burma, 28–30, 127–9

Campbell, J. H., 86
Canada, 84, 86, 124
Card holder, *plate 26*
Carums, 127–9, *figs. 101, 102*
Cent, American, 132
Ceylon, 1
Chess, Burmese, 28–30, *figs. 21–2, plate 7;* Japanese, 33–8, *figs. 24–34, plate 9;* Siamese, 31–3, *fig. 23, tailpiece p. 100, plate 8*
Chess and Playing cards, 52, 53
Chess group, 27–41, *figs. 19–35, plates 7, 8, 9*
Chess piece, deer horn, Scotland, *tailpiece p. 113*
China, 12, 33, 48, 56, 66, 68, 92, 93, 94, 99, 101, 102, 104, 105, 116, 137, 144, *figs. 9, 48, 59–69, 85, 86, 87, 89, 91, 92, 107, plates 5, 6, 12, 16, 23, 24, 25*

Chinese domino games, 101–6
Choro, 75, *fig. 73*
Chuki, 52–3, *fig. 45*
Cockfighting, 92–3, *fig. 85*
Come posso divertirmi?, 57
Counterfeit Medals Act, 141
Counting board, 138
Counters, 137–43, bone, *plate 18;* Metal, 138–43; *plates 27–8;* Mother-of-pearl, 137, *tailpiece pp. 116, 136, plate 24;* Porcelain, 137, *tailpiece p. 143*
Cowries, 1, 3, 31, 81, 82
Cribbage, 117–20, *fig. 98, tailpiece p. 122;* Four handed, 120; Three handed, 120, *plate 19*
Crokinole, 124–7, *fig. 100*
Cross and Circle games, 1–5, *figs. 1–4*
Culin, S., 3, 5, 52, 53, 78, 94

De Ludis Orientalibus, 12, 13
Dice, Chinese, 12, 92, 93, 94, *figs. 85, 86, plates 5, 6;* Six-sided 10, 11, 15, 16, 17, 18, 19, 44, 61, 83–91, *plates 4, 17;* Special, 97–100, *plate 15;* Two-sided, 78–83
Dicing Cup, 144, *plates 5, 6, 25*
Dittar Pradesh, 81–2, *fig. 79*
Djuka people, 73
Domino Loo, 111–13
Domino Pool, 111
Domino Whist, 110, *fig. 95*
Double-six domino games, 108–13, *figs. 93–5, plate 17*
Draughts, Turkish, 41, *tailpiece p. 54, plate 10*
Draughtsboard, *plate 10*
Druses, 2
Duff, D. I., 47
Dutch Guiana, 73

Eccentric Excursion to the Chinese Empire, 8–10, *fig. 6, plate 3*
Egypt, 49
Ends, 108–9, *fig. 94*
England, 6, 108, 114, 123, 130
English game, 15, *fig. 11*
Eskimoes, 135–6 *tailpiece, p. 122*

Fanorona, 24–6, *fig. 18*
Fidler, V., 135

Fifty, 83, *fig. 81*
Fish, Prawn, King Crab, 99–100, *fig.89*
Fithcheall, 45–6, *fig. 39*
Five in a row games, 57
Forbes, D., 44, 46
Four Field Kono, 42, *fig. 36*
Four-Five-Six, 84, *fig. 82*
Fox and Geese, 47
France, 19, 63, 115, 138, *plate 13*

Gambit chess club, London, 41
Game of Education, 94–7, *fig. 87*
Game of the Race, 11–12, *fig. 8, tailpiece 23, plate 4*
Gaming-counters, 137–43, Bone, *plate 18*; Metal, 138–43, *plates 27–8;* Mother-of-pearl, 137, *tailpiece pp. 116, 136, plate 24;* Porcelain 137, *tailpiece p. 143*
Gelli, J., 57
Genii's Game, 2–3, *fig. 2*
Germany, 138
Ghana, 55, 72
Go, 60 *frontispiece*
Gould, W. B., 149
Grand Hazard, 84–6, *fig. 83*
Grand Tric-trac, 19
Grasping Eight, 93–4, *fig. 86*
Groat, Edward IV, 124

Harris, J., 6,
Hawaii, 78
Hawkins, R. N. P., 142
Hearts, 100, *fig. 90*
Herskovits, M. J., 74
History of Chess (Forbes), 44, 46,
Holland, 138
Hoolim, H., 41
Hus, 76–7, *fig. 74*
Hyde, T., 12, 13,

Ibibio people, *plate 14*
Iceland, 19
Icelandic Backgammon, 19–23, *fig. 17*
I-go, 60
Immortals, Taoist, 144–6
Imperial game, 16, *fig. 13*
India, 46, *plate 10*
Ireland, 45, 46
Isle of Man, 46
Italy, 57, 115

Japan, 33–8
Jerusalem, 41
Jerk straws, 134
Jeton, 138
Jubilee game, 6–7, 8, *fig. 5, plates 1, 2*

Keno, 115, *fig. 97b*
Kerala, 3–5, *fig. 3*

Korea, 33, 42, 56
Kriegspiel, 39–41, *fig. 35*

Lasker, E., 60
Latrunculorum group, 48–9
Lead figures, 11, *tailpiece, p. 23*
Leggett, T., 38
Lombard game, 16, *fig. 12*
Lontu-holo, 73–4, *fig. 72*
Lost games, 52–4
Loto, 114–15, *fig. 96, plate 18*
Lu-lu 78, *fig. 75*

Ma-jong tile games, 106–7, *plate 16*
Madagascar, 24,
Malaya, 97, *plate 15*
Mancala games, 71–7; Four rank 75–7; Two rank 72–4
Maori, 149–50
Mon shi mo ut, 78–80, *fig. 76*
Montgomery, W., 25–6
Morris games, 55–6, *fig. 47*
Mu torere, 149–51, *figs. 112, 113*
Mulinello quadruplo, 57, *fig. 49*
Mylis, 18–19, *fig. 16, plate 6*

Netherlands, 138
New Mexico, 53
New Zealand, 149–50
Nigeria, 71, *plate 14*
Nine-pins, 132–3, *fig. 106*
Notation, Chess, 27; Fanorona, 24; Lontu-holo 73; Solitaire, 63; Tab, 50

Officers and Sepoys, 46–7, *fig. 40*

Pai kow, 102–3, *fig. 92*
Pakistan, 81, 82
Pancha Keliya, 1–2, *fig. 1*
Par, 91
Patience games, 63–70
Pitch and Toss, 80–1, *fig. 78*
Playing cards, 117–22, *plates 19, 20, 24, 26;* bone, *plate 17*
Poh, 97–8, *plate 15*
Poh kam, 97, *plate 15*
Pong hau k'i, 56, *fig. 48*
Pope Joan, 120–2, *plate 20*
Provincial game, 17, *fig. 14*
Pyramid, 57, *fig. 50*

Queen's game, 17–18, *figs. 15a, 15b*
Queen's Guard, 61–3, *figs. 52, 53*

Rengger, H. D., 41
Replacement games, 57–9
Rhodesia, 77
Rotation, 83, *fig. 81*
Round race games, 11–12

Royal Game of Goose, 6, 8
Running-fight games, 49–51, *figs. 43, 44*

Salta, 58–9, *fig. 51*
Scarne, J., 85
Scarne on Dice, 86
Scotland, 81, 108, 113
Shoffe-grotte, 123
Shove Ha'penny, 123–4, *fig. 99*
Shovel Board, 130–1, *fig. 104*
Sixteen Cowries, 82–3, *fig. 80*
Sixteen Soldiers, 48–9, *fig. 42*
Smith, A., 60
Snakes and Ladders, 10–11, *fig. 7*
Solitaire (French), 63–6, *figs. 54–58, tailpiece p. 77, plate 13*
Spellicans, 133–4, *fig. 107, plate 23*
Spinning Treasure, 97–9, *fig. 88, plate 15*
Spiral games, 6–7
Spooner, W., 8
Squails, 129–30, *fig. 103, plate 21*
Square board race games, 8–11
Stalemate, 30, 33
Sticks, casting, 50
Straits Settlements, 52
String games, 134–6, *fig. 108*
Svenskt brädspel, 19
Sweden, 19
Syria, 2

Tab, 49–51, *figs. 43, 44*
Tafl group, 43–8, *figs. 38–41*
Takagawa, K., 60

Tangram, fifteen-piece, 68–70, *figs. 63–69*
Tangram, seven-piece, 66–8, *figs. 59–62, tailpiece p. 70, plate 12*
Teetotum, 6, 8
Ten and a Half, 106–7, *plate 16*
Tenpins, 133, *fig. 22*
Territorial possession games, 59–63
Thailand, 31–3, 43, 137, *tailpiece p. 143*
The Times, 46
Throw-board, 43–5, *fig. 38*
Tien kow, 102, 105–6, *fig. 92*
Tiger Game, 47–8, *fig. 41*
Tigers and Oxen, 42–3, *fig. 37*
Tokens, Tradesmen's, 139
Tombola, 115
Totolospi (1), 5, *fig. 4;* Totolospi (2), 53–4, *fig. 46*
Tumbule, 115
Twi people, 72

Uganda, 75
United States of America, 5, 53, 79, 80, 84, 115, 132

Wales, 43
Walnut game, 80, *fig. 77*
Wei-ch'i, 59–61 *frontispiece*
Whyo, *plate 14*
Wisdom puzzle, 66–8, *figs. 59–62, tailpiece p. 70*

Yoe, S., 30

Zimbabwe, 77

A CATALOG OF SELECTED

DOVER BOOKS

IN ALL FIELDS OF INTEREST

A CATALOG OF SELECTED DOVER
BOOKS IN ALL FIELDS OF INTEREST

CONCERNING THE SPIRITUAL IN ART, Wassily Kandinsky. Pioneering work by father of abstract art. Thoughts on color theory, nature of art. Analysis of earlier masters. 12 illustrations. 80pp. of text. 5⅜ × 8½. 23411-8 Pa. $3.95

ANIMALS: 1,419 Copyright-Free Illustrations of Mammals, Birds, Fish, Insects, etc., Jim Harter (ed.). Clear wood engravings present, in extremely lifelike poses, over 1,000 species of animals. One of the most extensive pictorial sourcebooks of its kind. Captions. Index. 284pp. 9 × 12. 23766-4 Pa. $12.95

CELTIC ART: The Methods of Construction, George Bain. Simple geometric techniques for making Celtic interlacements, spirals, Kells-type initials, animals, humans, etc. Over 500 illustrations. 160pp. 9 × 12. (USO) 22923-8 Pa. $9.95

AN ATLAS OF ANATOMY FOR ARTISTS, Fritz Schider. Most thorough reference work on art anatomy in the world. Hundreds of illustrations, including selections from works by Vesalius, Leonardo, Goya, Ingres, Michelangelo, others. 593 illustrations. 192pp. 7⅛ × 10¼. 20241-0 Pa. $9.95

CELTIC HAND STROKE-BY-STROKE (Irish Half-Uncial from "The Book of Kells"): An Arthur Baker Calligraphy Manual, Arthur Baker. Complete guide to creating each letter of the alphabet in distinctive Celtic manner. Covers hand position, strokes, pens, inks, paper, more. Illustrated. 48pp. 8¼ × 11. 24336-2 Pa. $3.95

EASY ORIGAMI, John Montroll. Charming collection of 32 projects (hat, cup, pelican, piano, swan, many more) specially designed for the novice origami hobbyist. Clearly illustrated easy-to-follow instructions insure that even beginning papercrafters will achieve successful results. 48pp. 8¼ × 11. 27298-2 Pa. $2.95

THE COMPLETE BOOK OF BIRDHOUSE CONSTRUCTION FOR WOOD-WORKERS, Scott D. Campbell. Detailed instructions, illustrations, tables. Also data on bird habitat and instinct patterns. Bibliography. 3 tables. 63 illustrations in 15 figures. 48pp. 5¼ × 8½. 24407-5 Pa. $1.95

BLOOMINGDALE'S ILLUSTRATED 1886 CATALOG: Fashions, Dry Goods and Housewares, Bloomingdale Brothers. Famed merchants' extremely rare catalog depicting about 1,700 products: clothing, housewares, firearms, dry goods, jewelry, more. Invaluable for dating, identifying vintage items. Also, copyright-free graphics for artists, designers. Co-published with Henry Ford Museum & Green-field Village. 160pp. 8¼ × 11. 25780-0 Pa. $9.95

HISTORIC COSTUME IN PICTURES, Braun & Schneider. Over 1,450 costumed figures in clearly detailed engravings—from dawn of civilization to end of 19th century. Captions. Many folk costumes. 256pp. 8⅜ × 11¾. 23150-X Pa. $11.95

STICKLEY CRAFTSMAN FURNITURE CATALOGS, Gustav Stickley and L. & J. G. Stickley. Beautiful, functional furniture in two authentic catalogs from 1910. 594 illustrations, including 277 photos, show settles, rockers, armchairs, reclining chairs, bookcases, desks, tables. 183pp. 6½ × 9¼.   23838-5 Pa. $9.95

AMERICAN LOCOMOTIVES IN HISTORIC PHOTOGRAPHS: 1858 to 1949, Ron Ziel (ed.). A rare collection of 126 meticulously detailed official photographs, called "builder portraits," of American locomotives that majestically chronicle the rise of steam locomotive power in America. Introduction. Detailed captions. xi + 129pp. 9 × 12.   27393-8 Pa. $12.95

AMERICA'S LIGHTHOUSES: An Illustrated History, Francis Ross Holland, Jr. Delightfully written, profusely illustrated fact-filled survey of over 200 American lighthouses since 1716. History, anecdotes, technological advances, more. 240pp. 8 × 10¾.   25576-X Pa. $11.95

TOWARDS A NEW ARCHITECTURE, Le Corbusier. Pioneering manifesto by founder of "International School." Technical and aesthetic theories, views of industry, economics, relation of form to function, "mass-production split" and much more. Profusely illustrated. 320pp. 6⅛ × 9¼. (USO)   25023-7 Pa. $9.95

HOW THE OTHER HALF LIVES, Jacob Riis. Famous journalistic record, exposing poverty and degradation of New York slums around 1900, by major social reformer. 100 striking and influential photographs. 233pp. 10 × 7⅞.
                22012-5 Pa $10.95

FRUIT KEY AND TWIG KEY TO TREES AND SHRUBS, William M. Harlow. One of the handiest and most widely used identification aids. Fruit key covers 120 deciduous and evergreen species; twig key 160 deciduous species. Easily used. Over 300 photographs. 126pp. 5⅜ × 8½.   20511-8 Pa. $3.95

COMMON BIRD SONGS, Dr. Donald J. Borror. Songs of 60 most common U.S. birds: robins, sparrows, cardinals, bluejays, finches, more—arranged in order of increasing complexity. Up to 9 variations of songs of each species.
                Cassette and manual 99911-4 $8.95

ORCHIDS AS HOUSE PLANTS, Rebecca Tyson Northen. Grow cattleyas and many other kinds of orchids—in a window, in a case, or under artificial light. 63 illustrations. 148pp. 5⅜ × 8½.   23261-1 Pa. $4.95

MONSTER MAZES, Dave Phillips. Masterful mazes at four levels of difficulty. Avoid deadly perils and evil creatures to find magical treasures. Solutions for all 32 exciting illustrated puzzles. 48pp. 8¼ × 11.   26005-4 Pa. $2.95

MOZART'S DON GIOVANNI (DOVER OPERA LIBRETTO SERIES), Wolfgang Amadeus Mozart. Introduced and translated by Ellen H. Bleiler. Standard Italian libretto, with complete English translation. Convenient and thoroughly portable—an ideal companion for reading along with a recording or the performance itself. Introduction. List of characters. Plot summary. 121pp. 5¼ × 8½.
                24944-1 Pa. $2.95

TECHNICAL MANUAL AND DICTIONARY OF CLASSICAL BALLET, Gail Grant. Defines, explains, comments on steps, movements, poses and concepts. 15-page pictorial section. Basic book for student, viewer. 127pp. 5⅜ × 8½.
                21843-0 Pa. $4.95

BRASS INSTRUMENTS: Their History and Development, Anthony Baines. Authoritative, updated survey of the evolution of trumpets, trombones, bugles, cornets, French horns, tubas and other brass wind instruments. Over 140 illustrations and 48 music examples. Corrected and updated by author. New preface. Bibliography. 320pp. 5⅜ × 8½. 27574-4 Pa. $9.95

HOLLYWOOD GLAMOR PORTRAITS, John Kobal (ed.). 145 photos from 1926–49. Harlow, Gable, Bogart, Bacall; 94 stars in all. Full background on photographers, technical aspects. 160pp. 8⅜ × 11¼. 23352-9 Pa. $11.95

MAX AND MORITZ, Wilhelm Busch. Great humor classic in both German and English. Also 10 other works: "Cat and Mouse," "Plisch and Plumm," etc. 216pp. 5⅜ × 8½. 20181-3 Pa. $5.95

THE RAVEN AND OTHER FAVORITE POEMS, Edgar Allan Poe. Over 40 of the author's most memorable poems: "The Bells," "Ulalume," "Israfel," "To Helen," "The Conqueror Worm," "Eldorado," "Annabel Lee," many more. Alphabetic lists of titles and first lines. 64pp. 5 3/16 × 8¼. 26685-0 Pa. $1.00

SEVEN SCIENCE FICTION NOVELS, H. G. Wells. The standard collection of the great novels. Complete, unabridged. First Men in the Moon, Island of Dr. Moreau, War of the Worlds, Food of the Gods, Invisible Man, Time Machine, In the Days of the Comet. Total of 1,015pp. 5⅜ × 8½. (USO) 20264-X Clothbd. $29.95

AMULETS AND SUPERSTITIONS, E. A. Wallis Budge. Comprehensive discourse on origin, powers of amulets in many ancient cultures: Arab, Persian, Babylonian, Assyrian, Egyptian, Gnostic, Hebrew, Phoenician, Syriac, etc. Covers cross, swastika, crucifix, seals, rings, stones, etc. 584pp. 5⅜ × 8½. 23573-4 Pa. $12.95

RUSSIAN STORIES/PYCCKNE PACCKA3bl: A Dual-Language Book, edited by Gleb Struve. Twelve tales by such masters as Chekhov, Tolstoy, Dostoevsky, Pushkin, others. Excellent word-for-word English translations on facing pages, plus teaching and study aids, Russian/English vocabulary, biographical/critical introductions, more. 416pp. 5⅜ × 8½. 26244-8 Pa. $8.95

PHILADELPHIA THEN AND NOW: 60 Sites Photographed in the Past and Present, Kenneth Finkel and Susan Oyama. Rare photographs of City Hall, Logan Square, Independence Hall, Betsy Ross House, other landmarks juxtaposed with contemporary views. Captures changing face of historic city. Introduction. Captions. 128pp. 8¼ × 11. 25790-8 Pa. $9.95

AIA ARCHITECTURAL GUIDE TO NASSAU AND SUFFOLK COUNTIES, LONG ISLAND, The American Institute of Architects, Long Island Chapter, and the Society for the Preservation of Long Island Antiquities. Comprehensive, well-researched and generously illustrated volume brings to life over three centuries of Long Island's great architectural heritage. More than 240 photographs with authoritative, extensively detailed captions. 176pp. 8¼ × 11. 26946-9 Pa. $14.95

NORTH AMERICAN INDIAN LIFE: Customs and Traditions of 23 Tribes, Elsie Clews Parsons (ed.). 27 fictionalized essays by noted anthropologists examine religion, customs, government, additional facets of life among the Winnebago, Crow, Zuni, Eskimo, other tribes. 480pp. 6⅛ × 9¼. 27377-6 Pa. $10.95

FRANK LLOYD WRIGHT'S HOLLYHOCK HOUSE, Donald Hoffmann. Lavishly illustrated, carefully documented study of one of Wright's most controversial residential designs. Over 120 photographs, floor plans, elevations, etc. Detailed perceptive text by noted Wright scholar. Index. 128pp. 9¼ × 10¾.
27133-1 Pa. $11.95

THE MALE AND FEMALE FIGURE IN MOTION: 60 Classic Photographic Sequences, Eadweard Muybridge. 60 true-action photographs of men and women walking, running, climbing, bending, turning, etc., reproduced from rare 19th-century masterpiece. vi + 121pp. 9 × 12. 24745-7 Pa. $10.95

1001 QUESTIONS ANSWERED ABOUT THE SEASHORE, N. J. Berrill and Jacquelyn Berrill. Queries answered about dolphins, sea snails, sponges, starfish, fishes, shore birds, many others. Covers appearance, breeding, growth, feeding, much more. 305pp. 5¼ × 8¼. 23366-9 Pa. $7.95

GUIDE TO OWL WATCHING IN NORTH AMERICA, Donald S. Heintzelman. Superb guide offers complete data and descriptions of 19 species: barn owl, screech owl, snowy owl, many more. Expert coverage of owl-watching equipment, conservation, migrations and invasions, etc. Guide to observing sites. 84 illustrations. xiii + 193pp. 5⅜ × 8½. 27344-X Pa. $8.95

MEDICINAL AND OTHER USES OF NORTH AMERICAN PLANTS: A Historical Survey with Special Reference to the Eastern Indian Tribes, Charlotte Erichsen-Brown. Chronological historical citations document 500 years of usage of plants, trees, shrubs native to eastern Canada, northeastern U.S. Also complete identifying information. 343 illustrations. 544pp. 6½ × 9¼. 25951-X Pa. $12.95

STORYBOOK MAZES, Dave Phillips. 23 stories and mazes on two-page spreads: Wizard of Oz, Treasure Island, Robin Hood, etc. Solutions. 64pp. 8¼ × 11.
23628-5 Pa. $2.95

NEGRO FOLK MUSIC, U.S.A., Harold Courlander. Noted folklorist's scholarly yet readable analysis of rich and varied musical tradition. Includes authentic versions of over 40 folk songs. Valuable bibliography and discography. xi + 324pp. 5⅜ × 8½. 27350-4 Pa. $7.95

MOVIE-STAR PORTRAITS OF THE FORTIES, John Kobal (ed.). 163 glamor, studio photos of 106 stars of the 1940s: Rita Hayworth, Ava Gardner, Marlon Brando, Clark Gable, many more. 176pp. 8⅜ × 11¼. 23546-7 Pa. $11.95

BENCHLEY LOST AND FOUND, Robert Benchley. Finest humor from early 30s, about pet peeves, child psychologists, post office and others. Mostly unavailable elsewhere. 73 illustrations by Peter Arno and others. 183pp. 5⅜ × 8½.
22410-4 Pa. $5.95

YEKL and THE IMPORTED BRIDEGROOM AND OTHER STORIES OF YIDDISH NEW YORK, Abraham Cahan. Film Hester Street based on Yekl (1896). Novel, other stories among first about Jewish immigrants on N.Y.'s East Side. 240pp. 5⅜ × 8½. 22427-9 Pa. $6.95

SELECTED POEMS, Walt Whitman. Generous sampling from *Leaves of Grass*. Twenty-four poems include "I Hear America Singing," "Song of the Open Road," "I Sing the Body Electric," "When Lilacs Last in the Dooryard Bloom'd," "O Captain! My Captain!"—all reprinted from an authoritative edition. Lists of titles and first lines. 128pp. 5$^{3}/_{16}$ × 8¼. 26878-0 Pa. $1.00

THE BEST TALES OF HOFFMANN, E. T. A. Hoffmann. 10 of Hoffmann's most important stories: "Nutcracker and the King of Mice," "The Golden Flowerpot," etc. 458pp. 5⅜ × 8½. 21793-0 Pa. $8.95

FROM FETISH TO GOD IN ANCIENT EGYPT, E. A. Wallis Budge. Rich detailed survey of Egyptian conception of "God" and gods, magic, cult of animals, Osiris, more. Also, superb English translations of hymns and legends. 240 illustrations. 545pp. 5⅜ × 8½. 25803-3 Pa. $11.95

FRENCH STORIES/CONTES FRANÇAIS: A Dual-Language Book, Wallace Fowlie. Ten stories by French masters, Voltaire to Camus: "Micromegas" by Voltaire; "The Atheist's Mass" by Balzac; "Minuet" by de Maupassant; "The Guest" by Camus, six more. Excellent English translations on facing pages. Also French-English vocabulary list, exercises, more. 352pp. 5⅜ × 8½. 26443-2 Pa. $8.95

CHICAGO AT THE TURN OF THE CENTURY IN PHOTOGRAPHS: 122 Historic Views from the Collections of the Chicago Historical Society, Larry A. Viskochil. Rare large-format prints offer detailed views of City Hall, State Street, the Loop, Hull House, Union Station, many other landmarks, circa 1904–1913. Introduction. Captions. Maps. 144pp. 9⅜ × 12¼. 24656-6 Pa. $12.95

OLD BROOKLYN IN EARLY PHOTOGRAPHS, 1865–1929, William Lee Younger. Luna Park, Gravesend race track, construction of Grand Army Plaza, moving of Hotel Brighton, etc. 157 previously unpublished photographs. 165pp. 8⅞ × 11¾. 23587-4 Pa. $13.95

THE MYTHS OF THE NORTH AMERICAN INDIANS, Lewis Spence. Rich anthology of the myths and legends of the Algonquins, Iroquois, Pawnees and Sioux, prefaced by an extensive historical and ethnological commentary. 36 illustrations. 480pp. 5⅜ × 8½. 25967-6 Pa. $8.95

AN ENCYCLOPEDIA OF BATTLES: Accounts of Over 1,560 Battles from 1479 B.C. to the Present, David Eggenberger. Essential details of every major battle in recorded history from the first battle of Megiddo in 1479 B.C. to Grenada in 1984. List of Battle Maps. New Appendix covering the years 1967–1984. Index. 99 illustrations. 544pp. 6½ × 9¼. 24913-1 Pa. $14.95

SAILING ALONE AROUND THE WORLD, Captain Joshua Slocum. First man to sail around the world, alone, in small boat. One of great feats of seamanship told in delightful manner. 67 illustrations. 294pp. 5⅜ × 8½. 20326-3 Pa. $5.95

ANARCHISM AND OTHER ESSAYS, Emma Goldman. Powerful, penetrating, prophetic essays on direct action, role of minorities, prison reform, puritan hypocrisy, violence, etc. 271pp. 5⅜ × 8½. 22484-8 Pa. $5.95

MYTHS OF THE HINDUS AND BUDDHISTS, Ananda K. Coomaraswamy and Sister Nivedita. Great stories of the epics; deeds of Krishna, Shiva, taken from puranas, Vedas, folk tales; etc. 32 illustrations. 400pp. 5⅜ × 8½. 21759-0 Pa. $9.95

BEYOND PSYCHOLOGY, Otto Rank. Fear of death, desire of immortality, nature of sexuality, social organization, creativity, according to Rankian system. 291pp. 5⅜ × 8½. 20485-5 Pa. $8.95

A THEOLOGICO-POLITICAL TREATISE, Benedict Spinoza. Also contains unfinished Political Treatise. Great classic on religious liberty, theory of government on common consent. R. Elwes translation. Total of 421pp. 5⅜ × 8½. 20249-6 Pa. $8.95

MY BONDAGE AND MY FREEDOM, Frederick Douglass. Born a slave, Douglass became outspoken force in antislavery movement. The best of Douglass' autobiographies. Graphic description of slave life. 464pp. 5⅜ × 8½. 22457-0 Pa. $8.95

FOLLOWING THE EQUATOR: A Journey Around the World, Mark Twain. Fascinating humorous account of 1897 voyage to Hawaii, Australia, India, New Zealand, etc. Ironic, bemused reports on peoples, customs, climate, flora and fauna, politics, much more. 197 illustrations. 720pp. 5⅜ × 8½. 26113-1 Pa. $15.95

THE PEOPLE CALLED SHAKERS, Edward D. Andrews. Definitive study of Shakers: origins, beliefs, practices, dances, social organization, furniture and crafts, etc. 33 illustrations. 351pp. 5⅜ × 8½. 21081-2 Pa. $8.95

THE MYTHS OF GREECE AND ROME, H. A. Guerber. A classic of mythology, generously illustrated, long prized for its simple, graphic, accurate retelling of the principal myths of Greece and Rome, and for its commentary on their origins and significance. With 64 illustrations by Michelangelo, Raphael, Titian, Rubens, Canova, Bernini and others. 480pp. 5⅜ × 8½. 27584-1 Pa. $9.95

PSYCHOLOGY OF MUSIC, Carl E. Seashore. Classic work discusses music as a medium from psychological viewpoint. Clear treatment of physical acoustics, auditory apparatus, sound perception, development of musical skills, nature of musical feeling, host of other topics. 88 figures. 408pp. 5⅜ × 8½. 21851-1 Pa. $9.95

THE PHILOSOPHY OF HISTORY, Georg W. Hegel. Great classic of Western thought develops concept that history is not chance but rational process, the evolution of freedom. 457pp. 5⅜ × 8½. 20112-0 Pa. $9.95

THE BOOK OF TEA, Kakuzo Okakura. Minor classic of the Orient: entertaining, charming explanation, interpretation of traditional Japanese culture in terms of tea ceremony. 94pp. 5⅜ × 8½. 20070-1 Pa. $3.95

LIFE IN ANCIENT EGYPT, Adolf Erman. Fullest, most thorough, detailed older account with much not in more recent books, domestic life, religion, magic, medicine, commerce, much more. Many illustrations reproduce tomb paintings, carvings, hieroglyphs, etc. 597pp. 5⅜ × 8½. 22632-8 Pa. $10.95

SUNDIALS, Their Theory and Construction, Albert Waugh. Far and away the best, most thorough coverage of ideas, mathematics concerned, types, construction, adjusting anywhere. Simple, nontechnical treatment allows even children to build several of these dials. Over 100 illustrations. 230pp. 5⅜ × 8½. 22947-5 Pa. $7.95

DYNAMICS OF FLUIDS IN POROUS MEDIA, Jacob Bear. For advanced students of ground water hydrology, soil mechanics and physics, drainage and irrigation engineering, and more. 335 illustrations. Exercises, with answers. 784pp. 6⅛ × 9¼. 65675-6 Pa. $19.95

SONGS OF EXPERIENCE: Facsimile Reproduction with 26 Plates in Full Color, William Blake. 26 full-color plates from a rare 1826 edition. Includes "The Tyger," "London," "Holy Thursday," and other poems. Printed text of poems. 48pp. 5¼ × 7. 24636-1 Pa. $4.95

OLD-TIME VIGNETTES IN FULL COLOR, Carol Belanger Grafton (ed.). Over 390 charming, often sentimental illustrations, selected from archives of Victorian graphics—pretty women posing, children playing, food, flowers, kittens and puppies, smiling cherubs, birds and butterflies, much more. All copyright-free. 48pp. 9¼ × 12¼. 27269-9 Pa. $5.95

PERSPECTIVE FOR ARTISTS, Rex Vicat Cole. Depth, perspective of sky and sea, shadows, much more, not usually covered. 391 diagrams, 81 reproductions of drawings and paintings. 279pp. 5⅜ × 8½. 22487-2 Pa. $6.95

DRAWING THE LIVING FIGURE, Joseph Sheppard. Innovative approach to artistic anatomy focuses on specifics of surface anatomy, rather than muscles and bones. Over 170 drawings of live models in front, back and side views, and in widely varying poses. Accompanying diagrams. 177 illustrations. Introduction. Index. 144pp. 8⅜ × 11¼. 26723-7 Pa. $8.95

GOTHIC AND OLD ENGLISH ALPHABETS: 100 Complete Fonts, Dan X. Solo. Add power, elegance to posters, signs, other graphics with 100 stunning copyright-free alphabets: Blackstone, Dolbey, Germania, 97 more—including many lower-case, numerals, punctuation marks. 104pp. 8⅛ × 11. 24695-7 Pa. $8.95

HOW TO DO BEADWORK, Mary White. Fundamental book on craft from simple projects to five-bead chains and woven works. 106 illustrations. 142pp. 5⅜ × 8. 20697-1 Pa. $4.95

THE BOOK OF WOOD CARVING, Charles Marshall Sayers. Finest book for beginners discusses fundamentals and offers 34 designs. "Absolutely first rate . . . well thought out and well executed."—E. J. Tangerman. 118pp. 7¾ × 10⅝. 23654-4 Pa. $5.95

ILLUSTRATED CATALOG OF CIVIL WAR MILITARY GOODS: Union Army Weapons, Insignia, Uniform Accessories, and Other Equipment, Schuyler, Hartley, and Graham. Rare, profusely illustrated 1846 catalog includes Union Army uniform and dress regulations, arms and ammunition, coats, insignia, flags, swords, rifles, etc. 226 illustrations. 160pp. 9 × 12. 24939-5 Pa. $10.95

WOMEN'S FASHIONS OF THE EARLY 1900s: An Unabridged Republication of "New York Fashions, 1909," National Cloak & Suit Co. Rare catalog of mail-order fashions documents women's and children's clothing styles shortly after the turn of the century. Captions offer full descriptions, prices. Invaluable resource for fashion, costume historians. Approximately 725 illustrations. 128pp. 8⅜ × 11¼. 27276-1 Pa. $11.95

THE 1912 AND 1915 GUSTAV STICKLEY FURNITURE CATALOGS, Gustav Stickley. With over 200 detailed illustrations and descriptions, these two catalogs are essential reading and reference materials and identification guides for Stickley furniture. Captions cite materials, dimensions and prices. 112pp. 6½ × 9¼. 26676-1 Pa. $9.95

EARLY AMERICAN LOCOMOTIVES, John H. White, Jr. Finest locomotive engravings from early 19th century: historical (1804–74), main-line (after 1870), special, foreign, etc. 147 plates. 142pp. 11⅜ × 8¼. 22772-3 Pa. $10.95

THE TALL SHIPS OF TODAY IN PHOTOGRAPHS, Frank O. Braynard. Lavishly illustrated tribute to nearly 100 majestic contemporary sailing vessels: Amerigo Vespucci, Clearwater, Constitution, Eagle, Mayflower, Sea Cloud, Victory, many more. Authoritative captions provide statistics, background on each ship. 190 black-and-white photographs and illustrations. Introduction. 128pp. 8⅞ × 11¾. 27163-3 Pa. $13.95

EARLY NINETEENTH-CENTURY CRAFTS AND TRADES, Peter Stockham (ed.). Extremely rare 1807 volume describes to youngsters the crafts and trades of the day: brickmaker, weaver, dressmaker, bookbinder, ropemaker, saddler, many more. Quaint prose, charming illustrations for each craft. 20 black-and-white line illustrations. 192pp. 4⅜ × 6. 27293-1 Pa. $4.95

VICTORIAN FASHIONS AND COSTUMES FROM HARPER'S BAZAR, 1867–1898, Stella Blum (ed.). Day costumes, evening wear, sports clothes, shoes, hats, other accessories in over 1,000 detailed engravings. 320pp. 9⅜ × 12¼. 22990-4 Pa. $13.95

GUSTAV STICKLEY, THE CRAFTSMAN, Mary Ann Smith. Superb study surveys broad scope of Stickley's achievement, especially in architecture. Design philosophy, rise and fall of the Craftsman empire, descriptions and floor plans for many Craftsman houses, more. 86 black-and-white halftones. 31 line illustrations. Introduction. 208pp. 6½ × 9¼. 27210-9 Pa. $9.95

THE LONG ISLAND RAIL ROAD IN EARLY PHOTOGRAPHS, Ron Ziel. Over 220 rare photos, informative text document origin (1844) and development of rail service on Long Island. Vintage views of early trains, locomotives, stations, passengers, crews, much more. Captions. 8⅞ × 11¾. 26301-0 Pa. $13.95

THE BOOK OF OLD SHIPS: From Egyptian Galleys to Clipper Ships, Henry B. Culver. Superb, authoritative history of sailing vessels, with 80 magnificent line illustrations. Galley, bark, caravel, longship, whaler, many more. Detailed, informative text on each vessel by noted naval historian. Introduction. 256pp. 5⅜ × 8½. 27332-6 Pa. $6.95

TEN BOOKS ON ARCHITECTURE, Vitruvius. The most important book ever written on architecture. Early Roman aesthetics, technology, classical orders, site selection, all other aspects. Morgan translation. 331pp. 5⅜ × 8½. 20645-9 Pa. $8.95

THE HUMAN FIGURE IN MOTION, Eadweard Muybridge. More than 4,500 stopped-action photos, in action series, showing undraped men, women, children jumping, lying down, throwing, sitting, wrestling, carrying, etc. 390pp. 7⅞ × 10⅝. 20204-6 Clothbd. $24.95

TREES OF THE EASTERN AND CENTRAL UNITED STATES AND CANADA, William M. Harlow. Best one-volume guide to 140 trees. Full descriptions, woodlore, range, etc. Over 600 illustrations. Handy size. 288pp. 4½ × 6⅜. 20395-6 Pa. $5.95

SONGS OF WESTERN BIRDS, Dr. Donald J. Borror. Complete song and call repertoire of 60 western species, including flycatchers, juncoes, cactus wrens, many more—includes fully illustrated booklet. Cassette and manual 99913-0 $8.95

GROWING AND USING HERBS AND SPICES, Milo Miloradovich. Versatile handbook provides all the information needed for cultivation and use of all the herbs and spices available in North America. 4 illustrations. Index. Glossary. 236pp. 5⅜ × 8½. 25058-X Pa. $6.95

BIG BOOK OF MAZES AND LABYRINTHS, Walter Shepherd. 50 mazes and labyrinths in all—classical, solid, ripple, and more—in one great volume. Perfect inexpensive puzzler for clever youngsters. Full solutions. 112pp. 8⅛ × 11. 22951-3 Pa. $4.95

PIANO TUNING, J. Cree Fischer. Clearest, best book for beginner, amateur. Simple repairs, raising dropped notes, tuning by easy method of flattened fifths. No previous skills needed. 4 illustrations. 201pp. 5⅜ × 8½. 23267-0 Pa. $5.95

A SOURCE BOOK IN THEATRICAL HISTORY, A. M. Nagler. Contemporary observers on acting, directing, make-up, costuming, stage props, machinery, scene design, from Ancient Greece to Chekhov. 611pp. 5⅜ × 8½. 20515-0 Pa. $11.95

THE COMPLETE NONSENSE OF EDWARD LEAR, Edward Lear. All nonsense limericks, zany alphabets, Owl and Pussycat, songs, nonsense botany, etc., illustrated by Lear. Total of 320pp. 5⅜ × 8½. (USO) 20167-8 Pa. $6.95

VICTORIAN PARLOUR POETRY: An Annotated Anthology, Michael R. Turner. 117 gems by Longfellow, Tennyson, Browning, many lesser-known poets. "The Village Blacksmith," "Curfew Must Not Ring Tonight," "Only a Baby Small," dozens more, often difficult to find elsewhere. Index of poets, titles, first lines. xxiii + 325pp. 5⅜ × 8¼. 27044-0 Pa. $8.95

DUBLINERS, James Joyce. Fifteen stories offer vivid, tightly focused observations of the lives of Dublin's poorer classes. At least one, "The Dead," is considered a masterpiece. Reprinted complete and unabridged from standard edition. 160pp. 5³⁄₁₆ × 8¼. 26870-5 Pa. $1.00

THE HAUNTED MONASTERY and THE CHINESE MAZE MURDERS, Robert van Gulik. Two full novels by van Gulik, set in 7th-century China, continue adventures of Judge Dee and his companions. An evil Taoist monastery, seemingly supernatural events; overgrown topiary maze hides strange crimes. 27 illustrations. 328pp. 5⅜ × 8½. 23502-5 Pa. $7.95

THE BOOK OF THE SACRED MAGIC OF ABRAMELIN THE MAGE, translated by S. MacGregor Mathers. Medieval manuscript of ceremonial magic. Basic document in Aleister Crowley, Golden Dawn groups. 268pp. 5⅜ × 8½. 23211-5 Pa. $8.95

NEW RUSSIAN-ENGLISH AND ENGLISH-RUSSIAN DICTIONARY, M. A. O'Brien. This is a remarkably handy Russian dictionary, containing a surprising amount of information, including over 70,000 entries. 366pp. 4½ × 6⅛. 20208-9 Pa. $9.95

HISTORIC HOMES OF THE AMERICAN PRESIDENTS, Second, Revised Edition, Irvin Haas. A traveler's guide to American Presidential homes, most open to the public, depicting and describing homes occupied by every American President from George Washington to George Bush. With visiting hours, admission charges, travel routes. 175 photographs. Index. 160pp. 8¼ × 11. 26751-2 Pa. $10.95

NEW YORK IN THE FORTIES, Andreas Feininger. 162 brilliant photographs by the well-known photographer, formerly with *Life* magazine. Commuters, shoppers, Times Square at night, much else from city at its peak. Captions by John von Hartz. 181pp. 9¼ × 10¾. 23585-8 Pa. $12.95

INDIAN SIGN LANGUAGE, William Tomkins. Over 525 signs developed by Sioux and other tribes. Written instructions and diagrams. Also 290 pictographs. 111pp. 6⅛ × 9¼. 22029-X Pa. $3.50

ANATOMY: A Complete Guide for Artists, Joseph Sheppard. A master of figure drawing shows artists how to render human anatomy convincingly. Over 460 illustrations. 224pp. 8⅜ × 11¼. 27279-6 Pa. $10.95

MEDIEVAL CALLIGRAPHY: Its History and Technique, Marc Drogin. Spirited history, comprehensive instruction manual covers 13 styles (ca. 4th century thru 15th). Excellent photographs; directions for duplicating medieval techniques with modern tools. 224pp. 8⅜ × 11¼. 26142-5 Pa. $11.95

DRIED FLOWERS: How to Prepare Them, Sarah Whitlock and Martha Rankin. Complete instructions on how to use silica gel, meal and borax, perlite aggregate, sand and borax, glycerine and water to create attractive permanent flower arrangements. 12 illustrations. 32pp. 5⅜ × 8½. 21802-3 Pa. $1.00

EASY-TO-MAKE BIRD FEEDERS FOR WOODWORKERS, Scott D. Campbell. Detailed, simple-to-use guide for designing, constructing, caring for and using feeders. Text, illustrations for 12 classic and contemporary designs. 96pp. 5⅜ × 8½. 25847-5 Pa. $2.95

OLD-TIME CRAFTS AND TRADES, Peter Stockham. An 1807 book created to teach children about crafts and trades open to them as future careers. It describes in detailed, nontechnical terms 24 different occupations, among them coachmaker, gardener, hairdresser, lacemaker, shoemaker, wheelwright, copper-plate printer, milliner, trunkmaker, merchant and brewer. Finely detailed engravings illustrate each occupation. 192pp. 4⅝ × 6. 27398-9 Pa. $4.95

THE HISTORY OF UNDERCLOTHES, C. Willett Cunnington and Phyllis Cunnington. Fascinating, well-documented survey covering six centuries of English undergarments, enhanced with over 100 illustrations: 12th-century laced-up bodice, footed long drawers (1795), 19th-century bustles, 19th-century corsets for men, Victorian "bust improvers," much more. 272pp. 5⅜ × 8¼. 27124-2 Pa. $9.95

ARTS AND CRAFTS FURNITURE: The Complete Brooks Catalog of 1912, Brooks Manufacturing Co. Photos and detailed descriptions of more than 150 now very collectible furniture designs from the Arts and Crafts movement depict davenports, settees, buffets, desks, tables, chairs, bedsteads, dressers and more, all built of solid, quarter-sawed oak. Invaluable for students and enthusiasts of antiques, Americana and the decorative arts. 80pp. 6½ × 9¼. 27471-3 Pa. $7.95

HOW WE INVENTED THE AIRPLANE: An Illustrated History, Orville Wright. Fascinating firsthand account covers early experiments, construction of planes and motors, first flights, much more. Introduction and commentary by Fred C. Kelly. 76 photographs. 96pp. 8¼ × 11. 25662-6 Pa. $8.95

THE ARTS OF THE SAILOR: Knotting, Splicing and Ropework, Hervey Garrett Smith. Indispensable shipboard reference covers tools, basic knots and useful hitches; handsewing and canvas work, more. Over 100 illustrations. Delightful reading for sea lovers. 256pp. 5⅜ × 8½. 26440-8 Pa. $7.95

FRANK LLOYD WRIGHT'S FALLINGWATER: The House and Its History, Second, Revised Edition, Donald Hoffmann. A total revision—both in text and illustrations—of the standard document on Fallingwater, the boldest, most personal architectural statement of Wright's mature years, updated with valuable new material from the recently opened Frank Lloyd Wright Archives. "Fascinating"—*The New York Times*. 116 illustrations. 128pp. 9¼ × 10¾. 27430-6 Pa. $10.95

CATALOG OF DOVER BOOKS

PHOTOGRAPHIC SKETCHBOOK OF THE CIVIL WAR, Alexander Gardner. 100 photos taken on field during the Civil War. Famous shots of Manassas, Harper's Ferry, Lincoln, Richmond, slave pens, etc. 244pp. 10⅝ × 8¼.
22731-6 Pa. $9.95

FIVE ACRES AND INDEPENDENCE, Maurice G. Kains. Great back-to-the-land classic explains basics of self-sufficient farming. The one book to get. 95 illustrations. 397pp. 5⅜ × 8½.
20974-1 Pa. $7.95

SONGS OF EASTERN BIRDS, Dr. Donald J. Borror. Songs and calls of 60 species most common to eastern U.S.: warblers, woodpeckers, flycatchers, thrushes, larks, many more in high-quality recording.
Cassette and manual 99912-2 $8.95

A MODERN HERBAL, Margaret Grieve. Much the fullest, most exact, most useful compilation of herbal material. Gigantic alphabetical encyclopedia, from aconite to zedoary, gives botanical information, medical properties, folklore, economic uses, much else. Indispensable to serious reader. 161 illustrations. 888pp. 6½ × 9¼. 2-vol. set. (USO)
Vol. I: 22798-7 Pa. $9.95
Vol. II: 22799-5 Pa. $9.95

HIDDEN TREASURE MAZE BOOK, Dave Phillips. Solve 34 challenging mazes accompanied by heroic tales of adventure. Evil dragons, people-eating plants, bloodthirsty giants, many more dangerous adversaries lurk at every twist and turn. 34 mazes, stories, solutions. 48pp. 8¼ × 11.
24566-7 Pa. $2.95

LETTERS OF W. A. MOZART, Wolfgang A. Mozart. Remarkable letters show bawdy wit, humor, imagination, musical insights, contemporary musical world; includes some letters from Leopold Mozart. 276pp. 5⅜ × 8½.
22859-2 Pa. $7.95

BASIC PRINCIPLES OF CLASSICAL BALLET, Agrippina Vaganova. Great Russian theoretician, teacher explains methods for teaching classical ballet. 118 illustrations. 175pp. 5⅜ × 8½.
22036-2 Pa. $4.95

THE JUMPING FROG, Mark Twain. Revenge edition. The original story of The Celebrated Jumping Frog of Calaveras County, a hapless French translation, and Twain's hilarious "retranslation" from the French. 12 illustrations. 66pp. 5⅜ × 8½.
22686-7 Pa. $3.95

BEST REMEMBERED POEMS, Martin Gardner (ed.). The 126 poems in this superb collection of 19th- and 20th-century British and American verse range from Shelley's "To a Skylark" to the impassioned "Renascence" of Edna St. Vincent Millay and to Edward Lear's whimsical "The Owl and the Pussycat." 224pp. 5⅜ × 8½.
27165-X Pa. $4.95

COMPLETE SONNETS, William Shakespeare. Over 150 exquisite poems deal with love, friendship, the tyranny of time, beauty's evanescence, death and other themes in language of remarkable power, precision and beauty. Glossary of archaic terms. 80pp. 5³⁄₁₆ × 8¼.
26686-9 Pa. $1.00

BODIES IN A BOOKSHOP, R. T. Campbell. Challenging mystery of blackmail and murder with ingenious plot and superbly drawn characters. In the best tradition of British suspense fiction. 192pp. 5⅜ × 8½.
24720-1 Pa. $5.95

THE WIT AND HUMOR OF OSCAR WILDE, Alvin Redman (ed.). More than 1,000 ripostes, paradoxes, wisecracks: Work is the curse of the drinking classes; I can resist everything except temptation; etc. 258pp. 5⅜ × 8½. 20602-5 Pa. $5.95

SHAKESPEARE LEXICON AND QUOTATION DICTIONARY, Alexander Schmidt. Full definitions, locations, shades of meaning in every word in plays and poems. More than 50,000 exact quotations. 1,485pp. 6½ × 9¼. 2-vol. set.
Vol. I: 22726-X Pa. $16.95
Vol. 2: 22727-8 Pa. $15.95

SELECTED POEMS, Emily Dickinson. Over 100 best-known, best-loved poems by one of America's foremost poets, reprinted from authoritative early editions. No comparable edition at this price. Index of first lines. 64pp. 5³/₁₆ × 8¼.
26466-1 Pa. $1.00

CELEBRATED CASES OF JUDGE DEE (DEE GOONG AN), translated by Robert van Gulik. Authentic 18th-century Chinese detective novel; Dee and associates solve three interlocked cases. Led to van Gulik's own stories with same characters. Extensive introduction. 9 illustrations. 237pp. 5⅜ × 8½.
23337-5 Pa. $6.95

THE MALLEUS MALEFICARUM OF KRAMER AND SPRENGER, translated by Montague Summers. Full text of most important witchhunter's "bible," used by both Catholics and Protestants. 278pp. 6⅝ × 10. 22802-9 Pa. $11.95

SPANISH STORIES/CUENTOS ESPAÑOLES: A Dual-Language Book, Angel Flores (ed.). Unique format offers 13 great stories in Spanish by Cervantes, Borges, others. Faithful English translations on facing pages. 352pp. 5⅜ × 8½.
25399-6 Pa. $8.95

THE CHICAGO WORLD'S FAIR OF 1893: A Photographic Record, Stanley Appelbaum (ed.). 128 rare photos show 200 buildings, Beaux-Arts architecture, Midway, original Ferris Wheel, Edison's kinetoscope, more. Architectural emphasis; full text. 116pp. 8¼ × 11. 23990-X Pa. $9.95

OLD QUEENS, N.Y., IN EARLY PHOTOGRAPHS, Vincent F. Seyfried and William Asadorian. Over 160 rare photographs of Maspeth, Jamaica, Jackson Heights, and other areas. Vintage views of DeWitt Clinton mansion, 1939 World's Fair and more. Captions. 192pp. 8⅞ × 11. 26358-4 Pa. $12.95

CAPTURED BY THE INDIANS: 15 Firsthand Accounts, 1750–1870, Frederick Drimmer. Astounding true historical accounts of grisly torture, bloody conflicts, relentless pursuits, miraculous escapes and more, by people who lived to tell the tale. 384pp. 5⅜ × 8½. 24901-8 Pa. $8.95

THE WORLD'S GREAT SPEECHES, Lewis Copeland and Lawrence W. Lamm (eds.). Vast collection of 278 speeches of Greeks to 1970. Powerful and effective models; unique look at history. 842pp. 5⅜ × 8½. 20468-5 Pa. $14.95

THE BOOK OF THE SWORD, Sir Richard F. Burton. Great Victorian scholar/adventurer's eloquent, erudite history of the "queen of weapons"—from prehistory to early Roman Empire. Evolution and development of early swords, variations (sabre, broadsword, cutlass, scimitar, etc.), much more. 336pp. 6⅛ × 9¼. 25434-8 Pa. $8.95

AUTOBIOGRAPHY: The Story of My Experiments with Truth, Mohandas K. Gandhi. Boyhood, legal studies, purification, the growth of the Satyagraha (nonviolent protest) movement. Critical, inspiring work of the man responsible for the freedom of India. 480pp. 5⅜ × 8½. (USO) 24593-4 Pa. $8.95

CELTIC MYTHS AND LEGENDS, T. W. Rolleston. Masterful retelling of Irish and Welsh stories and tales. Cuchulain, King Arthur, Deirdre, the Grail, many more. First paperback edition. 58 full-page illustrations. 512pp. 5⅜ × 8½.
26507-2 Pa. $9.95

THE PRINCIPLES OF PSYCHOLOGY, William James. Famous long course complete, unabridged. Stream of thought, time perception, memory, experimental methods; great work decades ahead of its time. 94 figures. 1,391pp. 5⅜ × 8½. 2-vol. set.
Vol. I: 20381-6 Pa. $12.95
Vol. II: 20382-4 Pa. $12.95

THE WORLD AS WILL AND REPRESENTATION, Arthur Schopenhauer. Definitive English translation of Schopenhauer's life work, correcting more than 1,000 errors, omissions in earlier translations. Translated by E. F. J. Payne. Total of 1,269pp. 5⅜ × 8½. 2-vol. set. Vol. 1: 21761-2 Pa. $11.95
Vol. 2: 21762-0 Pa. $11.95

MAGIC AND MYSTERY IN TIBET, Madame Alexandra David-Neel. Experiences among lamas, magicians, sages, sorcerers, Bonpa wizards. A true psychic discovery. 32 illustrations. 321pp. 5⅜ × 8½. (USO) 22682-4 Pa. $8.95

THE EGYPTIAN BOOK OF THE DEAD, E. A. Wallis Budge. Complete reproduction of Ani's papyrus, finest ever found. Full hieroglyphic text, interlinear transliteration, word-for-word translation, smooth translation. 533pp. 6½ × 9¼.
21866-X Pa. $9.95

MATHEMATICS FOR THE NONMATHEMATICIAN, Morris Kline. Detailed, college-level treatment of mathematics in cultural and historical context, with numerous exercises. Recommended Reading Lists. Tables. Numerous figures. 641pp. 5⅜ × 8½. 24823-2 Pa. $11.95

THEORY OF WING SECTIONS: Including a Summary of Airfoil Data, Ira H. Abbott and A. E. von Doenhoff. Concise compilation of subsonic aerodynamic characteristics of NACA wing sections, plus description of theory. 350pp. of tables. 693pp. 5⅜ × 8½. 60586-8 Pa. $14.95

THE RIME OF THE ANCIENT MARINER, Gustave Doré, S. T. Coleridge. Doré's finest work; 34 plates capture moods, subtleties of poem. Flawless full-size reproductions printed on facing pages with authoritative text of poem. "Beautiful. Simply beautiful."—*Publisher's Weekly.* 77pp. 9¼ × 12. 22305-1 Pa. $6.95

NORTH AMERICAN INDIAN DESIGNS FOR ARTISTS AND CRAFTS-PEOPLE, Eva Wilson. Over 360 authentic copyright-free designs adapted from Navajo blankets, Hopi pottery, Sioux buffalo hides, more. Geometrics, symbolic figures, plant and animal motifs, etc. 128pp. 8⅜ × 11. (EUK) 25341-4 Pa. $7.95

SCULPTURE: Principles and Practice, Louis Slobodkin. Step-by-step approach to clay, plaster, metals, stone; classical and modern. 253 drawings, photos. 255pp. 8⅛ × 11. 22960-2 Pa. $10.95

THE INFLUENCE OF SEA POWER UPON HISTORY, 1660–1783, A. T. Mahan. Influential classic of naval history and tactics still used as text in war colleges. First paperback edition. 4 maps. 24 battle plans. 640pp. 5⅜ × 8½.
25509-3 Pa. $12.95

THE STORY OF THE TITANIC AS TOLD BY ITS SURVIVORS, Jack Winocour (ed.). What it was really like. Panic, despair, shocking inefficiency, and a little heroism. More thrilling than any fictional account. 26 illustrations. 320pp. 5⅜ × 8½.
20610-6 Pa. $8.95

FAIRY AND FOLK TALES OF THE IRISH PEASANTRY, William Butler Yeats (ed.). Treasury of 64 tales from the twilight world of Celtic myth and legend: "The Soul Cages," "The Kildare Pooka," "King O'Toole and his Goose," many more. Introduction and Notes by W. B. Yeats. 352pp. 5⅜ × 8½.
26941-8 Pa. $8.95

BUDDHIST MAHAYANA TEXTS, E. B. Cowell and Others (eds.). Superb, accurate translations of basic documents in Mahayana Buddhism, highly important in history of religions. The Buddha-karita of Asvaghosha, Larger Sukhavativyuha, more. 448pp. 5⅜ × 8½.,
25552-2 Pa. $9.95

ONE TWO THREE . . . INFINITY: Facts and Speculations of Science, George Gamow. Great physicist's fascinating, readable overview of contemporary science: number theory, relativity, fourth dimension, entropy, genes, atomic structure, much more. 128 illustrations. Index. 352pp. 5⅜ × 8½.
25664-2 Pa. $8.95

ENGINEERING IN HISTORY, Richard Shelton Kirby, et al. Broad, nontechnical survey of history's major technological advances: birth of Greek science, industrial revolution, electricity and applied science, 20th-century automation, much more. 181 illustrations. ". . . excellent . . ."—Isis. Bibliography. vii + 530pp. 5⅜ × 8¼.
26412-2 Pa. $14.95

Prices subject to change without notice.

Available at your book dealer or write for free catalog to Dept. GI, Dover Publications, Inc., 31 East 2nd St., Mineola, N.Y. 11501. Dover publishes more than 500 books each year on science, elementary and advanced mathematics, biology, music, art, literary history, social sciences and other areas.